The Heaven and the Afterlife

COLLECTION

2-in-1 Volume of True
Stories and Honest Answers
about the World Beyond

James L. Garlow *and* Keith Wall

BETHANYHOUSE
a division of Baker Publishing Group
Minneapolis, Minnesota

Previously published in two separate volumes:
  Heaven and the Afterlife © 2009 by James L. Garlow and Keith Wall
  Encountering Heaven and the Afterlife © 2010 by James L. Garlow and Keith Wall

Published by Bethany House Publishers
11400 Hampshire Avenue South
Bloomington, Minnesota 55438
www.bethanyhouse.com

ISBN 978-0-7642-3323-4

Bethany House Publishers is a division of Baker Publishing Group, Grand Rapids, Michigan

Printed in the United States of America

2-in-1 edition published 2018

The Library of Congress has cataloged the original editions as follows:
  Garlow, James L.
    Heaven and the afterlife: what happens the second we die? if heaven is a real place, who will live there? if hell exists, where is it located? what do near-death experiences mean? and more— / James L. Garlow with Keith Wall.
       p.   cm.
    Includes bibliographical references.
    Summary: "A comprehensive and straightforward exploration of beliefs about heaven, hell, and what happens when people die, written from a Christian perspective"—Provided by publisher.
    ISBN 978-0-7642-0576-7 (pbk. : alk. paper) 1. Future life—Christianity. I. Wall, Keith A. II. Title.
  BT903.G37   2009
  236'.2—dc22   2009014976

  Garlow, James L.
    Encountering heaven and the afterlife : true stories from people who have glimpsed the world beyond / James L. Garlow and Keith Wall.
       p.   cm.
    Summary: "True stories of spiritual encounters and near-death experiences offer glimpses into what happens when people die, written from a Christian perspective"—Provided by publisher.
    Includes bibliographical references (p.   ).
    ISBN 978-0-7642-0811-9 (pbk. : alk. paper) 1. Near-death experiences—Religious aspects—Christianity. 2. Future life—Christianity. 3. Spirits. I. Wall, Keith A. II. Title.
  BT833.G37 2010
  236'.2—dc22   2010011014

Cover design by Eric Walljasper

18   19   20   21   22   23   24   7   6   5   4   3   2   1

Heaven
and the
Afterlife

I dedicate this to the four people from my immediate
family who are now experiencing heaven:

My father Burtis
My sister Janie
My brother Bob
My wife Carol

Jim Garlow

To Ernie and Mary Wall, my dad and mom,
both fully alive in heaven.
Your love and legacy live on in everyone
who knew you.

Keith Wall

Contents

Part One

Through Death's Door

1

The Undiscovered Country

The Veil Between Life and the Afterlife Is Thinner Than We Think

> It is impossible that anything so natural, so necessary, and so universal as death should ever have been designed by Providence as an evil to mankind.
>
> Jonathan Swift

It is fitting that we begin with a true story involving three main characters: an elderly man nearing death, a kindhearted woman in robust health, and a deceased boy very much alive.

Five months earlier, physicians had diagnosed sixty-five-year-old Vernon Samuels with terminal lung cancer. They could do nothing but admit him to Rocky Mountain Hospice, in Colorado Springs, to live out his days with as much dignity and comfort as possible. Sadly, what relief palliative medicines could provide, human contact wouldn't. For decades, Vernon had been known to one and all as a cranky killjoy—a miserable person who made everybody around him miserable too.

And so almost no one came to visit him, despite the dwindling of his days on earth. Only the most intrepid family members straggled in from time to time, and they didn't stay long. Even the nurses braced themselves for barrages of criticism when they entered his room.

Vernon had just one regular visitor: Dee Ring Martz. A social worker with a cheerful disposition—in other words, Vernon's exact counterbalance—Dee stopped in daily to check on him. Undeterred by his toxic attitude, she would linger by his bedside and chat, assessing his moods and seeking ways to bring solace. Asked how he was doing, Vernon would scowl and complain about the asinine shows on TV, or the ruckus made by the kids who visited across the hall, or the nurses being incapable of doing anything right.

It came as a shock, then, when Dee arrived one Tuesday afternoon and found the withered, pajama-clad man sitting up in bed and smiling—you could almost say *beaming*. The room, usually stuffy and dark, was bright; the curtains were uncharacteristically pulled open.

"Hello, Dee!" Vernon called out. "Don't you look lovely today! And I want to tell you how much I've appreciated our daily visits."

Dee's first thought, naturally, was that the doctors had upped his medication. But they hadn't.

"Vernon, you're in high spirits today," she replied. "In fact, you seem happier than I've ever seen you."

"And with good reason," he said. "Joey came to see me. My son, Joey!"

Dee had talked with the occasional visiting relative, and there had never been a son—she was sure of it. She asked him to tell her more.

Joey, it turned out, was Vernon's long-dead child who'd drowned at age five. Vernon had always blamed himself for his beloved boy's tragic death and had vowed never to get close to anyone again. His grouchy disposition was an all-too-effective defense mechanism to keep others at arm's length.

"I'm telling you, Dee, Joey came into my room, just as clearly and visibly as you just walked in," the man went on, words tumbling from his mouth. "He told me my time on earth is short and that I should be nice to people."

Dee smiled at how seriously he took his son's admonition.

"Joey said something else," Vernon continued. "He's coming to get me at noon on Friday. That's when I'll die, and Joey will be here to escort me to heaven. He said he was *chosen* to be my guide. Isn't it wonderful?"

As much as Dee had been around dying people, she was no stranger to spiritual encounters: children who saw angels, semi-conscious people who reported heavenly visions, those who in their final moments called out, "It's so beautiful!" Still, she wondered about the specific timetable.

The next time she ran into the doctors overseeing Vernon's medical care, she told them of his experience and asked about his life expectancy.

"He's terminal, all right," one said. "But I'd give him three or four months. He's not so bad off that he'd die on Friday."

The other concurred: "You better be ready to tell him something on Friday when he expects to be in heaven but discovers he's still here."

Friday came, and Dee showed up at 11:30. She and Vernon chatted as usual, Vernon offering more compliments and encouragement. As the minutes ticked by, Dee didn't dare check her watch, knowing what he would think. She began rehearsing words of consolation.

Soon enough, the grandfather clock out in the hallway began tolling the noon hour. *Gong, gong, gong. . . .*

As if on cue, when the twelfth gong sounded, Vernon sat up, spread his arms wide, and shouted, "Joey!"

In that exact instant, the room filled with a palpable energy, as with the ionized air after a lightning strike. Dee felt the hairs on her arms stand up.

A split second later, Vernon slumped back on his pillows, his head lolled to one side, and the last gush of air escaped his lips. "Vernon? Vernon!" Dee shouted. No response. She pressed the emergency call button, and nurses scurried in. Checking his pulse, one announced, "He's gone."

Dee thought to herself, *Yes, he's gone—gone on to a better place with the son he longed to see again.*[1]

We usually don't dwell on thoughts of the afterlife. Life here and now is challenging enough, with obligations to cover and deadlines to meet and kids who need to be at soccer practice on time. Most of us don't want to think about death when there's so much to be enjoyed in life—and who can blame us?

But sometimes inklings of the afterlife intrude on our predictable orderliness. Maybe it's when you attend the funeral of your favorite aunt. Or when your mother calls and says, with perceptible desperation, "Dad's had a heart attack." Or when a close friend reveals that she has a life-threatening illness. Or when, on an otherwise typical rush-hour drive, you have a near collision that surely would've killed you.

It doesn't always come with grim circumstances, however. Perhaps you watch the sun rising over the ocean and can't help but ponder what heaven must be like. Or a radio show features someone who had a near-death experience, and the story stirs your heart and fires your imagination. Or you catch a magical glimpse into the wondrous innocence of your giggling child, and you hope beyond hope that you will spend eternity together, exploring, playing, laughing.

Most of us, when we hear the word *afterlife*, immediately assume this means heaven and hell. Those are the dominant features of the life beyond this one. But if you're like me, you acknowledge that there is a spiritual world buzzing all around us, every moment of every day, though we usually aren't aware of it and don't regularly take the time to notice it.

We're pretty sure spiritual beings, like angels, participate in our lives, but we don't know exactly how. Even though we've heard our parents say, "There's no such thing as ghosts," we wonder if there might be something more to it. We read reports about people "crossing over" through near-death experiences, and we think of gleaning insight about what awaits us. Deep down, we want to know:

- What happens when we die? What will transpire at the moment we expire—when we pass from life into death?
- What is heaven like? Certainly, it's more than the halos, harps, and hallelujah choruses portrayed in Sunday school versions.
- What about hell—must be more to it than fire, brimstone, and pitchfork-wielding creatures, right?
- What are angels and demons? What do they do for us or want from us?
- Could ghosts be real, and could people really see them?
- Is it possible to talk with dead people?
- So many people believe in reincarnation—is there anything to it?

These are some of the questions and ideas we'll explore in *Heaven and the Afterlife*. With one eye on the Scriptures, the other on credible accounts and research clues, let's pull back the veil and consider what we see.

The truth is, for a very long time people have been searching for the answers. With remarkably few exceptions, from the moment civilization began humans have upheld some kind of hereafter. For millennia, beliefs about the "geography" of the afterlife—and the road map we must follow to get there—have varied widely, but few cultures have doubted there *is* such a place or that human consciousness survives to see it. Funerals always have been rites of passage from this life to the next, ranging in form from a simple burial or cremation to immensely complex procedures lasting days or weeks.

Ancient Egyptians, for instance, took weeks to mummify their dead, carefully keeping the body and all its organs intact so that the soul would continue to have a place to live. After embalming was complete, they wrapped the body in strips of linen that bound charms, amulets, and talismans to the deceased.[2] Clearly, like the vast majority of those who have ever lived, they didn't subscribe to a lights-out philosophy of death.

For all our skeptical denial and rational thinking, beneath the modernistic veneers we've been no less preoccupied with the afterlife.

- A 2005 Harris poll revealed that 82 percent of Americans believe in God, 70 percent in life after death, and six out of ten in the existence of heaven and hell.[3]

- Medical studies say that 11 to 30 percent of all who survive a cardiac arrest report some kind of near-death experience (NDE) in which their conscious mind appeared to be independent of their physical body.[4]

- One out of three respondents to a 2007 *Associated Press/Ipsos* poll said they believed in ghosts. Nearly one in four claimed to have had a *personal* encounter with one.[5]

Even allowing for a broad margin of error, numbers like these are hard to ignore. Though we don't talk much about the matter, it seems real-life ghost stories are happening all the time. In your lifetime, the odds of encountering an apparition (one in four) apparently are better than rolling a six on your first try.

What's going on here? Have we forgotten the legacy of pioneering philosophers like René Descartes and Sir Francis Bacon, who helped us escape the "ignorance" and "superstition" of the Dark Ages? After enjoying the tangible fruits of the scientific revolution for centuries, do we still doubt that material reality is the *only* reality?

Seemingly, yes. And the reason may be that it's easy to demand verifiable "proof" of the afterlife—until you've had *your* turn to see an apparition or witness the appearance of a dead loved one or have your own near-death experience. In other words, brainy lab-coat logic might get revisited when it appears to contradict compelling, firsthand experience. People might not know how or why something "weird" happened to them, but those who've been there largely are adamant that something really did happen nonetheless.

Consider as a representative example the story of Brenda, who has degrees in both mathematics and physics and runs her own land surveying business. Well-trained in the scientific method of inquiry, Brenda makes her living by putting faith in hard, cold, precisely measurable facts.

Several years ago my kids and I moved into an old house in a small Colorado mountain town—a storybook Victorian-style home with lots of character. One night, not long thereafter, my teenage son came running into my bedroom, obviously terrified. From his room downstairs he had watched the bathroom door across the hall open all the way and then shut nearly to the point of latching—not once, but fifteen times in a row. Then he felt a "presence" enter his room and heard an audible sound like someone exhaling deeply.

I didn't know what to think. His fear was real, so I couldn't imagine he had made it up. Still, I thought there must be a logical explanation. At about the same time we began having electrical problems in the part of the house near his room. The lights were unreliable. They would go off and on at odd times, and the switches didn't always work right.

Then, not long after my son's encounter, I was standing near the kitchen where my kids were hanging out with a couple of friends. From the corner of my eye I clearly saw a tall male figure walk across the living room floor and disappear into the hallway toward my son's room. It wasn't just a vague impression. I had no doubt a real person had walked by.

My first thought was that my son's friend had slipped past me unnoticed. But when I looked, all the kids were there in the kitchen. No one else was in the house. It spooked me enough that we left and stayed at a friend's house that night.

Most of us similarly "don't know what to think" when we hear a story like this. Are there other possible explanations for what Brenda and her son saw besides a ghostly visitation from the afterlife? Sure, and a dedicated skeptic could come up with a dozen. But several years later, Brenda remains convinced there was more to the experience than drafty windows, creaky floorboards, or unexpected hallucinations. "I know what I saw," she says. "It was very real."

Whether or not we like it, testimony from credible sources just won't go away. On the contrary, in recent decades there has been an explosion of firsthand accounts that not only suggest an afterlife is real but also imply that the border between here and there is not the impassible iron curtain we perhaps have imagined it to be. Advances in emergency medical technology, for instance, have dramatically increased our chances of surviving a life-threatening illness or injury. And, thanks to the work of researchers (e.g., Elizabeth Kübler-Ross, Ray Moody, and Melvin Morse), more survivors are willing to talk about what they encountered at death's door. The result is a growing body of anecdotal evidence piling up in unavoidable heaps.

Once more, here's the point: Humans have a persistent belief in an afterlife, and a surprising number of us have had some encounter that keeps the fires of curiosity burning. Shakespeare's Hamlet said the "dread of something after death, the undiscovered country from whose bourn no traveler returns, puzzles the will." Are we forever stuck there, stymied in the dark, without a way to know more? Are we afraid of what we might find if we take a closer look?

Of course, some might say certain matters are tainted by association with "evil spirits" and should be avoided. They have a point; as we will see, there are hostile entities in the spirit world whose nature it is to make trouble. Certain kinds of recreational spiritual "dabbling" are like throwing open our doors and inviting that trouble into our lives. Caution is a good policy.

On the other hand, there is strong evidence that conscious contact with spiritual beings can be a helpful, healing experience. Could it be that informed knowledge is a better defense than ignorance when we're faced with realities we don't fully understand? After all, Jesus didn't teach the disciples to run from evil spirits but showed them how to take care of the problem. Is it possible that stubborn skepticism at one end of the spectrum, and blinding fearfulness at the other, actually cost us more in the long run than open-minded investigation?

I think the answer is yes, for at least three reasons.

Ignorance Promotes Fear

Norman Cousins said, "Death is not the enemy, living in constant fear of it is."[6] As children we learn that the best way to deal with fear of the dark is to turn on a light—in this case, the light of knowledge—and see what's really there.

Ignorance Prolongs Grief After a Loss

Ray Moody wrote,

> A number of studies . . . have established that a high percentage of bereaved persons have visions of the deceased. For instance, as many as 75 percent of parents who lose a child to death will have some kind of apparition of that child within a year of the loss. This experience is a relief for most of the parents and will greatly reduce their grief.[7]

Moody concluded that such visions are comforting because they provide us with another reason to trust that our loved ones are not "gone" but still survive—and thrive—in an afterlife. The more we know about these stories, the less likely we are to be wracked by prolonged, excessive grief when we lose someone we love.

Ignorance Leaves Us Unprepared for Our Own Death

In *On Death and Dying*, Elizabeth Kübler-Ross introduced a significant idea: Leaving this world with dignity is not so easy to do, and there are difficult stages in the process that all of us go through.

> It might be helpful if more people would talk about death and dying as an intrinsic part of life, just as they do not hesitate to mention when someone is expecting a new baby.[8]

That is to say, the more we know about all aspects of the afterlife, the easier it will be to make the trip when our turn arrives.

Belief in the afterlife is a cornerstone of Christian faith. Jesus told us, "God so loved the world that he gave his one and only Son, that whoever believes in him shall not perish but have eternal life."[9] We accept that Christ has conquered death—not just for himself but for anyone who repents and believes. It's normal to want to know more; however, when it comes to probing the mysteries of death and dying—and beyond—Christians are often just as afraid as anyone else. *Why should we be?* Fear is a well-known enemy to faith and freedom. Are there reasons to be prudent? Yes. Paranoid? I think not.

Freedom from fear generally is the fruit of knowledge, though this isn't always easy to come by. At times, the material in this book may make you uncomfortable. It may make you incredulous. It may even make you mad. All I ask is that you keep an open mind as you listen to the following stories and ideas. Let's go forward in the spirit of discovery, protected by God's perfect love that "drives out fear."[10]

2

There . . . and Back Again

The Near-Death Experience: A Miracle of Modern Medicine

We sometimes congratulate ourselves at the moment of waking from
a troubled dream; it may be so the moment after death.

Nathaniel Hawthorne

Imagine that you got up this morning knowing today is your day to kick
the bucket, pass away, check out, cash it in . . . *die*. There's no point
arguing over whether or not it's fair, or whether the timing could be
better, or any of a hundred other objections people typically raise when
confronting their mortality. As of now, you're simply out of time. Nothing
you can do about it.

Facing this imminent appointment, wouldn't it be nice to have some
idea of what to expect from the experience? Will it be painful? Comforting? Frightening? Exhilarating? Exhausting? Hot? Cold? Will you wink
out forever like a done-for light bulb? Or do you have a spirit that will
leave your skin and carry on? Given the magnitude of the journey you're
about to take, wouldn't you like to have a reasonably accurate map of the
terrain "over there"?

These days you can find a travel guide for even the most obscure earthly
destination. No one goes on vacation without reading up on what sights

to see, what local foods to eat (or avoid), and how to speak a few words of the language so as not to wind up in jail or a hospital. It's the prudent thing to do.

Why, then, do most of us approach this ultimate, inexorable adventure so thoroughly unprepared and ill-informed? Frankly, the reason is that we're just plain afraid of what we'll find. We've decided that instead of turning on the light, the best way to deal with unknown things going bump in the night is to keep our eyes glued shut and pray they'll go away. For lack of a clear alternative, a lot of people imagine dying to be like a bad horror movie in which Good Guy (you) gets tossed out of an airplane over moonless, vampire-infested Transylvania. It's not much fun to sit around and contemplate such an ending—so we don't.

Here's the million-dollar question: *Must* it be this way? Is our best metaphor for death really the black hole, a singularity in space with gravity so intense that nothing—not even light—ever bounces back with hints about what goes on in there? Is it actually true that "death devours all lovely things"?[1]

Increasingly, it appears the answer is a resounding *No way!*

It turns out there are clues lying around for anyone willing to take a look—convincing ones that may astonish and inspire. Even so, if you want to convince a jury of *skeptics* that we can know what happens after death, you need more than mere inference. You need hard-core evidence, which even dedicated investigators admit is in short supply. There is a burden of proof surrounding the subject that—so far—is difficult to satisfy.

This problem confronts us when we strain to see beyond the frontiers of material (observation) science. It's fuzzy, awkward territory where reason and intuition, knowledge and faith must work together if we hope to replace blind dogma—either naturalistic or religious—with resonant and relevant discovery. A willingness to consider clues and anecdotal evidence may be the nonnegotiable price of admission if we want answers to "What's it like to die?" That said, we're still not interested in any old scrap of speculation. We've set out to do the best we can with what we have, to honestly look at *what* we know and *how* we know it.

Which brings us to the intriguing subject of this chapter: what we might learn about the moment of death from eyewitness testimony.

That's right. It turns out lots of people—millions, in fact—have had a close encounter with death and lived to share about their experience with the rest of us. These days we call it a "near-death experience," or NDE, which sounds impressively contemporary. But judging from literature and other accounts, such stories have been around for ages. For instance, people taking care of the seriously ill or injured have long reported hearing them speak of seeing dead loved ones or about "angels of light" come to escort them to the other side. When it was more common for people to die at home, in the company of friends and family, these deathbed "visions" almost certainly were more regularly shared.

But when we started doing most of our dying in isolated hospital wards, surrounded by medical professionals whose training disallowed any notion of nonphysical reality, people became understandably reluctant to talk about having had a spectacular metaphysical episode. You can't really blame them; when they've just survived a narrow brush with death, why risk a trip to the psychiatric ward as well? As NDE researcher Melvin Morse wrote:

> Although George Gallup has estimated that 5 percent of the general population has had a near-death experience, people were afraid to talk about them for fear of being ridiculed. Far too often they themselves doubted the validity of what had happened to them.[2]

Five percent is a lot—roughly fifteen million Americans, at today's population levels. How have we managed to ignore so common an experience for so long?

This began to change, though, in the early 1970s. Led by Raymond Moody, author of the landmark bestseller *Life After Life*, a few specialists started paying attention to the occasional bedside NDE and started to be increasingly intrigued by the remarkable consistency in what they were hearing. Ignoring the prevailing medical wisdom and conducting the first systematic, scientific studies of the phenomenon, they discovered that while no two NDEs are precisely alike, there are startlingly significant similarities.

Now their file cabinets are bursting with documented cases that range from accounts of patients being temporarily "outside" their bodies to astonishing, multifaceted adventures that defy explanation. There were— and are—no accepted medical theories that provide a basis for human consciousness surviving, fully aware, after ER monitors indicate that the brain has completely ceased to function.

By listening to their patients with an open mind and then publishing their findings, these researchers have forever altered our perception of death and dying. Nearly four decades after the discussion went public, people who have a near-death experience are no longer as afraid to speak up. Medical professionals, still skeptical as a whole, at least have lost much of their hostility toward the idea of conscious survival after clinical death. In fact, hardworking doctors and nurses unwittingly have done more to advance the study of NDEs than anyone.

> It is ironic that the same medical technology that contributed to the degrading and humiliating conditions of dying patients allowed us to successfully resuscitate people so that they could report their near-death experiences. . . . Modern intensive-care medicine and rapid-response medic teams have made the cheating of death routine.[3]

This has created an amazing opportunity for us to pull back a veil we'd thought was impenetrable and get a peek at what perhaps is beyond. Keeping in mind that stories—even believable, compelling ones—don't constitute proof, let's check out the composite scenario they suggest. Very few people report each and every one of the elements that follow, but all of them frequently appear in NDE accounts from a wide range of people from diverse backgrounds. Buckle up and hang on.

Your adventure begins on a hospital gurney; you're in substantial pain and distress, being rolled into an emergency room. As vital signs plummet, the ER staff responds with flurried, energetic activity to resuscitate your body. Clearly they believe they're losing you. The monitors agree: you are flatlining.

Suddenly you realize you no longer feel any pain and are now looking down on the frantic scene from above, as if bobbing like a balloon near the ceiling. You see your body lying on the table, but for a moment you don't recognize it as yourself. You observe the doctors' attempts to bring you back. You attempt to communicate with the others in the room, but they can't hear you. (And later you will describe the procedures in accurate detail, even though your brain has ceased to function normally—and even though your "waking" self has no such knowledge or experience.)

After a moment of confusion, you become aware of sensing new freedom, clarity, and well-being. You still possess a body, but it's very different from the one in the room beneath you. You feel *good*.

Before long you see an opening appear nearby; it's a dark tunnel, and at the other end is an attractive bright light. Entering the tunnel, you quickly feel as if you're moving at incredible speed toward the light, which grows more and more intense. The brightest light you've ever seen doesn't hurt your eyes. In its warmth, you feel indescribable peace, joy, love, and contentment.

You notice that others are with you, and you recognize them as deceased people you have known: grandmother, sibling, and/or friend, there to help guide you through your experience. Their presence brings exceeding comfort.

Then, a being who is surrounded by (or perhaps made of) even more radiant light approaches and asks something along the lines of "How did it go?" or "What did you learn?" The question prompts your life's events to flash before your eyes in lightning-fast, 3D Technicolor. You not only see it all happening again, you also feel (for instance) the effects of your actions on others.

Throughout the review, even when reliving uncomfortable moments and realizing mistakes, you feel nothing but unconditional love from the being of light. You comprehend that only two things really matter during life on earth: your relationship with God, and how well you demonstrate love. Everything else is meaningless. You feel such joy and peace that you don't ever want to return to your previous life.

But you suddenly become aware of a boundary before you, and you know if you cross it you'll have moved on forever. Someone tells you now is not your time, that you must go back. The instant you reluctantly agree, you are back inside your physical body.

After your recovery, you attempt to tell people what you experienced, with frustrating results. For starters, language is completely inadequate to describe and illustrate what you've seen and felt; you usually start by saying, "Words just don't cut it, but. . . ." Further, most people don't know how to respond, and it's easier for them to think you're crazy or hallucinating than to expand their views of spiritual reality.

In addition, you're no longer afraid of death like you were before. You're not exactly eager for it to happen, but you know now what to expect when it *is* your turn to go for good. You're less likely to get caught up in petty dramas and trivial pursuits. You place greater importance on loving others and living each moment for God.

It's not hard to see why an experience like this might change how you live your life. Again, while there are many variations in the exact chronology and details, one thing nearly all people who've had an NDE share is the insistence that everything they saw and felt was *real*—often even more so than anything they've experienced in the "real world."

(There also are less frequently reported accounts of *unpleasant* experiences near death; we'll examine these in chapter 4.)

But what does all this *mean* in the grand scheme? Because, once more, so many people from all over the world reporting a remarkably similar experience does not prove the existence of life after death. Many scientists and religious leaders are equally unimpressed. As the pioneering death-and-dying researcher Kübler-Ross wrote in her foreword to the first edition of Moody's *Life After Life*:

> Dr. Moody will have to be prepared for a lot of criticism, mainly from two arenas. . . . Some religious representatives of a denominational church have already expressed their criticism of studies like this. One priest referred to it as "selling cheap grace." . . . The second group are scientists and physicians who regard this kind of study as "unscientific."[4]

True enough. Near-death experience researchers do get charged with everything from peddling crackpot theory to being tools of the devil.

As for objections on scientific grounds, studies conducted to investigate possible medical triggers of the NDE so far have not produced a smoking gun to settle the issue. Although a thorough discussion of these alternatives is outside the scope of this book, a short list includes oxygen deprivation, hallucination caused by drugs used in emergency situations, or deficiencies of calcium, potassium, and/or other essential bio-chemicals during resuscitation. Many have suggested the experience is purely psychological—the mind's defensive apparatus for coping during the trauma of serious illness or injury.

Interestingly, some researchers have found no correlation at all between physical factors and the NDE occurrence. For instance, during a Dutch study involving 344 cardiac arrest patients, 18 percent reported some kind of NDE, "including specific elements such as out-of-body experience, pleasant feelings, and seeing a tunnel." Yet the team found no link to drugs used during treatment, to the duration of the arrest, or even to the patient's previously held beliefs about dying. Lead researcher Pim Van Lommel said, "If there was a physiological cause, all the patients should have had an NDE."[5]

Others, doubting whether the NDE can be used to examine the afterlife, object on the grounds that walking up to a door is not the same thing as going through it. The prominent Catholic theologian Hans Küng wrote:

> What then do these experiences of dying imply for life after death? To put it briefly, nothing! For I regard it as a duty of theological truthfulness to answer clearly that experiences of this kind prove nothing about a possible life after death: it is a question here of the last five minutes *before* death and not of an eternal life *after* death. These passing minutes do not settle the question of where the dying person goes: into nonbeing or into new being.[6]

Good point; and most NDE researchers agree wholeheartedly. No account has been given by someone who actually *died,* since death, by definition, is an irreversible condition. That's why it's called a *near*-death experience.

As we have seen, this discussion, at least for the time being, is dominated by clues, hints, and suggestions—not proof—about what happens when we die. It's like examining something with only the benefit of peripheral vision—an oft-frustrating exercise that may not yield the clearest possible picture, but neither is it necessarily false. In fact, the most compelling facet of NDE narratives may be an aspect that the rational brain cannot see fully, no matter how much light we shine on it: the ineffable, almost mystical effect it has on those who've been there, and even on those who happen to hear the experiences firsthand.

After many months of research and countless hours of listening to people tell their stories, Moody put it this way:

> I am left, not with conclusions or evidence or proofs, but with something much less definite—feelings, questions, analogies, puzzling facts to be explained. In fact, it might be more appropriate to ask, not what conclusions

I have drawn on the basis of my study, but rather how the study has affected me personally. In response I can only say: There is something very persuasive about seeing a person describe his experience which cannot easily be conveyed in writing. Their near-death experiences were very real events to these people, and through my association with them the experiences have become real events to me.[7]

Christians, of course, are accustomed to discerning the reality of an experience by its effect on people. Salvation is "proved" authentic every day by its self-evident power to produce real change in even the most incorrigible life: "Faith is being sure of what we hope for and certain of what we do not see."[8] Then comes modern medicine—coupled with an increasing cultural openness about these issues—to give faith in life after death a boost through the firsthand testimony of those who have "been there."

Our quest for real knowledge about the afterlife is like following a trail of bread crumbs through the forest. They are there, but we must have our eyes wide open. The clues we glean from NDE stories may not clear up all our queries. Actually, like all expeditions to unknown territory, they raise as many new questions as they answer. But so many fellow travelers—millions of ordinary folks from every walk of life—have seen something promising that invites us to accept what people of faith have long believed: *Death is not an end but a doorway we walk through as automatically as we take our next breath*. The nonphysical part of us is not a mythical fantasy; it is our truest essence, created in God's image, the part of us that survives our travails in this life to begin a new journey in the next.

And who knows? These "crumbs" may well show us something we'd all like to see: a glimpse of heaven.

3

Hints at the Hereafter

For Most People, "Near Death" Is a Doorway to Indescribable Light and Love

Take all the pleasures of all the spheres, and multiply each through endless years—one minute of heaven is worth them all.

Sir Thomas Moore

Time for a field trip. Let's go *camping*.

Picture it: gathering the gear, stocking the cooler, loading up the car, driving to the woods, setting up the tent, gazing at the zillions of stars coming out above the pitch-black wilderness, crawling into your sleeping bag, drifting off to the mysterious sounds of nature.

Sound like fun? Well, depends on who you are.

To many, such an impromptu trip would be a dream come true, a nostalgic reprise of fond childhood memories or of outings with their own kids. They'd relish the quiet, the nighttime darkness, the comforting solitude.

But to others, this scenario represents their worst nightmare. Sleep on the ground? Eat beans straight out of the can? Risk facing a bear? Step on a snake? Get munched by bugs? Forget it!

What makes the difference between these two extremes? What separates those eager for an outdoor adventure from those who'd rate the prospect somewhere between a tax audit and a broken leg? Personal experience? Perhaps. Yet these days a majority on either side of the coin have never set foot in the wild or knowingly been within miles of a free-ranging bear. What accounts for their point of view? The answer can be given in a single word: *Stories*.

Chances are, your particular feelings about camping depend on the outdoors-related stories you've heard all your life—firsthand or through the media. Does the prospect of a weekend in the woods elicit romantic images of a thrilled Tom Sawyer on the Mississippi? Or of a lonely Tom Hanks hopelessly marooned on a deserted island?

Stories make the difference. By telling stories we gather up the threads of human existence and weave them together, seeking to create coherence out of what seems convoluted. Stories are how *meaning and belief* emerge from the confusing and sometimes contradictory tangles of everyday experience. Listen to master storyteller Robert McKee:

> The world now consumes films, novels, theater, and television in such quantities and with such ravenous hunger that the story arts have become humanity's prime source of inspiration, as it seeks to order chaos and gain insight into life. Our appetite for story is a reflection of the profound human need to grasp the patterns of living, not merely as an intellectual exercise, but within a very personal, emotional experience. . . . Why is so much of our life spent inside stories? Because as critic Kenneth Burke tells us, stories are equipment for living.[1]

Stories help us know how to live. For our purposes, let's carry that idea a step further: *Stories are equipment for dying as well.*

The tales we tell and take in about death—and beyond—form a blueprint for what we inevitably will believe about what happens when we die. Those who study the issue largely concur: "Because we learn about dying only indirectly by experiencing the death of others, it is reasonable to hypothesize that our attitudes about death and dying could be influenced by mass mediated messages."[2]

If McKee is right that the commercial "story arts" have become our prime source of insight into these mysteries, it's not hard to see why so many—Christians included—are deeply afraid of looking too closely at death. For most novelists and scriptwriters, dying is the mother of all worst-case scenarios, to be avoided by any heroic means available, whatever the cost. Think back to all the dramatic deaths you've "witnessed" via media, including the nightly news. How many were portrayed as painful, tragic, and terrifying? Nearly all. But is the portrait of death these stories paint an accurate one? Do they tell the truth? *No.*

We can answer so confidently because, as powerful as they are, mass-marketed stories are not the only ones available to us. As we've discussed, our era is unique to all of human history in that medical advances have made cheating death almost routine. It's as if ER techniques and technologies have lengthened the cord that tethers us to this life—just enough to permit a clearer view of what lies ahead. More people than ever have a close encounter with death and, as the saying goes, live to tell the tale.

The following pages, continuing into the next chapter, provide a sampling of these astonishing first-person stories. We want to see how they differ from the common societal message about death. What clues do they carry about the existence of heaven, or of hell? What light do they shed on the age-old question: *Where do we go when we die?*

We've noted that while those who've had an NDE—knocked on death's door only to be sent back to the here and now—give accounts containing different elements and variations, most include at least a few common aspects. What do they see and feel on the other side? Here are three prevalent answers.

Unparalleled Peace

Imagine you've come to the hospital today for a minor laparoscopic procedure. Your doctor plans to work using a tiny camera inserted through a small abdominal incision. It's strictly routine, you're told.

But something goes wrong. The surgeon accidentally cuts deeper than he intends, puncturing an artery and damaging your intestines. You are thrust instantly into a life-threatening emergency.

Be honest—just *envisioning* yourself in this situation is enough to fill you with fear and dread, right? Your body tenses at the very thought of such pain and trauma. Yet here is how Laurelynn told her real-life story to highly respected NDE researcher Kenneth Ring. As the dramatic situation unfolded, she suddenly found herself floating above the scene—outside her body—watching detachedly.

> The surgical team was frantic. Red was everywhere, splattered on the gowns, splattered on the floor, and a bright pool of flowing red blood, in the now-wide-open abdominal cavity. I couldn't understand what was going on down there. I didn't even make the connection, at that moment, that the body being worked on was my own. It didn't matter anyway. I was in a state of freedom, having a great time. I just wanted to shout to the distressed people below, "Hey, I'm okay. It's great up here." But they were so intent, I felt like I didn't want to interrupt their efforts.
>
> I then traveled to another realm of total and absolute peace. There was no pain, but instead a sense of well-being, in a warm, dark, soft space. I was enveloped by total bliss in an atmosphere of unconditional love and acceptance. . . . The freedom of total peace was intensified beyond any ecstatic feeling ever felt here on earth.[3]

Peace, love, freedom, ecstasy, bliss—hardly the words that leap to mind when you imagine seeing your own blood splattered everywhere during a brush with death. But such language shows up repeatedly in firsthand NDE accounts. Pain and fear instantly disappear, replaced by wellness far greater than ever felt on earth. Laurelynn put it this way: "I find it very difficult to describe where I was, because the words we know here in this plane just aren't adequate."

Raymond Moody shares representative testimony from people he interviewed for *Life After Life*. Below, the first is from a woman resuscitated after a heart attack, the second from a man recalling what he felt when he received a would-be fatal wound in Vietnam.

> I began to experience the most wonderful feelings. I couldn't feel a thing in the world except peace, comfort, ease—just quietness. I felt that all my troubles were gone, and I thought to myself, *Well, how quiet and peaceful, and I don't hurt at all.*

> A great attitude of relief. There was no pain, and I've never felt so relaxed. I was at ease and it was all good.[4]

Sally, who clinically died during surgery to repair internal bleeding after giving birth, left her body and looked back at herself in the bed from above. "I felt so loved, calm, peaceful, happy," she reported later. "I can't find words to express what it was like."[5]

Chris was only ten when he clinically died from complications after a kidney transplant. Afterward he told his mom, "I have a wonderful secret to tell you, Mother. I've been climbing a staircase to heaven. It was such a good and peaceful feeling. I felt wonderful."[6]

We could retell hundreds of these stories. What do they have in common with the sensationalized mass-media tales? Almost nothing at all. What can we conclude? Perhaps that, for many people at least, death is not the nightmare we've been led to fear. Maybe it's no more than an effortless step out of this world into the next—nearer to God's heavenly kingdom. Accordingly, is it really so surprising that our first sensation would be of indescribable peace and wellness? I think not.

> "Death has been swallowed up in victory."
> "Where, O death, is your victory?
> Where, O death, is your sting?"[7]

Unexpected Reunions

Elizabeth Kübler-Ross has said her patients most fear the prospect of dying alone. This is even more understandable when we consider how common it has become for people to approach life's end tucked away in bland, antiseptic hospital rooms with only complete strangers nearby. *Crossing the final threshold alone is not the same as being lonely when the moment comes.*

However, even when we face it without loving support from others, is death ever truly a solitary event? Not according to thousands of documented NDE stories. Those who have "died" and returned usually report being met and guided by people they know very well—even those already dead many years.

Donna clinically died on the operating table during emergency surgery to keep her gallbladder from rupturing. Her heart stopped; she had no blood pressure; when she suddenly felt herself float free of her body to a spot above the commotion, the distressed nurses said she was dead, but she felt "fine" and "free." As a team rushed through the door with electroshock equipment to try to restart her heart, Donna traveled through a tunnel away from the trauma:

> Suddenly I was in a place filled up with love, and a beautiful bright white light. The place seemed holy. Plants and flowers, I could see beautiful scenes.
> As I walked through this meadow I saw people separated in little bunches. They waved to me, and came over and talked to me. One was my father who had died about two years before. He looked radiant. He looked happier than I had ever seen him before, and much younger. My grandmothers and grandfathers were there too. Everyone was happy to see me. But my father told me it was not my time and I would be going back.[8]

Said a woman who'd hemorrhaged during childbirth and was near death:

> The doctor gave me up, and told my relatives that I was dying. . . . I realized that all these people were there, almost in multitudes it seems, hovering around the ceiling of the room. These were all people I had known in my past life, but who had passed on before. I recognized my grandmother and a girl I had known when I was in school, and many other relatives and friends. . . . I felt that they had come to protect or to guide me. It was almost as if I were coming home, and they were there to greet or to welcome me. All this time, I had the feeling of everything light and beautiful. It was a beautiful and glorious moment.[9]

Even skeptical Christians might be swayed by the words of Dwight L. Moody, one of history's greatest evangelists. In 1899, Moody was near death. At one point he lost consciousness, and the people gathered around him thought he'd passed away, but his doctor succeeded in reviving him. When Moody opened his eyes he exclaimed, "I went to the gate of heaven. Why, it was so wonderful, and I saw the children! I saw Irene and Dwight." He died a short time later, apparently in great peace and anticipation, having already seen his deceased children waiting for him in heaven.[10]

Many accounts suggest that it isn't necessary to undergo clinical death and return from a dramatic NDE to have visions of departed loved ones come to guide us to the other side. In her remarkable *Glimpses of Heaven*, hospice nurse Trudy Harris shares many memories she collected over a thirty-five-year career of helping terminally ill people die as gracefully as possible. As they draw nearer to the moment of death, her patients frequently speak of seeing someone in the room who has come to ease their passage.

Frank, suffering from inoperable lung cancer, told Harris during a routine visit, "My son, John, is here with me now; he said it's time for me to go. Can you see him? He's sitting over there in the chair; he is beckoning me to go with him." John had died many years earlier in Vietnam.[11]

Sometimes the guide is not a previously deceased human but an angelic spirit. Harris tells this story about a conversation with Lenora, a middle-aged woman dying of a brain tumor:

> One day while I was visiting, she [Lenora] asked to speak to me alone and, much to everyone's surprise, she excused her entire family from the room. "This big angel comes and stands near my bed," she said to me very sternly. "Right there," she said, pointing to the corner of her bedroom. "Ms. Nurse, when I see that angel, do you really think I see that angel?"
>
> "Yes, you do," I said. . . . I explained to her that this is a very common experience for people getting ready to go to heaven.[12]

Once again, these stories suggest death is not a lonely game of solitaire. The implication is that loved ones or spirits wait on the other side to take your hand and welcome you into familiar, warm, comforting arms—or to send you gently back to finish your time on earth. Why should it be any other way for God's children? God has promised: "Never will I leave you. Never will I forsake you."[13] That's as reliable in death as in life.

Unearthly Light and Unconditional Love

Don Piper, author of *90 Minutes in Heaven*, was as close to truly dead as anyone ever comes without finishing the journey and ending up in the cemetery (or urn). After an eighteen-wheeler ran head on into his Ford Escort on a rain-slicked Texas highway, EMTs on the scene declared that he'd died on impact. Unable to extract him right away from the crushed vehicle, they covered it with a tarp. He had no measurable heartbeat for *an hour and a half*—a fact for which medical science has no ready explanation. It remains a mystery.

Piper didn't view the scene from outside his body. He didn't travel through a tunnel. He simply "woke up" in heaven—bathed in the most wonderful light he'd ever seen.

I realized that everything around me glowed with a dazzling intensity. In trying to describe the scene, words are totally inadequate, because human words can't express the feelings of awe and wonder at what I beheld.

Everything I saw glowed with intense brightness. . . . I wasn't blinded, but I was amazed [as] the luster and intensity continually increased. Strange as it seems, as brilliant as everything was, each time I stepped forward, the splendor increased. . . . The light engulfed me, and I had the sense of being ushered into the presence of God. Although our earthly eyes must gradually adjust to light or darkness, my heavenly eyes saw with absolute ease.[14]

The amount of time Piper remained unconscious and without vital signs is highly unusual, even among growing numbers of reported NDEs. However, his experience of an ineffable light was not. Many people who have died and returned use similar language endeavoring to describe an encounter with a source of light that does more than transmit love.

Many say it *is* love.

Here is the testimony of a teenage girl who came near to death while undergoing treatment for leukemia:

All of a sudden I could feel myself being pulled upward. It was slow at first, then the pace became increasingly faster and faster. By this time I was in a black tunnel, but at the end of the tunnel was a light. As I got closer to it, it got brighter and brighter. It wasn't like any light I could describe to you. It was beautiful.

When I was almost to the end, I slowed down and then I was there. This light was so bright, and it surrounded me and filled me with a total love and joy. I don't know how else to describe it to you. I felt intensely pure, calm, and reassured. I just wanted to stay there forever.[15]

Consider the account of Betty Eadie, author of *Embraced by the Light*, who clinically died from complications following surgery.

As I got closer, the light became brilliant—brilliant beyond any description, far more brilliant than the sun—and I knew that no earthly eyes could look upon this light without being destroyed.

Eadie saw the figure of a man in the light and somehow *knew* she was in the presence of Jesus: "I felt as if I had stepped into his countenance, and I felt an utter explosion of love. It was the most unconditional love I have ever felt."[16]

Love and light are the essential fruits of a Christlike life. What else should we expect to see when the earthly veil is removed from our eyes and we no longer "see but a poor reflection as in a mirror"?[17]

Naturally, we would rather live, not die. We don't want to die alone or suffer terribly when our time comes. Even Jesus, facing death, prayed, "Take this cup from me."[18] But, again, wishing to avoid a lonely, painful death is quite different from the intense fear and foreboding many feel when they contemplate dying. The prospect is so terrifying that we rarely speak of it at all.

But now having heard a few accounts of what may await us, does it really stretch your imagination to see glimmers of heaven in them? Are these stories more than last-gasp hallucinations of oxygen-starved brains, as some scientists insist? More than trauma-induced dreams? More than wishful thinking?

As you ponder the evidence, remember this is by no means the first time Jesus has been described as being full of loving light:

> In him was life, and that life was the light of men. The light shines in the darkness, but the darkness has not understood it.[19]

Here's one thing we know for sure: The more you immerse yourself in the story of God's light in this life, the more likely you are to see it again on the other side.

4

A Taste of Torment

Not All Roads After Life Lead to the Light

Here sighs, plaints, and voices of the deepest woe resounded through the starless sky. Strange languages, horrid cries, accents of grief and wrath, voices deep and hoarse, with hands clenched in despair, made a commotion which whirled forever through that air of everlasting gloom.

Dante Alighieri, "Inferno"

These days, the term *near-death experience* has become practically synonymous with the word *light*. In the last chapter we saw why: So many who survive a close encounter with death tell a remarkably similar story, depicting the next world as being full of light, love, joy, and peace. Dying, they say, is by far the easiest, most pleasant thing they've ever done. Far from being dark, lonely, and frightening, the over-there landscape is full of familiar faces and radiant spirits to guide and welcome us when our time comes to move on.

Most books on the subject have titles like *Closer to the Light, The Light Beyond,* and *Lessons from the Light.* Even Raymond Moody's classic that helped launch the NDE revolution, the one that forever changed how our society views death, is optimistically called *Life After Life.*

It's settled then, right? So much compelling eyewitness testimony all but establishes that death is a joyous reunion; a child's sweet coming home to a Father's feast of unconditional love and acceptance. We all can relax and look forward to the embrace of a warm welcome at life's end.

Well, not quite. As it happens, the stories we've examined, the ones eagerly gleaned for heavenly glimpses, aren't the only ones being told by those who come close to dying. There is another, much less common version—and it's far less comforting. Some people reluctantly report an exact opposite experience to what we've considered so far, in surroundings that seem an "anti-heaven" in every way: dark, oppressive, extremely frightening. In short, they believe they've been to the brink of *hell:* a place like Jesus described where God's enemies would be thrown, where "their worm does not die, and the fire is not quenched."[1]

Before we get complacent and start thinking a soft, cushy afterlife is a done deal for everyone, we'd be wise to take a closer look at what these sobering stories have to teach us. Understandably, if you visit hell while near death, you might be hesitant to admit it, to share as readily as someone else who got to walk with angels in fields of heavenly flowers. What might that say about how you've lived so far? As cardiologist and NDE researcher Maurice Rawlings says, it's like getting an F on your report card—not something to brag about. What's more, many who have had a "taste of torment" found the experience so horrifying that they didn't want to speak of it once back on solid ground.

"I'm in Hell"

In *Beyond Death's Door,* Rawlings shares how his view of the afterlife forever changed on the day one of his heart patients "died" in his office. During a routine stress test on a treadmill, the man's heart stopped and he collapsed. Immediately, Rawlings and his staff began emergency resuscitation measures.

> The patient began "coming to." But whenever I would reach for instruments or otherwise interrupt my compression of his chest, the patient would again lose consciousness, roll his eyes upward, arch his back in mild convulsion, stop breathing, and die once more.
>
> Each time he regained heartbeat and respiration, the patient screamed, "I am in hell!" He was terrified and pleaded with me to help him.[2]

The man experienced clinical death—cessation of heartbeat and breathing—four times. Each time he was revived, he was anguished: "Don't stop! Don't you understand? I'm in hell! Each time you quit I go back to hell. . . . How do I stay out of hell?"

An unbeliever at the time, Rawlings replied, "I'm busy. Don't bother me about your hell until I finish getting this pacemaker into place." But he soon saw that his patient was immersed in extreme panic. Despite his own doubts about God and the reality of an afterlife, Rawlings told the man he should ask for God's forgiveness and turn over his life. They prayed together—the dying man and the agnostic—on the clinic floor. Soon, the man's condition stabilized, and he was transported to the hospital.

> Now I was convinced there was something about this life after death business after all. All of my concepts needed revision. I needed to find out more. . . .
>
> A couple of days later, I approached my patient with pad and pencil in hand for an interview. At his bedside I asked him to recall what he actually saw in hell. . . . What did hell look like?
>
> He said, "What hell? I don't recall any hell!" Apparently, the experiences were so frightening, so horrible, so painful that his conscious mind could not cope with them; and they were subsequently suppressed far into his subconscious.[3]

Rawlings surmises that this provides an example of why NDE literature contains relatively few hellish accounts—most people don't even want to remember the horrors they've seen, much less examine and discuss them. (This story, however, has a hopeful postscript: Rawlings reports the man is "now a strong Christian." Rawlings himself became a believer as a result of his patient's brush with hell.)

Fortunately, a courageous few who've been to hell and back have come forward to share what happened, most for the purpose of helping others avoid the fate to which they themselves came so close. In chapter 2, we drew a sort of composite *positive*–NDE sketch with elements that commonly appear in documented accounts. Though the reservoir of documented *negative* stories is much smaller, let's once again stitch them together and see what they could tell us about the reality and nature of hell. Once again, few people report an NDE identical to this one, but all the elements appear in multiple accounts.

As you read the following, don't do so from a safe, self-assured distance. Imagine yourself in this scenario with as much realism as you can muster.

You're on a hospital gurney, suffering in agony from a life--threatening illness or injury. Your body is in severe crisis, and despite their best efforts the ER staff is unable to stabilize your vital signs. Your heart stops beating; your blood pressure falls to nothing; your measurable brain activity ceases.

You suddenly realize you no longer feel any pain and are watching the frantic resuscitation attempts from outside your body. You observe the pandemonium with detached interest but experience no fear or regret.

After a moment you feel yourself sinking toward the floor; a dark tunnel has appeared, and you're being pulled into it. Involuntarily, you enter and move downward at incredible speed. As you go, the walls seem to close in tight around you. The atmosphere begins to grow disturbingly hot and stifling.

The first thing you notice after emerging at the other end is impenetrable darkness—deeper and blacker than anything you've ever seen on earth—seeming to radiate evil hostility toward you. The heat is now truly unbearable, leading you to wonder how anyone could possibly survive it. There's a sulfuric scent in your nostrils. Your thirst is beyond description.

Something in the darkness touches you or pulls at you. You can't see what it is; discerning vague movement, you feel the most intense terror imaginable. Despair and hopelessness close around your heart and mind like a vise.

You start to notice an orange glow, and a horrifying scene unfolds: a lake of fire that contains countless people, all screaming and thrashing about in agony. They plead for relief, but there is none. You know there never will be, and it fills you with anguished dread. Evil creatures are in the fire as well; they seem to delight in inflicting terror and torment on the souls imprisoned there.

In a flash of horror, you realize the fate you're witnessing is exactly what *you* deserve. The life you lived on earth has led you inevitably here.

Despite your sense of unworthiness, you cry out, "God, help me!"

Instantly, across the vast darkness, a light appears, as if from a great distance. As it approaches, you feel overwhelmed by unconditional love and forgiveness. The light lifts you away from the fire, out of the devastating blackness.

You accept and are taken into the light itself, where you experience many of the elements common to a "positive NDE." Afterward, you return to your body.

44

It is impossible to fathom a more horrifying fate. If you truly have succeeded in putting yourself in the shoes of someone who's been to the edge of hell, then you understand why D. L. Moody is quoted as saying, "When we preach on hell, we might at least do it with tears in our eyes."

Here again are the common elements present in hellish NDEs:

- Darkness
- Heat
- Terror and despair
- Souls in torment
- Evil, menacing creatures
- A way out of darkness and into the light for now, or so it appears.

As we'll see in the following stories, people usually are irrevocably changed by this experience. They are gripped by a determination to make the most of their second chance at life and to warn others in jeopardy of a tortured eternity. Most of all, they return to life convinced of one thing: *Hell is real.*

"The Sewer of the Universe"

Howard Storm was a survival-of-the-fittest kind of guy. He believed he'd been born into a dog-eat-dog world, so he "might as well be a winner instead of a loser." An artist and university professor, he sought greatness and immortality in his own creations, which would hang in museums and be adored forever.

> Why would I need to believe in a higher power? Who would put the needs of others ahead of their own needs? You have to watch your back always. Life is every man for himself. The one who dies with the most toys wins. Compassion is for the weak. If you don't take care of yourself, nobody else will. I thought I was the biggest, baddest bear in the woods. Wasn't I good enough?[4]

Storm would get an answer to that question sooner than he thought. During a trip to Paris with his wife, Beverly, he was overcome by intense pain in his abdomen; the cause was a tear in the lining of his stomach.

He was rushed to the hospital in agony . . . only to languish there, waiting for a surgeon to arrive. (At the time, Parisian hospitals typically were understaffed on weekends.)

After many hours of suffering with no relief, Howard Storm died, or so it seemed. He found himself standing up in the room, looking back at his body in the bed. Despite his bewilderment, he felt more alive and more real than ever before. He tried to communicate with his wife, who sat slumped in exhaustion beside him. But no matter how loudly he screamed, she could not hear him.

Then he heard voices calling his name in the hallway outside the room: "Come out here. Let's go, hurry up. We've been waiting for you a long time."

Confused and uneasy, at first he was reluctant to go. But when the voices promised to help him, he stepped into the hallway. There he saw several people motioning for him to follow; they were fuzzy and indistinct, as if he were looking through a dense fog. The longer he walked with them, the more belligerent and abusive they became, telling him to "quit moaning and hurry up."

Finally they reached their apparent destination. Storm recalls:

> When I looked around I was horrified to discover that we were in complete darkness.
>
> The hopelessness of my situation overwhelmed me. . . . I could feel their breath on me as they shouted and snarled insults. Then they began to push and shove me about. I began to fight back. A wild frenzy of taunting, screaming, and hitting ensued. As I swung and kicked at them, they bit and tore back at me. All the while it was obvious that they were having great fun. . . . I was aware there were dozens or hundreds of them. . . . They were playing with me, just as a cat plays with a mouse. Every new assault brought howls of cacophonous laughter. They began to tear off pieces of my flesh. To my horror, I realized that I was being taken apart and eaten alive, methodically, slowly, so that their entertainment would last as long as possible.[5]

As he lay on the ground, Storm heard a voice that sounded like his own, but what it said didn't come from his thoughts: *Pray to God.* At first he argued that prayer is stupid and pointless; nevertheless, by the third time the voice said, "Pray to God!" he was ready to try. He managed to string together bits and pieces of barely remembered Scriptures and prayers he'd heard, finishing with "Jesus loves me." As the words escaped his lips, he knew he wanted them to be true—*really* true—more than he'd ever wanted anything.

> Far off in the darkness, I saw a pinpoint of light like the faintest star in the sky. . . . The star was rapidly getting brighter and brighter. . . . I couldn't take my eyes off it; the light was more intense and more beautiful than anything I had ever seen. It was brighter than the sun, brighter than a flash of lightning.[6]

As the light approached, Storm realized it was not some*thing* but rather some*one*. Jesus picked him up off the ground and healed his wounds. Thus began the story's part 2: Jesus lifted him out and showed him the other possible end to life, a heavenly vision of inconceivable love and light. It was up to Howard Storm to decide which he would inherit.

When he returned to his body, he became a passionate believer and dedicated pastor. In the conclusion of his book, he writes:

> Why didn't I say "Yes" to God sooner? Why did I wait so long? How much of my life have I wasted with my eyes closed to the truth? If you make one step toward God, God will take a giant step to you.[7]

"The Place Where Hope Came to Die"

Angie Fenimore had struggled her whole life with what she called "the cycle," recurring periods of deep depression. Sexually abused as a child, she'd never escaped the toxic combination of shame and rage in her heart. She attended church off and on but didn't find lasting comfort there. After years of struggle and failure, she became convinced her husband and small children would be better off without her.

She took an overdose of medication. She killed herself. Free from her body, she was suddenly in darkness that "wasn't just blackness, it was an endless void, an absence of light." But that wasn't all.

> I landed on the edge of a shadowy plane, suspended in the darkness, extending to the limits of my sight. Its floor was firm but shrouded in black mist, swirling around my feet, that also formed the thick, waist-high barrier that held me prisoner. The place was charged with a crackling energy that sparked me into hyper-alertness. . . . The fog-like mist had mass—it

seemed to be formed of molecules of intense darkness. . . . It had life, this darkness, some kind of intelligence that was purely negative, even evil. It sucked at me, pulling me to react and then swallowing my reaction into fear and dread. In my life I had suffered pain and despair so great that I could barely function, but the twisting anguish of this disconnection was beyond my capacity to conceive.[8]

As she looked around, Fenimore became aware of many others "standing or squatting or wandering about on the plane. Some were mumbling to themselves . . . completely self-absorbed, every one of them too caught up in his or her own misery to engage in any mental or emotional exchange . . . they were incapacitated by the darkness."[9]

Then, like Howard Storm, just as she was about to abandon hope, a voice sounded in the dark:

. . . a booming wave of sound . . . that encompassed such ferocious anger that with one word it could destroy the universe, and that also encompassed such potent and unwavering love that, like the sun, it could coax life from the earth.[10]

The voice came from a point of light that appeared outside the veil of mist surrounding her. The light grew "far more brilliant than the sun," and she knew she was in the presence of God.

"Is this really what you want?" God asked.

Then they were joined by another, one she knew to be God's Son, Jesus.

He spoke to me through the veil of darkness, "Don't you understand? I have done this for you." As I was flooded with His love and with the actual pain that He bore for me, my spiritual eyes were opened. In that moment I began to see just exactly what the Savior had done, how He had sacrificed for me. . . . My trust had been violated so many times in my life that I had very little to spare. And so I had clung to my pain so tightly that I was willing to end my life rather than unburden myself and act on the chance that a Savior existed. . . . He had been there for me all through my life, but I had not trusted Him.[11]

Immensely sorrowful over the pain she'd caused her family, Angie Fenimore realized she was being given a second chance to live wisely. With a fierce determination not to waste the opportunity, she was returned to her body. Although she still needed to overcome old attitudes and patterns of behavior, she was no longer alone and at the mercy of the darkness.

"The Stench Was Terrible"

Ronnie Reagan (no relation to the former president) was a drug addict and a convicted criminal. His marriage was a wreck; his children were afraid of him. In the documentary *To Hell and Back*, Reagan said after all the pain and hardship he'd endured, he thought there was nothing left that could frighten him. All that changed one evening after a senseless brawl outside a neighborhood market left him bleeding to death.

Inside the speeding ambulance, the attending paramedic leaned close to his ear and said, "Sir, you need Jesus Christ."

Reagan responded to the suggestion as he always had—with angry curses. Undeterred, the medic repeated himself. "You need Jesus." Reagan recalls:

> As he was talking to me, it appeared like the ambulance literally exploded in flames. I thought it had actually blown up. It filled with smoke and immediately I was moving through that smoke as if through a tunnel. After some period of time, coming out of the smoke and out of the darkness I began to hear the voices of a multitude of people screaming and groaning and crying. But as I looked down the sensation was of looking down on a volcanic opening and seeing fire and smoke and people inside this burning place. They were burning but weren't being consumed.[12]

He instantly recognized some people he'd known who had already died. "The most painful part of it was the loneliness. And the depression was so heavy that there was no hope, there was no escape."

Then he awoke in the hospital. He could still feel hell's heat and smell its stench but had no clue what to do next. After his recovery, he tried to get drunk and stoned as usual but couldn't. Nothing worked to make him forget what he'd experienced. Finally, in desperation, after his wife became a Christian a few weeks later, Reagan followed her to church. The minister rose and said, "Behold the Lamb of God that takes away the sins of the world."[13] What happened next surprised even Reagan:

> I turned to leave, but instead I started down the aisle toward the front of that building. I didn't know the sinner's prayer. . . . But my prayer was this: *"God, if you exist, and Jesus, if you are God's lamb, please, please kill me or cure me. I don't want to live anymore, I'm not a husband, I'm not a father, I'm no good."* And at that instant, it was like the darkness and the blackness

49

left my life. Then the tears began to flow and for the first time since I was nine years old, the tears did run. The guilt left my life, the violence, anger and the hatred left my life. And Jesus Christ became Lord and Savior of my life that morning.[14]

Reagan no longer hears the tortured cries or smells the smoke, but he knows his life was spared so he can tell his story and warn others about the terrible torment he witnessed—about the *reality* of hell.

Some stories inspire in us the hope of heaven; others warn of hell's horrors. Does either qualify as admissible evidence in the court of scientific inquiry into the afterlife? No. Do they settle the theological questions (e.g., "Who goes where?") once and for all? Not that either. They certainly are suggestive, and in many respects they support biblical teaching. Still, in the mysteries that remain, there is ample room for differing interpretations.

In the previous two chapters, I wrote about the persuasiveness of elements that appear again and again in NDE accounts, full of light or full of darkness. You may have noticed there is one more commonality present in these stories, one not yet called to your attention. Of all the clues surfacing in NDE testimony, this is the most important to our understanding of what to expect when we die.

What's this common thread?

God's presence.

If you go toward the light at death—his love is there, enfolding you in a soothing blanket of acceptance and welcome.

Go into the darkness and return—God is still there, lovingly holding open the door to forgiveness and redemption.

Knowing what you know now, why cut it close? Why leave life's really important choices to the last minute? Why bother living through the hell on earth of separation from God when the kingdom of heaven is fully available?

As Howard Storm learned, it's as easy as saying and believing that "Jesus loves me. . . ."

Part Two

What Lies
Between Worlds

5

Things That Go Bump in the Night

Yes, Virginia, There Really Could Be a Ghost in the Attic

Penetrating so many secrets, we cease to believe in the unknowable.
But there it sits, nevertheless, calmly licking its chops.

H. L. Mencken

When David retired, he bought land in a remote corner of Colorado—nine thousand feet above sea level, fifteen miles from the nearest town, light-years beyond the stress and strain of urban life. From the front porch of his home—a rustic log cabin he built himself—he looked out over a forested valley rimmed in all directions by majestic mountains. Deer often grazed just outside his windows.

To David, it was the closest thing to paradise this side of heaven . . . and the last place on earth he expected to encounter a ghost. "I moved there to get away from people and enjoy a little peace and quiet," he said. "My nearest neighbors were two miles away. The nearest *living* ones, anyway."

On one side, his property abutted a national forest. He spent many hours there, walking the game trails and jeep roads crisscrossing the woods. An avid outdoorsman, he was at home in the wilderness—cautious, but not easily frightened. Even on the darkest night, he didn't hesitate to walk anywhere.

"But one spot was different," David recalled. "There's an old, overgrown logging road that hasn't been used in decades. From the top of a ridgeline, it drops into a narrow ravine, crosses a dry creek bed, and then climbs out the other side. The first time I walked there, it was after nightfall. The moon was bright, and I could see just fine. Yet when I descended toward the creek, suddenly the hairs on the back of my neck stood up. I had the overwhelming sensation I wasn't alone."

The feeling was so strong that he turned around and took a different route. By the time he returned home, he was convinced he'd imagined the whole thing. He laughed at his foolishness—and forgot all about it. Until a month later. Out again after dark, David came to the same road.

"It was the shortest way home, so without any thought I started down that path," he said. "Then, sure enough, at the exact same spot, I felt my skin start to crawl. Even then, I refused to believe there was anything to it. I gave myself quite a pep talk. 'Come on, you big sissy. When did you get afraid of the dark?' But this time there was more. I not only sensed someone was there, I had the feeling this 'someone' was really *angry*."

David didn't believe in ghosts or boogeymen—in fact, he scoffed at those who did. He believed God gave us five perfectly good senses for telling the difference between fantasy and reality. What happened next changed his mind.

"I was determined not to let my imagination get the best of me again," he said. "I decided to let my spine tingle if it wanted to and kept on walking."

When he reached the bottom of the ravine, David looked to his right. There he saw the figure of a man standing in the creek bed, looking up intently toward the ridgeline. His face was a mask of anxious concentration. He wore plain clothing—dusty pants and shirt—and a floppy cowboy hat.

"It's like he was there and not there, kind of luminous and see-through," he recounted. "Then he looked at me, and I knew he felt threatened by my presence. He turned and walked away from me—and just disappeared into the dark. I wasn't going to wait around for him to come back, I can tell you that. I got out of there."

David freely admits his experience doesn't prove the reality of ghosts. But the encounter was so convincing he decided to do a little digging to find out more about the area's history. He discovered his property was less than a mile from one of Colorado's forgotten so-called "ghost towns"— a late-1800s mining camp called Iris. In its heyday, Iris was home to five thousand prospectors, merchants, hoteliers, dreamers, gamblers, and other fortune-seekers. The surrounding hills and ravines were a patchwork of homesteads and claims, now abandoned and reclaimed by the forest. Many of the roads David hiked were originally built to carry fresh-cut timber to the town's sawmill.

By the turn of the century, the gold and silver were gone—and so was Iris. All that remains today are a half-dozen dilapidated log cabins and scattered piles of rusty tin cans and broken glass. Oh, and one more thing: There is a weed-choked cemetery on a rise overlooking the old town.

David mused, "Maybe the man I saw died out there defending his stake in the gold rush. Maybe he's still at it a century later, like one of those Japanese pilots who didn't know the war was over decades after getting shot down on a deserted island in the Pacific. All I know is what happened to me felt very, very real."

No Such Thing as Ghosts—Right?

It turns out that there are hundreds, perhaps thousands, of accounts similar to David's reported each year. Lots of sane, rational, otherwise highly skeptical people insist they've seen a ghost. What are we to make of this? As we saw in chapter 1, popular surveys indicate similar experiences are remarkably common—nearly one in four people claim to have had a personal encounter with a ghost or other apparition. Bookstore shelves are crammed with collections of well-documented tales about "hauntings" worldwide: spooks that scare the heebie-jeebies out of the living by gliding uninvited through the halls of damp castles . . . rattling windows, slamming doors, banging pipes everywhere from stately mansions to forgotten farmhouses . . . refusing to leave a tragedy-stricken hotel room decades after check-out time . . . or filling a room with an unexplainable scent—cigar smoke or lilacs or rotting meat.

Creepy stories are nothing new. Ghosts and demons have populated our imaginations from the dawn of storytelling. The Sumerian *Epic of Gilgamesh*, widely believed to be the earliest ghost story on record, was preserved for centuries on twelve clay tablets in the ruins of ancient Nineveh, with the earliest known versions dating back to around 2100 BC. Gilgamesh begs "the gods" for one last meeting with his fallen friend Enkidu, who reports on the horrors of the underworld. Enkidu says that the spirits of the "unloved dead" are present in the world and eat "the leftovers from the pot, the scraps of bread thrown into the gutter, things not even a dead dog would eat."[1]

Millennia later, William Shakespeare terrified Elizabethan audiences with the ghost of King Hamlet. The apparition appeared to his son at midnight, announcing that his death was no accident: He had been murdered by his own brother, Claudius, who'd poured poison in his ear. This knowledge propels young Hamlet into the classic story about the cost of vengeance.

Then there was "Old Jeffrey," a poltergeist said to have caused commotion during the year 1717 in Britain's Epworth Rectory. Over a period of weeks the "ghost" disturbed the peace with frightening "groans, squeaks, tingling and strange knockings in diverse places." A number of people heard sounds like breaking bottles and saw door handles rise and fall of their own accord. No rational explanation was ever found, though some have suspected a prank played by local parishioners. The story is famous in ghost lore, because at the time the rectory was home to Samuel and Susanna Wesley, among whose children was a young boy named John—who would go on to become a great evangelist and the founder of Wesleyan Methodism.[2]

Even Jesus' followers were prone to blame ghosts when they witnessed things their minds told them couldn't be real. One stormy night, they found themselves in a boat on a wind-tossed lake. Jesus had said to go without him.

> During the fourth watch of the night Jesus went out to them, walking on the lake. When the disciples saw him . . . they were terrified. "It's a ghost," they said, and cried out in fear.[3]

Let's face it—for as long as humans live in this world, we will continue to experience eerie things we interpret as visitations from the other side. So we might as well roll up our sleeves and tackle obvious questions: What's really behind all the goose bumps? All the sleepless nights? What *are* ghosts, anyway?

As you might have guessed, there isn't a single, definitive answer. Let's look at four possibilities.

(1) Nothing but Nonsense

In modern societies this likely would be the most common reply. "Nothing but nonsense" certainly is the most rational response to the notion of haunted houses, candles mysteriously igniting, and garbled voices recorded in empty rooms. When children cry out from their beds claiming to have seen a ghost, most parents offer comfort by invoking the materialist mantra: Anything you can't see, smell, taste, touch, hear, capture, measure, reproduce, dissect, and display in a museum simply does not exist. Now, go to sleep, dear.

"There is no such thing as a ghost."

"Your eyes were playing tricks on you."

"No more pizza before bedtime."

"It was only your nightgown hanging on the peg."

"It's all in your imagination."

We've heard the argument *ad infinitum*—from parents, teachers, ministers, and playground peers. The professor Geddes MacGregor summed this up in *Images of Afterlife:* "There can be no disembodied life. For mind, whatever it is, to exist there must be not only matter but life; that is, as we cannot have life without embodiment, we cannot have mind without life."[4]

To materialists, ghosts can't exist because material manifestation is the supreme, compulsory condition of being considered "real." Despite countless firsthand stories throughout history to the contrary, they dismiss as absurd the very idea of disembodied spirits that move, speak, and act without the physical apparatus to do so. Why, it's an affront to reason and logic.

"Ghosts?" they say, like Ebenezer Scrooge. "Bah!"

(2) A Glitch in the Matrix

The Matrix film trilogy is based on the premise that everything humans perceive as objective reality actually is an interactive neural computer program. People live out their lives blissfully unaware that the whole world is a grand illusion designed to hide the truth—that they're slaves to rogue machines, artificial intelligence gone bad. Within the matrix, "anomalies" in the code usually are "paranormal" experiences. So-called psychic phenomena often are really just programming relics that make perfect sense when the mechanisms of "reality" are truly grasped.

Many scientists studying the nature of consciousness think something similar is going on in our perception of the real world. Ghost sightings and other extrasensory encounters, they say, are not supernatural but are glitches in the mind's ultra-natural biological machinery. Accordingly, our lack of knowledge—a curable condition (with enough additional research)—is what makes us susceptible to all manner of superstitious speculation.

Melvin Morse introduces this in *Where God Lives*:

In 1997, neuroscientists from the University of California at San Diego bravely proclaimed that they had found an area of the human brain that "may be hardwired to hear the voice of heaven." In specially designed research, they found that certain parts of the brain—the right temporal lobe, to be exact—were attuned to ideas about the supreme being and mystical experiences. . . . This region is instrumental in facilitating mind-body healing. It is responsible for visions as well as psychic powers and vivid spiritual experiences.[5]

Here's the crux of the argument: If you have a ghostly "vision," you needn't look further than your own head for an explanation. Such an experience may suggest nothing at all about the existence of parallel spiritual realms, or whether you have a soul that survives beyond death. It might merely be the ordinary way the brain relates to its environment.

My analysis of more than ten thousand ghost stories convinces me that they represent complex interactions between the individual and universal memory. We tap into this universal memory in the same way that a radio receives radio waves. And just as the air around us is filled with radio and cell phone waves, it is also filled with thought and memory from people and events, both past and present. When tapping into this memory field, the right temporal lobe acts as a receiver because it is at times calibrated to receive memory that exists in the memory bank.[6]

The key idea is that human thoughts and emotions create an energy "imprint" that's preserved in the very fabric of the universe. All that has ever occurred is still present around us—in storage, so to speak. We don't have access to this information normally because our brains are concerned with more mundane tasks, like ferrying the kids and paying the bills. But that doesn't mean we *can't* see it. What Morse and others suggest is that some of us *do*; we all appear to be equipped with a receiver capable of translating this programming code into visible and audible forms. For whatever reasons, from time to time the receiver switches on. Being ignorant of how this mechanism works, we typically label the experience "paranormal" and pull the covers over our head.

If that thinking is correct, then ghosts are no more real than images on the cinema screen. They reveal more about the mind's impressive technology as a mental projector than about wispy visitors from the afterlife. Like moviegoers, we're sometimes drawn convincingly into the illusion and lose ourselves in the drama. But when the lights come on, nothing of any substance remains.

(3) Dead People—Sometimes Called "Disembodied Spirits"

Among possible explanations, the materialistic and mechanistic ones definitely are the new kids on the block. For most of history, few people would have hesitated to answer—fearfully whispering, maybe, so as not to attract otherworldly attention—that ghosts are "the restless dead."

Many diverse cultures have believed that successfully leaving this life and crossing over to the next at death is not as straightforward or automatic as it may seem. Spirits can become trapped on the earthly plane, held back by unfinished business, powerful attachments to people or objects, or a thirst for vengeance. Some believe victims of untimely or violent death are easily confused and may not even know they're dead. Not all are malevolent or threatening, though—just in need of directions. (There are many reports of spirits apparently hanging around to offer comfort to loved ones left behind. More about that in chapter 6.)

For this reason, complicated rituals and taboos concerning proper treatment of the dead can be found all over the globe. According to adherents, it's incumbent upon the living to make sure the departed have a safe trip—meaning that they actually reach their destination. They eagerly perform this service to avoid the terrible consequences of offending the spirit or of letting a lost soul stick around. As paranormal historian Brian Righi writes:

Intricate burials, festivals honoring the dead, and prayers for the departed served one basic purpose—to keep the dead in their graves. Man, both modern and ancient, has tempered his curiosity about the spirit world with a good dose of fear, which in turn has led to some rather colorful ways of dealing with returning ghosts.[7]

Here's a handful of examples:

- Ancient Greeks wouldn't have dreamed of burying a dead body without equipping the soul for the arduous journey ahead. Money was placed in the corpse's mouth as payment for "Charon, the Ferryman, to take it across the River Styx." Greek sailors at sea carried money with them at all times in the hope that if they drowned, the reward would entice whoever found their body to bury it properly.
- Romans assumed their dead relatives remained an important, albeit invisible, part of this world. They stocked ancestral tombs with food and drink and even invited the departed spirits, called *Lares*, into their homes to act as guardians.
- Pacific Islanders held vigil over the dead for at least seven days to be sure the devil didn't come and steal the body. They provided food and shelter in case the spirit grew hungry or tired of wandering.
- In most Spanish-speaking countries, the first day of November is *el Dia de los Muertos*—the Day of the Dead. People offer food and treats to dead relatives and attend prayer vigils, cleaning and decorating their graves.
- People in the British Isles believed someone who died violently or unexpectedly might return seeking retribution. To thwart them, the body was to be buried at a remote crossroads (to confuse the spirit about the way back) with a stake through the heart (to prevent it from getting up and causing mischief).
- The prospect of ghosts spooked the Danes so much that "before burial, the big toes of the corpse were tied together to hobble the spirit, pennies were placed on the eyes to blind it, and scissors were left on the stomach, opened in the form of a cross, to prevent evil."[8]

Clearly, "visitations" have been around a long time. With few exceptions, *our* ancestors blamed *their* dead ancestors when things went bump in the night.

(4) Evil Spirits—Often Called "Demons"

A great many of the hauntings reported in paranormal literature involve ghosts that are not overtly threatening. In fact, many appear oblivious to their earthly surroundings, as if it's just as uncommon for a ghost to "see" the living as for the living to see a ghost. That doesn't mean the experience isn't frightening, only that the apparitions show no apparent malice toward others present. They simply appear, and that's enough to send us scurrying to turn on all the lights.

But there is a subset of stories for which this isn't true. These encounters are characterized not by glimpses of figures in outdated clothes but by a terrifying experience of focused, purposeful, violent *evil*. In such cases, witnesses often become the target of physical and psychological attacks.

Ironically, materialist dogma—enjoining a nearly fanatical skepticism of all things unseen—objects forcefully to the possible existence of demons and their manifestation on earth. If suggesting that ghosts are disembodied *human* spirits can get you laughed at, then pointing the finger at *Satan's* minions can land you under heavy psychiatric care. Claiming demons are in your attic isn't widely accepted as a sign of mental health.

Before his own personal encounters with evil spirits, psychiatrist M. Scott Peck (*The Road Less Traveled*) certainly would have agreed with this diagnosis—describing himself as "99+ percent sure the devil did not exist." But in his *Glimpses of the Devil,* Peck tells the story of two patients under his care—both of whom he concluded were "possessed" by evil spirits. At substantial risk to his professional reputation, he agreed to participate in classic rites of exorcism for the women—one successful, one not. The most formidable obstacle to overcome was his rational resistance to the idea that such spirits even existed. What he saw and heard during direct confrontations with Satan was enough to do the trick:

> I had been converted . . . to a belief—a certainty—that the devil does exist and probably demons (under the control of the devil) as well. By the devil, I mean a spirit that is powerful (it may be many places at the same time and manifest itself in a variety of distinctly paranormal ways), thoroughly malevolent (its only motivation seemed to be the destruction of human beings or the entire human race), deceitful and vain, capable of taking up a kind of residence within the mind, brain, soul, or body of susceptible and willing human beings.[9]

61

That's as definitive a statement as you're likely to get from a trained scientist and medical doctor, and the Bible agrees with his "conversion." Jesus often confronted and drove out evil spirits that had invaded human beings. In one case, a man who spent his days wandering among tombs, crying out and cutting himself, saw Jesus coming from a distance and ran to meet him.

> He shouted at the top of his voice, "What do you want with me, Jesus, Son of the Most High God? Swear to God that you won't torture me!" For Jesus had said to him, "Come out of this man, you evil spirit!"
>
> Then Jesus asked him, "What is your name?"
>
> "My name is Legion," he replied, "for we are many."

The demons begged Jesus to send them into a nearby herd of pigs. He did; the herd ran off a cliff and drowned.[10]

To those who are the least bit spiritually oriented, that demons exist is indisputable. Their purpose is to harass, harm, and deceive. But is it reasonable to assume they're behind *all* ghostly phenomena? Authors of *The Kingdon of the Occult* say the answer is yes.

> Poltergeists (demons masquerading as humans) are usually imaginative in creating their manifestations: they slam doors, walk up steps, throw objects around the room, moan, cry, touch people, and materialize as dark clouds, red eyes, figures, or colorful moving orbs of light. . . . In some cases, foul smells or ice-cold temperatures manifest along with other phenomena.
>
> The world persists in its definitions, but the biblical revelation stands: poltergeists are *demons,* not lost human souls caught between this world and the next. They are not ghosts a la Patrick Swayze in the romantic tearjerker *Ghost.* Demons enjoy playing games with human beings, and they have had centuries to perfect their technique.[11]

It is unlikely anyone will ever prove beyond doubt that all ghosts are really demons in disguise. But, if nothing else, it certainly is the most prudent possible answer to our question. As C. S. Lewis once wrote, "There is no neutral ground in the universe: every square inch, every split second is claimed by God and counterclaimed by Satan."[12]

In other words, better safe than sorry.

Though I've had many other spiritual encounters, I am among the ranks that have never seen what I would call a *ghost*. That doesn't mean I'm not open to the possibility. As a grad student in the late '70s, I toured England, retracing the steps of John Wesley, born in 1703. I visited the hamlet of Epworth to see the house where Samuel and Susanna Wesley raised nineteen children.

Arriving on a cold, rainy day, I discovered I was the only visitor to the sprawling two-story house. Tired from long hours of air travel, followed by more via train and taxi, I finally viewed the place I'd read so much about and, completing my tour, prepared to leave.

Aware of my exhaustion, the curator said, "Guests are allowed to rent rooms in the house. Since no one else is staying here tonight, you can have your pick."

I thought how wonderful it would be to stay in the world's best-known rectory. Then I recalled all the stories—confirmed by the curator—involving "Old Jeffrey," who allegedly had roamed the corridors. Letters from family members specifically referred to the resident apparition and his shenanigans.

Suddenly I envisioned myself all alone in this drafty, creaky house on a cold, rainy night—and the thought of scurrying back to London sounded very appealing. I might as well admit it: I was too chicken to stay.

But perhaps you're among the 25 percent who say they've seen a ghost. I imagine the first words out of your mouth—after you regained the ability to speak—were, "What *was* that?" It's a curiosity many of us share.

While we still draw breath as living humans, we don't stand a ghost of a chance (forgive the pun) of knowing for sure what ghosts are. While many will theorize and speculate and pontificate, this will remain an intriguing mystery.

Here's the wisest course of action: Wrap yourself every day in the safety of God's love and protection. Again, as Paul wrote:

> I am convinced that neither death nor life, neither angels nor demons, neither the present nor the future, nor any powers, neither height nor depth, nor anything else in all creation, will be able to separate us from the love of God that is in Christ Jesus our Lord.[13]

There's no brighter night-light than that, no matter what's in the shadows.

6

Grace-Filled Guests

*A Visitation From a Deceased Loved One
Is a Gift to Be Accepted Gratefully*

Miracles do not happen in contradiction to nature, but only in contradiction to that which is known to us of nature.

Augustine

Nearly seventy years after his comic-book debut, Casper the Friendly Ghost is still a popular character. He has starred in theatrical shorts, Saturday morning cartoons, even a feature-length film. Casper's always the same. He's a ghost, but not a typical one. He's about as spooky as the Pillsbury Doughboy.

Unlike his three spectral uncles—Fatso, Stinky, and Stretch—who delight in terrifying every mortal in sight, all Casper wants is to be someone's friend. But that's easier said than done when you're a ghost. One look at Casper and people's hair stands on end; then they run for their lives.

The character has enjoyed endurance in part because the premise is so ironic. Even people who completely disbelieve in ghosts are just as sure there's no such thing as a *friendly* ghost. The kinds of scary stories we've examined certainly contribute to that belief. But what if it's wrong?

- What if many people have had a pleasant encounter with the "friendly ghost" of someone who is deceased?
- What if that someone is a person they knew well and loved in life?
- What if nearly everyone who's had the experience describes it as comforting and healing after a painful loss?
- What if prominent grief counselors and hospice caregivers have said that after-death encounters like these are remarkably common?

There's no need to speculate, because all of the above is true. This isn't to say there is scientific proof of after-death communication. As we've already seen, that goal may always remain just over the horizon. It simply means convincing, firsthand testimony continues to accumulate about spontaneous communication with the spirit of a deceased loved one.

Notice that key descriptive word: *spontaneous*. We're not talking about people who seek out communication with the dead through psychics, mediums, or other means (we'll start addressing this in chapter 7). These encounters come unbidden to people of all ages, sometimes within moments of the death of their loved one, sometimes months or even years later. There is no obvious trigger other than an ongoing state of grief over their loss.

Evelyn's father, a retired English teacher and high school principal, died of a heart attack at eighty-nine, and despite his advanced age, losing him was a heavy emotional blow. Several months later, Evelyn still felt depressed and empty. Then something happened to break the logjam of sorrow.

It was the first time my mother and siblings had all come to my house after Daddy died. We were missing him but not talking about it much. After all, he'd raised us to face adversity with a stiff upper lip. It was a beautiful spring day, but it might as well have been overcast and rainy, considering our mood.

One of Daddy's favorite things was to gather around the piano together and sing our way through a couple of hymnals. This was somewhat stressful for me, since I don't play the piano very well, and he had a knack for picking the most difficult hymns. But that was easily overcome by his pure delight, his lovely tenor voice, and the way we bonded through the music. Eventually, other people would drift in and join us.

I'm not sure how it happened without him there to get us started, but that day we all wound up around the piano. It was as if singing his favorite hymns was a safe way to let our feelings out.

After a while, I slipped away from the group for a moment (my sister was playing the piano) and went into the living room. I stopped in my tracks when I saw Daddy sitting there in his old rocking chair. He looked younger and healthier than he was before he died. He had a glow about him that's hard to describe. The look on his face was one of deep satisfaction, as though he was enjoying the music as much as ever, with no sense of regret that he wasn't still with us. He said, "It's so good that you are still singing."

All I could manage to say was, "Daddy!" He smiled, and I *knew* he was happy and well wherever he was now. Then suddenly, he was gone. But the room was filled with deep peace and love that I have trouble expressing. Although I missed him, I can't say that I grieved for him after that. I knew he was still, for lack of a better word, *alive* and that we'd be together again.

After her father's death, Evelyn thought she'd never see him again on earth. But when she did, the experience filled her with new hope that *death is not an end but merely a transition to a new state of life.* Until then she'd struggled with the fear that her daddy was lost forever and that with him had gone the love they'd shared. Within seconds that fear was dispelled and her healing began in earnest.

Psychotherapist Dianne Arcangel is former director of Houston's Elizabeth Kübler-Ross Center and chaplain for The Hospice at the Texas Medical Center. Over the years she's heard hundreds of stories like Evelyn's from people grieving over a painful loss. She calls these *afterlife encounters* and says they can consist of anything from a strong impression of a loved-one's presence to detailed conversations with visible, even tangible, apparitions. Sometimes they come as meaningful dreams, symbols, sounds, or smells, and frequently the experience is shared by more than one person, which tends to lend credibility.

Many of Arcangel's grieving clients turned to her after such an event and asked, "Am I going crazy? Should I be afraid of this?"

After scouring the existing literature for answers—and coming up empty-handed—Arcangel launched a five-year international study called "The Afterlife Encounter Survey." Her purpose wasn't to prove continuation of life after death; she set out to determine the prevalence of after-death communication and its effect on those who experience it. Does it bring comfort or more pain? Does it facilitate closure or prolong grief? Do we have anything to fear in this arena?

Arcangel published the results in *Afterlife Encounters: Ordinary People, Extraordinary Experiences.* Here she reports that 64 percent of the bereaved who responded had an afterlife experience following the death of a loved one. Furthermore, an astonishing 98 percent of those said the encounter had brought much comfort and helped them cope with their grief, even many years later.[1]

These numbers suggest the phenomenon is much more widespread than most would readily believe and almost universally beneficial to those who experience it. If so, why is it not taken more seriously? Given its potential therapeutic value, why haven't researchers done more to investigate it as a standard part of the grieving process?

Professor Louis LaGrand, with over thirty-five years' experience in hospice care, death education, and counseling, offers a possible answer:

People fear ridicule and rejection. Again, in our materialistic culture, what lies outside the naturalistically defined boundaries of reality is considered to be imaginary—or worse, delusional. Few want to compound the pain of their loss with the sting of scorn from others, especially friends and family. And few scientists wish to risk their reputation on research that their peers consider to be quackery.

> One of my fantasies is that someday we will be able to demystify the ADC [after-death communication] so that it is looked at by all as a normal part of human wholeness and not an aberration to be endlessly debated. . . . It's a shame [that] we still have people who have an ADC and they have to be very careful about sharing it with others. Why? Because they feel the stabbing non-verbal responses of rejection—sometimes even from counselors. So they learn not to talk openly about it. We lose much valuable data when this happens.[2]

With this in mind, let's look at some of the "data" that has not been lost but is preserved in the following stories. These fall into three broad categories.

Signs and Symbols

Not all afterlife encounters involve direct communication with visible ghosts. Sometimes contact is made through objects or occurrences that are more subtle but no less meaningful to those who experience them. For example, when Donna lost her husband of forty-five years to a heart at-tack, she was nearly overwhelmed by shock and sadness—until a bedside lamp eased her mind.

> My husband and I always slept with a touch light on the lowest setting because I did not like to sleep in the dark. Since his death, this light has come on by itself on many days, especially when I am having a very bad time. We have had this lamp for sixteen years and it has never come on by itself. I have tried to stamp on the floor near the lamp; I have banged the dresser where it sits and it will not come on unless it is touched. One day, I just could not bring myself to turn it off because I always believed it is my husband turning it on. So I left the light on. That night when I went into my bedroom, the light was on the second level setting. When I left for work it had been on the first level.[3]

While many skeptics would dismiss her experience as coincidental or chalk it up to faulty wiring, Donna accepts it as comforting proof of there being more to reality than she had realized. For her it's a sign that her husband's soul—his essence—did not vanish just because his body died.

In another example, Loretta was devastated when she lost two grand-sons in a tragic car accident. In the following months several encounters convinced her that the boys' spirits were still very much alive and well:

> [When he was alive] Tommy used to hold the [house's] front door shut on the other side of my daughter's front door when I was trying to leave. Well, he did this several times even after his death, and as soon as I would say, "Tommy, stop it," the door would suddenly open by itself. On his birthday in May, he would have been sixteen, and he had been looking forward to getting his driver's license. I was over at my daughter's house [and] Tommy started a clock that hadn't been wound since the boys died six months earlier. It continued to run for three hours. It helped both of us so much.[4]

Numerous variations exist in such stories: a music box played unex-pectedly even though it hadn't been wound in years; a young woman's car started by itself while she visited her father's gravesite; meaningful objects were inexplicably moved or rearranged; flowers bloomed out of season.

Here's the important part: No matter how small or trivial such signs appear to casual observers, they regularly have profound significance—and bring much-needed comfort—to those on the receiving end.

Dreams

When Mary's granddaughter, Amanda, died during the summer, the family knew Christmas would be especially hard that year.

In my box of decorations I found a single jingle bell tied to a red ribbon for wearing around my neck. I slipped it over my head remembering that Amanda had made it several years before. I wore it all day. . . . Early the next morning, I had a beautiful dream of Amanda. I do believe I had a visitation as I remember all of it in great detail.

She was standing in our bedroom smiling at me. She was beautiful! . . . She stood very straight, almost regally, with a faint glow around her. I finally said, "Amanda, is that you?" She replied in a voice I well remember, "Yes, Grandma, it's me!" And to my great disappointment, I awakened.

When we were on our way to church that Christmas Eve, I told Jim and Jane [Amanda's parents] about my beautiful dream. "Oh yes," I said, "I remember something else. Amanda's hair was braided—I could see it on one side." I had never seen her hair braided and thought that was unusual, but Jane replied softly, "Mother, we braided her hair in the hospital because it was so long and in the way. She died with a braid down her back." So I am quite certain that I did, indeed, have a visit from Amanda.[5]

Mary's story provides an example of what researchers call an *evidential encounter*—one that includes information previously unknown to the mourner. In a few cases, details from the deceased even have been instrumental in identifying the person guilty of their murder. While most instances are less dramatic, they're no less intriguing. Consider Jerri's story: When she was a young girl her grandmother died of a heart attack shortly before Christmas.

We were all so sad that we hardly had any Christmas at all. But that night, Grandma came to me in a dream and told me to go get my present from her. She said she'd wrapped it and hidden it away. The next morning, when I told my mom and grandpa, Mom said, "It was just a dream." My grandpa teased me . . . laughing about it, but it *seemed* so real to me. I looked and looked everywhere but I couldn't find any present, so I knew Mom was right—it was just a dream.

I was looking out my window that night, and I could've sworn I saw my grandma shining through the top of the trees, coming from the moonlight. That may sound weird, but then I heard her say, "Go get your present before something happens to it. It's a watch. Look in the bottom of my big sewing box in the back of the closet. . . . You'll see it—it's wrapped in a red and green box."[6]

The next morning Jerri again told her family what had happened. This time her grandfather said, "Let's go see!" They followed Grandma's instructions and found the gift—a wristwatch—wrapped in green and red paper, exactly where Jerri had been told it would be. A young girl received a final present that brought her immense joy; the experience was a re-assuring gift to the whole family as well and helped ease their grief.

According to LaGrand, such dreams are among the most common vehicles or modalities for after-death communication. "Many, many more dreams than we realized—both symbolic and those that can be literally interpreted—do occur and bring peace and strength to continue on."[7]

Elizabeth Kübler-Ross agrees:

> Our dreams show us that our loved one is not in essence the sick person to whom we tearfully said good-bye in the hospital. Neither is he or she the body we saw at the funeral home. . . . When people dream of a loved one, they often report feeling a sense of peace afterward, a reassurance beyond words.[8]

Apparitions

So far we've looked at instances of indirect communication through inanimate objects or via the highly subjective realm of dreams. But, like Evelyn, who saw her father in his old rocking chair, many people insist they've been visited by the ghost of a loved one while wide awake. Such encounters can involve one or more of the physical senses, even tactile contact. Consider Fred's experience, after the loss of his son.

> Forty-five days after Eric's death in a car accident, I awoke at 6:45 A.M. along with my wife, Marilyn. . . . At 7:15 I got up off the bed—fully awake and up for one-half hour. My mind was clear. I was not crying and not under any stress. As I took my third step toward the bathroom, I felt a tremendous squeeze and hug on both sides of my body that stopped me in my tracks. Eric appeared right in front of my face, smiling, and the whole room was full of energy. It's like the molecules, atoms, and air are all moving at a tremendous speed. It was forceful, explosive, loving, highly energized—the most exhilarating experience I've ever had! I hugged Eric. . . . I kissed him

on his right cheek and felt his beard/whiskers on my lips. . . . My mind was ecstatic, lucid, fully awake and aware of what was happening. I could see the tremendous love that Eric brought with him. I knew this was real, on purpose, planned by Eric as I could never have written or wished the events in this spontaneous experience.[9]

Like most people who have an afterlife encounter, Fred was comforted by what he believes was proof that his son was not dead and *gone* but had merely moved on to a "different plane or dimension"—and that he was happy there. The experience empowered him to cope with his grief and get on with his own life.

Sooner or later we all will lose someone we love. Grief is a universal human experience. Do afterlife encounters constitute proof that our spirits live on after death and sometimes offer comfort and healing to the living? No. The skeptics among us also will say, "What grief-stricken person, overwhelmed by emotion and perhaps sleep-deprived, wouldn't *want* to see their deceased family member or friend in a happy state? It's a matter of *projection* or *wish fulfillment*, a trick played by the mind." In some cases that's probably true. But can we so easily explain away the thousands of reported experiences that occur each year—often by people who were themselves skeptical at one point? I don't believe we can. Maybe it's enough to judge such encounters by the overwhelmingly positive effect they have on grieving people.

Joel Martin and Patricia Romanowski have spent years collecting stories of after-death communication. They believe such encounters are, by far, the most common—and most beneficial—of all so-called paranormal occurrences.

> Rather than turn away from these experiences in fear, doubt, or disbelief, we should learn to embrace and treasure them. While we do not always know the exact purpose of these trans-dimensional contacts, those who have experienced them gladly attest to the results. Even the most beautifully crafted words barely capture the joy, the comfort, the peace of mind one derives just from knowing that there is something beyond, that life does go on.[10]

LaGrand's interactions have led him to the same conclusion:

In all the years I have been around people who have had an ADC, I have never heard of a single case in which the ADC resulted in spreading evil and discouragement. Instead, love wins out—there is no more powerful antidote for grief. A quiet reassurance begins to reign.[11]

Sometimes "ghostly encounters" aren't sinister or spooky—sometimes they represent *grace* in the form of a comforting visitation from beyond the grave to bring peace and relieve distress. As Jesus said to his followers when he appeared after his death and resurrection: "Don't be alarmed. . . . Peace be with you. . . . Why are you troubled, and why do doubts rise in your minds?"[12]

7

Calling Long Distance

Death May Be the Last Word in Life . . .
But Can Communication Continue?

What the eyes see and ears hear, the mind believes.

Harry Houdini

At the end of 1847, an American blacksmith named John Fox needed a change of scenery. With his wife, Margaret, and two daughters, Maggie (15) and Kate (11), he moved to Hydesville, New York, a tiny hamlet in a rural area. While a place of their own was under construction, Fox rented a small house in the middle of town; owned by descendents of the village founder, Henry Hyde, it had been home to a steady stream of semi-transient renters for years.

Fox hoped the move would bring a new beginning. He got his wish but not in the way he imagined. Never in his wildest dreams could he have foreseen how life was about to change—for his family and for millions of others.

In the spring, the rental house was beset by inexplicable noises: "thumps on the ceiling, bumps on doors or walls, sometimes raps sharp enough to jar bedsteads and tables."[1] Curiously, the knocking happened only at night when the family was in bed in the single room they shared. Fox did his best to discover the cause, suspecting loose shingles or siding banging in the wind, an animal nesting in the attic, or perhaps a prank played by neighborhood kids. But despite his determined efforts he was unable to locate the source of the persistent clamor.

The story might have ended there—just an ordinary "haunting"—no different from countless other noisy mysteries that ever have been part of human experience. But on March 31, 1848, the episode took a dramatic turn. After several consecutive disquieting nights, Margaret decided the family had lost enough sleep. She put Maggie and Kate to bed early with strict instructions: If the noises return, pay no attention to them. Margaret herself would fatefully ignore that sage advice before the evening was done.

When the sounds did return, Kate playfully started to mimic them by snapping her fingers. This went on a few minutes until the roles suddenly reversed, and the mysterious raps began to follow *her* lead; knocks on the ceiling and walls repeated whatever patterns of sound she produced. Maggie quickly joined in, telling the unseen source to "do this just as I do." And it did, counting out knocks as if in direct response.

The girls became terrified by this development, huddling together on their bed. It was their mother who seized the initiative, telling the "spirit" to count to ten. It did. She asked the ages of her daughters. It replied with the right number of knocks. She recounted what happened next:

> I then asked if it was a human being that was making the noise . . . and if it was, to manifest it by the same noise. There was no noise. I then asked if it was a spirit . . . and if it was, to manifest it by two sounds. I heard two sounds as soon as the words were spoken. I then asked, if it was an injured spirit . . . to give me the sound, and I heard the rapping distinctly.[2]

Continuing along this line, Margaret discovered that the spirit had been killed near the house, that its murderer was still living, and that its remains were buried in the basement. (In subsequent weeks, the spirit would reveal that it had been a traveling peddler when alive. It spelled out its mortal name by rapping when someone called out letters of the alphabet. And it identified its killer, a former resident of the house named John Bell who still lived in Hydesville and who firmly denied any such crime.)

Finally, Margaret asked if the spirit would continue communicating in this way if she called her neighbors to witness it. *Yes,* said the knocks.

Running to a friend's house nearby for backup, she unwittingly triggered an avalanche of fame and notoriety that would sweep over her family, especially the two girls.

Over the next few weeks, ever-growing crowds gathered to hear the knocks for themselves and to ask questions about the afterlife. By then it was apparent that the disturbances only occurred when Kate or Maggie were present. Of course, this led many observers to scoff and declare it an adolescent prank. Yet even the most skeptical could never uncover *how* the girls were producing the sounds—if they were. The house was turned upside down, the girls were searched and examined by doctors, but no clear-cut trickery ever was exposed.

News of the phenomenon traveled fast. People all over the country took philosophically opposing sides in the developing debate. Many hailed the Fox sisters' experiences as the long-sought proof of life after death; others ridiculed "believers" as the gullible victims of an obvious hoax; some denounced the entire business as the devil's dangerous work.

In any case, the genie was out of the bottle—modern spiritualism had arrived in the US. Hundreds of mediums sprang up, claiming similar abilities and using various techniques for communicating with the dead. Within a few years the Fox sisters themselves, for a fee, began giving public demonstrations of their percussive conversations with the dead. *Séance*—French for "session"—became a household word nearly overnight.

Christianity always had inspired people to put their hope in life after death. It's likewise something people have wanted to believe, especially if they've lost loved ones and longed for assurance that the departed is well cared for. But under this life's grinding pressures, belief in spiritual immortality often has required prodigious levels of courageous faith.

Now, in the form of two seemingly innocent girls, along came visible *proof*. At a time when astonishing scientific discoveries were transforming our view of the material world, Maggie and Kate Fox were at the leading edge of an ideological revolution about nonmaterial realms. The enticing message was clear: Not only do our loved ones survive death in a spiritual dimension, but they're also still present with us, ready (even eager) to go on communicating as before. All we need is a go-between, someone with a natural—many say God-given—spiritual sensitivity. In other words, we need a *medium*.

"Why Have You Disturbed Me?"

Of course, this wasn't a new idea at all, only a repackage. Necromancy—raising spirits of the dead to solicit a glimpse of the future or to keep in touch with a departed loved one—was a common (if not always acceptable) practice in many of the world's earlier cultures. Shamans or priests on every continent have claimed the ability to speak with the dead through a wide variety of methods.

Israel's King Saul himself sought an audience with the recently deceased prophet Samuel's spirit. Facing the formidable Philistine army, he was terrified and wanted Samuel's help, just like in the good old days. Having "expelled the mediums and spiritists from the land" (in accord with the Law), Saul, in disguise, approached a woman called the Witch of Endor. He asked her to awaken Samuel, and she complied.[3]

> When the woman saw Samuel, she cried out at the top of her voice and said to Saul, "Why have you deceived me? You are Saul!"
>
> The king said to her, "Don't be afraid. What do you see?"
>
> The woman said, "I see a spirit coming up out of the ground."
>
> "What does he look like?" he asked.
>
> "An old man wearing a robe is coming up," she said.
>
> Then Saul knew it was Samuel, and he bowed down and prostrated himself with his face to the ground.
>
> Samuel said to Saul, "Why have you disturbed me by bringing me up?"
>
> "I am in great distress," Saul said. "The Philistines are fighting against me, and God has turned away from me. He no longer answers me, either by prophets or by dreams. So I have called on you to tell me what to do."[4]

Unswayed, Samuel told Saul both he and his sons would be killed in the ensuing battle, and that's exactly what happened.

This story offers valuable insight into *why* people throughout history have sought counsel and comfort from the dead. Who hasn't endured "great distress" from time to time, feeling that God has turned away and no longer answers? The temptation to reach actively through the veil of death during hard times and lean on someone you trusted in life can be appealing. What else explains the practice's persistence throughout the centuries?

The Greeks, for instance, strove to solicit information from the dead. Every village had an "oracle," one or more who for a price would reveal a person's future. Ephyra, however, was different: the city stood over caves thought to be the entrance to Hades. There, it was believed, a supplicant could speak directly to the dead—if he were willing to undertake an ordeal (no doubt costly) that lasted up to twenty-nine days.

The seeker would enter a temple called a Necromanteion, which means "oracle of death." After offering the appropriate sacrifices, he was led to a dark subterranean room where he remained alone for many days, eating only foods associated with the dead: beans, pork, mussels, barley. (The diet also included narcotic substances.) At the appointed time, the priest returned to administer a ritual bath; then, thoroughly disoriented, he was taken to a chamber deep within the earth where he could finally speak with an "apparition" that mysteriously appeared from a cauldron suspended above the ground.

The message from beyond typically was a cryptic verse requiring a heavy dose of interpretation. After contact with the dead spirit, the living seeker was taken back to the surface and out into the blinding light of day—thankful to have survived a trip to the underworld.[5]

Few people now would go to such lengths (though attempting to connect with the dead is more popular than ever). Many present-day "oracles" have online sites, toll-free numbers, and TV shows. Since the Fox sisters of the nineteenth century enlivened modern spiritualism, peering into the beyond has grown into a profitable industry. Psychics and seers have steadily proliferated—and so have their communication techniques. Let's look at five in use today.

Crystal Gazing

Chances are, the first image that pops into your head when you hear the word *fortune-teller* is of a cloaked old woman in a darkened tent waving her hands over a crystal ball. Hollywood certainly has done its part to plant that picture. Yet crystal gazing—also known as *scrying*—has been used since antiquity to open a window between this world and the next. Any reflective surface will do: a pool of water, a cup of wine, a polished stone. In *Snow White*, the wicked queen scries when she asks, "Mirror, mirror, on the wall, who's the fairest of them all?"

The sitter—as the living person seeking contact is called—comes with questions of her own. If all goes according to plan, a spirit appears in the murky reflected patterns and answers through the medium.

Table Tilting

Much like spirit rapping, in table tilting, the dead make their presence known via tangible physical manifestation. Sitters—with or without a medium—place their hands on a tabletop and ask a question; the spirits respond by moving, rattling, or even levitating the table. It's easy to see how "feeling the spirits" with your own hands might have a powerful psychological effect. As historian Brian Righi explains:

> Table tilting became so popular in its heyday that doctors and scientists thought the craze dangerous to the public's mental health. In reaction, a committee was formed to study the fad. . . . After heated debate, the committee's findings concluded that table tilting was due to the unconscious muscular activity of the sitters and not to any real spiritual presence.[6]

Predictably, that verdict did little to dampen enthusiasm for the practice.

Talking Boards

Known today as a Ouija board, some accounts claim this device dates back 3,200 years to its use in China. The design is simple: letters of the alphabet are printed on a flat, portable board, along with the ordinal numbers plus the words *yes* and *no*. Sitters place their fingers lightly around the edges of a disc—called a *planchette*—that can glide easily over the board's surface. They ask a question and then allow the planchette to move where it will, spelling or marking out a response, presumably under a spirit's influence.

Like so many techniques for contacting the dead, the talking board gained popularity in the mid-nineteenth century, during the early days of the spiritualist movement. Today, it can be purchased in most toy departments; the box of the Parker Brothers edition has read, "*It's all just a game—isn't it?*"

Scientists studying the phenomenon maintain that any "messages" thus received originate in subconscious human minds, not with a discarnate spirit. Interesting but harmless, they say. But others warn the device is no mere parlor plaything; Christians believe using a talking board invites demons to masquerade as benevolent spirits in order to mislead or gain influence. Many secular researchers—for example, the well-known paranormal investigators Ed and Lorraine Warren—have come to the same conclusion.

> Ouija boards are just as dangerous as drugs. . . . Séances and Ouija boards and other occult paraphernalia are dangerous because "evil spirits" often disguise themselves as your loved ones—and take over your life.[7]

It isn't uncommon for a "conversation" with a spirit through a talking board to turn suddenly harsh, obscene, and abusive. Consider: *If it's a game, then with whom do we play, and for what purpose do they accept the invitation?*

Automatic Writing

Using this technique, a medium enters a trance and allows the contacted spirit to control his hand to write a message. The medium often is unaware of what he writes until after "coming to" again. Sometimes, the handwriting or language style dramatically differs from the medium's own. In this way, he claims the ability to channel an eager-to-communicate spirit.

Again, scientists think the only opened "channel" lies between the mind's conscious and subconscious regions. Some psychologists even have begun using automatic writing as a therapeutic tool to help patients access painful feelings and memories they're otherwise unable to face. However, as with talking boards, many warn of the danger of inviting an unknown spirit to enter one's mind and manipulate one's body.

Psychic Readings

Many mediums claim the ability to directly sense the spirits of dead people and communicate with them—without rapping or writing or other methods. When a sitter seeks contact with a dead person, the medium doesn't summon the spirit but simply acts as a go-between should it show up on its own. The assumption is that the ghost is as zealous to converse as the sitter.

This is the technique used by most "psychics" today, including famous ones who work in front of a studio audience. They commonly appear to access information about the sitter that only the dead person could have known, leading observers to conclude they must be "for real."

Skeptics, on the other hand, charge that the "medium" frequently is a mere con artist using pre-gathered data by snooping and scrounging around in *this* world. Advances in technology—transmitting information via hidden microphones and cameras, Internet searches, and wireless communication devices—have made the task easier than ever.

It's more likely that most psychics are skilled at a process called *cold reading*. This requires knowledge of basic psychology, body language, and old-fashioned theatrics—but not genuine communication with the dead. By prodding the sitter with vague and suggestive questions, the medium fishes for clues that can lead her to seemingly remarkable "hits"—presumed info from the other side. Furthermore, ambiguity is no obstacle when the sitter desperately wants the medium to succeed. As Robert T. Carroll writes:

> Clients of mediums who claim to get messages from the dead are very highly motivated clients. Not only do they have an implicit desire for immortality, they have an explicit desire to contact a dear loved one who has died. The odds are in favor of the medium that the client will find meaning in many different sets of ambiguous words and phrases. If she connects just a couple of them, she may be satisfied that the medium has made a connection to a dead relative. If she doesn't find any meaning or significance in the string, the medium still wins. He can try another string. He can insist that there's meaning here but the client just isn't trying hard enough to figure it out. He can suggest that some uninvited spirit guests are confusing the issue. It's a win-win situation for the medium because the burden is not on him but on the client to find the meaning and significance of the words.[8]

Of course, that some or even most psychics employ cold reading to fool the sitter does not necessarily mean all do. Gary Schwartz, professor of psychology and neurology at the University of Arizona, decided to put his reputation on the line attempting to settle the question once and for all. Properly designed experiments, he reasoned, could remove cold reading and previously gleaned info from the medium's toolbox. He wanted to know: If a psychic were prevented from seeing or even speaking to the sitter but still gave an accurate reading, could that prove the existence of afterlife communication?

To summarize, over the course of many carefully controlled sittings with well-known mediums, Schwartz calculated they retrieved accurate information 80 to 90 percent of the time, on average. These results were far better than we could expect from random chance or guessing.

> We delight in having professional magicians fool us. They have mastered the tricks for deceiving our senses—tricks developed over many, many years. How could I truly be sure I was not being fooled by these mediums in a similar way . . . ?
>
> Other scientists would demand incontrovertible proof before even beginning to accept what we thought we had witnessed. As a scientist myself, I had a nagging certainty I could not yet answer all the challenges that might be thrown at me. . . .
>
> Yet for the time being, I could hardly help but feel elated. In this territory so unknown to us, we had planned and carried out a significant experiment with fairly elaborate safeguards. The results were decidedly impressive, certainly enough to give us confidence and the strong desire to continue.[9]

As Schwartz predicted, most observers complained that the research raised far more questions than it answered. Still, it managed to keep the issue alive when it might just as easily have killed psychic interest on the spot.

Practitioners of modern spiritualism in all its forms have been hounded every step of the way by allegations of deception and chicanery. Escape artist Harry Houdini spent much of his career using what he knew about theatrical illusion to expose the fraudulent. "It takes a flimflammer to catch a flimflammer," he said.

In 1888, Maggie Fox stunned the world by admitting that she and Kate had perpetrated a fraud: They'd hatched the prank as children to frighten their mother. Then events took on a life of their own, and they didn't know how to stop—and perhaps didn't want to, especially once it became clear they had stumbled on a lucrative way to make a living at a time when most women had few such opportunities. How? By cracking the knuckles in their toes, Kate said. Maggie even went on tour to demonstrate the technique.

It was proclaimed in the skeptical press and scientific communities as a death blow to spiritualism.

But—as has been the case throughout the long history of necromancy—there was more strangeness to come. Two years later, the sisters recanted and again took up the work of helping people communicate with dead loved ones. Supporters claimed they'd previously been threatened or even paid to denounce the movement. Many of the "psychic" phenomena attributed to them remain hard to explain even considering their short-lived confession. In any case, they never again achieved similar popularity and died impoverished within ten years.

Where Do We Go From Here?

Is it *possible* to communicate with the dead? The honest reply is "Probably, though who knows for sure?" Despite centuries of investigation and debate, a definitive, intellectually satisfying answer seems elusive. But assuming for a moment that the answer is yes—which the story of Saul and Samuel suggests—a more important question arises: Is seeking out such communication *advisable*? On that point it's far easier to reach a reasonable conclusion: No.

The mere possibility—convincingly raised by many researchers and firsthand witnesses—that necromancy amounts to an open invitation for evil spirits to make themselves at home in our lives is grounds enough to steer clear. God warned the Israelites to have nothing to do with one who "practices divination or sorcery, interprets omens, engages in witchcraft, or casts spells, or who is a medium or spiritist or who consults the dead."[10] Zero wiggle room!

Another reason to shy away might be found by asking, Why bother?

When men tell you to consult mediums and spiritists, who whisper and mutter, should not a people inquire of their God? Why consult the dead on behalf of the living? To the law and to the testimony! If they do not speak according to this word, they have no light of dawn.[11]

In other words, what can a medium, speaking for a dead person, possibly tell you that you can't hear in Scripture and in prayer? With God there is no potential for fraud, deception, contamination, or disaster.

When it comes to communication with the dead, while many mysteries remain unsolved, one thing is clear: God has already granted you access to the wise guidance and comforting counsel you might want from a lost loved one. It is there for the asking—in your relationship with *him*.

8

Angels Among Us

God's Messengers Provide Protection and Provision

Philosophers have argued for centuries about how many angels can dance on the head of a pin, but materialists have always known it depends on whether they are jitterbugging or dancing cheek to cheek.

Tom Robbins

Ever been rescued by an angel? I have . . . in a manner of speaking.

I grew up three miles from a town—Ames, Kansas—with a population that numbered less than a hundred. One mile south of our farm was a dirt-road intersection graced by a small church, Morgan Chapel Wesleyan Methodist. That is where I experienced all my early spiritual training. One of the biggest events was the annual Christmas program, where you could count on nearly all town residents attending, far more than our average attendance of sixty-five.

To give a more professional ambiance, from a number nine wire strung across the front of the church hung curtains that opened and closed for various acts. When I was five, I had the opening recitation; something simple like "We welcome you to our Christmas pageant" with three rhyming lines to follow.

As the show was to begin, and the small varnished sanctuary filled with excited anticipation, the curtains parted three feet wide, just enough room for me to appear but not enough to reveal the nativity scene on the darkened stage. I stepped forward through the gap, as obediently as David going to face Goliath, though with far less confidence. After clearing my throat, I began to recite my carefully memorized lines. I got through the first two with hardly a wobble.

But suddenly I felt as if I were standing before a hundred *thousand* gawking onlookers. As my mind raced, my mouth froze. I stood motionless. The audience stirred nervously, as did my brain. When no words came, I cried. And cried some more. Then I cried louder.

When it became apparent that my distress would continue unabated, an "angel" suddenly appeared. My mother, standing out of view backstage, dressed as an angel for her appearance in the nativity scene, came to rescue her troubled child. She dashed toward the curtain opening, swooping in from her assigned position, and scooping me up with a long circular motion of her right arm. In an instant, the whimpering lad was cradled in an angel's arms. The winged white messenger then pirouetted with a ballerina's grace back to her original mark. The figure of deliverance and the relieved young thespian clung to each other as the curtains fully parted and the show commenced.

The crowd was awed by the intervention. Some became convinced that the weepy opener and the angelic appearance were part of the plan. Many said it was the best beginning of a Christmas program they'd ever seen.

That, I must confess, is the closest I'm aware of having come to an "angelic visitation." But I have no doubt that honest-to-goodness, God-sent angels do indeed exist and participate in our lives, probably far more than we realize. Dozens of absolutely convinced people have told me of their encounters. Many more such accounts are recorded by credible books, magazines, and Web sites.

What do you envision when you think of an *angel*? A white-robed being with halo and harp, standing knee-deep in clouds? An effervescent and glittering figure of the Victorian variety, perched atop an opulent Christmas tree? Or perhaps you see the twentieth-century George Bailey's bumbling but loveable angel, Clarence (*It's a Wonderful Life*). Or maybe the more contemporary imagery from *City of Angels*: dark, long-coated beings straddling skyscrapers . . . ever watching, influencing, occasionally falling from grace and even in love. Hollywood strikes again! Let's try to form a more accurate perception of who angels are and what they do.

Background on Heavenly Beings

The term itself comes from the Greek *angelos*, which means "messenger." In ancient times, when travel was slow and communication limited, personally delivered messages were coveted and critical; battles could be won or lost due to a courier's expedience or delay. It's not surprising that Greek mythology has a winged messenger as one of its gods: Hermes also was known as Mercury in later Roman times. Other cultures and religions included the idea of messenger gods; Hebrew literature, regarding the people of Israel, also is full of stories about angelic messengers with names like Michael, Gabriel, and Raphael.

As for the New Testament, you've probably heard of Gabriel, who told Mary she would be the mother of Jesus. Through the ages, many angels described in Hebrew and Christian writings are depicted artistically as winged, superhuman beings, from the stoic, iconic, gold-haloed medieval figures to the cute little winged cherubs of the Renaissance.

Mormonism's roots trace to the story of an angel's alleged message to their nineteenth-century founder; a statue of this angel, named Moroni, adorns most Mormon temples.

Interestingly, having moved beyond passé modernist culture's rigid naturalistic doctrines, popular (postmodern) Western culture once again is embracing the supernatural and these beings in particular. Books like Doreen Virtue's *How to Hear Your Angels* encourage people to contact "angels" and harness their powers for assistance in life's journey.[1]

Angelic Appearances in Scripture

The Bible has much to say about angels, in more than three hundred references—about a hundred in the Old Testament and over two hundred in the New. Although no single passage gives us a complete picture, we can piece together snippets and glean much about the nature of angels from Scripture.

Could they be metaphorical figures, inserted to illustrate abstract ideas about truth or moral behavior? *The Bible portrays angels as literal, personal entities who play a role in historical events and individual lives.* They appear both in dreams and visions as well as to fully conscious people; the result of the encounters is always dramatic and life-changing, regardless of the manifestation. The life of Jesus especially points to literal angels: herein they tell others about Jesus, they help Jesus, and Jesus himself talks matter-of-factly about them.[2] They don't reproduce sexually, and they don't die;[3] they are immortal.

The book of Daniel is a combination of history and prophecy, written several centuries before Jesus' birth. Daniel was a young Jewish captive in the land of Babylon (modern-day Iraq). At one point, Daniel found himself in a tight spot and prayed to God for help. Some twenty-one days later, an angel showed up, and Daniel's astonishment is clear from his description:

> His body was like chrysolite,[4] his face like lightning, his eyes like flaming torches, his arms and legs like the gleam of burnished bronze, and his voice like the sound of a multitude.[5]

Here we learn that angels are powerful, knowledgeable, and helpful; breathtaking in appearance, not always fully visible. They can communicate with people. Some have names and rank—*Michael*, the *arch*angel. As the word implies, Daniel's angel was sent to deliver a message. But he couldn't be everywhere at once or do everything at once.

Then there's Revelation, which is filled with angelic descriptions. In about AD 95, John, one of Jesus' closest followers, received a glimpse of heaven, and what he saw (among many other details) were angels—*lots* of angels: "Then I looked and heard the voice of many angels, numbering thousands upon thousands, and ten thousand times ten thousand."[6] A literal interpretation would yield a hundred million angels. If we take this as figurative language, it affirms that heaven has *throngs* of angels.

Elsewhere John, awed by an angel's presence, fell down to worship but the angel stopped him: "Do not do it! I am a fellow servant with you and with your brothers. . . . Worship God!"[7] Unlike the mythological Hermes, angels are *not* divine; as impressive as they may appear, they serve God, just as mortals do.

In Luke 16, a foundational passage to what we know about heaven, we see the role played by angels even in our getting there: "The time came when the beggar died and the angels carried him to Abraham's side."[8] In

Hebrews, a sort of theological treatise, the author speaks of angels via rhetorical question: "Are not all angels *ministering spirits* sent to serve those who will inherit salvation?"[9] So what exactly does this mean—how do angels minister?

Nature of Angels

The ambiguous word *spirit*, along with descriptions in the passages above, might cause us to wonder about the difference between angels and humans, with whom angels share some traits.

First, angels also are creatures, meaning God-*created* (they're not divine).

Second, they likewise have *personality*—intellect (thought), emotion (feeling), and will (choice).

Third, they *exist in time and space*. They function within time and space, although they have much more freedom than we do. In Psalm 148, a song of praise, the writer says the angels should praise God because God created them.[10] Another song of praise says humans were made "a little lower than the heavenly beings." (Even so, God "crowned [us] with glory and honor."[11])

Like us, angels are personal creatures: responsible, accountable, and dependent upon God. Again, as theologian C. Fred Dickason puts it, a person is not just a "human being" but a being that has the qualities of personality (intellect, emotion, and will).[12]

Though existing in time and space, angels seem able to appear and disappear suddenly or get from one place to another very quickly.[13] Biblically, they often appear in some kind of glorified humanlike form—with unusual brightness resembling fire, lightning, polished metal or precious stones, and/or blindingly white linen.[14] Other angels, not resembling humans at all, are likened to unusual beasts.[15] In the sixth century BC, the prophet Ezekiel had an astounding heavenly vision;[16] interestingly, the creatures John and Ezekiel saw had wings but didn't use them to fly.

There's no question angels are superhuman. Daniel's angel was stronger, smarter, and faster than any human; he could fight heavenly battles, see into the future, and, even though it took time, go between Persia to Babylon without breaking a sweat. But they aren't all-powerful or all-knowing,[17] and they cannot be everywhere at once.[18] Only God has these qualities.

Occupation of Angels

God created angels to help carry out his work, much of which occurs in heaven. There are mysterious things we don't know about and/or can't see—for instance, Ezekiel's cherubim and Isaiah's seraphim. Apparent guardians of the holy places, they're like priests—heavenly priests whose role and mission it is to glorify God. But while we don't know everything angels do, the Scriptures present them as being variously occupied worshiping God, carrying out his judgment, and ministering to humans by bringing messages and protection.[19]

Due to the biblical depiction of these beings as protectors, many have speculated as to whether there are "individualized," one-on-one angels. The early church seemed to think so, and this tradition is especially strong in Catholicism.[20] It's not such a farfetched idea, and there are a few allusions that some believe support the existence of guardian angels.[21] Protecting and caring certainly are among the angelic character traits; they often arrive to comfort God's people at their lowest point,[22] as with Jesus himself on a few occasions.[23]

The Angelic Army

How do angels carry out all this strengthening, encouraging, guarding, and protecting? They are numerous, and they are highly organized; they have positions and ranks, as in the military. Jesus used Roman terminology, *legion,* to indicate the profuse array of angels, and he explained to the disciples and the crowd who wished to take him by force that it wasn't necessary to resist. After all, if he desired, God would supply backup with twelve legions of angels.[24] A Roman legion was comprised of six thousand soldiers, plus their slaves, so Jesus could have had the help of at least seventy-two thousand angels, though the point was not the literal number but the overwhelming available force.

As for angelic ranks, Paul tells us the names of some divisions: *rulers, authorities, powers, thrones,* and *dominions.* Regarding everything that has been created in heaven and on earth, some things are visible, while some, like thrones, powers, rulers, and authorities, are not.[25] God uses his people, the church, to reveal wisdom "to the rulers and authorities in the heavenly realms."[26] Peter links these invisible divisions with angels when

89

he says Jesus is in heaven "at God's right hand—with angels, authorities and powers in submission to him."[27]

There are two known angelic offices as well: angel and archangel. *Arche* is Greek for "ruler"; the archangel is the head angel, or at least head of one rank. Michael, an archangel,[28] also is called a prince.[29] This office is mentioned only twice, and only once in connection with Michael or any other name.[30]

Some speculate that the six-winged seraphim hovering above God's throne may have the highest office of all.[31] Others say the cherubim are the highest ranking, present in Ezekiel's account of beast-like creatures with multiple wings and intersecting wheels.[32] Theologians through the ages have puzzled over angelic ranks and offices. A sixth-century mystic, Dionysius, proffered his ideas in *The Celestial Hierarchy*, placing seraphim and cherubim on top. He took his ideas from the Bible but added a lot of hocus-pocus.[33] Thomas Aquinas, one of history's most brilliant theologians, added to this work; earlier, Augustine had found the topic interesting but was reluctant to comment, pleading ignorance.[34] More recently, Billy Graham's organizational chart conversely placed angels and archangels on top, above the seraphim and cherubim.[35]

No matter what, we know these all are part of a larger group called the "heavenly hosts." This includes God himself, the angels, archangels, cherubim, seraphim, and the thrones, powers, authorities, dominions, and rulers that are God's army, the "extension of His power and providence."[36]

As the military terminology suggests, there also are enemies. The Bible refers to a rebellion in heaven led by one very high-ranking angel;[37] other angels joined him and were banished.[38] It also depicts an unseen spiritual battle between angelic and demonic powers. (We'll delve more deeply into this dark realm in chapters 9–10.[39])

Active and Among Us

Let's bring all this back down to earth: Is there reason to believe angels still interact with us? The Bible indicates there is. Recall the reference to "ministering spirits sent to serve *those who will inherit salvation*."[40] Why wouldn't angels, as immortal creatures serving God, continue working to help his people?

Gary Kinnaman, who was senior pastor at Word of Grace Church in Mesa, Arizona, for several decades, shares stories of encounters gathered during a study he undertook for his doctoral work.[41] While Kinnaman cautions that this study was not scientific, he found commonality and credibility in the experiences described by people who didn't know each other. He confirms that angel visitations are rare, and for those few who have seen or sensed an angelic presence, it's usually a brief, unexpected, once-in-a-lifetime event.

As for *appearance*, among the similarities found in the descriptions is that angels are very tall—"as high as the ceiling," as one man put it.[42] In form they appear sufficiently humanlike, enough to be recognizable—as to Daniel—but their faces are such that they can't be distinguished as male or female.[43] Long hair is a frequent feature; often so is a robe-like garment, with a sash or belt. They are bright, glowing, and transparent. Respondents rarely reported wings.[44]

Regarding *actions*, often the angel imparted some kind of message, though not always with audible speech, somehow "communicating" so that the person would be as sure of the words as if they were spoken aloud. Usually the angel didn't appear to look directly at the person or solicit attention; the descriptions almost sound as if the viewer was being permitted to glimpse an angel going about mysterious business. Often, whatever that business might be was indiscernible at the time, though the person speculated about it thereafter.

Again, nearly everyone who reported such an encounter felt it to be life-altering. Some would discern the significance years later, after reflecting on events or changes in their outlook that had occurred since the visitation. For example, some became Christians as a result of their angelic encounter; for some, the process took years or even decades.[45]

Entertaining Angels Unaware

What about angels appearing in human form? It happened to Abraham and Lot, but that was a long time ago—what about now? Once again Hebrews advises: "Do not forget to entertain strangers, for by so doing some people have entertained angels without knowing it."[46] It should still be possible for us to encounter angels who have assumed human form.

While there are many anecdotal stories to support this, though, how could anyone know for sure? Nearly all who report such an experience say something like, "I think it must have been an angel." Usually it's later, when they've had time to puzzle over the unlikely "coincidence" that a stranger "appeared" to help them at a desperate time. Maybe their old clunker broke down on a remote road. Or they were camped beside a cliff where a landslide was about to occur. Or were being stalked by hoodlums. Help shows up just in the nick of time and then—poof!—the disappearance is as sudden as the arrival. Not into thin air—but into the nearby woods . . . around a corner . . . or when heads were turned.[47]

This is common with missionaries. Ruth Graham told of growing up as the daughter of missionaries in China; her family experienced such providential encounters.[48] In addition to much anecdotal evidence, there is biblical implication that angels would be watching out for missionaries especially.[49] Angels do not preach, teach, or counsel; humans do those jobs. As we've seen, angels assist those who do God's work on earth.[50]

Kinnaman reports that on occasion parishioners have reported seeing an angel standing near him while he stood preaching.[51] I had such an experience when a woman who attends my church shared what she witnessed during a service; she was visibly impacted.

> My husband and I sensed an unusual presence last Sunday morning. I noticed some movement around you as you began to preach, but I dismissed it. A few minutes later I felt a cool breeze, then experienced a weight so heavy I could barely sit upright. I asked God what he was trying to tell me or show me. Then I saw a quick flash of light that moved behind your left shoulder. Every so often the light would reappear. It moved with great speed, darting back and forth behind you. Then as I looked across the platform, I saw it was filled with angels moving about. My hearing became so acute that I could hear you speaking even though the sound the angels were making was almost deafening. Not in a bad way—not like loud music you hear in someone's car at a stoplight but thunderous noise of angels in motion.

When you hear someone tell a story like that, are you skeptical? If so, know that I am too. While open to unexplainable and bona fide miraculous happenings, I have a natural bent toward skepticism. But be assured that if this woman, and her husband—a respected police detective—did not have credibility with me, I would not report the encounter. (Besides, if we truly

92

believe God's messengers are active and involved in our world, why should we be surprised when we hear of such experiences from reliable sources?)

Another account comes from my friend Gary, an electrical engineer and business owner. Heading home after an extended road trip, towing a house trailer, Gary crossed the Cascade Mountains in darkest night, heading east into the high plains of Washington State. He struggled to stay awake by talking on the CB radio to his sister, who was driving behind him. In the first car were Gary, Gary's father, and Gary's two daughters. In the second car, besides Gary's sister, were his mother and his wife. Everyone but the drivers were asleep.

Dreaming that the car towing the trailer was veering off the road, Gary's father suddenly reached across and yanked the steering wheel, semiconsciously attempting to avoid an accident. At sixty-five miles per hour, pulling a heavy load, there was no way to correct the abrupt swerve in time. The car and trailer hurtled off the road, overturned, and came to rest right-side-up, flattened like an accordion, in the bottom of a ditch. The trailer had practically disintegrated—pieces of it were strewn across two hundred yards of roadway.

Gary's sister, observing the entire incident, had stopped some distance back. Afraid at what they might find if they ran down to the wreck, the three women, now wide awake, stood by their vehicle, repeating in stunned disbelief, "Oh no. Oh no. Oh *no*—"

Inside the smashed, rolled-over car, now half its original height, the four passengers struggled to get out through the one working door. Miraculously, no one was hurt. They were dirty, frightened, and stunned into near silence, but hardly a scratch could be found on any of them.

Back up on the highway there was complete quiet. No other traffic, no one around—not for miles and miles. No sound at all . . . except for a voice coming out of the darkness. A very tall man in a long black coat appeared, approached the mother and sister, put his arms around them both, and said, "Don't worry. Everyone is okay. They will be fine. No one is hurt." And then, just as suddenly, he disappeared back into the darkness.

Overcoming their shock, the women ran to the ditch, helping the struggling victims—now looking like coal miners with dirt-smeared faces—back onto the road and quickly verifying the truth of the stranger's statements. Everyone was indeed unharmed.

Minutes later, after the babble of voices recounting details had finally subsided, Gary's mother asked, "Where is the man who told us you were okay?"

"What man?" Gary and his father asked.

In the 2:00 AM stillness, in the middle of nowhere, in the midst of a near tragedy, the question repeated through the ages by God's children again was asked: "*Who was he?*"

To them there's no doubt about the answer: They'd encountered an angel.

Angels at Death's Door

Deathbed stories are replete with angel sightings, reports of which frequently are less about details of tall beings and more about brief comments of "I see an angel," accompanied by peacefulness on the face of the dying individual. Billy Graham, who has presided at the deathbeds of many people, both believers and nonbelievers, says the first is a "glorious" experience, while the latter can be "terrible."[52] At his own grandmother's death, just moments before she died, the room filled with light; she sat up and said, "I see Jesus . . . I see the angels!"[53]

One of Kinnaman's survey respondents, a young father, recalls the birth— and death—of his prematurely born daughter. Every day she survived was a miracle. After one week, he began to hold out some hope that she would live.

When he came to the hospital, he was stunned to see her incubator flanked by two very tall, luminous visitors. He ecstatically related this to his wife, assured now that their baby had angels to safeguard her tenuous existence. But the tiny girl died the next day, and for weeks he felt betrayed—until he and his wife noticed Graham on television talking about angels. The bereaved father was comforted that his child had been escorted to heaven, just like Lazarus.[54]

We all will face physical death sooner or later. When that day comes for me, I want to be able to affirm this text: "I am sending an angel ahead

94

of you to guard you along the way and to bring you to the place I have prepared."[55] Understanding the angelic role in life's great crossover extracts some of death's sting *and* gives confidence as we live here on earth.

When this life is over, we do not go alone. For the people who reported end-of-life sightings, there was comfort. It should be the same for us who may not be at death's door but know we someday will be. It is good to understand—as best we can on this side—the reality of angelic protection by God's provision.

9

More Than a Pitchfork
and a Pointy Tail

The Great Adversary, Satan, Prowls Like a Hungry Lion

I often laugh at Satan, and there is nothing that makes him so angry
as when I attack him to his face, and tell him that through God I am
more than a match for him.

Martin Luther

If you're a fan of *The Twilight Zone,* you might recall the 1960 episode
"The Howling Man." David Ellington, an American, is on a walking
trip through central Europe after World War I. Caught in a fierce storm,
he chances upon an imposing medieval castle where he meets a reclusive
brotherhood of monks.

At first they turn Ellington away. But after he passes out, they reluctantly
take him in. As he's reviving, he hears someone or something howling. The
brothers insist they hear nothing.

Later that night, the American discovers a man locked inside a cell. An
ancient wooden staff holds the door closed. The prisoner claims he's held
captive by the "insane" head monk, Brother Jerome, and pleads for his
release. His kind face and gentle voice convince Ellington to help.

96

Ellington confronts Jerome, who says the prisoner is Satan himself, "the Father of Lies," held captive by the Staff of Truth, the one barrier he cannot pass. This incredible claim convinces the visitor Jerome is indeed crazy. As soon as he gets the chance, he returns to the cell and opens it. Big mistake—the former captive instantly transforms into a hideous creature that vanishes in smoke.

The stunned American is mortified upon realizing what he has done. Jerome responds sympathetically, "I'm sorry for you, my son. All your life you will remember this night and whom you have turned loose upon the world."

"I didn't believe you," Ellington replies. "I saw him and didn't recognize him."

"That is man's weakness—and Satan's strength," Jerome muses solemnly.

Shortly after Satan's release, World War II breaks out. Ellington devotes his life to recapturing the devil and finally succeeds. As he makes arrangements to ship him back to the brotherhood, he tells his housekeeper to ignore the howling. But as soon as he leaves, she lifts the bar on the door, and it swings open.

The episode ends with Rod Sterling's ominous warning, "Ancient folk saying: 'You can catch the devil, but you can't hold him long.' Ask Brother Jerome. Ask David Ellington. They know, and they'll go on knowing to the end of their days and beyond."[1]

It's a cautionary tale, an allegory for those who acknowledge the devil's power but don't always recognize him for what he is.

AKA Satan

Stephen King, who's made a career of scaring the wits out of people, once said, "The beauty of religious mania is that it has the power to explain everything. Once God (or Satan) is accepted as the first cause of everything which happens in the mortal world, nothing is left to chance. . . . Logic can be happily tossed out the window."[2]

Lucifer, Abbadon, Asmodai, Antichrist, the Beast, Beelzebub (Lord of the Flies), Belial, Iblis, Lord of the Underworld, Mephistopheles, Old Scratch, Old Nick, Old Hob, Prince of Darkness, the Serpent . . . the being most commonly known in Western culture as either Satan or the devil has a long alias string that stretches through human history. And that's not including his many incarnations in Eastern religions.

Does a belief in Satan really mean logic has been "happily tossed out the window"? How relevant is the slithering, seductive serpent of Genesis today? Most modern skeptics argue he is at most a metaphor—a boogeyman of a bygone era who has no place in our rationalistic times.

Yet Satan remains a constant character. You might say he's a regular guest on every available medium, from classic literature to television, pop music to film.

Consider some of our heritage. The medieval German legend of Faust tells of a man who makes a pact with the devil in exchange for knowledge. In the seventeeth-century epic poem *Paradise Lost*, John Milton brilliantly portrays Satan as a protagonist reminiscent of Greek heroes. In the first scene the fallen angel proclaims defiantly to his just-banished followers, "Better to reign in hell, than serve in heav'n."

Two American legends featuring Satan in a prominent role are Washington Irving's *The Devil and Tom Walker* (1824) and Stephen Vincent Benét's *The Devil and Daniel Webster* (1937). Other incarnations include the Charlie Daniels Band's "The Devil Went Down to Georgia"; *The Simpsons* episode "The Devil and Homer Simpson"; and Tenacious D's rock opera, *The Pick of Destiny*.

The devil has starred in numerous contemporary movies as well. *Constantine* (2005) presents earth as a neutral war setting in God and Satan's wager over who will win the most souls. In *The Passion of the Christ* (2004), Satan carries a demon baby during Christ's flogging, perversely mocking Madonna and Child. You'll find thousands of such satanic "appearances" with a quick Google search.

Western ideas about Satan are mostly exaggerated, cartoonish, and inaccurate—based on medieval art and human imagination rather than on what the Bible says. Thus we have lighthearted stories, songs, films, illustrations, and games that glamorize the Prince of Darkness. He has become a stereotype that's more symbol than substance, even among many professing Christians. Indeed, Americans' belief in the devil fell from 68 percent to 59 percent between 2003 and 2008, approximately the same decline as beliefs in God, heaven, and hell.[3]

Origins of Darkness

Many argue that Satan is merely a concept adapted by Christians from ancient pagan religions with a dualistic approach to good and evil. There is, however, a distinct difference: Christianity asserts there is one God, the Supreme Creator, who is all-powerful, perfect, unchanging, just, loving, and completely good. Satan is an inferior, created being—not an opposing god.

In arguing against the reality of Satan, many have asked how a good and loving God could allow such an evil being to exist. Augustine of Hippo struggled with this very question, because while affirming the goodness of God's creation, he couldn't deny the existence of evil. Augustine came to understand evil as an *absence* (privation) of goodness; when angels or humanity turn away from God and choose sin, they turn from the source of goodness.[4] An analogy would be light and darkness, repeatedly used in Scripture to describe good and evil. Just as darkness is the absence of light (i.e., darkness is not a thing itself), so evil is the absence of, or lack of, good.

The Bible does not depict God and Satan as competing forces in a power struggle (like ontological dualism does). Though real, Satan is not an equal power but a created being who is part of the fallen creation and is utterly opposed to God. Jesus Christ, Light of the World, makes it clear that darkness can never overcome the light, in either the spiritual or physical realm.[5]

Another argument seeking to discount Satan is that only ignorant people would believe in such "superstition." This implies that Jesus was primitive or that he presented his message to accommodate the worldview of his audience. However, calling a belief primitive or superstitious assumes it's outdated or in error. Countless careful students of the Bible are convinced Jesus spoke of timeless truths.

In the last one hundred years, there have been many attacks upon Scripture in academic circles. These don't alter the Bible's teachings; the eternal truths revealed in God's Word will not change.

The Stuff of Legends

During the Middle Ages ordinary people didn't have access to God's Word as we do today. Monasteries, not universities, were the centers for learning. The monks and priests who served the local parishioners could not overcome the illiteracy and lack of education among their "flocks." The uneducated population (the majority of Europeans at the time) knew little about the Bible or church doctrine and quite often had little idea what Christianity is about.

Without solid biblical faith, people were easily convinced that folktales, legends, and sensational stories revealed the true nature of their world. They were fascinated by widespread beliefs about Satan, demons, angels, and other supernatural beings like fairies, trolls, werewolves, vampires, and witches. They didn't understand the difference between pagan myth and the tenets of authentic doctrine. They weren't able to examine Scripture and read for themselves the truth about Satan.

A Fallen Angel

The biblical authors agree: There is a supernatural entity that constantly seeks to destroy God's creation, especially those persons who have chosen to love and serve their Creator. This demonic personality was present, for instance, when the first humans sinned against God, when Jesus went into the wilderness for forty days, and when Judas met with the chief priests to betray Jesus.[6]

In the Old Testament's earliest writings, this entity is called "the Satan" (which means "adversary"). *Satan* is not a name but a title that describes a particular set of characteristics, just as *the Christ* is a title that identifies Messiah or King. Satan is the embodiment of evil—the one *farthest* from God. As one progresses through Scripture, the title *Satan* becomes synonymous with an angel named *Lucifer*, which is Latin for "light-bearer" or "day star."[7]

We know from three different parts of the Bible that pride and jealousy led this highly ranked angel to forsake his special relationship to God in order to corrupt humanity.[8] We don't know exactly when, where, or why this happened; Scripture leaves these questions unanswered. There are, however, intriguing clues about Satan and the fallen angels.

> Now there was a day when the sons of God came to present themselves before the Lord, and Satan also came among them. And the Lord said to Satan, "From where do you come?"
>
> So Satan answered the Lord and said, "From going to and fro on the earth, and from walking back and forth on it."[9]

100

The "sons of God" have been interpreted as being part of a heavenly host. Notice that although Satan is with these "sons," his status in heaven is unclear. The author of Job seems indifferent to Satan's motivations.[10]

At the time Job is believed to have been written, the Hebrews did not yet identify Satan as a completely evil entity. His personality wasn't fully defined until the time of three important prophets: Isaiah (c. 740 BC), Ezekiel (c. 597 BC), and Zechariah (c. 519 BC). Today's reader benefits from the full biblical revelation and can easily see Satan's furious, hate-filled animosity toward humankind.

The Anointed Angel

It happens every Halloween. If you live in a neighborhood, you get trick-or-treaters dressed as superheroes, princesses, witches . . . and devils. The latter are outfitted with horns, a pointy tail, a pitchfork, maybe even red skin. This is pop culture's most prevalent visual image. But the spiritual entity who became "the Satan" was created as a glorious heavenly being of indescribable beauty:

> This is what the Sovereign Lord says:
>   "You were the model of perfection,
>   full of wisdom and perfect in beauty.
> You were in Eden,
>   the garden of God;
>   every precious stone adorned you. . . .
>   Your settings and mountings were made of gold;
>   on the day you were created they were prepared.
> You were anointed as a guardian cherub,
>   for so I ordained you.
>   You were on the holy mount of God;
>   you walked among the fiery stones.
> You were blameless in your ways
>   from the day you were created
>   till wickedness was found in you."[11]

This angel was not only magnificent but also very important. He walked on the holy mountain with God. The anointing upon him signifies he was special.

Isaiah describes this angel's beauty in terms of sounds: astonishing music flowed from him. Both Ezekiel and Isaiah say God blessed him with perfect beauty and gave him a place of honor. Like the archangel, he was created good and was bestowed with the ability to choose whether or not to love and serve God.

Several passages help explain the motives behind the disobedience. From Isaiah:

> How art thou fallen from heaven, O Lucifer, son of the morning!
> How art thou cut down to the ground, which didst weaken the
>   nations.
> For thou hast said in thine heart, I will ascend into heaven,
> I will exalt my throne above the stars of God: I will sit also upon
>   the mount of the congregation, in the sides of the north:
> I will ascend above the heights of the clouds; I will be like the most
>   High.
> Yet thou shalt be brought down to hell, to the sides of the pit.[12]

A similar description of this fall is found in Ezekiel:

> In the abundance of your trade you were filled with violence, and you sinned;
> so I cast you as a profane thing from the mountain of God, and the guardian
> cherub drove you out from the midst of the stones of fire.
>
> Your heart was proud because of your beauty; you corrupted your wis-
> dom for the sake of your splendor. I cast you to the ground; I exposed you
> before kings, to feast their eyes on you.[13]

The Original Tempter

Both Genesis and Matthew highlight cunning and cleverness:[14]

> The serpent was more subtle than any other wild creature that the Lord
> God had made.[15]

> Behold, I send you out as sheep in the midst of wolves; so be wise as serpents
> and innocent as doves.[16]

In the New Testament, the relationship between Satan and the garden of Eden's serpent is revealed. John identifies Satan as "the dragon, that ancient serpent, who is the devil, or Satan."[17] And Paul warned the Corinthians to be watchful against the temptations of the same snake that tempted Eve:

I am afraid that as the serpent deceived Eve by his cunning, your thoughts will be led astray from a sincere and pure devotion to Christ.[18]

That this tempter was Satan makes these words from Genesis very provocative:

God said to the serpent, "Because you have done this, cursed are you above all cattle, and above all wild animals; upon your belly you shall go, and dust you shall eat all the days of your life. I will put enmity between you and the woman, and between your seed and her seed; he shall bruise your head, and you shall bruise his heel."[19]

What does it mean when God refers to a future "enmity between you [Satan] and the woman [Eve]"? This refers to something greater than the two personalities. The next phrase, referring to "your seed and her seed," clarifies that Eve's descendants will hate Satan and his demons; this animosity, then, will always exist between Satan and people.

God's statement to Satan that "he shall bruise your head" is the first foretelling of the devil's ultimate destruction. The injury (the cross) Satan would inflict on Eve's descendent would be akin to a bruise on his heel, because the resurrection followed the crucifixion. In defeating death and darkness, the Christ would crush Satan completely.

Our Adversary

Zechariah joins Job in describing Satan as part of the heavenly court:

Then he showed me Joshua the high priest standing before the angel of the Lord, and Satan standing at his right hand to accuse him. And the Lord said to Satan, "The Lord rebuke you, O Satan!"[20]

Note the adversarial role of Satan as accuser, and this reality is made much clearer in later biblical writings. Peter uses vivid imagery that leaves no doubt as to Satan's intent: "Your enemy the devil prowls around like a roaring lion looking for someone to devour."[21] To the church at Rome,

Paul describes the relationship between God and those who love him as inseparable, despite the adversary's best efforts.

> We are more than conquerors through him who loved us. For I am sure that neither death, nor life, nor angels, nor principalities, nor things present, nor things to come, nor powers, nor height, nor depth, nor anything else in all creation, will be able to separate us from the love of God in Christ Jesus our Lord.[22]

Among the things that might try to part us from God's love, Paul includes "angels," "principalities," and "powers." He uses similar terms in another letter, this time to the church in Ephesus, when he reminds us we're not fighting against people . . .

> . . . but against the principalities, against the powers, against the world rulers of this present darkness, against the spiritual hosts of wickedness in the heavenly places.[23]

Paul is speaking about personal spiritual forces that seek to destroy a person's relationship with God. These have turned away and strive to corrupt the goodness within his creation, and this message is consistent with the whole Bible's teachings: *Nothing* can stand between Christ and those who love him. However, there are powers that will try. I've heard it said that "when Satan tries to remind us of our past (failures and sins), we're to remind him of his future (ultimate destruction)."

Satan has indescribable animosity toward those who desire to follow Christ and live out his example. His plan is basic: he wants to tempt you into self-destructive choices and behavior. He and his demonic entities are actively trying to undermine (or prevent) your relationship with Jesus Christ. While God wants to enjoy fellowship with you now and forever, Satan is determined to keep you from this spectacular destiny.

Humans must choose between God and Satan. The nineteenth-century French poet Charles Baudelaire said it well: "There are in every [person], at every hour, two simultaneous claims, one towards God, the other towards Satan."[24]

In his renowned satire *The Screwtape Letters*, C. S. Lewis says,

There are two equal and opposite errors into which our race can fall about the devils. One is to disbelieve in their existence. The other is to believe, and to feel an excessive and unhealthy interest in them. They themselves are equally pleased by both errors.[25]

The evil one is no match for God. When you're following God and filled with his life, Satan is no match for you either.

10

Demons in the Dark

Emissaries of Evil Bring Chaos and Confusion

Demons do not exist any more than gods do, being only the products of the psychic activity of man.

Sigmund Freud

Years ago I conversed with a friend who had been my undergraduate classmate. We'd parted ways to pursue graduate degrees and now had met again. During our visit, the topic of demons came up.

"You actually believe they're for real?" he said. "Everybody knows that when the Bible speaks of demons it doesn't mean *literal* demons. Ancient peoples were primitive in their understanding, and all those stories refer to psychological aberrations. Two thousand years ago people weren't as sophisticated as we are."

"What about Jesus?" I asked. "He seemed to believe in demons."

"Certainly Jesus knew better," he replied. "Jesus understood he was dealing with people whose beliefs were primitive, so he talked about demons in order to relate to their worldview. Obviously, Jesus would have known there is no such thing. Demons can't possibly exist."

While I disagree with my friend's interpretation, he did make an accurate observation: The way we see the world depends on our point of view

. . . our worldview. For example, the Christian worldview is that God and creation are not the same. Trees, rocks, spiders, and eagles are not God, nor can they become God after several lifetimes or by spiritual achievement.

Many contemporary Westerners believe there is a spiritual realm in addition to the physical world, and in America the overwhelming majority believes there is a God. However, fewer people believe supernatural forces can enter material, earthly reality.

Scripture presents creation as a three-tiered universe: the unseen (spiritual) realm, the seen (material) world, and a third dimension that allows the seen and unseen to intersect. Paul Hiebert refers to this interactive realm as "the excluded middle," since it's been excluded from the thinking of many people.[1]

The Excluded Middle

If your worldview incorporates this excluded middle, you won't need to remove the supernatural from the biblical record. That's why there's a chapter on demons in this book about the afterlife—the topics of heaven and hell take us into unseen dimensions. These are not merely vacuous regions waiting for people; they have intended occupants and participants, whether angels or demons.

The Bible contains so many references to demons, demon possession (see below), demonization, unclean spirits, exorcisms, healing, and the casting out of evil spirits that even well-educated, sophisticated believers must allow for the possibility that the universe is more complex and mysterious than it may appear to our senses. If Jesus encountered demons and evil spirits during his lifetime, his followers likewise may face them.

Who Still Believes?

Sometimes it seems *everybody* believes in angels. It's an extremely widespread conviction, generating a flood of related shows, books, magazines, films, and all manner of merchandise. The belief that benevolent supernatural beings watch over innocent earthly souls continues to gain followers—even in (and at least partially in response to) our naturalistic age.

Ask someone if she believes in demons, however, and she'll probably say *no*. The widespread popularity of angels doesn't extend downward, although most religions that include angels also depict their evil counterparts. Among Christians, few want to openly discuss demonic activity or accept that demons are as real as ever. Perhaps we don't want to sound naïve or backward; belief in dark spiritual forces may seem ignorant or paranoid.

Looking from the vantage point of the demonic world, it would be to their advantage if we denied their reality or wallowed in a lack of knowledge. Maybe the old saying is true: The greatest lie the devil ever told is that he doesn't exist. Those in doubt about demons should consider this historical account:

> They [Jesus and his disciples] came to the other side of the sea. . . . And when he had come out of the boat, there met him out of the tombs a man with an unclean spirit, who lived among the tombs; and no one could bind him any more, even with a chain; for he had often been bound with fetters and chains, but the chains he wrenched apart, and the fetters he broke in pieces; and no one had the strength to subdue him. Night and day . . . he was always crying out, and bruising himself with stones. And when he saw Jesus from afar, he ran and worshiped him; and crying out with a loud voice, he said, "What have you to do with me, Jesus, Son of the Most High God? I adjure you by God, do not torment me." For he had said to him, "Come out of the man, you unclean spirit!" And Jesus asked him, "What is your name?" He replied, "My name is Legion; for we are many." And he begged him eagerly not to send them out of the country. Now a great herd of swine was feeding there . . . and they begged him, "Send us to the swine, let us enter them." So he gave them leave. And the unclean spirits came out, and entered the swine; and the herd . . . rushed down the steep bank . . . and were drowned in the sea.[2]

Possessed or Afflicted?

Over time the terms and phrases Scripture uses to describe human encounters with supernatural evils have changed somewhat in meaning. For example, the term *possessed*, utilized several times in some translations,[3] might be better stated today as *afflicted*, one of the many ways some versions describe a person captive to a demonic force. For example, "the people also gathered from the towns around Jerusalem, bringing the sick and those *afflicted* with unclean spirits, and they were all healed."[4]

Note that these people could distinguish sickness/disease from demonic affliction. In a similar passage, we find another term:

> [Jesus] came down with them and stood on a level place, with a great crowd of his disciples and a great multitude of people . . . who came to hear him and to be healed of their diseases; and those who were *troubled* with unclean spirits were cured.[5]

Here again, those who presented themselves for healing recognized a difference.[6]

Affliction can be explained as a spectrum that ranges from demonic influence "on" a person to the extreme of a demon actually "in" a person's body. One way to understand this concept is to consider the way alcohol makes a person drunk. Using medical instruments to study its effects on the brain, we would find that the first sips cause changes and reactions. As more and more is consumed, the body's responses become more pronounced and noticeable (bloodshot eyes, slurred speech, loss of coordination). Our investigation would utilize a spectrum that measured *levels* of inebriation: sober . . . tipsy . . . drunk.

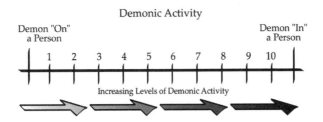

Demonic Activity

This type of model can describe the progression from demons *on* a person to a demon *in* a person (the final stage is the only time a person is truly possessed). This continuum is demonstrated as a gradual progression of influence, from low-grade affliction to eventual possession. (Complete bodily possession generally is rare, despite Hollywood's fascination with it.)

Demonic possession and various stages of demonization have been documented for thousands of years in cultures worldwide. The anthropologists, psychologists, sociologists, ministers and priests, and dedicated laypersons who have devoted their lives to studying such supernatural activity report an amazing consistency in the encountered cases. There are universal patterns, symptoms, behaviors, and rituals associated with affliction, and these phenomena are real.

What Is a Demon?

The Bible contains more details about the destruction and chaos around demonic affliction than about demons themselves. This isn't an oversight; the New Testament focus is on people being set free. In addition, the demonic world does not want to be understood—demons don't want to be revealed as a source of suffering and misery, preferring to see men and women directing their anger at one another or blaming God. On the other hand, it's erroneous to see demons in every circumstance or problem and behind every sin. Inexplicable behavior should not be prematurely labeled "demonic." Bible knowledge, spiritual discernment, and prayer are necessary tools to distinguish supernatural evil from natural misfortune or from the results of poor choices.

Jesus and his followers knew how to recognize what is truly demonic and how to set people free from demonic affliction. Demons don't have earthly bodies; they were often "in" the bodies of those Jesus healed. They seem to have a hierarchy that depends on their wickedness:

> When the unclean spirit has gone out of a man, he passes through waterless places seeking rest, but he finds none. Then he says, "I will return to my house from which I came." And when he comes he finds it empty, swept, and put in order. Then he goes and brings with him seven other spirits more evil than himself, and they enter and dwell there; and the last state of that man becomes worse than the first.[7]

110

The accounts of possession also reveal that demons can wield control in several ways: speaking, screaming, laughing, shaking, convulsing, seeing, and hearing. Most troublesome are the accounts of demons entering into a person and controlling thoughts, manipulating emotions, and creating visions and delusions.

Demonic affliction and possession also can distort a person's ability to make rational decisions:

> Then Satan entered into Judas called Iscariot . . . [who] went away and conferred with the chief priests and officers how he might betray him [Jesus] to them. And they were glad, and engaged to give him money. So he agreed, and sought an opportunity to betray him to them in the absence of the multitude.[8]

> During supper, when the devil had already put it into the heart of Judas Iscariot, Simon's son, to betray him, Jesus . . . rose from supper, laid aside his garments, and girded himself with a towel.[9]

It's not surprising that Satan, the very "source" of evil, had an active role in the betrayal of the man Judas knew to be Messiah. At the same time, *Christians do not need to fear demons—at all.* God has given us power over them; we must only understand what to do and how to do it.

Demons of Biblical Proportions

Although many ancient manuscripts contain elaborate myths about demonic forces, Christians uphold the Bible as the ultimate source for revealed truth.[10] Therein God doesn't reveal much about the origin or appearance of demons but emphasizes their weaknesses, trickery, and deceitfulness. Demons are dangerous only until they are confronted by the power of Jesus.

We know that demons can kill, are strong, and have what's been called a "Luciferian spirit"—that is, "It's all about me." Egregious self-absorption says, "I will, I want, I will get what I want, I will exalt myself."[11] We also know that numerous demons can afflict. As noted, when Jesus demanded a name from the spirit that possessed a man, it replied, "My name is Legion, for *we are many*."

Although demons can be crafty and skillfully deceptive, it appears they have varied levels of intelligence. At times, they can be remarkably dumb. Once, a demon "shouted at the top of his voice, 'What do you want with me, Jesus, Son of the Most High God? Swear to God that you won't torture me!' For Jesus had said to him, 'Come out of this man, you evil spirit!'"[12]

This is amazing: The spirit acknowledged Jesus as God's Son, then it tried to get Jesus to "swear to God" he wouldn't act! The demon was invoking God's help against whatever Jesus might do to him, apparently thinking he could leverage one against the other.

In the early '80s, I visited a Houston church for a conference where the speaker was talking about demons. Suddenly, without warning, a man in the audience stood up, terror on his face. He left his chair, moved quickly to a column in the auditorium, positioned himself behind a supporting pole, and peered around it toward the stage, seeming to hope the speaker couldn't see him.

Making the scene comical was that the pole was a fraction of the man's body width—he couldn't hide behind it at all. Sadly, however, he demonstrated the characteristics of a demonically afflicted person. The speaker, not flustered in the least, easily took control. With the confidence of Jesus, he commanded the demons to come out of the man.

Stupidity or ignorance had led the demon to believe the man could hide behind the column. And, after the speaker had said, "I command you, by the authority of Jesus, to leave this man and to go to the dry places," someone asked, "Why did you send the demon there?" He said this phrase was from an exorcism in which demons shrieked, "Please don't send us to the dry places."

"As a result," he said, "we've been sending them there ever since."

How dumb is it for a demon to use the vocal chords of the afflicted person to name the very place he doesn't want to go! Later I realized that Scripture confirms what the demon said: "When an evil spirit comes out of a man, it goes through arid places seeking rest and does not find it."[13]

Although it's important to know some facts about demons, we don't need to dwell on them or focus on finding more details. History has shown repeatedly that any obsession with the demonic will always lead to tragedy.[14] One might even argue that, according to Genesis, the very first disobedient human choice was acting on something God had chosen to keep hidden.[15]

Many biblical narratives also reveal God's absolute authority over all creation. *There is not a balance of power or a struggle for control—God is in charge.* Demons fear the power of Jesus Christ, and even speaking his name can rebuke evil.

How Should We Respond?

Once again, Christians need not fear demons, "for he who is in you is greater than he who is in the world."[16] The Spirit of the living Christ lives in those who believe and trust in him; demons may not possess such a person.

> There was in their synagogue a man with an unclean spirit; and he cried out, "What have you to do with us, Jesus of Nazareth? Have you come to destroy us? I know who you are, the Holy One of God." But Jesus rebuked him, saying, "Be silent, and come out of him!" And the unclean spirit, convulsing him and crying with a loud voice, came out of him.[17]

The spirit could do nothing but obey Jesus' command. Invoking his name gives his disciples power over demons, so that even in the face of demonic activity believers can go forward without fear.

The first response in helping others suffering unusual havoc and chaos is to determine if the source of their problems is demonic. People can get into all kinds of trouble through sin, without any help from demons. One overarching biblical theme is that people have the choice to serve God or serve themselves. Mere belief in God is not the ticket to heaven: "Even the demons believe—and shudder."[18] Anyone can believe God exists but still maintain a life apart from him.

Sinful habits or lifestyles may open a person, unknowingly, to increasing degrees of affliction. Immoral acts repetitiously committed over long periods can create opportunities for demonic forces to influence behavior and turn habits into bondage (a form of possession), weakening one's resistance to demonic influences.

So, demonic activity can occur in an individual's life through actions and attitudes contrary to God's clearly defined pattern for our lives. There is, however, another somewhat more complex way in which demonic activity can intrude. Though this isn't noted in Scripture, it's certainly not in conflict with Scripture; it comes from those who have studied and experienced the reality of demonic affliction.

Intrusive demonic activity unrelated to personal sinful practices seemingly can occur when a person has a highly traumatic experience, particularly one associated with extreme fear. An example might be an abusive parent's locking a small child in a dark closet. Years later, attempting to discern how his affliction began, the victim reflects on the terror with awareness that something tragic and significant happened in that moment.

How is this possible? Some think trauma of such intensity creates a fissure or weak spot—some type of break—in our natural "psychological armor." An unexpected tragedy or severe grief resulting from events beyond our control apparently can bring emotional and spiritual vulnerability to demonic intrusion.

This category is not the norm, however; *we* initiate most demonic activity. In addition to some obvious and common sinful practices, we can make ourselves more vulnerable by participating in biblically forbidden activities. Interest and participation in occult practices can be the door through which demons influence a person or become active in her life.

Scripture issues more than forty warnings about magic and witchcraft. Ouija boards, séances, fortune-telling, white magic, horoscopes, and tarot cards are just a few prohibited dark-arts tools. Many people report curiosity having turned into an obsession that has caused them damage and havoc.

Again, Jesus has taught his followers the disciplines needed to discern God's will: prayer, study of Scripture, baptism, tithing, Communion, worship, fasting, and service to one another. If a person appears to be demon-afflicted, and the practice of these disciplines makes no positive difference in her life, demonic activity is a real possibility. Signs may include bizarre behavior, prolonged depression, abnormal fears, even a persistent illness that cannot be diagnosed.

Simply recognizing evil influence is not sufficient for freedom. In most cases, a person suffers from demonization because of a spiritual blockage that has undermined her relationship with God. Bitterness, resentment, and unconfessed/unforgiven sin build a fortress behind which a demon has a legitimate claim—it's as if the spirit has the right to be there. Once a person experiences forgiveness, resentment and bitterness will leave; the fortress that protects the demon will be destroyed.

Mental and emotional blockages that protect evil spirits are not easily dislodged. Often there must be prayer for spiritual healing before deliverance can begin. Repentance and acceptance of God's forgiveness removes the barriers to physical healing and deliverance. It is during this process that the afflicted person may undergo physical displays or manifestations.

After reception of inner healing, physical healing and final deliverance can happen. Tools used during deliverance are prayer, the laying on of hands, the reading of Scripture, and the reverential use of Jesus Christ's name. This deeply personal and intimate process should not be opened to an audience beyond the participants. The dignity of the afflicted should be protected at all times.

A Deliverance Observed

Several decades ago I traveled to Southern California to attend a large church conference on the topic of demons, a subject on which I was quite naïve. On the second night, about two hundred people were praying near the front of the church, and many were praying out loud, so it got pretty noisy. Suddenly, over these sounds came an extremely loud voice, yelling one word. We were all startled to hear the F-word in a church.

Looking up, I noticed four or five men quietly surrounding another man—the source of the profanity—and gently leading him off the platform. Wanting to learn and to pray with them, I followed. We went to a confined room, where a man who seemed to have related and relevant experience immediately took leadership in praying for the man to be set free from a demonic presence.

What occurred over the next hour was one of the most amazing episodes of my life, my first and thus far only time to witness a fully possessed human being. This otherwise sophisticated gentleman would snap his teeth (trying to bite) and growl, his eyes glowing with hate. Then he would return to normal, and during those brief moments he would say, "Guys, I don't know what's happening. I'm not like this. This is not me. I'm not doing this." The fear in his eyes was exceeded only by his pleading: "Help me!" Suddenly he again would become demonically infused, growling and snapping.

The others didn't seem surprised—they'd dealt with this before. I hadn't and was stunned. I'd only read about such encounters. The men worked as a team, praying, alternately calling out for deliverance. However, no improvement occurred. The afflicted man continued to vacillate between ghoulish behavior and a kind of fearful innocence.

Finally, after nearly one hour, the demon cried out hauntingly, gutturally, *"Don't go get Becky!"* This made no sense to me, but the others instantly looked at each other, obviously knowing a Becky involved with the conference. One man went to get her. (Again, the stupidity of demons.)

Moments later Becky arrived. We'd been praying a long time; not having succeeded, we'd prayed louder. In the confines of a small, stuffy room, with several men praying in desperation and one demonized man terrorizing us all, we'd worked up quite a sweat. I remember being somewhat embarrassed that this well-dressed woman was entering what smelled like a postgame locker room.

Becky knew what was going on, took control of the situation with poise, and ordered the demonized man to sit down. He'd been leaning against the wall but now sat down facing her. She then ordered the demon not to speak or make itself evident in any way. She said to the man, "These men have prayed for you nearly an hour. The demon should have come out. The only thing that could allow it to stay in your life would be if it was hiding behind a fortress. And the likely fortress will be related to a lack of forgiveness. We are going to end this session. You are to go be alone with your Bible and with God. Ask God what areas in your life need forgiveness. Come back tomorrow morning at nine. They will meet you here and pray over you at that time."

Then she left. Her entire monologue had lasted less than two or three minutes. I thought, *So this is the "Becky" the demons fear?*

The next morning the afflicted man came on time to meet the team of men who'd prayed extensively the previous day. After just seconds of commanding the demon to come out, the man began to sense something had left him. He was joyful and certain that he'd been delivered.

116

Before long, the others went on their way. But I stopped him and asked if we could talk, as there was much I didn't understand. Graciously he consented, and we stood in the hallway as I asked questions: who was he, what was his job, where was he from, and above all, what exactly had happened, moment by moment, during his two-day ordeal?

He was a pastor in Canada, but was familiar with this area. As a child and youth he'd lived within a mile of this very Anaheim church building.

As a young teenager, with another boy his age, he had cornered his own younger sister in the garage, forced her into the backseat of a car, and assaulted her. Sometime later, he and his family moved away.

Decades passed. Now when he'd come back to the vicinity of the crime, a demonic presence consumed him and caused him to yell a horrible curse that described his own actions toward his sister.

Becky's words about forgiveness issues were true and twofold: He had never asked his sister for forgiveness, and he had involved a neighbor boy. The night before his deliverance, he had finally placed phone calls, seeking to make right what he had perpetrated many years before. His confession and repentance seemed to be the key to tearing down the fortress and breaking free from the demon.

I have since seen and sensed demonic affliction in many forms, but none compared with the intensity of this one. It became a model for me. Unforgiveness, resentment, and bitterness can give an excuse for demonic activity to remain in a life. With a cleansed heart, and with confession and forgiveness, a person can be set free from even the most insidious intrusion.

During his traveling ministry on earth, Jesus sent out seventy-two of his followers to tell others who he was. They returned with excitement and pride about what they'd accomplished, especially casting out demons. He said,

> I saw Satan fall like lightning from heaven. I have given you authority to trample on snakes and scorpions and to overcome all the power of the enemy; nothing will harm you. However, do not rejoice that the spirits submit to you, but rejoice that your names are written in heaven.[19]

In other words: "Don't get obsessed with your power over demons. That's truly not the big deal. Be excited that you have a relationship with *me*."

Part Three

Crossing Over

The Upward Call

11

A Delightful Detour

The First Heaven Is a Temporary Stopover Before Permanent Paradise

We talk about heaven being so far away. It is within speaking distance to those who belong there. It is a prepared place for a prepared people.

D. L. Moody

I f you build it, they will come."

Recognize that statement? If so, you've probably seen *Field of Dreams*, a film that manages to intertwine three universal interests: the pursuit of a dream, the nature of heavenly bliss, and the love of baseball (which may or may not be a love of yours). This whimsical movie requires us to suspend disbelief, what with the "voice" talking from a cornfield, old baseball players walking in and out of a centerfield "heaven," and time travel back to a Midwestern town in 1972.

The story centers on Ray Kinsella, who's struggling to scratch out a living on his farm. One day he hears a voice instructing him to build a baseball field in the middle of his cornfield. His long-suffering wife, Annie, encourages him to go for it despite her own misgivings. Townspeople suspect he's a few kernels short of a full cob. No matter—he heeds the mysterious voice's direction and pursues his dream, which catalyzes several paranormal events.

In the closing scene, Ray prepares to meet his long-dead father, John. They gather on the field Ray has carved out of his farmland. Ray stands along the chalk lines with Annie, their gaze turned toward home plate. There, standing with his back to them and pulling off his old-fashioned catcher's gear, is a young man dressed in the loosely fitting uniform he once wore as a minor leaguer.

Suddenly it dawns on Ray that he is witnessing a miracle. John Kinsella, his own father, has returned from "baseball heaven." John begins walking toward his son, looking around as if taking in the novelty of earth's air, the setting sun, and the smell of the grass.

Ray turns to Annie and says, "I only saw him years later, when he was worn down by life. What do I say to him?"

Father and son soon stand face-to-face.

"It's so beautiful here," says John. "For me, it's like a dream come true. Can I ask you something? Is this heaven?"

"It's Iowa," Ray answers.

"I could have sworn it was heaven."

"Is there a heaven?"

"Oh, yeah—it's the place where dreams come true."

After a moment the two shake hands, but as the father walks away, Ray calls out, "Hey, Dad, want to play catch?"

"I'd like that," John replies.

They walk back onto the field together, Ray standing by the plate, John on the mound, and they begin tossing the ball. Just a little taste of heaven on earth.[1]

Movies like this, besides being fun escapist entertainment, may stir some questions after we shut off the DVD player and turn out the lights. What will my final destination look like? Will I recognize loved ones? What will I do there? Nearly all of us have an innate curiosity about where we'll end up.

Indeed, if you believe in life after death, you're in good company. Most religions uphold some form, whether that "life" is described as heaven, hell, reincarnation, soul sleep, limbo, or purgatory. Of the eight major religious groups, only two—atheists and certain Christian subsets—believe in annihilation, that after death we completely cease to exist.

Considering all the people claiming to believe in heaven, there's not a lot of solid instruction taking place regarding the destination most of us think we're heading toward. We can understand why there's not a lot of

Beliefs About What Happens After Death

Christian Protestant		
In Christ	→	To Heaven
Outside Christ	→	To Hell
Christian Catholic		
Sanctified	→	To Heaven
Partially Sanctified	→	To Purgatory
Unbaptized or In Sin	→	To Hell
Historical Catholic		
Death Before Christ	→	Limbo Until Resurrection
Infant Death	→	Limbo Permanently
Christian Subsets		
Outside Christ	→	Annihilation (Cease to Exist)
Conditional Immortality	→	Annihilation (Cease to Exist)
Christian Sect		
In Christ	→	Soul Sleep
Cultural Secularist		
All People	→	Heaven
Atheists		
All People	→	Annihilation (Cease to Exist)
Eastern/New Age		
All Believers	→	Reincarnation

talk about hell—with its nightmarish imagery, we'd rather avoid the topic altogether. But what about heavenly wonders and glories? We should be wildly eager to learn as much as we can. Still, the information we get usually is sketchy and generalized. John Gilmore wrote that "silence on heaven by clergymen is puzzling. The pulpit is where one would expect to hear more about heaven. Yet . . . the matter is passed over briefly, if mentioned at all."[2]

Even in seminaries and classrooms, discussions of heaven are strangely absent. I've spent a lot of time in those classrooms, having earned six degrees in religious studies—an associate of arts in religion, a bachelor of arts in religion, a Master's in New Testament, a Master's of divinity, a Master's of theology in church history, and a doctorate of philosophy in historical theology. Throughout all those years I never took a single class on heaven. What's more, I don't recall a course on heaven even being offered. To make matters worse, I don't remember a single lecture on heaven or hell or even one vigorous discussion on the topic! As a result, when I became a college professor, I didn't lecture on the subject either. It wasn't until after pastoring for several decades that I finally began to study and preach on heaven.

Believing in heaven is one thing, but what do we really *know*? It seems to me that most of us know more about the vacation spot we'll be visiting next summer than we do about the place we're planning to spend eternity.

Indeed, many of our perceptions of heaven come from the media. How can we form our opinions about something as important as "forever" from talk show hosts, celebrities on *Larry King Live*, fantasy books, or late-night guests? One man identified the concoction as "cosmic sausage." Our image of heaven, he wrote, is a combination of "childhood memories, tidbits from intellectual chopping blocks, and choice cuts from poetic doublespeak. Mixed in with the eclectic mass are down-home anecdote spices to add aroma and individual flavor."[3]

I enjoy baseball and have fond memories of growing up on a farm, even playing sports in the pasture (though not in a cornfield). Maybe there will be baseball and cornfields in heaven—but I know there will be far more than that. Surely far more than we can imagine.

So where *do* we turn for solid answers about heaven? It does make sense to take in the stories of people who have died and returned. As we've learned, those who have had near-death experiences and come back to share details about heaven provide helpful glimpses. I believe many of these reports are legitimate and credible. Yet they don't provide a complete picture, only disparate pieces we can attempt to put together. We need to turn to the most authoritative source of information if we want to get close to a true and accurate perspective.

Our Guidebook to the Great Beyond

It may not surprise you, this suggestion that we should go confidently to Scripture for insights into heaven, but you may be surprised at the reason. It's not just that the Bible is at the epicenter of theological belief for the faith with the greatest number of followers on earth. *We can go confidently to the Bible for answers about heaven because it's a completely trustworthy document.*

We know this because, while Scripture contains many spiritual claims that cannot be verified, it also contains countless statements that *can* be historically proven. When the provable statements are tested and prove to be accurate, we can know the "unprovable" statements have credibility.

This is not an unfamiliar concept. You and I make decisions all the time based on such reasoning. For example, if we've done business for years with someone who—every single time we've checked up on him—has showed himself trustworthy and honest, we know we can believe him when he tells us something that needs to be taken on faith, something that, for whatever reason, can't be double-checked.

Likewise, when it comes to Scripture's accuracy, the provable statements in its pages have been challenged repeatedly through the years and found to be historically, archeologically, and geographically correct. Using every accepted method of historical verification, the Bible has passed with flying colors. Is it any wonder, then, that we also can embrace unprovable claims and statements?

With this in mind, let's consider how Scripture answers two questions that, if we're honest, are foremost whenever we think of the afterlife:

Where will I go when I die?
What will I look like when I get there?

The Bible doesn't talk about just one heaven but three. Our first clue that there are multiple heavens could not be found any earlier. We see it from the start: God created the *heavens*—plural—and the earth.[4]

If you scanned this book's table of contents page, you may have been curious about two different chapters addressing two different heavens. Can that be right? Most of us have grown up hearing that when we die we go to heaven—that's it, end of story. But the Bible has much to say about what I'll call the *first heaven* and the *permanent heaven* (which we'll delve into at length in chapter 13).

It's clear that while the first heaven is temporary, the second heaven is permanent. Paul (in a letter to Christians in Corinth[5]) additionally makes reference to a third heaven, which we don't know much about.

Do these three heavens refer, as some have suggested, to layers of space in the universe? Some believe the first heaven is the space surrounding our stars and planets, the second heaven contains the galaxies beyond our own, and the third is where Christ-followers end up when they die.

Others believe the first heaven is the kingdom of heaven that is here now dwelling within us, while the second heaven is the one discussed in this chapter, meaning a temporary place believers go immediately after death until Christ returns, gathers his church (those who've died and those yet to die), and takes them to their permanent home in the third heaven described by Paul.

That viewpoint is certainly appealing. However, throughout *Heaven and the Afterlife* we're going to limit our discussion to what we know for sure by focusing on the two heavens directly pointed to in Scripture: a temporary heaven and a permanent heaven. If we were to number these, they'd be either numbers one and two or numbers two and three, depending upon your theological perspective. For our purposes, let's call them the first heaven and the permanent heaven; that seems to line up best with how the Bible refers to them.

First Heaven: The Initial Stop After Death

What happens immediately after we die? Apparently, we leave our present earthly bodies and depart for someplace else, someplace better than where we are now, someplace where we're instantly in the presence of God. As Jesus was dying on the cross, he looked at the repentant thief next to him and said, "I tell you the truth, today you will be with me in paradise."[6] And when Paul wrote to the church in Philippi, he said, "I am torn between the two: I desire to depart [this life] and be with Christ, which is better by far; but it is more necessary for you that I remain in the body."[7]

One of the most fascinating passages regarding the first heaven is found in Luke's gospel, where Jesus tells a story about a beggar named Lazarus. About the time Lazarus died and went to heaven, a wealthy man also died, but he went to a very different place. While some would argue this is a parable and shouldn't be taken literally, it's the only occasion on which Jesus told a parable using an actual name, suggesting Lazarus may have been a real person. In any case, here's what Jesus had to say about the matter.

In hell, where he [the wealthy man] was in torment, he looked up and saw Abraham far away, with Lazarus by his side. So he called to him, "Father Abraham, have pity on me and send Lazarus to dip the tip of his finger in water and cool my tongue, because I am in agony with this fire."

But Abraham replied, "Son, remember that in your lifetime you received your good things, while Lazarus received bad things, but now he is comforted here and you are in agony. And besides all this, between us and you a great chasm has been fixed, so that those who want to go from here to you cannot, nor can anyone cross over from there to us."

He answered, "Then I beg you, father, send Lazarus to my father's house, for I have five brothers. Let him warn them, so that they will not also come to this place of torment."[8]

It seems the first heaven, to which we're transported immediately after death, is separated from hell by an impassible gulf. Furthermore, the people there are not only conscious and aware, but they also have memories of events and people from their years on earth.

Heavenly Bodies: Fact or Fiction?

This raises another matter, having to do with our bodies. After all, how can we see without eyes? How can we talk without lips? Don't we leave these bodies behind when we die? Do we have any kind of body at all at that point, or are we disembodied spirits who can't kick the habit of using words and phrases that made sense back when we had forms that could hear and touch and thirst?

Actually, many verses suggest we will have some sort of physical body in this temporary (first) heaven. Randy Alcorn, author of an exhaustive work on heaven,[9] makes this case by noting the same account of Lazarus and the wealthy man, who certainly appear to have physical forms. Alcorn also references Christ's conversation with the thief on the cross, explaining that "today you will be with me in paradise" implies not only an immediate transition but a very personal one, pointing to a conscious, bodily existence on the other side.

Finally, Alcorn cites people coming and going from the first heaven *wearing bodies*. For example, when Enoch was caught up into heaven, he didn't leave anything behind[10]—can't we assume he took his body with him? When Moses and Elijah descended on the Mount of Transfiguration, they had bodies.[11] Did this apply only to them, or does it apply to the rest of us as well?

Whatever kind of body we'll have, one thing we know for sure: It's not the final, permanent, perfected, resurrected body we'll receive later when taken into the permanent heaven. I believe this is what Paul implies:

> We know that if the earthly tent we live in [our physical bodies] is destroyed, we have a building from God, an eternal house in heaven, not built by human hands. Meanwhile [after our earthly bodies are gone and before we get our eternal bodies] we groan, longing to be clothed with our heavenly dwelling.[12]

He apparently is giving us a glimpse into when, if not disembodied spirits, we're at least spirits clothed in something imperfect and temporary. This is the season between our individual death and Christ's triumphant return, when our spirit longs for perfection and completion, when we yearn to be clothed in permanent, resurrected bodies worthy of dwelling forever with Jesus in an eternal heaven.

Britain's N. T. Wright, one of the world's foremost Bible scholars, affirms that "Paul speaks of 'the redemption of our bodies' [Romans 8:23]. There is no room for doubt as to what he means; God's people are promised a new type of bodily existence, the fulfillment and redemption of our present bodily life."[13]

But when? When do we transition from the first to the permanent heaven, the point at which we finally get our redeemed and resurrected bodies? *When Christ returns to earth.* In this moment, Jesus will descend from the clouds, and those who believe on him—the living and the dead—will rise together to meet him.[14] For this grand event, if we are alive and well on earth, these bodies will be transformed into our new, permanent ones.[15] If we have already died (and have been waiting in the first heaven for this day) our bodies will be resurrected from the grave, clothed in glorified bodies, and transported to meet Jesus in the sky.

You might wonder: What if a person's earthly body is long gone? What if he died a very long time ago? Or drowned at sea? Or was cremated? *How* would he be raised from the grave?

Paul, asked this question, answered with an analogy from the harvest:

When you sow, you do not plant the body that will be, but just a seed. . . .
So will it be with the resurrection of the dead. The body that is sown is
perishable, it is raised imperishable; it is sown in dishonor, it is raised in
glory; it is sown in weakness, it is raised in power; it is sown a natural body,
it is raised a spiritual body.[16]

In other words, our decomposing earthly bodies are like seeds planted
in the ground, and even though they're "sown in dishonor," in time returning to the dirt, they will be gloriously raised. From the seed comes
the flower. Our new bodies will be wonderful, and they will never die
or fade away.

New and Improved?

Paul uses the illustration of Christ being the "firstfruits," which means
exactly what it sounds like. The firstfruits of the harvest is important as
a sign of what will come—it's a prototype of what will follow. Paul says,
in essence, "If you want to know what resurrection will be like for you,
look at Jesus."

Some have asked, since there are isolated cases in both Testaments of
people being brought back from the dead before Jesus was resurrected,
wouldn't they technically be the firstfruits? No. While some people did
come back to life, they were brought back into their earthly bodies, which
eventually had to experience death again. Without diminishing the miracle
of these events, these people were divinely *resuscitated*, not raised as Jesus
was into a new body and immortality. Complete *resurrection* means being
raised and never dying again.

While we're on the subject of people who were raised from the dead,
there is one most unusual verse in the Bible—so unusual (some would say
disturbing) that it's rarely spoken of. Yet it's there, and it deserves to be
examined.

According to Matthew, at the moment Jesus died, an earthquake rocked
Jerusalem, and many tombs split open. People who'd been buried outside
the city came back to life and began making their way back into town.[17]
Maybe this sounds like a low-budget horror flick, but there it is, in Scripture. This story is so profound that it's easy to miss the point. What in the
world happened? And more important: *why?*

I believe this was God's way of saying, "I'm showing you that what I say is true. It's too soon to bring *all* of you out of the grave, but I want you to know who I am, so I'm giving you a small sampling of what is yet to come. The power you see around you today—you will experience firsthand in your own life."

Jesus paved the way; you and I will one day follow in his steps. We will be like him. So what is his resurrected body *really* like? For starters, it's not limited by time and space. After all, on earth, following his resurrection, he entered a locked room without using doors or windows; he disappeared from the believers in Emmaus and reappeared elsewhere.[18]

Jesus' resurrected body *also* was tangible and physical in every sense. After his resurrection he could speak and be heard by human ears. He could be seen by human eyes. His body could be touched. Assuring his frightened disciples that it was actually him standing before them, he said, "Look at my hands and my feet. It is I myself! Touch me and see; a ghost does not have flesh and bones, as you see I have."[19] And there's something humorous about his asking, "Do you have anything here to eat?"[20] He enjoyed meals with his friends.

Jesus' body was still, well . . . *him*. Sure, it may have been transformed, changed, immortal—but Jesus was still Jesus. He looked like himself; he was recognized by Mary Magdalene and others. His transformed body still bore the scars from what had happened to him during his earthly life.

Fear of death is universal to every people, era, and culture; we often associate dying with pain and loss. The good news is that, beyond the veil, we don't have to be afraid. Immediately after death, you and I, conscious and alert, will be transported to a new place. We will be able to remember and reason. Whether we experience a season of being spirits without bodies or are given a "temporary body," we eventually will be clothed in transformed, resurrected, glorified bodies just like the one Jesus modeled for us after his resurrection.

But before you and I get to relax and enjoy the next hundred thousand millennia—and beyond—in the permanent heaven that's to be our home forever, one more event must occur. The very name—judgment day—strikes terror into the hearts of many. But have no fear: it's an awards banquet, really. And once you realize what it's about and truly grasp what's going to happen, you will never look at your life—or your death—the same way again.

12

A Rewarding Experience

God's Children Have Nothing to Fear of Judgment Day

God examines both rich and poor, not according to their lands and houses, but according to the riches of their hearts.

Augustine

Susan edged as gracefully as she could across the threshold of the CEO's office door. Ms. Anderson's e-mail had asked her to come ASAP, but then she'd added a postscript with the reassuring words: "Don't worry—it's good news." The leader of the entire worldwide corporation had then punctuated that P.S. with a smiley face. That was a good sign . . . right?

At the appointed time, Susan arrived to find John—Ms. Anderson's admin—standing at the door, holding it open to usher Susan in, with a broad smile that seemed to offer reassurance. Then why was she so nervous?

"Welcome, Susan! Thank you for coming promptly." Ms. Anderson glanced up, this time offering an actual smiley face. She motioned for Susan to sit in the chair beside the desk as her eyes went back to her monitor. "Give me just a moment—I need to finish this."

Susan sank warily into the comfortable leather without a word—with hardly a breath. And she waited, as if perhaps Ms. Anderson might even forget she was there. For what seemed an eternity—a full thirty seconds—she glanced about the office, only her eyes moving. She scanned book titles from a shelf behind the massive oak desk. But she couldn't seem to distract herself from the nagging voice in the back of her mind, warning with despondency, *This can't truly be good. It feels like being called to the principal's office.*

"So, Susan," Ms. Anderson's voice halted the musings. "We need to talk."

Here it comes.

"I have great news for you," she said. "You've been doing superb work lately. How long has it been since you joined us?" Her expression still seemed warm and sincere.

"Um, six months, ma'am," Susan replied.

"Well, you've been achieving remarkably. And your manager has brought you specifically to my attention."

Just what I don't want.

"Susan, we want to reward you."

Susan responded quickly, almost interrupting. "Oh—you don't need to."

Ms. Anderson paused, still smiling, but cocked her head quizzically.

"I mean, that's not why I've been working hard," Susan said. "I didn't do it for a reward."

The boss nodded as her smile broadened. "I know, Susan."

"I know you know, ma'am," Susan responded. "So you really don't need to do anything more for me. I'm just happy to be a part of this company. That's honor enough."

There was an awkward pause for another few eternal seconds as the CEO continued to hold that smile, then said, "Susan, I know I don't have to." She glanced down at a folder. As she opened it, without looking up, she added—rather firmly—"But I *want* to. So let me tell you what I'm going to do for you. . . ."

Rewards Earned

What if I were to tell you that God the Father, CEO of the universe, for his own reasons wants to reward *you*? Many Scriptures tell us this is true. Realize that we're not talking about getting into heaven; that happens because of what Jesus has done. We don't and couldn't ever *earn* entrance into heaven.

So here you are, a part of God's people already, and you're thankful to be serving the kingdom. Your place is secure. Then you see this memo from God—his Word. And it tells you in no uncertain terms that you're going to meet him face-to-face and will discuss your evaluation. Intimidated?

The good news is you're very close to the boss's son—Jesus. And he's made it clear to you what's important to his Father. Let's prepare for the job review and see what God himself says—the criteria by which you'll be weighed. It's no secret, and what's more, he wants you to succeed. He's rooting for you!

So here we are, right now, living this life. The question that should be driving us daily is *What are those things God wants me to invest in that will bring rewards in heaven?* The great news is he's given you all the directions you need.

Understanding the Judgments

Several years ago I attended a relative's funeral and afterward stood around talking with family members. We were commenting about the fact that this man had become a Christian so late in life—in his seventies. The frankness of his son's next comment surprised me. He said, "I have no question about where he'll spend eternity. But I certainly doubt he'll get any rewards."

His bluntness aside, my cousin apparently understood the issues. Salvation comes about only by what Christ did on the cross. We cannot add to it; it's provided for us as we accept the forgiveness his death affords us. However, having been saved, there *are* actions that can result in heavenly rewards. One might think getting to heaven is all the reward we need. Possibly so. But God views it differently, and he openly discusses the rewards many will receive.

In all candor scholars and theologians do not agree on certain matters about judgment day, including how rewards or punishment will be handed out. Here are the key areas of dispute: Are there two judgments—one called "the great white throne judgment" (only for unbelievers) and the other called "the judgment seat of Christ" (for those "in Christ")? Or do these refer to one judgment for all people?[1] Why is the judgment seat referred to as the "bema seat"? Is the bema seat only for affirming and rewarding, or could it be for issuing punishment as well?

Paul said, "We must all appear before the judgment seat [Greek: *bema*] of Christ, that each one may receive what is due him for the things done while in the body, whether good or bad."[2] He shed more light on this in an earlier letter:

> If any man builds on this foundation using gold, silver, costly stones, wood, hay or straw, his work will be shown for what it is, because the Day will bring it to light. It will be revealed with fire, and the fire will test the quality of each man's work. If what he has built survives, he will receive his reward. If it is burned up, he will suffer loss; he himself will be saved, but only as one escaping through the flames.[3]

The word *bema* is used in contemporary Greek culture to refer to the stage area in a synagogue or church. This is the place occupied by a pastor and a choir in a Christian church. But in Bible times, the term referred to a "judgment seat"[4]; in simplest terms, it was a raised platform, occupied by a ruler, from which decisions, sentences, or punishments were announced. Influenced by Greek athletic contests, Paul used *bema* in a different fashion: he viewed it more like a judge's place at the end of an event, rewarding the athletes for their levels of accomplishment. Highlighting this theme, he wrote:

> Do you not know that in a race all the runners run, but only one gets the prize? Run in such a way as to get the prize.
>
> Everyone who competes in the games goes into strict training. They do it to get a crown that will not last; but we do it to get a crown that will last forever.[5]

Adopting *this* understanding of *bema,* as opposed to that of a Roman magistrate issuing judgments, leads many people to view the judgment seat of Christ as a place of reward. Considering the "reward" language in Paul's letters, we might conclude that this event sounds dramatically different from John's reference to the great white throne judgment[6] and allusions to the "lake of fire" (more on that in chapter 15).

All of this raises an obvious question: For *what* will we be rewarded? The Bible is straightforward on this topic, and the following is a partial list.[7]

Influencing Others for Righteousness

The Old Testament uses poetic language to explain God's priorities: "Those who are wise will shine like the brightness of the heavens, and those who lead many to righteousness, like the stars for ever and ever."[8] God wants us to influence other people to righteousness—to have a right relationship with him.

And God promises to remember this work when evaluation time comes in the life hereafter: "God is not unjust; he will not forget your work and the love you have shown him as you have helped his people and continue to help them."[9]

When it comes to influencing others to righteousness, though, perhaps you're thinking, *Billy Graham—sure, he'll get a big reward. He preached to stadiums full of people. And those old-time missionaries, who used to pack all their belongings in pine coffins knowing they probably wouldn't go home alive. And the martyrs who died at the stake for believing in Jesus.*

Actually, though, the rewards will be distributed widely. This is because we participate in righteousness vicariously. Jesus himself plainly said as much:

> Anyone who receives a prophet because he is a prophet will receive a prophet's reward, and anyone who receives a righteous man because he is a righteous man will receive a righteous man's reward. And if anyone gives even a cup of cold water to one of these little ones because he is my disciple, I tell you the truth, he will certainly not lose his reward.[10]

Amazing! It's like a championship basketball team: you might be the one who swishes the winning shot at the buzzer or the one sitting on the end of the bench waving a towel and shouting encouragement. You're all going to get a ring.

If we have received a saint sent from God, we are going to participate in that saint's level of reward. So if your church received Billy Graham when he came to your community, you will receive the same reward as Billy for that. This is because of the honor shown to those who have been sent by God.

Caring for Others

There's also the significance of hospitality to strangers—specifically, how we've cared for the downtrodden and the poor. Jesus told a parable about the King separating the sheep (those with faith in Christ) from the goats (those without). He spoke of the hungry, thirsty, naked, sick, and alienated. This reward goes to those who cared for these people, whom he describes as "the least of my brothers." Caring for the needy is the same as caring for Jesus himself.[11]

We want to hang out with the desirable people, don't we? But Jesus says,

> When you give a luncheon or dinner, do not invite your friends, your brothers or relatives, or your rich neighbors; if you do, they may invite you back and so you will be repaid. But when you give a banquet, invite the poor, the crippled, the lame, the blind, and you will be blessed. Although they cannot repay you, you will be repaid at the resurrection of the righteous.[12]

We will be rewarded for how we treated outcasts, outsiders, and the oppressed.

Responding to Those Who Hate Us

Another way we'll receive rewards involves our response to suffering, mistreatment, and injustice. James says, "Blessed is the man who perseveres under trial, because when he has stood the test, he will receive the crown of life that God has promised to those who love him."[13] Our reaction to being treated poorly is factored into the equation of heavenly compensation.

On persecution, consider Jesus' Sermon on the Mount, in which he says,

> *Blessed* are you when people insult you, persecute you and falsely say all kinds of evil against you because of me. Rejoice and be glad, because great is your reward in heaven, for in the same way they persecuted the prophets who were before you.[14]

Some have sacrificed enormously for the faith. God says they're going to be rewarded for that—if not here, then in the life to come. The Bible is clear in its admonishment to "love your enemies."[15] There are eternal rewards for doing so.

Using Our Gifts

We'll also be held accountable—and receive rewards—for the appropriate use of our abilities, time, and resources. In one parable, a rich man entrusted his servants with different amounts of money, according to each man's ability. One invested his share, succeeded exponentially, and was rewarded greatly. Another doubled his share and was rewarded accordingly. The third just buried his portion in the ground and didn't do anything with it—didn't invest, didn't develop what he was given at all. The deeply displeased master took away his share and gave it to another.[16]

Jesus told this parable to illustrate that we should fully utilize the gifts and resources he has given us. We are responsible to develop these to their potential, and we can expect to receive rewards accordingly.

What ARE These Rewards?

The Bible refers to our rewards as "crowns."[17] Literal crowns, or is this figurative language? I suspect they're not literal, though from our vantage point it's impossible to know for sure. One thing we *can* know: When we get them—whether literal or figurative—we'll be thrilled to receive them.

We know these crowns won't pass away but will last forever. Ever gone to a garage sale and seen a whole tableful of trophies selling for a nickel apiece? They once seemed important but are virtually worthless now. Conversely, eternal rewards will not diminish in value.

Many biblical passages talk about crowns, and there are at least five crown-types involved in heaven's reward system.

The Crown of Life

This is awarded to those who have endured suffering, those men and women who "gutted it out" through hardship and adversity. Jesus told the church in Smyrna: "Do not be afraid of what you are about to suffer. . . . Be faithful, even to the point of death, and I will give you the crown of life."[18] James also mentions this crown: "Blessed is the man who perseveres under trial, because when he has stood the test, he will receive the crown of life that God has promised to those who love him."[19]

137

The Crown of Glory

This is for church leaders who lead and guide with humility. Peter wrote,

> Be shepherds of God's flock that is under your care, serving as overseers—not because you must, but because you are willing, as God wants you to be; not greedy for money, but eager to serve; not lording it over those entrusted to you, but being examples to the flock. And when the Chief Shepherd appears, you will receive the crown of glory that will never fade away.[20]

The Crown of Rejoicing

This is given to those who pour their lives into other people—uplifting, encouraging, serving, mentoring, and caring for others. That's a great name for it too. We'll see all those people we invested our lives in and joyfully dance on heaven's streets. As Paul says, "What is our hope, or joy, or crown of rejoicing? Is it not even you in the presence of our Lord Jesus Christ at His coming?"[21]

The Crown of Righteousness

This is given to those who crave intimacy with God. It's the special award for those who yearn for Jesus' coming: "There is in store for me the crown of righteousness, which the Lord, the righteous Judge, will award to me on that day—and not only to me, but also to all who have longed for his appearing."[22]

The Imperishable Crown

Using athletic competition to illustrate, again Paul explains,

> Do you not know that those who run in a race all run, but one receives the prize? Run in such a way that you may obtain it. And everyone who competes for the prize is temperate in all things. Now they do it to obtain a perishable crown, but we for an imperishable crown.[23]

This crown is called imperishable to contrast it with the temporal awards Paul's contemporaries pursued. The olive wreath—the "crown" for competitors—was sure to wither away. The ever-enduring "endurance crown" is given for profound examples of self-denial and perseverance.

The Purpose of the Crowns

Suppose you end up with a few heavenly crowns—maybe even a whole cartload. What exactly will you do with them? We'll be given accolades for some reason, but what is it? John gives a clue:

> The twenty-four elders fall down before him who sits on the throne, and worship him who lives for ever and ever. They lay their crowns before the throne and say:
> "You are worthy, our Lord and God,
> to receive glory and honor and power,
> for you created all things,
> and by your will they were created
> and have their being."[24]

The crowns will be given us so that we can give them back to the Creator of all things. Scripture suggests we will be so awestruck by Almighty God—we will find him so awesomely all-consuming and entirely sufficient—that with rejoicing we will return rewards to him as an act of worship.

Are you one of those who dread the thought of judgment day, when the celestial CEO will deliver your performance review? The thought justifiably gives us pause—and motivates us to carefully consider our actions and attitudes. But God's children need not fear that day, for it will be a day of reward, not punishment. I appreciate the perspective of Frederick Buechner:

> The New Testament proclaims that at some unforeseeable time in the future, God will bring down the final curtain on history, and there will come a day on which all our days and all the judgments upon us and all our judgments upon each other will themselves be judged. The judge will be Christ. In other words, the one who judges us most finally will be the one who loves us most fully.[25]

Jesus himself said, "I tell you the truth, whoever hears my word and believes him who sent me has eternal life and will not be condemned; he has crossed over from death to life."[26] The equation is simple, really: Influence others toward righteous living, care for the poor and oppressed, love your enemies, and use wisely your God-given gifts. Then anticipate a delightful reward.

13

Beyond Halos, Harps, and Hymns

Permanent Heaven Is a Place of Riches, Rest, and Rewards

The best is yet to be.

John Wesley

Suppose you go downtown tomorrow and select a busy corner to conduct a survey. With clipboard and pen, you'd say to passersby, "Excuse me, can you tell me the first things that pop into your head when you think of heaven?"

Assuming people actually stopped to answer, I imagine you'd discover recurring themes in their responses. In fact, you'd probably hear, over and over, the words *clouds, pearly gates, angels, harps, halos, streets of gold, St. Peter, white robes,* and *choirs.* Some may add idyllic images of rainbow-filled skies, majestic mountain peaks, and sunsets over oceans. Perhaps a few would speak of reunions with deceased family members, friends, and pets.

With these prevalent "heavenly" images floating through our minds, it's no wonder we don't get more excited about floating up to heaven. Talking with Christians and non-Christians over the years, I've discovered that most in *both* groups have a lackluster impression of heaven. I like how John Eldredge puts it:

Nearly every Christian I have spoken with has some idea that eternity is an unending church service. We have settled on an image of the never-ending sing-along in the sky, one great hymn after another, forever and ever amen. And our heart sinks. *Forever and ever? That's it? That's the good news?* And then we sigh and feel guilty that we are not more "spiritual." We lose heart, and we turn once more to the present to find what life we can.[1]

What do *you* think heaven will be like? Ever hoped there's more than what many seem to believe—that we'll spend eternity sitting on clouds, wearing white robes? Some people believe we will turn into angels, which might be an improvement over the monotonous harp-hymn scenario—hey, at least we could fly from cloud to cloud and visit friends.

When you think of heaven in these terms, what emotions do they evoke? Boredom? Disinterest? Even dread? We need to press the delete button on our misguided, mundane notions of what eternity holds in store. To that end, let's spend some time exploring—and correcting—misconceptions about heaven and begin painting a more accurate portrait of what we can expect.

Dispelling Myths

Where do some of these crazy ideas and images come from? Are they from the Bible? Surprisingly, the answer is yes. Well, sort of. While many of these impressions come from Scripture, they've been mis-applied and miscon-strued. Unfortunately, the resulting outlook many of us carry around is a far cry from the rich realities that await us. C. S. Lewis addressed this:

> There is no need to be worried by facetious people who try to make the Christian hope of heaven ridiculous by saying they do not want "to spend eternity playing harps." The answer to such people is that if they cannot understand books written for grown-ups, they should not talk about them. All the scriptural imagery (harps, crowns, gold, etc.) is, of course, a merely symbolic attempt to express the inexpressible.
>
> Musical instruments are mentioned because for many people (not all) music is the thing known in the present life which most strongly suggests ecstasy and infinity. Crowns are mentioned to suggest the fact that those who are united with God in eternity share His splendor and power and joy. Gold is mentioned to suggest the timelessness of heaven (gold does not rust)

and the preciousness of it. People who take these symbols literally might as well think that when Christ told us to be like doves, He meant that we were to lay eggs.[2]

Many images we get hung up on were recorded in the Bible—mainly by John in Revelation—in *attempts* to convey what heaven is like. Human language has severe limitations, especially for describing the indescribable. I suppose we could say John and other biblical writers did the best they could with the tools at their disposal—words on paper. So when considering heaven, we can use the biblical account as a framework and let our imaginations run wild. Even then, we probably can't get close to God's everlasting wonders and delights.

Try this for starters: If you want to know what heaven *feels* like, think of your deepest longings, those insatiable soul-cravings for love, acceptance, purpose, worth, intimacy, belonging. Now imagine what it would feel like to have those longings satisfied in a more abundant fashion than you've ever dreamed. Now multiply that feeling by infinity. Suddenly, heaven starts to sound exciting and enticing.

No Boredom Allowed

In his book *Heaven*, Randy Alcorn helps us see eternity in new and fresh ways, unabashedly setting before us a topic that's been circumvented by most erudite contemporary thinkers. But he goes beyond why-aren't-you-talking-more-about-heaven; his greatest contribution might be portraying heaven as fun. Yes, *fun!*[3]

Why we would think of heaven in any other way is beyond me. The Master Designer of all creativity and all things good would never have his most loved friends (us) in unending boredom, slogging through an eternity of navel-gazing, chanting, and yoga. Now *that* would be hell.

Heaven is for rest, riches, and reward. There will be plants, animals (perhaps even pets), music, games—everything that's good and wonderful *now* will be better *then*. There will be cities, or one major city. There will be buildings, art, culture, and music. There likely will be goods, services, major events, transportation, and communications.

What's more, there will be education. You'll continue to develop and grow. You'll have no impairments, no aversions for learning. We often associate learning with drudgery (probably from being stuck in stuffy classrooms with stern teachers), but learning and discovering will become most pleasurable.

One obstacle to learning adequately now is time. There, you'll have plenty of "time." A great frustration for me here on earth is being kept from so many books I want to read. I plan to spend part of my eternity reading every book worthy of my attention.

Let's be honest—we have a hard time grasping the concept of *forever*. We get dismayed at thinking eventually heaven's newness and excitement will wear off. What then, sitting around with nothing to do? That's our earthbound mind talking. We find it tough to fathom that God, endlessly creative and imaginative, will introduce new, amazing things for us to enjoy throughout eternity.

What Will We Do in Heaven?

Envision standing in a throng of billions, everyone's breath held with anticipation, inspiration like the wind sweeping the multitudes, and suddenly a song—stirred in our souls by God himself—begins to swell. Imagine the sound of several *billion* voices raised in worship of every style. In heaven, we will sing, but not just any song: new music written for us by the Holy Spirit himself.[4]

And if music isn't your particular source of inspiration, take heart—heaven will feature far more. Everything we *do* will be passionate, heartfelt worship, including leadership tasks and roles we'll be privileged to assume. God created us to be his heirs and inherit the earth and reign over the land—not with the power-hungry leadership prevalent here on the first earth but with the servant-leadership that so characterizes the very heart of our Lord Jesus Christ.

In heaven you'll be involved in leading. You will be a ruler. Governance there is not about being the boss of somebody else to lord it over them. No! Our ruling will be part of the *serving* plan of the entire universe over which God has ordained us to be coeternal rulers.[5] If you've wanted more responsibility, you're about to get it. Consider just a few promises:

If we endure, we will also reign with him.[6]

To him who overcomes and does my will to the end, I will give authority over the nations.[7]

143

To him who overcomes, I will give the right to sit with me on my throne, just as I overcame and sat down with my Father on his throne.[8]

In addition to some kind of ruling responsibility, I also believe we'll enjoy something nearly all of us like to do—eating. After all, we know that Jesus—in his resurrected body—ate and drank with the disciples.[9] John creates a bountiful image: "On each side of the river stood the tree of life, bearing twelve crops of fruit, yielding its fruit every month. And the leaves of the tree are for the healing of the nations."[10]

We'll Be Thrilled to Go to Work

Some believe there will be no work in heaven, and perhaps here the fear of boredom surfaces: What will we *do*? I believe work indeed will be part of our heavenly experience, though in a much different way than we typically think.

Want to understand what heaven will be like? Look at earth *before* the fall, before the distortion of sin. Here's what we discover: work predated evil. That's because we're made in God's image, and he is creative. In his image, we are creators. Thus we will "work."

Heavenly work will *not* be drudgery. Everything—and I mean *everything*, including work—changed after sin entered this planet. The ground, upon which an agrarian economy is based, was "cursed." Not that dirt is somehow evil—rather, to work the soil, to produce crops from it, now requires toil and strain and aching muscles. Whereas humanity once knew only a spectacular garden, now we face thorns and thistles. Work requires the "sweat of your brow."[11]

If you're thoroughly fulfilled with your vocation, then you're experiencing a little slice of heaven here and now. You already know work can be joyous and gratifying. If you find work arduous and dull, you have much to look forward to, for your work in heaven—what God has arranged for you—will be a delight!

It's inherently inadequate to envision heaven with earthly examples, but to stimulate your imagination, do two things. First, *picture what work would be like without your associated negatives.* Strip out the downsides and detriments. Never again will you have a demanding boss, crabby colleagues, relentless deadlines, mountains of paper work, income taxes, customer complaints, snarled commutes, backaches, or tedium. No more chore and bore—work is continually invigorating and inspiring. Sound like something you could enjoy for a long, long time?

Next, *think of your dream job—the absolute best description you could write for yourself.* If you're passionate about gardening, you might be in charge of designing and tending botanical gardens. If you love to cook, perhaps you'll be a chef at one of heaven's many fine restaurants. If you enjoy nothing more than being around animals, you might run a stable full of celestial creatures. Be sure, too, that there will be many fascinating roles we as yet know nothing about.

What About Those Robes and Harps?

It's both amusing and frustrating to see how harps and heaven have become so interconnected. Let's see where the whole harp idea comes from.

> I saw what looked like a sea of glass mixed with fire and, standing beside the sea, those who had been victorious over the beast. . . . They held harps given them by God and sang the song of Moses the servant of God and the song of the Lamb.[12]

Another harp reference comes where John describes the four living creatures, along with the twenty-four elders, holding harps.[13]

Obviously, the harp was a familiar instrument for John. In the original language, *harp* is similar to the word that gives us *guitar*. John saw stringed and wind instruments. Since the ancient writers didn't know about guitars and pianos and many other instruments, it seems reasonable to assume that the harps and horns represent music and worship in general. We'd have a different image of heaven if the biblical text described creatures holding saxes and bongo drums. The point is that there will be music—and plenty of it—for every taste and preference.

Similarly, to these writers accustomed to traveling hot, dusty roads, robes were the clothing they would have found familiar and comfortable. That the robes they saw were white—and could *stay* white—simply made them more special than anything they'd seen or worn. Likewise, your heavenly wardrobe will be something you're used to, something you find familiar, comfortable—but with an unexpected flair that exceeds anything you've ever owned.

Humans Are Not and Will Not Be Angels

We've seen what Hollywood has portrayed. We know what Oprah says. We've heard comforting words from well-meaning but uninformed friends at funerals. But the definitive source on this matter—the Bible—gives us the answer we can rely on, and that answer tells us people will not become angels.

To be sure, there are angels in heaven—"thousands upon thousands, and ten thousand times ten thousand."[14] In one passage, Jesus says in heaven we will be *like* the angels in that we'll have no need for marriage. Some misinterpret this to mean we will turn into angels, but this text is comparing marital status, not species. Over and over the fact is driven home that angels and humans have never been—and never will be—one and the same.

Our creation stories are different. Angels were created before humankind was given opportunity to walk the earth. Man showed up on the scene later, was created in God's image, and then was ranked a little lower than the angels.[15]

Our purposes are different. Again, angels are "ministering spirits, sent forth to minister for them who shall be heirs of salvation."[16] Humankind was created to enjoy fellowship with God, becoming his heirs and joint-heirs with Christ.

Our destinies are different. The first angel to fall into rebellion talked a third of the angelic forces into joining him. The destiny of the devil and his fallen angels is to be cast into an eternal fire prepared especially for them.[17] In contrast, when Adam and Eve rebelled and led all humankind into a state of sin, God took a much different approach, taking the punishment upon himself so that we could be redeemed and restored back into intimate fellowship with him. While he didn't take on the nature of the angels in order to rescue them, he became a man to rescue us.[18] The angels will not be given dominion in heaven; when God created man he gave him authority over the earth and one day will give him authority in heaven (the new earth).[19] Paul says in heaven we'll even receive authority to judge angels.[20]

Heaven's Location

We talk of heaven being "up there" or even "in the clouds." Clouds *are* mentioned in conjunction with heaven. For instance, when Jesus returns, we will see him descending on the clouds of the sky.[21] God spoke from a cloud at the transfiguration.[22] But the idea that heaven is *in* the clouds, and that we might spend eternity reclining on them, is misdirected.

We shouldn't think of heaven as a long way away; it may be much, *much* closer than we think. "In the beginning God created the heavens and the earth."[23] He looked on all he had created and said it was very good.[24] Then sin sent his handiwork spiraling toward death and decay; one day, the first heavens and earth would need to be destroyed, replaced with a heaven and earth that would be forever indestructible and perfect.

The Bible is filled with related references. God said, "Behold, I will create new heavens and a new earth."[25] Peter, comforting close friends, said despite the tough times they faced "we are looking forward to a new heaven and a new earth."[26] Jesus' dear friend John described having seen "a new heaven and a new earth, for the first heaven and the first earth had passed away."[27]

Why a new earth? Well, ours was created perfect. The heavens were perfect too. But sin entered—first through angelic rebellion and then through human disobedience—and with it came disease, pain, heartache, suffering, and death. Today, creation's breathtaking beauty is but a vestige of what it was at the start. Paradise *has* been lost. Our earth *is* broken, and it groans to be made new.

Where will the new heavens and earth be? *How* can paradise be redeemed?

Dennis Kinlaw, former president of Asbury College, is one of the most brilliant Old Testament scholars I know. One day, talking about the nature of death and the location of heaven, he said, "The Bible seems to imply that the new heaven is here—on this earth."

At the time, I was still processing my own brother's untimely death. Bewildered, I looked at Dr. Kinlaw and said, "Are you saying that they—the dead—are here? On *our* turf?"

"Oh, no," he said quickly. "I'm saying that *we* are on *their* turf."

We can't now see into that dimension, but it's possible we might be "intersecting" with heaven itself. When the new heaven and earth are made, they'll likely be right here, where the old earth currently winds down its life.

Scripture too seems to indicate there will be no need for a separate heaven and earth. They will be one and the same, meaning that if the new earth is created where the earth currently resides, the new heaven will be here also:

They will inherit *the earth*.[28]

Those the Lord blesses will inherit *the land*.[29]

Abraham . . . received the promise that he would be heir of *the world*.[30]

They will reign on *the earth*.[31]

Finally, the new heaven and new earth already are under construction. Two thousand years ago Jesus said,

> Let not your heart be troubled: ye believe in God, believe also in me.
>
> In my Father's house are many mansions: if it were not so, I would have told you. I go to prepare a place for you.
>
> And if I go and prepare a place for you, I will come again, and receive you unto myself; that where I am, there ye may be also.[32]

This means the new heaven is not "up there somewhere." It is intertwined with this earth, now, in another dimension—heaven *is* here. As Paul Marshall explains, "Our destiny is an earthly one: a new earth, an earth redeemed and transfigured. An earth united with heaven, but an earth, nevertheless."[33]

The point is heaven and earth intersect, so much so that while we can't see into heaven from where we stand today it appears heaven can see us. Every time someone becomes a new member of God's kingdom, angels in heaven rejoice.[34] When the martyrs, killed for their faith, observe happenings here, they cry out to God, "How long will you let this continue?" To which God responds, "A little longer."[35] Finally, those who have gone before us are like a "cloud of witnesses."[36] They well could be—in their own dimension—moving among us even now,[37] celebrating our victories, weeping over our persecutions, observing our struggles and our growth.

Praying to and Talking to People in Heaven

We are not to pray *to* those in heaven. God alone has power to answer our prayers. Again, he strictly forbids *seeking out* communication with the dead.

However, this is not to say they cannot contact us. If/when we sense the presence of a loved one who's now in heaven, who's to say that's not exactly what we're sensing? This isn't something to be feared—neither is it something to be pursued. My belief is that God sometimes allows this to encourage and comfort us; it's part of the rich experience of the doctrine called the "communion of the saints." This oneness, said to extend to all believers in Christ Jesus, whether on earth or in heaven, is a profound reminder that there is life after death and that those who've gone on ahead have not ceased to exist. Absent from the body, they are very much alive and enjoying the Lord's presence.

My dear friend Gerard Reed, a respected university professor, was in deep grief from the loss of his beloved wife following a battle with cancer. He expressed to me the profound comfort he felt when he sensed her clear presence. This man of Native American descent, not given to displays of emotion, said with tear-filled eyes, "I believe in the communion of the saints." He meant that even though his wife had gone on to heaven, he was still enjoying meaningful communion with her. Following scriptural directives, he was not seeking out contact with her; he simply was aware of her periodic presence.

Extreme Makeover, Heaven Edition

In chapter 11, we talked about our resurrected bodies and how they will be like the resurrected body of Jesus. But what age will we be? Science tells us we tend to peak physically somewhere in our late twenties or early thirties. Scripture doesn't give us many clues, but it's worth mentioning that when God created Adam and Eve, he created them in their childbearing years. And when Jesus was raised, he was recognizable, so he was probably an age similar to that when he died, around thirty-three. Do these examples reveal anything about the age we will appear to be in heaven? Maybe, maybe not.

What about children? We can't assume that when someone dies they enter heaven at the same age and appearance with which they leave the earth. But neither can we assume heaven will be filled with thirty-somethings who never change or grow. Once more, heaven will be a perfect earth filled with, among other things, foliage and trees that bear fruit. So growth and change could apply to us as well.

And while we tend to think of heaven as timeless—after all, what better way to describe eternity—perhaps there is some concept of time. When one of the seven seals is opened, "There was silence in heaven for about half an hour."[38]

What age will we appear? And will we stay that age for eternity, or will we experience change? Some things we will have to wait to know for sure.

Marriage and Sex

When we are resurrected and living in the new heaven on earth, we will not marry.[39] This is why, during our marriage vows, we commit ourselves to our spouses "till death do us part."

I suspect some people think about the question of marriage in heaven and are relieved to envision heaven *without* their spouse. However, for most (including me), the thought of going to heaven and not being married is painful. Still, *in heaven you will know oneness with your spouse beyond what you could ever know on this earth.* You will know and live the very nature of *oneness.* You will *know* your spouse, and you will enjoy more oneness than ever before—pure, unsullied, unimaginably wonderful.

Will we keep our gender? Yes. "God created man in his own image, in the image of God he created him; male and female he created them."[40] In other words, gender distinction predated the fall; God created us that way from the beginning, and pleased with his design, he affirmed it. When Jesus was raised, he didn't stop being a man. His body was recognizable, down to the wounds in his hands and feet.

At the risk of turning you off to the idea of heaven forever, let me respond, from my earthbound perspective, to the matter of sex in heaven. The short answer is no, it won't be a feature of heaven. Biblically, sex is designed for the context of marriage, and since there's no marriage in heaven, the context for sex is missing as well.

But don't stop here. Let's take a closer look at the mysteries of marriage and sex as they relate to heaven. Sex between husband and wife is holy. It's beautiful. It pleases God. So why would anything *that* wonderful, *that* sacred, be absent in heaven? And if sexual expression is missing, what will fill the void? We are told there can be no void in heaven, no sadness or longing.[41] In reality, heaven not only will encompass the best our old earth has to offer, but these delights will be refined to levels we can't yet begin to comprehend.

Consider four wondrous benefits we receive from healthy sexual expression here on earth, and how they may be exceeded in heaven.

On earth, sex is given to us for intimacy, but *in heaven, all barriers to emotional intimacy will be removed.* We will recognize our loved ones and enjoy all the relationships we have now, except without sin's destructive influences, whether sin of our own or of others. In heaven you will experience unity and belonging beyond what you have ever known on earth.

On earth, sex is given to us for procreation, in order to keep the species alive, but *since no one will ever die in heaven, procreation won't be necessary.*

On earth, sex is given to us for joy and even ecstasy. Although this may be difficult for us to grasp and accept until we get there, *heaven itself will contain such inherent ecstasy that the delight of sex will not be missed.*

I believe the fourth benefit of earthly sexual expression holds the greatest key to the mystery of why sex will not be missed in heaven. The intimate, surrendered relationship—sexual and otherwise—between husband and wife was designed by God to represent the intimate, surrendered relationship between Jesus Christ and his bride, the church. Now, granted, human marriages are tainted and sometimes riddled with the effects of sin, meaning the worst marriages may reflect nothing of Christ's relationship with his body, while even the best marriages are a cracked and broken mirror at best. In fact, think of the happiest couples you know. Even *their* marriages—stellar by human standards—are mere shadows of the marriage to come between Jesus and his bride. *The delight of human sexual intimacy is an imperfect depiction of the perfect, all-fulfilling wonder we will experience when united with Christ.*

Human sexuality and our longing for intimacy is God's way of giving us a glimpse of what it's going to be like when Jesus is finally and fully with us in ways we cannot yet fathom. This may be part of the meaning of "You will fill me with joy in your presence, with eternal pleasures at your right hand."[42]

Longing for Home

How about you? Do you long for heaven? If your honest answer is no, I have another question: What *do* you long for? And would it surprise you to discover that the things you long for are precious to you beyond understanding because they remind you, in some fashion, of coming home? Not to the home of your childhood or even to the home you've created for yourself as an adult, but the *other* home—that elusive place of utter welcome and well-being you've always sensed was out there somewhere?

You undoubtedly have experienced moments—perhaps while watching a shaft of sunlight, hearing a moving refrain of music, watching your child lost in the pure abandon of play—when something stirred inside your soul that felt new and old all at once; something that seemed part anticipation, part distant memory, as if you were standing on the threshold of the very thing you'd been seeking your entire life. You recognize the feeling, as inconceivable as it seems. You're homesick for someplace you've never been.

What will heaven feel like?

Take your deepest longings. Think of what you crave, what fills you with delight, joy you've never experienced but yearn for just the same. Remember your longing for home, for a lover of your soul, for the contented wholeness that leads you to the place you've never been yet can't forget—the place where your every desire is satisfied more abundantly than you've ever dreamed.

Heaven is that home.

Part Four

Crossing Over: The Dark Descent

14

Going From Bad to Worse

Hades Is a "Horrible Holding Tank" for Those
Awaiting a Final, Fiery Destination

Hell isn't merely paved with good intentions, it is walled and roofed
by them.

Aldous Huxley

In the movie *Bridge to Terabithia*, ten-year-old Jesse is befriended by
Leslie, the new girl in town. Together they create an imaginary world
they call Terabithia.

At one point Jesse invites Leslie to attend church with his family, provided she wears a dress. With the congregation, they sing "The Old Rugged
Cross," during which Leslie gazes at the light streaming through stained
glass and pretends to capture the rays in her purse. Soon the church bells
ring as people file out.

On the way home, Leslie, Jesse, and his younger sister May Belle ride
in the back of the family's pickup truck.

"I'm really glad I came," says Leslie. "That whole Jesus thing—it's
really interesting, isn't it?"

"It's not interesting," May Belle responds, "it's scary. It's nailing holes through your hands. It's 'cause we're all vile sinners that God made Jesus die."

"You really think that's true?" Leslie asks somberly.

"It's in the Bible, Leslie," Jesse says.

"You have to believe it, and you hate it," she replies. "I don't have to believe it, and I think it's beautiful."

"You have to believe the Bible, Leslie," May Belle warns. "If you don't believe in the Bible, God will damn you to hell when you die."

"Wow, May Belle," Leslie says, sounding dismissive. "Where'd you hear that?"

"That's right, isn't it, Jess?" she prods. "God damns you to hell if you don't believe in the Bible."

"I think so," the boy answers.

"Well, I don't think so," Leslie proclaims. "I seriously do not think God goes around damning people to hell." She then spreads her arms wide and looks at all the scenery. "He's too busy running this."[1]

A discussion about hell—whether by children or grownups—is bound to raise questions, spark debate, and reveal conflicting perspectives. Perhaps most of all, any serious dialogue about hell is sure to make most people uncomfortable. If you believe it's a real place, you probably don't want to end up there, and you don't want anybody you love to go there either. If you don't believe in it, you may laugh it off or avoid talking about it because it's something only religious people could really ponder.

The concept of hell has been around since Old Testament times. The biblical descriptions of hell sound like a horror movie: burning lakes, dark pits, and shadowy realms filled with dragons, serpents, demons, and three-headed beasts.

These images don't fit well with today's naturalist-minded world, and some Christians even find them embarrassing. Such beliefs may come across as superstitious, ignorant, backward, or unenlightened, and people who take these passages seriously are often labeled fanatics. Many people rationalize that hell can't exist—it's an old wives' tale. Others feel a loving God couldn't possibly allow anyone to suffer eternal torment (more on this in chapters 17 and 18).

Skepticism about hell is not a unique development of the rationalistic world. Christian beliefs have been attacked and mocked for centuries by those whose faith is in human knowledge and human reason. In the West today, it isn't acceptable to openly believe in the supernatural, and many Christians either have changed or hidden certain beliefs to fit in with intellectual trends.

But if hell is a real place, it's a supernatural one, and no afterlife discussion would be complete without asking about the evidence for its reality. A crucial information source about hell is the Bible, which is rooted in history that tells of real persons, in real places, experiencing real events. Unlike other religious texts, Scripture is not a collection of stories unrelated to historical reality, so its historicity gives it additional credibility.

The Bible says much about hell and several related places. The terms for these don't translate very well into English, and they vary in their origins and meanings:

- *sheol*—Old Testament Hebrew word; can mean a place of torment, hell, or the grave
- *hades*—New Testament Greek word; also can mean place of torment, hell, or the grave
- *gehenna*—also New Testament Greek; usually means hell

Sheol, Hades, and Gehenna

Greek Orthodox, Roman Catholic, and Western Protestant confessions of faith (creeds) all include belief in the reality of physical and spiritual life after death. Creeds identify the core of accepted ideas held by a group of people. They define what is believed (*orthodoxy*) against what is considered incorrect (*heresy*). The most basic truth about Christ needs to be understood before believers can grow in maturity and "distinguish good from evil."[2]

One of the most popular confessions, the Apostles' Creed, is said to have been written by Jesus' disciples, but that's unlikely. This creed, officially adopted by the Roman Catholic Church several hundred years after Christ (in the eighth century), has been an almost universally foundational statement of the Christian faith.[3] It's used today by many churches in its original form:

I believe in God the Father almighty, creator of heaven and earth;

And in Jesus Christ, His only Son, our Lord, Who was conceived by the Holy Spirit, born of the Virgin Mary, suffered under Pontius Pilate, was crucified, dead and buried.

He descended to hell, on the third day rose again from the dead, ascended to heaven, sits at the right hand of God the Father almighty, thence He will come to judge the living and the dead;

I believe in the Holy Spirit, the holy catholic Church, the communion of saints, the forgiveness of sins, the resurrection of the body, and the life everlasting.

Amen.[4]

This creed embodies the basic beliefs of the Christian faith: the crucifixion and resurrection, heaven, hell, bodily resurrection of believers, judgment, and eternal life. Perhaps the most difficult statement in this creed is that Jesus "descended to hell."

God's perfect son went to hell? Why?

The crucifixion and resurrection are commonly known. Jesus had a real physical body and suffered a true human death.[5] But Jesus also was sinless, so it seems strange he wouldn't go directly to paradise, as he promised the repentant thief hanging on the cross next to him.[6] We know that if Jesus went to hell, he didn't stay there but was "exalted to the right hand of God."[7]

Inspiration for the creedal statement about Christ's time in hell is in 1 Peter:

Christ also died for sins once for all, the righteous for the unrighteous, that he might bring us to God, being put to death in the flesh but made alive in the spirit; in which he went and preached to the spirits in prison, who formerly did not obey, when God's patience waited in the days of Noah, during the building of the ark, in which a few, that is, eight persons, were saved through water. . . . They will give account to him who is ready to judge the living and the dead. For this is why the gospel was preached even to the dead, that though judged in the flesh like men, they might live in the spirit like God.[8]

Even Martin Luther admitted he didn't know what preaching "to the spirits in prison" meant; he called this "obscure."[9] It's sometimes interpreted to mean that during the time between his crucifixion and resurrection, Jesus traveled to where the spirits of the dead were held, awaiting judgment. In this holding place or prison—often called *sheol* (Old Testament) and *hades* (New Testament)—he preached to the captive spirits.

Whether those spirits could respond to the gospel or whether it was instead a triumphant appearance—"victory lap"—by the one who had defeated the demonic hordes, we cannot know.[10] What's important is this passage's first-century glimpse of hades. Peter later defines the spirits in prison as the "dead."[11] Hades appears to be an intermediate location for the spirits of all who died before Christ's life and ministry. Others view it as a "holding tank" for those who die without believing in him.

This is in contrast to hell, or *gehenna* (see chapter 16). Hell is a place of eternal torment created by God for the devil and his fallen angels. Tragically, it also is a permanent and final destination for unrepentant souls following judgment.[12]

Our concern here is more with hades. In the Apostles' Creed, the original Latin word for hell was *infernos*, which can be translated *underworld, nether world, sheol, grave,* or *hell*.[13] The word *hades* can mean "hell" or simply "underworld." An alternative creedal wording might be "He descended to the underworld . . ."

Sheol in the Old Testament

The concept of hell is not well developed in the Old Testament. When sheol is mentioned, it appears to have been understood as a dark, shadowy place. *Sheol* is a term for the place of the dead; it is best translated *grave*. The Psalter poetically reads,

> Truly no man can ransom himself, or give to God the price of his life, for the ransom of his life is costly, and can never suffice, that he should continue to live on for ever, and never see the Pit [the grave, or death]. Yea, he shall see that even the wise die; the fool and the stupid alike must perish and leave their wealth to others.
>
> *Their graves are their homes for ever, their dwelling places to all generations,* though they named lands their own. Man cannot abide in his pomp; he is like the beasts that perish. This is the fate of those who have foolish confidence, the end of those who are pleased with their portion. Like sheep they are appointed for Sheol; Death shall be their shepherd; straight to the grave they descend, and their form shall waste away; Sheol shall be their home.

But God will ransom my soul from the power of Sheol, for he will receive me.[14]

Remarkable! This not only reflects the ancient Hebrew understanding of death, it also points to a time when God will rescue souls from sheol and from Death, the "shepherd of sheol." About a thousand years before Christ, David had a prophetic glimpse of salvation beyond sheol, although he didn't know how it would happen:

> Therefore my heart is glad, and my soul rejoices; my body also dwells secure. For thou dost not give me up to Sheol, or let thy godly one see the Pit. Thou dost show me the path of life, in thy presence there is fulness of joy, in thy right hand are pleasures for evermore.[15]

Though they didn't fully understand God's plan to take our sins so we wouldn't have to go to hell, still he was preparing the readers of this psalm for the revelations that would come centuries later.[16]

The Hebrews did not identify sheol specifically as a place of punishment, like we think of hell; sometimes it was just where the dead went. When Joseph's father, Jacob, was told the lie that his beloved son had been killed, he rejected comfort and said, "No, I shall go down to Sheol to my son, mourning."[17] Jacob believed that upon Joseph's death, his spirit went to sheol, and that he also would go there when he died.

Longsuffering Job spoke of hoping he might die and be safe from God's wrath in sheol.[18] Yet Job later acknowledged that sheol cannot hide someone from God's all-powerful vision: "The shades below tremble, the waters and their inhabitants. Sheol is naked before God, and Abaddon [destruction] has no covering."[19]

The words of Psalm 88 describe sheol as a place of darkness and forgetfulness. As the psalmist endured some kind of suffering, he imagined what it might be like:

> I am reckoned among those who go down to the Pit; I am a man who has no strength, like one forsaken among the dead, like the slain that lie in the grave, like those whom thou dost remember no more, for they are cut off from thy hand. Thou hast put me in the depths of the Pit, in the regions dark and deep.[20]

The Old Testament certainly doesn't portray sheol as a pleasant place; it never has any association with heaven or rewards or the like.

Progressive Revelation

Although hell isn't a well-developed Old Testament doctrine, God reveals truths to his people when they are prepared to hear them, just as Jesus held back from the disciples certain truths they weren't yet ready to grasp:

> I have yet many things to say to you, but you cannot bear them now.
>
> When the Spirit of truth comes, he will guide you into all the truth; for he will not speak on his own authority, but whatever he hears he will speak, and he will declare to you the things that are to come.[21]

One intriguing scriptural facet is the way God takes us by the hand and shows us more truth when we can handle it. With each passing century in biblical history, God revealed more and more of his character. This gradual unveiling of truth is called "progressive revelation." The disciples had only the Old Testament and the words of Jesus they heard in his presence. First-century believers also had letters from Paul and the other great writers whose works became the New Testament. Today we have the benefit of two thousand years of hindsight as we study both Testaments.

The truth revealed by God is unchangeable; what *does* change is our human understanding, which continues to mature. On the topic of hades, we see a gradual development as information is added—we know far more about it by the end of the New Testament than we do halfway through the Old Testament.

Hades in the New Testament

The New Testament Greek word *hades* occurs ten times. Twice it simply means "grave," like *sheol*. However, usually it portrays a place where persons not destined for heaven will be held until the final judgment.[22] One writer has noted that "Hades is like the county jail, where inmates await their trial date, final sentence, and transfer to the penitentiary or prison where they will serve their time."[23] (See chapter 16 on the "permanent penitentiary," generally called hell, *gehenna,* or sometimes the "lake of fire.")

Immediately Following Death

In the previous chapters on heaven, I made the case that immediately following death, a believer is fully aware and alert, even if she hasn't passed into the permanent heaven in her glorified body. In the same way, an unbeliever is fully alert and aware after death—that's part of the message we will see in Luke 16.

There are some who believe Jesus' story of the fates of two men who died—one a believer, the other an unbeliever—shouldn't be used as evidence for this awareness. However, Jesus himself seems to use the story partly for that purpose, addressing it to the Pharisees, who placed more importance on religious rules than on following truth.

Whether literal or metaphorical, this story's message is the same: The dead men's conversation gives significant insight into the state of the spirit following death.

Lazarus, a poor man who suffered greatly during his life, lay outside the gate of a very rich man. The rich man lived luxuriously and ignored the needs of others, even those who suffered on his own street. When Lazarus died, the angels carried his spirit to a place of comfort to be with God's faithful servant Abraham. The rich man also died, but his fate was different: "in Hades, being in torment, he lifted up his eyes and saw Abraham far off and Lazarus at his side."[24]

The rich man cried out for help, but Abraham told him there was an uncrossable chasm between them. The man then asked Abraham to help save his family from hades:

> He answered, "Then I beg you, father, send Lazarus to my father's house, for I have five brothers. Let him warn them, so that they will not also come to this place of torment."
>
> Abraham replied, "They have Moses and the Prophets; let them listen to them."
>
> "No, father Abraham," he said, "but if someone from the dead goes to them, they will repent."
>
> He said to him, "If they do not listen to Moses and the Prophets, they will not be convinced even if someone rises from the dead."[25]

The rich man didn't need to go to the place of torment; he chose it by ignoring what Moses and many other people of God had taught. When God showed up in human flesh—as Jesus—the rich man (like the Pharisees) missed him.

Even before Christ's death, many people knew and served God and, like

Lazarus, were spared from the darkness of hades. Others refused to heed the warnings of the Old Testament prophets and paid dearly.

God gave us free will because he wants us to *choose* him. All parents want their children to love them, not from a coerced response but out of genuine devotion. God *is* love, and he designed us with the capacity to love him back. But he won't force the issue. We have the freedom to choose him or turn away. Our choice is what determines where we will go after death. God wants us to choose heaven and eternity with him.

15

Called to Account

The Great White Throne of Judgment—
Where Punishment Is Handed Out

When the day of judgment comes, we shall not be examined as to what we have read but what we have done, not how well we have spoken but how we have lived.

Thomas à Kempis

It was end of semester, and Daniel dreaded logging on to check his chemistry grade. He'd blown his second year of pre-med, wasting study time on video games and shooting hoops. He'd ignored warnings— from his girlfriend, his mom, even Eli, the grad student who assisted him on lab days. They'd all noticed he wasn't even trying. He'd just assumed somehow it would all work out, that he was getting by, that the TA would pass him because he was a decent guy.

Now he crossed his fingers for luck and sat down at the computer, hoping he wouldn't have to tell his parents his academic career was over and their hard-earned money had gone for nothing. Maybe he'd get another chance. But what came up on the screen made his heart sink: even worse than a score of 55 on the final exam was an F for the course.

Disappointment turned to anger. It wasn't his fault—*my prof is a jerk!* he thought. *Doesn't even know how to teach. Always uses grad students to fill in for him.*

Daniel knew what would happen next, though. Chloe and his mom would remind him of all those squandered hours. His dad would shake his head and sigh, weary of a son who refused to do what was necessary to reach goals. The last thing Daniel needed was to be told how lazy he'd been for neglecting to follow through. He knew the consequences were serious. It was judgment day, and that meant losing the opportunity for med school. It was over. This was it.

Failing a class is one thing—failing "life's final exam" is quite another. We humans get one chance at making decisions about our eternal future. That chance, presumably, lasts as long as we're in this life, and "after that comes judgment."[1] Unlike with reincarnation or annihilation, the Bible tells of a "great white throne judgment." What is it, and why should we care?

The Great White Throne Judgment

Of all the biblical topics, hell and final judgment seem especially likely to turn people off. Few seek to study these issues or flock to hear a sermon about them. "Hellfire and brimstone" are held up for ridicule by many and rarely are taken seriously in the twenty-first century.

For Christians, the simple word *judgment* can be intimidating, even without *great white throne* before it. Few (except for trial lawyers) are enthusiastic about appearing in any kind of court for any type of judgment. What if the judge is unfair? What if the evidence is misrepresented? What if the witnesses lie?

And why is this judgment called *great*? If you stop to ponder this word's meaning, it could be anything from *wonderful* to *dreaded* or even *awful*. It could refer to the size of the throne, to the masses that will appear before the throne, or to God himself. In this context, the word inspires awe, if not outright panic.

Our trepidation is confirmed when we examine the language surrounding the biblical depiction. Found near the end of Revelation, John's words leave little room for doubt as to the seriousness of the unfolding drama:

> Then I saw a great white throne and him who was seated on it. Earth and sky fled from his presence, and there was no place for them. And I saw the dead, great and small, standing before the throne, and books were opened. Another book was opened, which is the book of life. The dead were judged according to what they had done as recorded in the books. . . . Then death and Hades were thrown into the lake of fire. . . . If anyone's name was not found written in the book of life, he was thrown into the lake of fire.[2]

In examining the event, we can pose the same questions a journalist might ask: When? Who? What? Where? and How?

When?

The chronology[3] suggests this judgment will happen on the heels of *the millennium*—a term coined for a thousand-year time of peace—and the casting of Satan, antichrist, and false prophet into the lake of fire. This is one of the final events in biblical prophecy.

Who?

As noted in chapter 12, there is much disagreement about who will appear at the great white throne. Some claim it's a judgment that includes everyone. According to this view, the final separation of the "sheep" (believers in Christ) and the "goats" (unbelievers) will take place at the great white throne.

> When the Son of Man comes in his glory . . . he will separate the people one from another as a shepherd separates the sheep from the goats. He will put the sheep on his right and the goats on his left.[4]

Some contend this separation actually refers to a different event—a third judgment—in which the nations are judged, perhaps based on their treatment of Israel. Others complicate the topic even more by naming seven judgments.[5] For our purposes we have one issue: Are there two separate judgments (the great white throne *and* the judgment seat of Christ), or are these two aspects of one event? The answer is significant—if these are two events, believers in Christ do not go before the great white throne. If there is one event, all will experience it.

A clue to "*who* appears" is that this group includes "the dead," as well as a curious reference to those dead who were "delivered up" by the sea, death, and hell.[6] It is possible Christians could be included, but the case is not closed.

So what will happen to those who appear before the throne? We are told that "books will be opened" at the judgment. John refers specifically to a "book of life" where our deeds are recorded. If he were living in today's society, he might have referred to computers being booted up and documents being opened for all to view, as God scrolls through what appears to be a record of each life. God judges individuals "according to what they had done as recorded in the books."[7] Those whose names are not found in the Book of Life are banished.

Note what's missing in this passage. Where is there any hint of rewards or of heaven? The only destination mentioned in the text—and it's mentioned twice—is the ominous-sounding lake of fire. Could that mean this judgment is an event only for those outside of Christ?

Perhaps the great white throne judgment of each person "according to what he had done" refers exclusively to the nonbeliever's deeds. That would explain the absence of any reference to heaven or rewards. And this makes sense if the judgment seat of Christ is exclusively for believers.

On the other hand, if there is only one judgment, of Christians and unbelievers together, it might be charted as follows:

If There Is Only One Judgment

However, it appears more likely that the Bible indicates two separate judgments with separate, parallel "tracks."

What?

Assuming the great white throne judgment is only for nonbelievers, what happens to them? As we saw, books are opened, including "the book of life." We don't know the names of the other books, but we're told they contain a record of the deeds of those being judged. It isn't clear whether the Book of Life is the same as the "Lamb's book of life,"[8] but let's assume it is. This book contains names, and anyone whose name isn't recorded there is sent to the lake of fire.

Are the books figurative or literal? Will they appear as a scroll or as a thick volume? Are they a reference to the mind of God? It makes little difference. What's important is the content: the deeds of the dead and the names of the righteous.

On ABC's *Nightline*, interviewer Cynthia McFadden asked former President George W. Bush whether he believed the Bible is literally true. "Probably not," he responded. ". . . No, I am not a literalist. . . ."[9]

Perhaps a better answer would be "The Bible should be taken literally when it is clear that the writer is expressing himself literally." As literature, the Bible contains (among other things) history, poetry, symbolism, and imagery. It's relatively easy to tell which is which, and certainly all Scripture should be accepted as truth by those who believe it is God-inspired. Here's a safe rule: When uncertain, err on the side of caution and accept the literalness of inspired writing until it's clearly and convincingly proven otherwise.

Whether the "books" are codices, scrolls, or in the mind of God—what exactly is in them, and how are they filled? Is there a celestial record keeper or court reporter typing away for each person? Will video footage show everyone what we did? Will our thoughts and feelings be recorded too? The Bible says only that the books contain a record of what each person has done—his or her "deeds."

And what about our words? Your mama probably used to tell you, "If you can't say something nice, don't say anything at all." Good advice, especially in light of what Jesus says:

> I tell you that men will have to give account on the day of judgment for every careless word they have spoken. For by your words you will be acquitted, and by your words you will be condemned.[10]

Suddenly, we're all recalling the times we let words fly that should've stayed in.

Think of it this way: Anytime we delete our e-mails, we assume they've disappeared forever. Phew! But most of them are still out there "somewhere." It may not be easy to retrieve them, but it's possible. Would you want all your messages recovered and read publicly? Neither would I. Yet Jesus states plainly that our words matter and are recorded on some kind of heavenly hard drive.

Moreover, the Book of Life apparently is a record of names—those of Christians. We could stretch the details a little and imagine that everyone's name is written in this book until death. Then a nonbeliever's name would be erased or blotted out.

"Blotting out" is not uncommon throughout Scripture.[11] And while most of these verses aren't pleasant to read, they give insight into the judgment books. The final reference to blotting out puts the term in a more positive light: "He who overcomes will, like them, be dressed in white. I will never blot out his name from the Book of Life, but will acknowledge his name before my Father and his angels."[12]

Not all passages using the term also refer to the book of life. What's notable, however, is the consistent pattern of something being erased. The conclusion we must draw is that what was already written can be deleted.

Did you notice what's absent? There are no references to anything being *added* to the Book of Life. Instead of a grand book with names being written down as people are coming to Jesus—a book that grows throughout history—we see a book that originally contained the name of everyone who has ever existed. If people die without choosing to believe and follow Christ, their names are erased.

The writing and the erasing must be both thrilling and heartbreaking to a loving heavenly Father. God is excited about the potential of our entrance into this life, and he's even more excited about spending eternity with us. With the grand hopes of a father before a child's birth, he notes our names in his book; then, as our lives progress, he reaches out to us. What he wants is our love and our acceptance of his Son. And our names stay in the book until our last breath. Then, if we depart without having acknowledged and accepted him as our Savior, you can imagine how his heart breaks to blot out the name of one who is his precious creation.

The "what" of the great white throne judgment is simple: The deeds of those who come will be reviewed, and their names will not be in the Book of Life. That's why they are here—at *this* judgment.

Where?

Though this judgment could take place on earth, more likely it's a heavenly event. God sits on the throne; his realm is in heaven. All the dead from the beginning of time will be there, and that number will be in the billions. We can't determine the location for sure, and it isn't important to know.

How?

Rather than ask "How did it *happen?*" let's address "how to *avoid*" the great white throne. The evidence points to an event only for the dead who died without Christ, so the key question is "How can I miss this one?" The fact is this will be the single most terrifying event *ever*. If such a scene could be adequately portrayed on the big screen, multitudes would repent with fervor—or as the evangelists of yesteryear would say, "attempt to flee the wrath to come."

If you do not believe, this chapter is written in actual hopes of "scaring the hell out of you." If you die without accepting Christ's provision for eternal life, you will stand before the most formidable judge you can imagine. And you will do so aware that he did not put you in this inescapable predicament. Like Daniel, the failed pre-med student, you will have put yourself there.

Your belief system may not embrace the great white throne judgment. That doesn't make it any less real. You may scoff at it or choose to ignore it; makes no difference. It's real, it's coming, and every person who has not placed faith in Jesus Christ will be judged and found wanting.

16

The Heat Is On

Hell Is an Indescribable Punishment for Those Who Reject Salvation

What is hell? I maintain that it is the suffering of not being able to love.

Fyodor Dostoyevsky

There is plenty of disagreement about hell—whether it's a real physical place with real flames, whether people will be fully conscious there, whether it's temporary or permanent, whether it's all a metaphor.[1] The previous chapters on heaven and hades showed that people will be fully conscious and aware after death, not resting in soul sleep. If your destination is heaven, this is a magnificent thought; if it's hell, you should be terrified.

Let's revisit the story about the dead man who looked up from his "agony in the fire" and saw Abraham far away, with Lazarus by his side. He called for water to cool his tongue and asked Abraham to send word to his brothers so they wouldn't end up where he was. But Abraham couldn't cross the gulf between them and said that even if he could communicate with the brothers, they wouldn't listen.[2]

Taken as Christ's own words, this account tells us clearly what happens to those who die outside of meaningful relationship with him. They go to hades, where they're aware of their misery and conscious that they don't want their loved ones to be there.

Separation Anxiety

Paul points out that there are two parts to suffering in hell: "They will be punished with everlasting destruction and shut out from the presence of the Lord and from the majesty of his power."[3] Hell is not just a place of torment; additionally it's a place of separation from God.

What's the big deal about this isolation? Some people are so overwhelmed by their sense of brokenness that the thought of being *with* God is intimidating. If they hear "In hell you'll be away from God," their reaction might be "That's how I am now—why would I care about it then?" But many people take for granted the goodness all around them. Separation from God after death means separation from everything that's right, true, and wonderful; he is the source of all that is good. Eternity without God means exposure only to what is wrong, false, and horrible.

Imagine stepping out of your house one morning only to discover that every bit of beauty is gone from this earth. All that you like, that makes you feel great, that makes life worth living has disappeared. All that's left is the hideous and the obscene.

Mortified, you realize you could have kept this from happening by making one important decision, but you didn't think it was important and/or you didn't believe the truth about it. You see now what's happened, but it's too late to change things. You're stuck—no way out.

The absence of God, of goodness and light, means being forever in the presence of evil and darkness. We weren't created for that destiny—*he made us to be with him.* As Jerry Walls wrote, "God could not make rational creatures such as ourselves in such a way that they would not need him for their fulfillment and happiness."[4]

In discussions of hell, the same question almost always comes up: If God is so loving and gracious, why would he torment people? The answer is so simple it may seem ridiculous, but it's true: *God never has sent any human to hell, and he never will.*

If you've ever hired someone to do a job, you know he expects to be paid his wages when the work is done. This life could be described as having wages—wages for living our lives as we please and wages for choosing to follow love and truth. We can choose everlasting death without Christ, or we can choose everlasting life with him.[5] Although each person makes this choice during life, the ramifications are delayed, so it's easy for some to deny that there ever will be any real results or consequences.

Hell *wasn't* made for people; God doesn't want anyone to go there. But he is utter goodness—absolute holiness—and evil cannot be in his presence. Without Christ, our "goodness" isn't good enough. So he allows us to choose: eternal life or eternal death.

Those Who Have Never Heard

Another question: What about people who die without hearing the good news? What if no one has ever told them about Jesus? This seems like a real dilemma, because if we see God as righteous—as justice itself—how could it be fair to punish someone for being born in a place and time where he or she couldn't hear the truth?

An answer is found in John's gospel, regarding "the true light that gives light to every man."[6] At some point, each is touched by awareness that he or she needs God and that he has made a provision. This insight may be basic, but God doesn't leave anyone in the dark. In that light-burst, that divine appointment, it becomes clear there is a personal, moral Creator— one beyond and above us, one who has made us and cares for us.

Picture a tribal hunter picking his way through heavy jungle foliage outside his village in the early morning hours. In the tangle of vines and branches, he sees an iridescent butterfly perched motionless on the edge of a leaf. Its delicate beauty takes his breath away, and in that moment he senses that *Someone made it*—Someone bigger and more powerful than anyone he's ever known. It occurs to him that this Someone has provided for *everything*. He has known the difference between right and wrong since he was a child, but now he's overwhelmed by a feeling that there's something more, and that all he has to do is say *yes* to this Someone. He has received the light; it is sufficient. If he embraces it, he will receive eternal life, even though he doesn't yet know that this gift has a name: Jesus Christ.

Paul wrote about this situation also.

What may be known about God is plain to them [those who suppress the truth], because God has made it plain to them. For since the creation of the world God's invisible qualities—his eternal power and divine nature—have

173

been clearly seen, being understood from what has been made, so that men are without excuse.[7]

Although it seems there will be some who enter heaven based on such an experience, God wants his people to keep telling others about him. That's one reason believers may come across as compulsive about sharing their faith or sending out missionaries. Coming to Christ may be as simple as seeing a beautiful butterfly on a morning hunt, but these moments will be ignored or overlooked by many.

Words for Hell

In chapter 14, we looked at the Hebrew word *sheol*, which usually refers to a holding place for the dead. A second word is the Greek *hades*, which normally denotes a place of torment, the way most people think of hell.

Though its exact meaning is ambiguous, hades appears to be a temporary location or, again, a "horrible holding tank." It's where those who die without Christ go at the moment of death. They remain there until the great white throne judgment.[8]

For those who have rejected God's offer of salvation, the worst part comes after this judgment, when what was temporary becomes permanent.

The Abyss and Tartarus

Three New Testament terms essentially mean "hell" or something related to it. There's the bottomless pit—the Greek word denotes "abyss."[9] It's not for humanity but rather a holding place for Satan and his demons.

A curious word used only once (by Peter) and translated "hell" is *tartarus*: "God did not spare angels when they sinned, but sent them to *tartarus*, putting them into gloomy dungeons to be held for judgment."[10] Jude uses a different description of this temporary place for fallen angels.[11]

Gehenna

If hades holds lost souls until the great white throne judgment, then eventually these souls must go to a permanent place. Biblically, the term used most often for what comes after hades is *gehenna*, which literally means "Valley of Hinnom." *Gehenna* surfaces thirteen times in the Old Testament, a dozen times in the New.

Jerusalem today is modern and metropolitan, but you can still see vestiges of the ancient city. It's perched on the southeast corner of a raised area, with steep drop-offs on two sides. On the southwest is a deep crevice—a ravine. For centuries the Valley of Hinnom was used as a trash depository; the bodies of animals and criminals were discarded there. This dumpsite, always smoldering, gave off a putrid smell.

But it was also more. In Old Testament times, children were sacrificed there during pagan worship of Molech. The practice, involving fire, truly is too horrific to comprehend. When writers, prophets, or priests of that time spoke about hell, they would say, "It's like *gehenna*." Thus the lake of fire (Revelation) and *gehenna* (rest of the New Testament) are regarded as essentially the same thing.

Hell's Location

We can't pinpoint the exact location of hell—God doesn't tell us whether it's a part of our earthly realm. Paul mentions "lower, earthly regions"[12] and also those "in heaven and on earth and under the earth."[13] Although scientists believe earth's inner core is solid, perhaps with a molten outer core, popular thought among some is that hell actually is beneath our feet.

Years ago a story went around that a drilling crew had drilled down to hell. According to this tale, some had even heard the screams of the damned. Unfortunately, the story was picked up by a major Christian television network and passed along by certain preachers. That turned out to be an urban legend with no basis in fact; gullible people had turned it into something more. Regardless, what we need to know is that *there is a real place called hell, and God has made a way for us to avoid going there.*

A Place of Endless Torture

Ever burned your finger? Even a minor burn can keep you awake at night. Most anyone can relate to the agony of scorched skin, and no one likes to think of everlasting torment involving fire. Spending one day alive and conscious in a flaming jail cell would be intolerable—imagine being in that situation forever. Man has never invented such a torture—we find the very thought of it offensive, even as punishment for the most heinous criminals. Yet Scripture tells us the fiery torment prepared for the devil and his cohorts also will be peopled with unrepentant humans.

How do we handle the concept of unending torture? We have two choices:

(1) Deny the New Testament, even though it "will not allow us to wiggle out of confrontation with the fact that the wicked will pay a penalty."[14]

(2) Believe what Scripture says.

Those who claim to have "seen" hell report real fire there; Bill Wiese is one of these. In his controversial *23 Minutes in Hell*, he asserts, "I saw the pit. . . . I saw the liquid fire that falls like rain. I felt the extreme heat, and I smelled the stench of burning things. I do not believe the Scripture references are merely symbolic or allegorical."[15]

In contrast, biblical scholar Jerry Walls has said,

> The suffering of hell is the natural consequence of living a life of sin rather than arbitrary chosen punishment. In other words, the misery of hell is not so much a penalty imposed by God to make the sinner pay for his sin, as it is the necessary outcome of living a sinful life. . . . I do not think the fire of hell is literal, nor do I think hell is an ingeniously contrived place of the greatest possible pain and agony.[16]

Even Pope John Paul II, following that line of thinking, redefined hell as a post-death psychological state: "Hell is not a punishment imposed externally by God, but the condition resulting from attitudes and actions which people adopt in this life."[17]

Lest one think this view of suffering is somehow "better," Walls continues with an equally sobering assessment:

> What about physical pains of sense? Is there any good reason to think hell must also include bodily pain as many traditional theologians have insisted? I do . . . think hell includes physical distress. My reason for this involves an appeal to the traditional Christian belief that the damned as well as the blessed will be resurrected in their bodies. If the damned will have bodies in

hell, it seems only natural to suppose that there will be a bodily dimension to their suffering.[18]

Literal or Metaphorical?

When Bill Crocket, my classmate years ago at Princeton Theological Seminary, gathered four theologians (himself included) to reflect on hell, he not surprisingly received four different views.[19] One (Zachary Hayes) was the classic Catholic take on purgatory;[20] another (Clark Pinnock) was annihilationism, wherein people will cease to exist.[21] John Walvoord expressed a third outlook: "There is sufficient evidence that the fire is literal. . . . Scripture never challenges the concept that eternal punishment is by literal fire."[22] People object to this concept, he said, out of a personal aversion, not because the biblical text doesn't support it.

Crocket represented the fourth view, which contends that the New Testament's references to hellfire are overwhelmingly figurative. For example, it speaks of hell as the "blackest darkness";[23] how could it be dark and yet be filled with fire, which is bright? Physical fire affects physical beings, not spirit beings, which is what Crocket believes entities will be in hell.

Although we don't know for sure whether the New Testament writers were referring to literal or figurative flames, we can do our best to interpret their meaning. Hermeneutics, the science of interpretation, tells us to examine context. If context indicates a literal interpretation, we should understand it that way. For example, there's an enormous difference between saying, "I put on my sweats and ran five and a half miles today" and "I probably walked a million miles today—my feet are killing me." The first statement, without further explanation, can be taken at face value; the second, given the sweeping "million miles" and "killing me," is meant to be taken figuratively.

It appears to me that the New Testament intent is metaphorical. Crockett points to an at-that-time example of such figurative speech:

> When Jesus says, "If anyone comes to me and does not hate his father and mother, his wife and children . . . he cannot be my disciple" (Luke 14:26), he does not mean we must hate our parents to be proper disciples. That is a language vehicle used to convey . . . that loyalty to him is supreme.[24]

Such biblical admonitions as "take the plank out of your own eye" or "let the dead bury their own dead" are instances of figurative yet powerful speech.[25] Fire frequently is referenced non-literally in ancient Jewish writings.[26] Again, however, a figurative view of hell's flames needn't diminish their very real effects. One is neither less punishing nor "better" than the other.

We've noted that hell ultimately is separation from God—not only separation from all that is good but also integration with all that is evil. Hence, the punishment of hell may be less about how God designed a place for torturous suffering and more about how "the damned will inflict physical pain on one another. . . . Those whose characters have been shaped by violence may continue to feed on violence in hell."[27]

Why the Hellish Choice?

People tend to fixate on a question we addressed earlier: Why would God create a world in which we have the capacity to choose something so horrifying? If ever there was a theological obsessive-compulsive disorder, it's on this point. Answering seems akin to filling a bottomless pit, because the asking never ceases. Once again, though, it can't be overemphasized: *God did not make hell for humans, but for those who deserve it: the devil and his demons. Yet we can will it for ourselves.*

God *is* love, and God *desires* love from us—unconditional love, freely given. Genuine love requires the freedom to choose. He created humans as sentient beings with free will, able to reject him. This choice reveals something profoundly mysterious and tender: God longs for intimacy with us. Let that settle in for a moment. *God—the all-knowing, all-powerful, everywhere-present One—wants closeness with you and me!*

This desire in God is so strong that he made the issue plain in the beginning:

> I'm making this as easy as I possibly can. I'm giving you a garden and inviting you to pick any fruit you want. All you see is yours. Enjoy!
>
> I made just one rule, so you will understand what it is to obey and depend on me. There is one tree you may not touch. Just one! This is for your own good, and you must trust me.
>
> I'll even explain why I don't want you to eat from that tree. It is called the Tree of Knowledge of Good and Evil. If you were to eat from it, you would be choosing to decide for yourself what is good and what is evil. That's my role. You have yours: Care for and enjoy the rest of the garden.

But do not try to be me. Don't try to decide on your own what is good and what is evil. I'll handle that.

You know the rest of the story. Adam and Eve found their way to that tree—with a little outside help—and blew it for the rest of us. They chose separation from God, who wanted intimacy with them. With capacity to choose came capacity to turn away.

Forever Is Forever

Must hell be eternal?[28] Some say no. Gerry Beauchemin contends that Christian teaching on hell is like

> a "crazy uncle" that the Church, with justifiable embarrassment, has kept locked in the back bedroom. Unfortunately, from time to time, he escapes his confinement, usually when there are guests in the parlor. . . . It's no wonder that the guests run away never to return. But instead of shunting the "crazy uncle" back to his asylum, and trying to cover our embarrassment . . . we need to get "our crazy uncle" healed.[29]

Beauchemin insists hell is temporary, that "though men will weep and even gnash their teeth, they will not do so forever."[30]

Randy Klassen agrees, stating succinctly, "An eternal hell serves no purpose."[31]

However, in contrast to those who reassure us that hell is "for a while," Jesus says the future promises only two prospects: "eternal punishment" for some, but for the righteous, "eternal life."[32] Later we're told again about the fate of those who reject God: "They will be tormented day and night for ever and ever."[33]

It may be popular to hand out comfort by assuring that hell is temporary, but when pop theologians deny hell and make heaven the one and only destination, they also deny our freedom to choose. This erodes the basis for authentic love: choice. If heaven can't be chosen, it becomes devoid of the one thing heaven *must* have: love.

God grants us the right to embrace or reject him. This literally is a hell of a decision. What on earth are you going to do about it, for heaven's sake?

Part Five

Hell-Avoidance Strategies

17

The Ultimate Escape Hatch

Universalism Suggests That All Will Be Saved in the End

Disbelieve hell, and you unscrew, unsettle, and unpin everything in Scripture.

J. C. Ryle

A tax lawyer was lying on his deathbed, frantically thumbing through a little-used Bible. A friend who visited during his final hours mused, "Harvey, I didn't know you were religious." The lawyer replied, "I'm not—I'm looking for a loophole."[1]

Much of history regarding the doctrine of hell has been concerned with just that—a loophole. In my lifetime, I've only met one person who actually thought he was going to hell. Everyone else seems either to ignore the whole idea or to expect heaven.

Plato proposed that a person's soul lasts forever and ends up *somewhere*; some Supreme Good Entity figures that out. Many people since have discarded any notion of an eternal hell and hold to the idea of a cozy afterlife in some sort of heaven where everyone goes. That is, they believe heaven is *universal*. To understand how this became popular, let's look at how belief in hell has gone in and out of favor over the centuries.

A "History of Hell"

In the time of Christ, and through God's revelation in him, hell was under-stood as a physical destination and punishment for those who rejected him. There were alternative views of hell, but within the faith they remained on the fringes.

In the third century, Origen, a scholar and apologist from Egypt, of-fered a new suggestion: that hell is not a place of eternal punishment but a temporary place where sinners will be rehabilitated. All unredeemed creatures—demons and humans alike—would go through a cleansing pro-cess and be reunited with God in heaven. Even Judas, who betrayed Jesus, could be forgiven. God, a consuming fire, will consume evil, not people. Origen's theory of restoration is called by its Greek name: *apokatastasis*.

Not long thereafter, the church began to hold ecumenical councils—theological conferences to discuss concepts of orthodoxy ("right belief"). There was also a negative component: learning to refute heretical teach-ings. *Apokatastasis* was rejected at the fifth ecumenical council; Origen's universalist views have been considered heresy ever since.

Belief in hell as eternal punishment for the damned held firm through the Middle Ages and into the Reformation. Medieval life was harsh and uncertain; powerful (and often corrupt) clergy often used the fear of hell to control the illiterate masses. There was so much superstition in the church and such misery and oppression among the common folk that everlasting punishment for the wicked was quite acceptable. People longed for the relief that heaven offered but lived in terror of hell's torment.

In the early eighteenth century, Jonathan Edwards, a third-generation New England preacher and later president of Princeton University, deliv-ered a hellfire-and-brimstone message titled "Sinners in the Hands of an Angry God."

> The wrath of God burns against them, their damnation does not slumber; the pit is prepared, the fire is made ready, the furnace is now hot, ready to receive them; the flames do now rage and glow.[2]

Most sermons are quickly forgotten by both speaker and audience. Edwards' words, however, were so memorable that after almost two cen-turies a plaque was placed at the site where he preached. The sermon's influence is so significant that I traveled some distance out of my way to

Enfield, Connecticut, to view the small bronze marker in commemoration of its having been given some two hundred sixty-seven years earlier. Then I traveled to Yale University's Beinecke Rare Book and Manuscript Library in New Haven, where a skilled archivist, with a heart surgeon's precision and concentration, opened the original handwritten sermon notes.

What gripped Edwards' listeners and caused "Sinners in the Hands of an Angry God" to be so revered was his graphic portrayal of hell. He emphasized the metaphors of *fire* and the *pit* so urgently that even "strong men clung to the pillars of the meetinghouse and cried aloud for mercy."[3]

Before this time, theologians were beginning to question and reject an eternal hell. A European sect called the Socinians, which later became the Unitarians, argued that hell is unjust and against God's character. Yet even these intellectual elite approved of preaching about hell to the masses, believing it kept people in line.[4]

Victorian Sensibilities

Most people in the late nineteenth century went to church, and overall an aura of decency and family values prevailed. Underneath all the civility, however, a theological crisis was brewing: The Bible's inspiration was suspect. God was still good, but what about hell? Typically, Victorian fathers reigned supreme over their families, yet didn't discipline too harshly, and it was difficult for people to accept God as an all-loving father who sent his wayward children to eternal damnation.

The chaplain to Queen Victoria pronounced hell a "blasphemy against the merciful God."[5] Another prominent Anglican, F. D. Maurice, arguing that eternal (spiritual) death is more consistent with God's character than eternal punishment, introduced the theology of "conditional immortality," a brand of annihilationism.[6] Lewis Carroll, author of *Alice in Wonderland*, dismissed the inspiration of Scripture and insisted that God's goodness precludes hell. In an unpublished essay titled "Eternal Punishment," Carroll said that if one believes in hell, it's illogical to believe in God.[7]

In contrast to the fiery Jonathan Edwards, Victorian preachers preferred to shelter their congregations from the distasteful, indecent concept of a literal hell. Charles Spurgeon, a British Reform Baptist, was an exception, who didn't shy away (though, unlike Edwards, he injected humor into his sermons). Spurgeon specifically challenged the notion that hellfire is metaphorical:

. . . a metaphorical fire: who cares for that? If a man were to threaten to give me a metaphorical blow on the head, I should care very little about it; he would be welcome to give me as many as he pleased . . . [and so the wicked] do not care about metaphorical fires.[8]

Modernist Hell

Theologians continued to search for "acceptable alternatives" in the twentieth century. Rudolph Bultmann, a New Testament professor in Germany, had a solution: "demythologize" the Gospels. Anything that didn't fit with "scientific" understanding was discounted as myth. But mainstream theologians who still believed in authentic biblical inspiration weren't willing to accommodate; they searched for ways to explain hell without dismissing the New Testament's authority.

Meanwhile, two world wars intensified discussions of the problem of evil. Conditions in developing countries inspired liberation theology, which links "sin" to poverty and oppression. Herein salvation no longer is the saving of a soul; replacing that discarded notion was social activism addressing "social sin." Psychology claimed people couldn't be blamed for wrongs—genetics, upbringing, and environment were responsible. Rehabilitation, not punishment, was the answer to criminal behavior.

So evil was society's fault, a mindset that spawned certain theological offspring:[9]

- Anyone who speaks for God must also defend him against evil, suffering, and intolerance.
- *Love* is God's primary attribute—separate from justice, authority, constancy.
- God's justice is redefined by human standards.
- Human freedom and choice are elevated above God's holiness.

Both scholars and ordinary people were affected by these theological shifts. British New Testament scholar John Wenham agonized over the horror of hell—he saw it as worse than the horror of sin. In his quest to find a viable alternative to the doctrine of eternal punishment, he couldn't gain support for universalism and instead concluded (as had F. D. Maurice) that God created man as *inherently mortal* but grants immortality to those who choose Christ. Those who choose otherwise, then, cease to exist after death; this again is conditional immortality.[10]

Universalism—the belief that all go to heaven after death—isn't scripturally supported, but it's trendy. The Church of England jumped on the bandwagon in 1995, concluding that hell is incompatible with God's love and that the privilege of salvation should include everyone.[11]

By the turn of the century, the theological cleanup of hell had trickled down to the average person. A 1991 survey for *U.S. News & World Report* said that 60 percent of Americans believed in some kind of hell[12] but differed widely in beliefs about its nature. Almost without exception, people believed hell to be for others, not themselves.

A God of love who doesn't judge or condemn is easier to sell. In the 1990s, Robert Brow and Clark Pinnock offered a new-millennium take on doctrine in *Unbounded Love: A Good News Theology for the 21st Century*.[13] Wanting to freshen up antiquated ideas like Christ's death, sin itself, and the wrath of God,[14] Pinnock argued that the doctrine of hell needed revamping so people wouldn't dismiss it.[15] Both men supported annihilationism as kinder and gentler than eternal punishment.[16]

The world-renowned psychiatrist Karl Menninger warned against the loss of a sense of *sin* at a time when well-known preachers were abandoning the very word.[17] Norman Vincent Peale preached "the power of positive thinking," while his disciple Robert Schuler emphasized "possibility living." Some mega-church pastors have championed explosive ministry in which seeker-sensitive services avoid terms or phrases such as *salvation, born again,* and *accepting Jesus.*[18]

Hell Disappears

A prominent, dynamic pastor named Carlton Pearson also had an alternative vision. A gifted gospel singer, skilled author, and profound speaker, Pearson studied at Oral Roberts University in Tulsa, and started a church soon after; the congregation of Higher Dimensions Family quickly swelled to five thousand. He certainly had my attention—I loved his music, I listened to him speak, I read his books.

But as Pearson wrestled with the harshness of hell, he became convinced that universalism is true—that while hell is a corrective measure for some people, no one will stay there. He rejected the "classical version of hell" as "completely out of character with what we know about God,"[19] calling his variation of Origen's theory "the Gospel of Inclusion."[20] He eventually claimed that even Satan could repent. Pearson succinctly sums up his views:

> Will hell for some people last 10 minutes or 10 million years . . . ? We don't know. But this we do know; hell will not last for eternity; it will not be endless. . . . Don't sin. Be reunited with God now, rather than after you have put yourself (and those you love) through hell.[21]

When Pearson's council called his idea heretical, his influence began to wane, and he lost his church. Despite this, he has predicted that within five years every pastor in America will be preaching his doctrine.

Universalism: Escape Hatch for All

Universalism is based primarily on optimism and an over-simplistic view of God. The motivation is understandable: compassion for fellow humans and revulsion toward the very concept of hell. The multiple brands of universalist thinking embrace the same rationale but with different theologies and varying levels of sophistication. J. I. Packer defines three categories: secular, pluralistic, and postmortem.[22]

Secular Universalism

Secular universalism doesn't involve sin, atonement (Christ's death on the cross), or salvation but instead maintains that everyone will have a pleasant eternal existence. This category includes the belief that people become angels after they die—a view upheld by Oprah Winfrey just after the tragedy of September 11, 2001. Such eschatology may entail New Age philosophy or merely wishful thinking.

Pluralistic Universalism

The pluralistic approach to universalism is based on the view that there is a god of some sort and all roads lead to him. Here, all religions and belief systems have validity; the overlapping of lifestyles and practices is nothing more than a positive and enriching cultural experience; holding any worldview as superior is arrogance. All religions have equal merit and access to God, and *even Christians*, who claim salvation comes exclusively through Jesus, probably would be pardoned for this error and allowed access to the universal heaven.

Universalistic pluralism is appealing because most people would like heaven to be open to those we live, work, and play with, despite their beliefs and choices. However, it isn't compatible with Scripture.

Postmortem Universalism

Postmortem universalism, the "Christian version" (Origen's *apokatastasis*), assumes inherent human sinfulness and acknowledges our need for a savior, but it holds that God's loving patience wills to give repeated opportunities to anyone who dies without accepting Christ's atoning work. It also accounts for those who die without hearing the gospel, an issue that troubles many believers.

According to postmortem universalism, hell will be a temporary correction spot. The stop-off will last as long as necessary; rejects from purgatory can hang out there while they think things over. Eventually, though, even the most resistant atheist, the most heinous terrorist, and the most hateful mass murderer will choose salvation.

Nels Ferre, this view's most enthusiastic twentieth-century promoter, says God will tighten the screws until the recalcitrant soul relents. No one ultimately can resist his grace and goodness.

- If God *could not* save everyone, he's not all-powerful.
- If God *would not* save everyone, he's not good.
- Since God *is* all-powerful and good, everyone will be saved.[23]

This logical conclusion has flaws. For one, an omnipotent God still won't violate his own principles, which are what they are as based on his own essence. If he created human beings with the power to choose, then he cannot also make their choices for them. The annihilationist Pinnock rejects universalism for that very reason: "How can God predestine the free response of love? This is something even God cannot do."[24]

Apparently, in the postmortem scenario of hell-as-halfway-house, people can exercise free will after death. But why wouldn't some souls, having a choice, still reject God? Why *must* truly evil people choose differently, given more time?

The apostle John speaks of people who are in hell because they turned against God, and even there they curse his name and refuse to repent.[25] Pinnock agrees: "In the end he [God] will allow us to become what we have chosen."[26]

Ferre's logic also is faulty in that he defines God's goodness on his own terms. Postmortem advocates argue that God's love precludes any sort of permanent judgment or punishment because such action is unworthy of him. They insist that a God who would allow any of his creatures to go to hell is not a God of love and goodness.

But this ignores other attributes intrinsic to God's perfect character and inseparable from his love—holiness, justice, sovereignty, and, yes, anger. Any good parent knows when to show love and when to express legitimate, appropriate anger. It's the same with our heavenly Father.

There isn't much (if any) biblical justification for universalism. Several passages that speak of Christ's atoning work, taken out of context, can *seem* to support the idea that God will save everyone.[27] For instance, they speak of Jesus drawing all persons, God restoring everything, having mercy on them all, wanting all to be saved, not wanting anyone to perish—*all* people, the *whole* world. But careful examination shows that each statement is limited by the context of the passage and the intent of the writer.

If I say I'm "inviting everyone" to my birthday party, I'm not including everyone in the world—that's not the context of my statement. I'd be referring to everyone within a smaller group: people in my office, my church group, my neighborhood, my family, or similar group. You wouldn't know which of these I meant without learning the context.

Sometimes "all" *is* inclusive—God *does* want *all* to be saved and *everyone* to come to repentance; he offers salvation to *all*. But not everyone will accept what is offered. Some will reject it.

On one local freeway, the final exit ends with a sharp curve that requires slowing to about fifteen miles per hour. A mile before the curve, there's a warning sign to reduce speed. Another sign stands a little farther along, and then there's also a series of arrows that light up at night so no one will miss the curve and continue in a perilous way. But some people have ignored the signs and arrows, and they didn't brake until it was too late. Skid marks show where they've gone off the road. People can and do ignore warning signs, whether on the freeway or those given to us by God.

Remember the story Jesus told that illustrates the finality of hell, the one about the rich man and Lazarus? The rich man didn't ask Abraham to release him from his place of misery. He knew it was too late for him—he was stuck there.

The writer of Hebrews likewise confirms there won't be an opportunity to change your mind after death: "Just as man is destined to die once, and after that to face judgment, so Christ was sacrificed once to take away the sins of many people."[28] Note that Jesus takes away the sins of *many* people; forgiveness depends on our response.

Universalist teaching is soothing to those who hate the idea of hell, but it's based on a misunderstanding of God's nature. It starts and stops on one attribute—love, which certainly is central—while ignoring justice. It ignores the clear words of Jesus and the New Testament writers not only on God's love and provision of salvation but also on those who will be forever separated from God as a result of rejecting him.[29]

When you don't like something that's clearly taught in the Bible, you have two choices: embrace it despite your dislike or try to rationalize it away. Nels Ferre has felt so strongly about his position that he claimed the disciples couldn't have understood God's love and sovereign purpose. They may even have misrepresented it, and perhaps Jesus himself misunderstood. But why does Ferre assume that *he* gets it? We can hardly uphold the Bible as testimony to God's nature and as his Word to us while assuming we understand it better than those who wrote it.

The temptation to whitewash or "air-condition"[30] hell can be strong, even among believers. But as a Christian and a pastor responsible for my congregation's welfare, I can't adopt any brand of universalism. The Bible is too explicit about hell's reality.

18

Disappearing Acts

Annihilationism Proposes That Those Without Faith Will Cease to Exist

Eternity is really long, especially toward the end.

Woody Allen

In C. S. Lewis's spiritual autobiography, *Surprised by Joy*, he relates an incident from his boyhood while a boarding school student in Britain. Such schools were hotbeds of humiliation and bullying, and this one was no exception. Lewis recalls being "dragged at headlong speed through a labyrinth of passages . . . beyond all usual landmarks . . . [as] one of several prisoners into a low, bare room lit by a single gas jet." He noted a row of pipes blocking the opposite wall.

> I was alarmed but not surprised when the prisoner [each boy] was forced into a bending position under the lowest pipe, in the very posture for execution. But I was very much surprised a moment later. The two gangsters gave the victim a shove; and instantly no victim was there. He vanished; without trace, without sound. . . . Another victim was led out; again the posture for a flogging was assumed; again, instead of flogging—dissolution, atomization, annihilation![1]

192

Of course, young Lewis's classmates were not annihilated, much to his relief. When it was his turn to be pushed, he found himself sliding down a chute into a coal cellar, reunited with dirty classmates, a little banged up but intact.

In *conditional annihilationism*—espoused by theologians like John Wenham, John Stott, Edward Fudge, Robert Brow, David Powys, and Clark Pinnock—it's not unsuspecting schoolboys who are snuffed out but sinful humans who die without saving faith in Christ. Only those who accept salvation through Jesus will continue to exist. In this way, annihilationism contrasts with universalism, which proposes that everyone finally will be saved.

Both ideas are alternatives to the orthodox view of hell; both are based on the premise that hell as eternal punishment is contrary to God's nature. As defined here, conditional annihilation is different from the ancient Epicurean view of death as nonexistence. The Epicureans believed that upon death, a person's particles eventually would dis-sociate from the body and disseminate throughout the universe. Nothing more would happen—just a peaceful transition into nonbeing. No God, no soul, no afterlife for *anyone*.

Annihilation as such might make sense if there were no God. But unlike this perspective, which applies in-the-end nonexistence for everyone, we're looking at the Christian (conditional) view, which says:

- Believers are granted eternal life by God when they die.
- Unbelievers, not receiving this gift, disappear into oblivion.

This brand is also known as *conditional immortality,* and its most influential recent advocate has been John Stott. Although highly orthodox in other areas—for example, regarding the deity of Christ and the sufficiency of his atoning sacrifice—Stott wrestled emotionally with the strain of supporting hell as traditionally taught. He concluded that hell *is* a place of eternal damnation; however, to be damned means to be annihilated rather than punished.

Evangelicals for Annihilationism

Over the last few decades a surprising number of mainstream theologians have adopted conditional immortality. After John Wenham outlined it in

The Goodness of God (1974), an impressive number of evangelical scholars "converted." Universalism, though, is still considered unacceptable in most evangelical circles.[2]

Supporters are convinced that, for the damned, the biblical hell is not a place of eternal suffering. They base their opinions on interpretation, moral reasoning, the issue of God's character, and an appeal to emotion.[3]

The controversy over whether unrepentant sinners are annihilated or tormented is related to Scripture as well. Several New Testament Greek words, found in verses about hell, usually are translated *destruction*.[4] However, the Greek term for "destroy" has a wide range of meanings;[5] much depends on the object of destruction. For example, if I "destroy" a piece of furniture by smashing it with a sledgehammer, I can no longer use it for its intended purpose, because I now have a pile of splintered wood. But I'll still have to clean up the pieces—"destroying" the table didn't make it vanish.

Charles Hodge explains how to better understand passages used in support of annihilationism: "A soul is utterly and forever *destroyed* when it is alienated from God, rendered a fit companion only for the devil and his angels."[6]

In language that's hard for us to hear, Jesus says those alienated from God will go "into the eternal fire prepared for the devil and his angels."[7] These people will "go away to eternal punishment,"[8] which implies consciousness and existence, because you can't be punished after you've ceased to exist. Those humans who cohabit with the devil and his followers in hell will be destroyed but still will be aware of their own destruction.

Explaining the terrible fate of lost sinners, Jesus spoke to Jews who already understood from their ancient writings that there was an eternal place of suffering for the wicked. Jesus didn't refute this impression; we would expect him to, if it weren't true. The New Testament writers could have denied it as well, but they consistently describe hell as a final and everlasting state of torment for those who will not repent. We don't need further confirmation of hell's reality, and we aren't given the option of changing the Scriptures or the intents of these passages.

God's Justice and Patience

Despite the Bible's clear affirmation and descriptions of hell, many Christians have wrestled with the seeming contradiction between God's perfect love and the sheer awfulness of never-ending torment. Isn't God gracious and compassionate? If he can't tolerate sinful humans, why not just incinerate them? Their sins lasted a lifetime; everlasting punitive measures seem like overkill.

Only the most hardhearted or self-righteous people wouldn't struggle over these tough questions. If hell were an easier doctrine, biblical scholars wouldn't be wrangling over its meaning and searching for other explanations. How *can* we resolve the daunting issue of God's justice for wicked and unrepentant persons?

Justice: Fair Is Fair

We all want what's "fair." The younger child gravitates toward fairness when his older sister gets the larger piece of cake. Not fair? She gets punished for not cleaning her room, while he can leave his toys strewn around the living room. Not fair. Each of us sees justice in terms of our own perceived best interests.

How can we judge what's fair or unfair in terms of sin? We can't, and that isn't our job. Furthermore, we humans will always under-estimate the grievousness of sin and fail to see that the seemingly smallest act can have serious consequences. And the seriousness of the result is not always related to the intent.

Our own justice system requires payment for crimes, and God is an infinitely better judge than we are. How could annihilation pay for years of wickedness or a lifetime spent rejecting Christ? That would be a reward. Think about Adolf Hitler, a man responsible for the deaths of *millions*. In 1945, Hitler swallowed a cyanide capsule and shot himself in the head; annihilationism says that was the end for him (no consequences). Even with our limited sense of justice, *that* doesn't seem fair.

Ancient Perspective on God's Justice

In biblical times, people didn't spend a lot of energy debating injustice regarding the wicked. The concern of prophets like Jonah and Habakkuk was in fact just the opposite: Why does God apparently allow people to keep getting away with evil deeds? Why is he so patient? Why doesn't he punish them immediately? In that mindset, God's judgment didn't cause moral dilemmas—it solved them!⁹ The gods of Greek and Roman mythology, modeled after human weaknesses, were capricious and spiteful; the theistic God is perfect *and* just.

You may be familiar with Rabbi Harold Kushner's *When Bad Things Happen to Good People*, the very title of which raises many questions. We find it upsetting when calamity befalls those who don't deserve it. But equally perplexing is why *good* things happen to *bad* people. That alone might be justification for hell.

Persecuted Christians of the first century and beyond had a different take on New Testament statements about God's judgment than we do today.¹⁰ Paul wrote to the new believers in the Macedonian city of Thessalonica, who were experiencing persecution for their faith:

> God is just: He will pay back trouble to those who trouble you and give relief to you who are troubled. . . . This will happen when the Lord Jesus is revealed from heaven in blazing fire with his powerful angels. He will punish those who do not know God and do not obey the gospel of our Lord Jesus. They will be punished with everlasting destruction and shut out from the presence of the Lord.¹¹

This sounds excessively harsh to most of us. But these people had the concern of the prophets: Why is God so patient with those who hate him? What's taking him so long? Paul's words encourage and give strength to persevere in the faith, to have confidence that God certainly will take care of evil—and evildoers.

Peter, a trusted friend of Jesus, wrote, "The Lord knows how to rescue godly men from trials and to hold the unrighteous for the day of judgment."¹² He wasn't saying God is vindictive but that God is *just*. Those who mock him and persecute his people will receive their due punishment.

Eat, Drink, and Be Merry?

What if God didn't exact judgment upon sin after death? If he annihilates the wicked—vaporizes unrepentant sinners into oblivion—then it's true that "nothing is better for a man under the sun than to eat and drink and be glad."¹³

Conversely, God says to such a careless person, "You fool! This very night your life will be demanded from you."¹⁴ Such a man's existence *won't* end with death; his soul will live on to be judged for his commitment to falsehood and repaid for his rejection of God. Jesus also says, "What good is it for a man to gain the whole world, yet forfeit his soul?"[15] If unrepentant people are annihilated after death, why *not* attempt to "gain the whole world"—there would be nothing to lose. Likewise, Hebrews refutes annihilationism in warning that "it is a dreadful thing to fall into the hands of the living God" after death.[16]

Sam Mikolaski, a Baptist minister and professor of theology, graphically sums up the rightness of God's perfect judgment: "Unless God is angry with sin, let us put a bullet in our collective brain, for the universe is mad."[17]

The annihilationist view of death and hell doesn't solve the dilemma of God's justice; rather, it redefines justice by human standards. This is compatible with our twenty-first century "tolerance" obsession and our fervent desire to explain God so as to render him tame and approachable. Nonetheless, annihilationism is inconsistent with reality.

Trying to Grasp Eternity

One of our greatest difficulties in contemplating hell is that it lasts forever. How can we comprehend a tormented, tortured existence with no end and no resolution, where time is meaningless?

My daughter Josie used to ask me a certain question frequently, late at night, in those before-I-go-to-sleep conversations. She'd say, "Dad, how long is forever? I just can't understand forever. How long is it?" I wasn't sure how to answer, except to say, "I don't know. It's just that—forever."

Human beings, caught up in time, can't truly fathom anything without beginning or end. But Jesus clearly says there is eternal existence for all: The wicked "will go away to eternal punishment, but the righteous to eternal life."[18]

Despite our inability to grasp the concept of never-ending anguish, none of us seems to have the same problem pondering never-ending joy. It's easy for universalists to postulate an all-inclusive, everlasting heaven. And it's easy for annihilationists to imagine an utter end of being for those who reject God. Hell stands for everything our culture would like to reject:

- Human beings are sinful.
- God is holy and just.
- Sin must be paid for.
- Only Jesus paid the price for sin, and nothing else will work.
- We must accept Christ's atoning sacrifice.
- If we don't, we must pay the penalty ourselves, outside of Christ.

Several New Testament writers speak about this penalty; it *is* eternally real. Jesus himself is the chief spokesperson for the doctrine of hell. You can't reject his teaching on hell without rejecting his other words and, ultimately, his authority.

C. S. Lewis said,

> There is no doctrine which I would more willingly remove from Christianity than this [hell], if it lay in my power. But it has the full support of Scripture and specially of our Lord's own words.[19]

While we all agree with this reservation, we are compelled—if we are consistent—to accept also this conclusion.

Lewis struggled with God for many years before he "gave in and admitted that God was God, and knelt and prayed."[20] He concluded,

> There are only two kinds of people in the end: those who say to God, "Thy will be done," and those to whom God says, in the end, "Thy will be done." All that are in hell, choose it.[21]

The good news about hell is this: It wasn't intended for you, and you weren't intended for it. You don't have to go there. Choose otherwise.

19

The Celestial Waiting Room

Is Purgatory Really a Stopover on the Way to Heaven?

If I have to spend time in purgatory before going to one place or the other, I guess I'll be all right as long as there's a lending library.

Stephen King

Most of us have chuckled at jokes involving someone who arrives at the Pearly Gates and meets St. Peter. This one is updated for our technological age.

When Sue finds herself at heaven's gates, she is surprised to find not Peter but a lone computer terminal. On the screen are the words "Welcome to *www.heaven.com*," with instructions to enter User ID and Password. Sue suddenly feels panicked—she has neither. But she's comforted to see "Forgot your ID or Password? Click here." She follows the instruction.

Then new requirements appear: "Please enter your name, date of birth, and date of death." When Sue complies, another message appears: "Sorry, no match found in database. Would you like to register with us?" Delighted that she has an option to correct this obvious error, she quickly clicks "Yes."

To her disappointment, though, an exhaustive form now appears with dozens of questions to answer. Although exasperated, she complies, meticulously handling each inquiry. At last, she finishes and clicks "Submit."

To Sue's horror, the screen reads: "Service temporarily unavailable. Please try again later."

She notices a "Back" button and with great hope, clicks on it.

But the new page says, "Welcome to *www.purgatory.com*. Please enter your User ID and Password."

That little (very little) attempt at humor aside, this chapter explores some serious questions about the in-between place most often called *purgatory:* Is there any other option besides heaven and hell? Are there second chances? Is there an opportunity, after death, to try to get it right?

Again, most people believe in the afterlife. In fact, 74 percent of Americans believe in life after death, though only 59 percent believe in hell.[1] Apparently, many people have other options in mind.

What Is Purgatory?

The short answer is: Purgatory is where one is cleansed or purged (hence the name). *Purgatory* is the noun describing a place; *purging* is the verb describing what happens there. According to this view, upon the death of someone who should not go to hell but isn't yet ready for heaven, she goes for a time to face moderate punishment in which sins are "burned away" or cleansed.

Let's look at where the idea of purgatory comes from: it starts with a brief history of Protestants and Catholics. A significant schism, Split #1, occurred within Christianity in 1054, when an East-West eruption resulted in the (Eastern) Orthodox Church and the (Western) Roman Catholic Church.

It's Split #2 that's important for our present discussion. One of Western (i.e., the Western Hemisphere) Christianity's most significant divisions occurred in 1517, with the start of the Protestant Reformation. After that, we see two distinct streams: Catholic and Protestant. Catholics trace their historical and ecclesiastical ("churchy") beginnings to Jesus and his first followers, with slow but continual developments of tradition. Protestants contend their beliefs and teachings are rooted squarely with Jesus and the New Testament accounts.[2]

On major issues—regarding such matters as Christ's divinity, death, and resurrection—the groups agree. In fact, all three (including the Eastern

Christian Church History

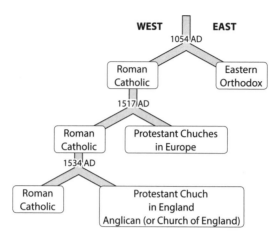

Orthodox) affirm many foundational aspects regarding Jesus. However, there are several key issues upon which Protestants and Catholics differ, and purgatory is one of them. To most Protestants, at death one goes to heaven or hell. To most Catholics, one might go to heaven or hell or purgatory.[3]

This gulf is demonstrated in two quotes; the first from a Catholic, the second from a Protestant:

- "We absolutely believed in Heaven and Hell, Purgatory and even Limbo. I mean, they were actually closer to us than
- Australia or Canada, that they were real places" (Irish author John McGahern).[4]
- "If I were a Roman Catholic, I should turn a heretic, in sheer desperation, because I would rather go to heaven than go to purgatory" (British preacher Charles Spurgeon).[5]

Can't We All Just Get Along?

Thankfully, for the sake of peace and harmony, many if not most Catholics and Protestants today have agreed to focus on their commonalities rather than their discrepancies. Despite this effort, however, there do remain a few significant differences—one involving the Bible. Protestant Bibles have sixty-six books, while the Catholic Bible includes thirteen additional books.[6]

Protestants argue that the Jewish faith (which regards the Old Testament as sacred) has never regarded the thirteen "extra" books as authentically God-inspired so as to be considered part of Scripture. Further, it was not until 1548 that Catholics officially regarded the Apocrypha (which means "hidden" or "secret") as being part of God's Word. Perhaps most important to Protestants is that the apocryphal books are never quoted in the New Testament, an indicator of their non-canonicity.

Our focus is not to resolve the validity of disputed texts (many books have been written on that subject). Simply note that Catholics and Protestants have disparate takes on this issue. This is vital for understanding the disparity in views regarding purgatory.

Why the Maccabees Matter

In the Catholic Bible are two books called 1 Maccabees and 2 Maccabees, and the latter contains a story of a Jewish hero named Judas Maccabeus, the leader of an uprising (c. 165 BC) named the Maccabean revolt in his honor. A highly acclaimed soldier, he's in the "Warrior Hall of Fame" alongside such luminaries as Joshua, Gideon, and David. On one occasion, Judas Maccabeus was in a fierce battle with a particularly high casualty rate.

> On the following day, since the task had now become urgent, Judas and his men went to gather up the bodies of the slain and bury them with their kinsmen in their ancestral tombs.
>
> But under the tunic of each of the dead they found amulets sacred to the idols of Jamnia, which the law forbids the Jews to wear. So it was clear to all that this was why these men had been slain.
>
> They all therefore praised the ways of the Lord, the just judge who brings to light the things that are hidden.
>
> Turning to supplication, they prayed that the sinful deed might be fully blotted out. The noble Judas warned the soldiers to keep themselves free from sin, for they had seen with their own eyes what had happened because of the sin of those who had fallen.
>
> He then took up a collection among all his soldiers, amounting to two thousand silver drachmas, which he sent to Jerusalem to provide for an expiatory sacrifice. In doing this he acted in a very excellent and noble way, inasmuch as he had the resurrection of the dead in view; for if he were not expecting the fallen to rise again, it would have been useless and foolish to pray for them in death.

But if he did this with a view to the splendid reward that awaits those who had gone to rest in godliness, it was a holy and pious thought.

Thus he made atonement for the dead that they might be freed from this sin.[7]

Why is this passage important? Because it indicates that (1) the living did something intended to impact those who were already dead, and (2) the dead were in a place where they could still be freed from their sin. This seemingly points to an impermanent place one can go after death. In other words, one can die, go somewhere other than hell, and later ascend to heaven.

Here's the crux of the matter with belief or disbelief in purgatory: This story is found in a text considered insufficiently reliable for biblical inclusion by the Jews and by the early Christians. Also, a place or stage called *purgatory* is not mentioned in the passage. Judas and his companions attempt to atone for the sins of the fallen by offering sacrifices, but there is no forthright explanation that this is to get them out of a purgatorial condition.

There's another issue too: Roman Catholics distinguish between venial (forgivable) and mortal sins. *Mortal* means "death," indicating a sin so egregious that it causes an irreparable rupture in one's relationship with God; by contrast, venial sins are burned away by purgatory. In the account involving the dead soldiers, what was their sin? Each possessed an idol. This is, by Catholic doctrine, a mortal sin, the type purgatory cannot cleanse. Standard Catholic belief underscores the seriousness of mortal sin, believing that, minus the act of penance, a person goes directly to hell. This is the only text in the Catholic Bible that might reference purgatory, yet it does not teach the doctrine of purgatory.

Protestants and Purgatory

A tiny Protestant minority has affirmed purgatory or its equivalent. Surely the best known pro-purgatory comments are from C. S. Lewis.

Our souls demand Purgatory, don't they? Would it not break the heart if God said to us, "It is true, my son, that your breath smells and your rags drip with mud and slime, but we are charitable here and no one will upbraid you with these things, nor draw away from you. Enter into the joy"? Should we not reply, "With submission, sir, and if there is no objection, I'd rather be cleaned first." "It may hurt, you know"—"Even so, sir."

My favorite image on this matter comes from the dentist's chair. I hope that when the tooth of life is drawn and I am "coming round," a voice will say, "Rinse your mouth out with this." This will be Purgatory. The rinsing may take longer than I can now imagine. The taste of this may be more fiery and astringent than my present sensibility could endure. But . . . it will [not] be disgusting and unhallowed.[8]

Other pro-purgatory Protestants include Jerry Walls, formerly a professor at a major evangelical theological seminary. Walls argues for a type of purgatory based in part on the reality that "Christians are imperfect lovers of God and others at the time of their death."[9]

Biblical Backing?

The primary Protestant contention is that purgatory is not in Scripture. To this, Catholics respond that neither are many accepted theological terms or concepts—say, *Trinity* or *incarnation*. Catholic theologians argue that the *concept* is present in the Scriptures, even if the *word* is not.

Pro-purgatory Christians also cite Christ's words that one's sins will be forgiven "either in this age or in the age to come,"[10] which they consider to be a clear purgatory reference. Protestants insist this actually is an affirmation that forgiveness (or the refusal of forgiveness) impacts one's life now and in eternity.

Another statement used in support of purgatory is in Paul's first letter to the believers in Corinth:

[A man's] work will be shown for what it is, because the Day will bring it to light. It will be revealed with fire, and the fire will test the quality of each man's work. If what he has built survives, he will receive his reward. If it is burned up, he will suffer loss; he himself will be saved, but only as one escaping through the flames.[11]

Protestants insist that Paul is not talking about cleansing sins after death but about a loss of rewards that comes at the judgment seat of Christ.

So if purgatory isn't explicitly in the Bible, how did the concept become so rooted within Catholic theology?

204

Scripture and Tradition

Herein lies one key difference between Protestants and Catholics: The former affirm the Bible as the sole authoritative source of truth, while the latter affirm Scripture and "tradition." In other words, "official" church history has equal authority with the Bible.[12] If a pope or a church council affirms purgatory, then purgatory is considered to be real (unless another pope or church council changes the course).

Catholics also argue that there are examples, by way of the Jewish faith (which forms the foundation for Christianity), where praying for the dead would presume a temporary or purgatory-like place. And some early Christians in the first centuries after Jesus did indeed pray for the dead.

The concept of purgatory became more widespread and highly developed under the sixth-century leadership of Gregory the Great. Citing the "age to come" reference in Matthew, Gregory wrote:

> As for certain lesser faults, we must believe that, before the Final Judgment, there is a purifying fire. He who is truth says that whoever utters blasphemy against the Holy Spirit will be pardoned neither in this age nor in the age to come. From this sentence we understand that certain offenses can be forgiven in this age, but certain others in the age to come.[13]

Gregory did not view purgatory as a second chance for unrepentant sinners but rather as a place for Christ-followers to get rid of the stain of sinful nature and/or for those who are guilty due to ignorance of truth. Regardless of Gregory's "greatness," though—and he was profoundly influential, well beyond this concept—most Protestants believe purgatory cannot be biblically validated.

With the passage of time, teaching about purgatory lent itself to tragic abuses. Commonly recalled is the manipulation of naïve and unschooled peasants by unethical priests, who collected fees allegedly to get people's relatives out of purgatory sooner if adequate fees were paid. The split between Protestants and Catholics historically traces to Martin Luther's reaction to a sixteenth-century monk, Johann Tetzel, who offered chances to buy, for cash, deceased relatives an earlier escape from purgatory.[14]

How Long Is the Wait?

All of us have found ourselves sitting in a crowded waiting room or standing in a serpentine line at the bank—we check our watch and think, *Wow, how long is this going to take?* The same question comes to mind when we consider purgatory: How long must people stay in the "celestial waiting room"?

The answer is, "It depends." It depends on what *you* do. And it depends on what *others* do for you. And there is the rub. Notice the you-centeredness of the answer. The most correct response to "How long in purgatory?" depends on:

(1) the number of one's sins;
(2) the deliberateness with which those sins were committed;
(3) the penance performed for those sins;
(4) the actions (accelerating the "purging") of the living for the dead.[15]

To most Protestants, this seems a tragic distraction. The concept of purgatory ultimately robs us of the sufficiency of the cross. The real response to the problem of human sin must always be that *I cannot do anything to erase it.* In all honesty, we are powerless to eradicate it. But the breathtaking answer to human sin is that Jesus *can* take care of it. And he *did.*

Posted over the cross of Christ should be a sign reading, "I did this for you, because you cannot do it for yourself. I set you free—from your sin. No stopover in purgatory needed. Embrace what I did, and go straight to heaven."

Three Guiding Words

A point made earlier bears repeating: Catholics and Protestants by and large have chosen to focus on similarities instead of differences. I have many dear Catholic friends whom I deeply respect and whose faith I admire.[16] We simply differ on the issue of purgatory.

To me, the strongest argument against purgatory is something beyond the presence or absence of the word or concept in the Bible. It has to do with the epicenter of our faith: the death of Jesus. The most fundamental teaching of historic Christianity is the fact that Christ's death cancels out the result of sin in the hearts and lives of those who by faith embrace the Savior. Jesus took the responsibility for our sins upon himself. His death, so many years ago, was given to handle whatever purgatory supposedly is meant to purge.

Let's focus on three words: *assigned, actual,* and *accomplished.* When one chooses to accept that Jesus' death truly does have relevance to one's life—now, here, today—then he has what would be called *assigned* righteousness. In other words, God in his mercy *assigns* the goodness of Christ to him. We are not righteous. However, God assigns it to us, entirely by grace, without merit. Why? Because he loves us and because we have responded to him with loving faith.

That's only the beginning. As an individual continues to grow in spiritual maturity, in her understanding of biblical truth and its application to holy living, there is more than just assignment; she begins to demonstrate *actual* righteousness. She begins to act, think, and speak more like Jesus. This is tremendously encouraging, this practical realization of personal progress.

At the same time, the holier one's life, the more she becomes attuned to God's pure holiness. With this comes awareness of one's failures, even in the midst of personal improvements. We become aware of how far we are from the perfection of Christ, the type of perfection that would merit heaven.

Here we become aware of our need for *accomplished* righteousness or purity. Only persons with complete righteousness would ever enter heaven.

In more common terminology, these phases (*assigned, actual,* and *accomplished*) are referred to as "initial salvation" (justification) on-going "sanctification," and then, at death, "glorification." Viewed as a timeline:

Righteousness

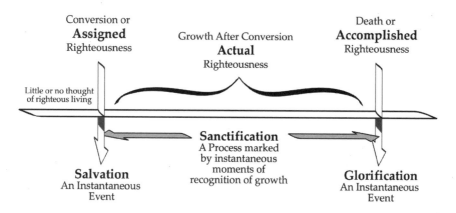

207

And that's what happens at death. Once again, purgatory isn't needed.

Paul says absence from the body means to be at home with the Lord.[17] Leaving this life is being immediately with Christ.[18] Not even a hint of purgatory.

His enthusiasm for an instant post-death reunion with Jesus is compelling. If one faces death having accepted the reality of Christ's accomplishment on the cross, then a spectacular reunion awaits. Not later, but sooner.

The well-known Monopoly card says "Do not pass Go. Do not collect $200." In effect, Christ's work seems to say, "Do not go to purgatory. No need." His sacrifice in effect allows you—each of us—to receive a card that says "No purgatory. Go directly to heaven."

20

Recycling Plan

*If Millions of People Believe in Reincarnation,
Could There Be Something to It?*

Reincarnation is making a comeback.

Bumper sticker

Julius Caesar was one frustrated general. He was battling the fearless Celts, who were more courageous than any force he had encountered. His difficulties were rooted in the staunch Celtic belief in reincarnation—that "souls do not become extinct, but pass after death from one body to another."[1]

The soul of a soldier killed in battle would move on to inhabit another body. This assurance of an endless cycle of life presented no small problem for a military leader.

But the Celts were not alone in believing one could return to earthly life, and several religious groups today uphold reincarnation: Hindus, Buddhists, and Sikhs, for example, along with some smaller sects and an assortment of New Age groups. Differences emerge quickly: Some contend that souls were created by a "god-force," while others argue that the soul has its own intrinsic being—a preexistence.[2]

At its core, reincarnation is "the belief that a living being . . . after cessation of existence on earth, will experience a new birth and enter existence again in the form of another being." In some variations rebirth applies only to human beings. Jack London, author of *Call of the Wild* as well as a reincarnation classic called *The Star Rover*, wrote,

> I did not begin when I was born, nor when I was conceived. I have been growing, developing, through incalculable myriads of millenniums. All my previous selves have their voices, echoes, promptings in me. Oh, incalculable times again shall I be born.[3]

Reincarnation is based on two assumptions: First, time is cyclical—sometimes termed "timelessness"—therefore, whatever happens will happen again. Second, the class of a given birth depends on the deeds of the previous life.[4] This is called *karma*, viewed essentially as a law of cause and effect, echoing collectively through an ongoing series of lives, rebirths, and deaths.

Reincarnation is an ancient concept, certainly dating to before the incarnation,[5] with roots in the Hindu Vedas (scriptures). Most other reincarnation forms—for instance, Buddhist (half of all Buddhists live in China, Japan, and Thailand) and Jainist or Sikh (both mainly in India)—spring from this common source. There is some tracing of the teaching to Greek philosophy as well. Reincarnation's more Western expressions, such as Transcendental Meditation, also find their source in Hinduism.

It's not a biblical notion, but reincarnation has enjoyed increasing popularity as Eastern and New Age religions have become chic. Wide acceptance in the U.S. has been furthered by personalities like Edgar Cayce, Jeanne Dixon, and Shirley MacLaine; other well-known fans have included Henry Ford, George Patton, Salvador Dali, Mark Twain, George Harrison, John Denver, and Deepak Chopra. Consider these statistics:

- 92 percent of Americans believe in God
- 85 percent believe in heaven
- 82 percent believe in miracles
- 71 percent believe in the devil's existence (up from 63 percent in 1997)
- 34 percent believe in ghosts
- 29 percent accept astrological forecasts
- 25 percent believe in reincarnation[6]

At first glance, 25 percent may not seem like a high rate of belief, compared to the other categories. Yet in some surveys as many as 83 percent of Americans claim to be Christian.[7] Since we'll later see that the Bible denies reincarnation, it's remarkable that one in four Americans affirm it.

Why is the concept of rebirth so embraced? Its appeal lies partly in the promise of having multiple opportunities to "get it right." Renowned botanist Luther Burbank spoke glowingly in this regard:

> The theory of Reincarnation . . . is one of the most sensible and satisfying of all religions that mankind has conceived. This, like the others, comes from the best qualities of human nature, even if . . . its adherents sometimes fail to carry out the principles in their lives.[8]

Evidence for Reincarnation

One of America's best-known reincarnation scholars is Ian Stevenson, a psychiatrist whose long career focused on children between ages two and five who purportedly were able to recall vivid details from past lives.[9] Stevenson's extensive academic articles covered more than three thousand study cases, and many people have claimed he proved reincarnation conclusively.[10]

His research is so extensive and technical that it's helpful to read what others have said.[11] The suggested evidence for reincarnation fits into several categories:

- Memories of previous lives
- Xenoglossy, the ability to speak a language one does not know
- Presence of birthmarks or physical deformities matching a deceased person
- Personation—full identification of the living person with the deceased person's identity
- The Bible's supposed affirmation of reincarnation (we'll come back to this).[12]

Although Stevenson's work seemed to support the possibility, he was careful to refer to it as "suggestive of reincarnation."[13] Do the cases studied by such a distinguished scholar really confirm such rebirth? *Not* conclusively, he thought. He provided an alternative, one he claimed should be taken seriously: "Possession of the living by a foreign spirit."[14] This can't be overstated: *One of the world's top research scientists in the field acknowledged that a foreign spirit could occupy a living person.*

Gary Habermas,[15] a Christian scholar, is quick to caution that Stevenson is not suggesting *demonic* possession. Instead, Stevenson is explaining the phenomenon as possession by the disembodied "spirit of the actual person who had previously died."[16]

Stevenson himself acknowledges that "the distinction between reincarnation and possession becomes blurred."[17] Here is how he defines the terms:

. . . if the previous personality seems to associate itself with the physical organism at the time of conception or during embryonic development we speak of *reincarnation*; if the association between previous personality and physical organism only comes later, we speak of *possession*.[18]

It's possible that what we think of as reincarnation is really a foreign spirit taking hold of, or possessing, a living person. This causes the person to *think* he or she was someone else in a previous life. Habermas observes:

Researchers and theorists have not proved that these cases demand reincarnation. . . . There are several cases where either discarnate or demonic possession serves as the best explanation and seems to be accepted as such by most researchers, including Stevenson himself.[19]

Sometimes the deceased person (supposedly reincarnated) died *after* the birth of the individual who was later influenced. This sequence dispels any notion of "I died" and then "I was reborn." The timing is simply off. As Stevenson says, "No matter how you look at it, reincarnation gets the short end of the evidential stick."[20]

Xenoglossy, or speaking a previously unlearned language, can be accounted for by possession, so it doesn't constitute solid evidence for reincarnation. Neither does sharing birthmarks or a physical defect with a dead person. Stevenson cites mystics who sometimes develop stigmata, or wounds corresponding to those suffered by Jesus on the cross. Having those wounds does not make them reincarnations of Jesus. Similarity does not prove sameness.[21]

The Bible doesn't teach reincarnation; it affirms the reality of demonic influence and warns against "familiar spirits,"[22] demons who pose as someone with whom you are familiar, perhaps a deceased spouse or parent. They are *not* deceased loved ones but rather spirits under Satan's direction. Scripture says to have nothing to do with them.

You may recall that in a previous chapter we stated that although one should never seek to communicate with the dead, a bereaved person might sense the presence or even witness the appearance of a deceased loved one. Does that contradict this warning regarding "familiar spirits"? No, it doesn't. Being aware of the presence of a loved one, which provides comfort and solace, is considerably different from *deliberately seeking* information from the dead. Demons do not comfort—they attempt to deceive. It is in the seeking of information that one becomes prone to error and vulnerable to deception.

Do not confuse soliciting information from spirits—which is dangerous and to be avoided—with the God-provided solace from the sensed presence of a deceased loved one.

Habermas concludes:

> Reincarnation has no real data in its favor. . . . Reincarnation simply does not offer any true or distinctive answer to the nature of life after death.
>
> It is certainly debatable if any case of reincarnation could ever be proven, due to the possibility that possession could also account for pre-birth examples of a spirit's entering another's body.
>
> . . . Even if there is no evidence for reincarnation, our discussion still produced another sort of consideration in favor of an afterlife. Since there is evidence for possession of a body by another spirit, this would appear to constitute some "back door" data in favor of a spiritual world of some sort where life after death is distinctly possible, if not likely.[23]

Can Reincarnation and Christianity Coexist?

Advocates say reincarnation is in complete harmony with the spirit of Christianity. They claim it was taught in the days after Jesus until some began to suppress it in the sixth century. Leslie Weatherhead, pastor of London's City Temple for more than thirty years, contended that since reincarnation was the prevailing belief during the time of Jesus, and he never denied it, then he must have accepted it.[24]

Reincarnationists claim sound biblical support for their beliefs. The most commonly cited verses are:

- John 3:3, in which Jesus urges Nicodemus to be born again (interpreted as a reference to the capacities for additional lives)
- Matthew 11:13–14, in which Jesus seems to say John the Baptist was Elijah (seen as evidence of reincarnation)
- Hebrews 7:1–3, in which the writer appears to be saying Jesus had a previous life in the person of Melchizedek
- John 9:2, in which the disciples ask Jesus if a man was born blind due to sin (implying they believed in karma)

Do these Scriptures show that the Bible teaches reincarnation? In the John 3 passage, Nicodemus was bewildered by Jesus' reference to a second birth. Jesus made it clear this birth was spiritual, not physical. If Jesus believed in reincarnation, this would have been the time to teach it. Instead, he refuted it.[25]

Matthew 11:14 is equally mishandled. Reincarnationists fail to note that John himself denied he was Elijah. When asked, "Are you Elijah?" he said, "I am not." He stated flatly that he was not "the Prophet."[26]

Jesus' clear explanation that John would come "in the spirit and power of Elijah"[27] means John would be *like* him. Elijah was taken to heaven without undergoing a normal physical death,[28] which is necessary for the life-death-rebirth cycle. When he made an appearance with Moses at the Mount of Transfiguration,[29] Elijah appeared as himself, not as someone who had been reborn in another body. (Likewise, Hebrews 7:2–3 clearly says Melchizedek was *like* Jesus, not that he *was* Jesus.)

Of John 9:1–3, reincarnationists claim, "They [the disciples] were among the most knowledgeable men of Christian doctrine . . . because they got it straight from the Master; and yet these learned men asked if the man was born blind because of a previous sin."[30] However, Jesus' explanation plainly refuted any law of karma.

Is reincarnation taught in the Bible? Again, no, but let's take the question a step further. Does the Bible straightforwardly teach that reincarnation is false?

James, half brother of Jesus, certainly would have been one to know what Jesus taught. He wrote that one's life is like a mist that appears for a little while and then vanishes.[31] Had he believed in reincarnation, James might have written that life is like a persistent fog that never lifts! Hebrews says, "Man is destined to die once, and after that to face judgment,"[32] which again reinforces that death comes only once.

Can one be an authentic believer in both the Bible and in reincarnation? Since we've seen that they aren't compatible, the answer is no.

The Big Picture

To comprehend the most significant difference between Christianity and reincarnation, we need to first grasp the terms *monism* and *pantheism*.

Monism holds that "all is one," that everything that exists is one. Pantheism says, "All is one, one is all, all is god." *Pantheistic monism* affirms that everything—all the created order—is god and is one with god. There is no personal God who is separate from his creation, and this is part of the reincarnationist paradigm. A pantheistic monist wouldn't say, "In the beginning God created the heavens and the earth."[33]

In sharp contrast, the *monotheistic* ("one God") faiths—Christianity, Judaism, Islam—reject pantheistic monism and affirm two distinct entities: (1) a personal Creator God, and (2) everything else, which He created.

Eastern and New Age religions are largely monist, believing in a type of all-encompassing godlike force. Reincarnation involves three cycles: first, living things die; then, based on their state of mind at death (e.g., positive or negative), they experience a deep, drugged sleep; then, they are reborn.[34] Reincarnation supposedly is impacted only by the good or bad karma of the previous life or lives.

Reincarnational View of History: Cyclical

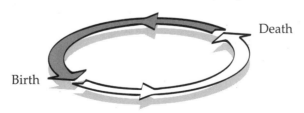

Death

Birth

A Simplistic Biblical View of History: Linear

This cyclical portrayal is antithetical to Scripture's linear, upward historical movement toward an end-of-time crescendo: starting point ("In the beginning"); unfolding storyline (God's intervention in human affairs and his coming to earth in the person of Jesus); and end, or climax (the ultimate, final destiny of all humans).

Of course, in some ways history is bound to repeat itself. Picture the line, then, as always moving upward toward an end yet not on a two-dimensional, flat surface—more like a spiral. Think of the wire in a spiral notebook. While it comes back around to a point similar to where it was one cycle ago, it's truly not at the same place and it's closer to the top. Such is history: It may feel like "everything is the same," but it isn't. With each passing moment, we are moving closer to what Scripture calls the "great day of the Lord,"[35] the culmination of history, when time as we know it will be no more.

A Complete Biblical View of History: Spiral

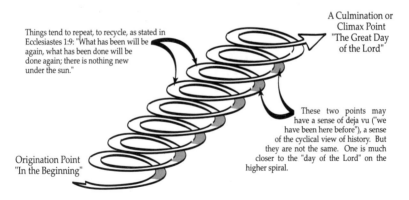

Based on the biblical view of God, an understanding of his involvement in creating the cosmos, his personal involvement in our lives, and his nudging history toward closure, we see that Christian faith and reincarnation are mutually exclusive.

Belief in reincarnation means saying "no, thanks" to a loving, tender, heavenly Father. Monism says *you* are god and god is *you*, but we humans were created to need someone bigger, greater, better, and stronger than we are. We need the one God, who loves us, cares about us, and wants us— *created* us—to belong to him.

Part Six

Confident Before the King

21

Forever and Ever, Amen

God Wants You to Be Comfortable With Him in This World and the Next

> Time is short. Eternity is long. It is only reasonable that this short life be lived in the light of eternity.
>
> Charles Spurgeon

Years ago the speaker at my brother's funeral said, "The older we get, the more we realize that fewer and fewer things are truly important."

In reality, life is like a funnel. When we're young we think everything is significant. In our thirties, we discover that much less is crucial. At fifty, the "really important things" have greatly reduced in number. This continues in our seventies, eighties, and beyond.

If only a few things make a difference when we end this life, how about living for those things *now*, no matter where you are in the age continuum?

What will matter when you take your last breath? Only one thing: that you are ready to meet God. How about learning to know and enjoy him *now*, so the crossover won't be such a jolt?

When I was in high school, my pastor asked me unexpectedly, "Jim, are you ready to die?"

"I dunno," I muttered, taken aback by his abruptness.

"Because," he continued, "you aren't ready to live till you're ready to die."

At the time I thought maybe he was just posing the kind of soul-searching dilemma pastors are supposed to bring. But I've never forgotten that question, and I've realized the wisdom contained in it.

I decided I wanted to be ready to die. How about you? Are you ready?

We've explored some fascinating territory: NDEs, heaven, hell, ghosts, angels, demons, and much more. All this material could be *theoretical* or even *theological*, but nonetheless it should be highly *personal* and *practical*. Each of us one day will cross over from here to the afterlife. Becoming clear about there and then will greatly influence how we live here and now.

Characterizing the Creator

There are lots of perceptions about God: powerful . . . mean . . . loving . . . preoccupied. Many see him as perpetually angry, scowling, condemning their every move. Others see him as a syrupy celestial Santa, handing out gifts and affirming everything. If what the Bible says is true, neither is accurate.

The latest Harris poll reveals that 80 percent of adult Americans believe in God, which represents no statistical change over the previous three years. However, barely a majority of adults believe *all or most* of the Old Testament (55 percent) and the New Testament (54 percent) are the Word of God. Only 37 percent (Old Testament) and 36 percent (New Testament) believe *all* of these texts are God's Word.[1] Apparently, many aren't sure they can have confidence in the Bible.

Let me pose a critical question: What's the most credible source for knowing about God? The Bible? Islam's Qur'an? Hinduism's Bhagavad Gita? Buddhism's Buddhavacana? *Bruce Almighty*? Whatever book Oprah Winfrey endorses? *Touched by an Angel*? Deepak Chopra? How do we know about God? How are we to form our understanding of him?

Deep within, we all long to know that the one true God is knowable. In case you don't already, assume with me for now that the Bible *is* the source for knowing God.

You may ask why, in a book about life hereafter, I'm concluding with a discussion on God's nature. *The afterlife, properly understood, is all about God.* It's about his desire to be with us. It's about the great plans he has for us. It's about the close friendship he's eager to experience with us.

Therein is the question. Just how comfortable are you with God? Allow me to tell you a story—God's story. When we better understand his character and heart, we'll become clearer about his intent for our afterlife—mine and yours.

The Story of God #1: Two Key Words

The first part of the story involves two words. One is the Old Testament Hebrew *chesed* (pronounced *KHEH*-sed, with a hard K, or guttural sound from deep in your throat). The other is the New Testament Greek *agape* (ah-GAW-pay). Both mean "love," or, as we're using them here, "the love of God," which cannot possibly be explained in a few pages. *Chesed* means "unending, unswerving loyalty"; God uses the term to try to convey his fierce loyalty to us.

In order to explain this term, I need to tell you about Joe and Georgette. Joe was consumed with Georgette's beauty. They fell in love. They married. However, when their first child was born, Joe had a sinking feeling. Observing his wife's conduct, he wondered if this really was his child. He watched as other men exchanged glances with her. A second child came. Same question. Then a third. Now there was no doubt. The babies were not Joe's. He was devastated.

Then Georgette abandoned Joe and their young children to become a prostitute. Joe was stunned and crushed. His heart broke as he tried to explain to three sobbing children why Mommy had walked away. As best as he could, he kept alive his heart's dream that someday she would return.

The passage of time was hard on Georgette. The toll taken by prostitution stole her beauty. Fewer and fewer men sought her services. She sank so low in the ranks that she was functioning virtually as a slave. After years of no contact, one day Joe caught a split-second glimpse of her on a crowded street. As his eyes met hers, he still recognized what once had been a breathtakingly beautiful girl.

He'd found her! After negotiating with her pimp, he bought her freedom.

As he led her back to the home she'd once known, he held her hand tenderly. It was the first time a man had treated her kindly since she'd left him. He cherished her as his honored wife. At first she was suspicious, waiting for his wrath. When it never came, she began to receive his affirmation and love.

I didn't make up this story. It actually happened 2,700 years ago. The man's name wasn't Joe but Hosea. The woman's wasn't Georgette but Gomer.

Chesed, used in the book of Hosea, means "love that just will not give up or let go." It's the kind of love Hosea had for Gomer. To Hosea, God says, in essence, "Just as you had love that would not give up on Gomer, even though she was unfaithful, had run away, and lost her beauty, so I will not give up on people who have been unfaithful to me, have run away from me, even if they have messed up everything in their lives." *That is God's commitment to you.*

Agape, used over and over in the New Testament, means love that's spontaneous, lavish, freely given, and undeserved or unwarranted. *That is the love God has for you.*

There's another important dimension to such love: it confers great value on you. That God—the Creator of everything—loves *you* adds enormous value to your life. That's what *agape* truly is. And this word repeatedly conveys how special you really are.

The Story of God #2: He Cried

Jesus is divine; he's God. But if we're not careful we can miss out on his humanness, which is no less important than his divinity. There are perhaps few more distinctly human expressions than tears, and Jesus cried at least twice.

Lazarus was a close friend of Jesus.[2] When news of his life-threatening illness reached him, Jesus delayed coming to his aid. Martha, one of Lazarus's sisters, was thoroughly perturbed that Jesus had waited so long. *Why?* she wondered. Finally, a messenger brought word that Jesus was on the outskirts of Bethany, where Lazarus had already died—crossed over from life to the afterlife.

Martha turned to her sister Mary and said, "Do you want to go meet Jesus?"

"I can't," sobbed Mary, too heartbroken to walk across the little town.

Martha ran to meet him. Coming over the crest of the last small hill, all her other emotions were overcome by resentment. Why had Jesus not made an effort to come earlier? Gruffly, she said, "If you'd come quickly when we sent word, my brother would still be alive."

She was shocked at the abrasiveness of her own tone. Feeling a twinge of guilt, she offered a consolation statement: "But God will give you now what you ask of him." She believed that—at least she wanted to. After all, Lazarus had been dead four days.

"It will be all right. He'll rise again," Jesus responded. His declaration wasn't boastful, and something about how he said it caused her to believe him.

"Yes," she meekly responded, "everyone will rise someday."

"I'm not talking about *someday*," he told her. "I'm telling you I *am* the resurrection." He paused, looked at her eye to eye, and without flinching asked, "Do you believe that?"

She paused, not out of doubt but attempting to understand both his question and her answer. "Yes," she whispered.

Nothing more was spoken then. She ran the short distance back to the house. "Mary, come now! Come, right now! He wants you to come. *Now.*"

The grieving Mary was half-pulled by her sister to Jesus. Trailing them was a score of mourning friends and relatives.

Moments later, she was giving a hug to her good friend. Unaware of Martha's chastisement, she parroted what had been said only moments before: "If you'd been here, Lazarus would have lived." Not answering the accusation a second time, Jesus simply waited. And they awaited his response.

Then his eyes welled with tears. "Where is he?" Barely audible.

Without words, Mary motioned toward the burial cave holding her brother's body. No one spoke in the four minutes it took to get there.

Then the crowd stood still. Exactly what did they expect? Depends on which mourner you asked. But no one expected what occurred next. Jesus just stood there. He did not say a word. And then those gathered heard a sound few had ever heard before—the sound of a man crying.

Men don't like to cry—and certainly not in public. But he cried. Audibly. The sounds were those of a man feeling the loss of a friend, a brother. Standing at a burial site containing the body, along with grieving friends, was too much. As recorded in what would become the Bible's shortest verse, "Jesus wept."[3]

He's human. He feels pain. He feels your humanness, your hurt. *He cares.* And he wants to spend a time called *forever* with you.

The second episode came as the end of Jesus' ministry was approaching. He was coming into the great capital of Jerusalem, always a challenge. A group of hypocrites tried to run the place, theologically speaking. And there was the Sanhedrin, a combination of Harvard elites and a religious supreme court—about seventy of the most nitpicky guys you could ever meet. Then there was Roman interference and oppression. Would the Jews *ever* be free from intruders?

But this trip was different: It would be Jesus' last. He knew. Most others didn't. He'd tried to explain, even to his closest friends. He was the only person who'd been born to die; his *purpose* was dying. This final foray would be "it."

Cresting the hill on the road that would take him to the Mount of Olives on the city's eastside, he tugged slightly on the reins of the small colt he rode. The crowd that had been busy singing and shouting praises noticed something was wrong. They quieted.

He didn't move. The colt, at his bidding, stood motionless. Sensing something significant, everyone froze.

And then they heard it. Barely audible. A sound was coming from Jesus.

One lone figure—or so I picture in my mind—among the crowd dared move, ever so slightly. Amani turned to his younger brother and whispered, "I've heard this before. I know it."

"What is it?" his brother asked.

Amani hesitated to speak the words, but finally they came, so quietly as to be hardly heard. "He's crying. I was there that day—when he came to Bethany. He's crying again."

And he was. Jesus cried over a city, over its people. He saw what could have been. He saw what it had become. The gap was enormous. All the dreams, the hopes . . . but Jerusalem had made its decision. The "city of peace" was just hours from rejecting the only one who could bring peace. Its destruction would come. Soon—in just four decades. The unthinkable—Jerusalem would be destroyed. And Jesus' words about no stone left on another would prove true.[4]

And he was brokenhearted. He wanted to be with them. He wanted to be close to them. The incarnation of God wanted to be with those he had created. And this same One wants to be with you.

The Story of God #3: A Plane Crash, an Adoption, and Cancer

Bob and Bill were my twin brothers, eight years my junior. They were college freshmen in Kansas City when I was a graduate student in New Jersey.

One evening as I left our house with my wife, Carol, I heard the phone ring inside. But as I turned to reenter, I realized I'd locked the door with the keys inside. I stood there helpless and exasperated, knowing I couldn't respond to the caller.

With nothing to be done at the moment, we left with our friends in their car, went to our evening engagement, and returned hours later to climb through a window. Then the phone rang again. Whatever else my father said, I do not now recall. The words I did hear were "Bob has been killed in a plane crash."

Crumpled on the floor, I heard a sound come out of me that I'd never heard before and have not heard since. It was utter, devastating shock and grief escaping my lips. My brother was suddenly dead, along with my cousin Rick and Bob's college roommate, Dave.

The funerals—plural—were excruciating. The sight of three gleaming caskets containing the remains of nineteen-years-olds was overwhelming, first at their college and then as we made our way three and a half hours to North Central Kansas, where nearly a thousand people filled the Concordia High School auditorium. Only eleven months before, Bob had graduated there.

In the days that followed, well-meaning sages waxed philosophic as to reasons for the deaths of three young men. I was well aware of the standard talking points in moments like this. I recalled the rationales I'd read for my sister's death—Janie died before I was born. Loved ones had written poems trying to help my parents through their questions and struggles; they'd only been married two years when this tragedy befell them.

One poem stands out in my mind to this day. It compared my sister to a rose that God, when seeing it, liked so much he simply picked it. Comforting to others, perhaps, but dreadful to me. What kind of God would "pick a rose" just because he liked it, with no thought for the consequences of his action?

With regard to the deaths of Bob, Rick, and Dave, the explanations were more standard fare. The defense of their deaths contained such phrasing as "Well, when you see how many youth came to know God through their funeral, you can see his hand, his plan in it all."

Plan! What kind of plan? If God wanted students to be drawn to him, he didn't need to kill three kids to do it. He could have sent Billy Graham to town! The price seemed too high. I wanted my brother back.

My struggles were not those of a rebellious juvenile. They were the heart renderings of a theology graduate student, one deeply committed to God but profoundly bothered by some of his arch-apologists.

To add insult to injury, I was told I shouldn't ask why. My response: "Why not? Why can't I ask why?"

They said, "That shows your lack of faith."

"Nonsense," I retorted. "The very fact that I'm asking *God* is proof in itself that I have confidence *in him, in God.* If I thought the devil had the power, I'd ask the devil why. But I know *God* has all power. My asking isn't evidence of insufficient faith—it shows I affirm his omnipotence. Asking why *honors* God."

I have always regarded Jesus' disciple Thomas as my hero. Many preachers say he was the doubter. I say he was the questioner. The questions Thomas asked are the exact ones I would have asked.[5]

Vigorous questions asked of God do not bother him. He's secure. He can handle it. *He understands the "Why, why, why—I wanna know why!" cries of his kids.*

In time, I had a realization. What if . . . what if God would somehow tell me the *why* of Bob's death? Would I be satisfied? No. Bob would still be dead.

I realized my key question was not "why?" but "where?" As in, "Where were you? Did you lose control? Could you not stop the plane from going down? Where were your angels that sometimes rescue people in peril?" My questions pertained more to having future confidence than trying to figure out what to do about the past death of a brother. Bottom line: Could I trust God?

About that time, a wise Kansan cowboy from Abeyville named Harv Schmucker called our home. (Harv always said Abeyville was a "poke and plum town"—if you poked your nose around the corner, you was plum out of town.)

My dad answered. Harv said, "I'll bet you wonder where God was when Bob's plane was going down that day, now don't ya?"

"Yes, that has crossed my mind," Dad responded.

"Well," Harv continued, with his distinctive twang, "God the Father was on his throne, in charge, the exact same place he was when *his* son died."

For reasons I cannot fully explain, Harv's brief down-home homily accelerated my healing, or at least moved me from one question to another. It answered the question, "Did you lose control? Could you just not stop it?"

God did not lose control. I'd not been able to answer the why to my satisfaction. And I don't understand why he didn't exercise his control. But deep in my spirit I felt I could believe that God truly *has* control of the world around me. It did not spin out of his hand.

Fast-forward several years to a different life season with different challenges. Carol and I had two adopted children, and we wanted a third. Multiple attempts ended in disappointment, but finally one seemed to be coming through. Our dreams were about to be realized.

Hearing the words "you can come now" caused us to load up our two children and drive several hundred miles to see our just-born baby girl.

Arriving the next day in a town we'd never visited, we entered the doctor's office expectantly. One glance at the nurse in the waiting room told us something was wrong. My attempt to pry information failed. Stone-faced, she escorted us to a private room. Our excitement evaporated instantly.

Finally the doctor came with the dreaded words, "There's been a problem." Cutting to the chase, the teenage birth mother who'd said "tell them to come, the baby is theirs" had changed her mind moments before we got there.

The doctor and nurses were as apologetic as possible. They seemed to fully empathize with our disappointment. We knew we would never meet "Melissa," the baby girl with a name we'd already chosen.

Then we had the long drive home. I called ahead and asked people from our church to go into our Dallas-area house, dismantle the crib, and remove all the baby items assembled in anticipation of our joyous homecoming.

That drive seemed far longer than the outbound trip. Deep into the night I drove, attempting to cover each of the miles as quickly as possible. Carol and our children had fallen asleep, their eyes stinging from crying. A light snow was falling. The roads somewhere south of Alva, Oklahoma, seemed unusually winding and hilly. Finally, at around midnight, my resolve to hold it together and be the strong one that others could lean on gave out.

I cried. I cried long and hard, trying to drive safely through both snow and tears as they fell. And in the midst of my heartache, I said, "Do you care, God? Do you really care?"

At that moment I realized I'd just taken another step in the grief journey. I had begun my questioning with "why?" regarding Bob's death, only to slowly move on to "Did you lose control?"

Now I saw that the human heart isn't adequately consoled by "No, son, I have not lost control." I needed something more . . . emotive. I wanted to know, "Do you give a rip? Does it matter? Do you see my pain? *Do you care?*"

In the Oklahoma night, on a dark, slick two-lane highway, as my family slept, I met God. Or God met me. And do you know what he said? He said, *"Jim, I care. I do care."* I learned much about him that night, and I've not been the same since. He *does* care. He wants to be with me. And he wants to be with you. He has a "forever party" planned for us. It is called the *afterlife.*

Jump ahead once again to June 20, 2007. The phone rang, and Carol was on the other end. I'd been with her all night in the emergency room, trying to find out why she felt so awful. Waiting on a doctor, she finally sent me home to get our teenagers ready for school. The 7:09 call was somber and straightforward.

"Come now," she said. Knowing she must know more, I asked, "Why?"

She responded, "A mass."

"A mass?" I mumbled. "You mean, like cancer?"

She said the one word I did not want to hear: "Yes."

It was not a mass but *many* masses. Over one hundred tumors were removed in an eight-hour surgery. Due to massive resections, a series of other problems began. The subsequent nine months would be some of the most challenging I have ever known.

I should mention that Carol's shocking call came exactly one week after I'd met with my publisher and coauthor to discuss a book about heaven and the afterlife, topics that long had intrigued me. Amazing how an "interesting" subject can become unspeakably relevant and personal with the diagnosis of a serious illness. Anyone who's heard the word *cancer* (or a similar word) come from the mouth of their doctor or the doctor of a loved one knows life instantly turns upside down. "Life as usual" is gone, replaced by endless treatments, endless research, endless concern.

The days after Carol's diagnosis were two of my darkest. Her prognosis seemed so uncertain. I was trying to hang on to her. I was grasping. I was fighting for her life.

I was about to be taken through the knothole, which involves "letting go and letting God." Alone in my home, I had to release my wife. For the first time, I faced the reality of losing her. Emotionally and spiritually, I released her to the arms of God. Through many tears, I crossed a kind of dividing line. In that process, I told God I will not, like Job's wife, "curse God and die."[6] I would love him, no matter what.

Once I crossed that boundary, I was able to fight for Carol's life again, but this time with freedom. I didn't have to walk in fear. I now walked in confidence that all would be well. And fight for her I did. Succinctly stated, she made it through the long year and did well during the many months I was working on this book. (However, on the final day of writing, we received heartbreaking news of another setback—a recurrence. So we continue on with this battle.) The key point is that I passed through "Phase 4" in understanding God. This is when you say, "*God, I will love you and serve you, no matter what.*"

The previous three phases (above) are all about who God is. This phase is when you respond back to him. This one is about you. Will you trust him? I mean, *really trust him*. If you will, it prepares you for this life. And it prepares you for the life coming thereafter. Your relationship with God will move to a level in which you become amazingly comfortable being with him.

231

The Story of God #4: Ponder This

My friend Ponder Gilliland is aptly described by his first name. He is ponderous. Brilliant but ponderous. He's a thinker. As I write these words, he's in his nineties, and his mind has been affected by age. But before Ponder's slow descent, he was a marvel of intellectual insight and incisive ideas. As a pastor, he never used notes to preach. Attorneys, recognizing his cogent debate skills and logical aptitude, would bring their cases to him so he could help craft their arguments.

What has impacted me most about him, though, isn't his mind but his view of God. One line echoes over and over in my spirit. He'd say, "My Father likes me. He likes to be with me. He wants to spend time with me."

Saying "God loves me" is not nearly as powerful as "My Father *likes* me. . . . He wants to spend time with me."

This is precisely what God wants. And that is why he offers us eternity. He wants no one in hell. He wants you with him. In heaven. Forever.

If you've spent any time in Sunday school you've probably heard—maybe even memorized—one of the Bible's most familiar verses: "For God so loved the world that he gave his one and only Son, that whoever believes in him shall not perish but have eternal life."[7] That's what this whole discussion about the afterlife boils down to: God has prepared an unimaginable place for you to spend eternity, and he wants to enjoy it with you.

God's desire? For you to become comfortable with him. Here. *Now*. It will make the next life even more wonderful.

He likes you. He wants to be with you. *Now*.

Acknowledgments

Books are almost always a collaborative effort. This one is no exception. I am deeply indebted to an incredible team who helped so very much.

I am so grateful for Tracy Burger, my administrative assistant, who from her first day on the job—due to my wife's unexpected battle with cancer—had to assume an exorbitantly heavy load. Her thoroughness, heart of service, and uncomplaining and joyous spirit are important components in how this book came to be. Thank you, Tracy.

A special thanks to Priscilla Hammond, who with such a gracious spirit helped in so many ways, too numerous to mention. In addition, a heartfelt thank-you to Ray Christenson, whose graphs and charts are used throughout this book.

Special thanks to April Williams, who has worked with me on so many projects, along with Bill Coe and Kate Murray, who were willing to open up their calendars on very short notice to research and write with great skill. And they did so with joy and delight. It is always special to work with persons with exuberant attitudes. In addition, thank you to Adam Palmer for some hastily requested research and writing. Thank you, April, Bill, Kate, and Adam.

I am deeply indebted to Craig Bubeck, with whom I have worked on numerous projects. Craig's definitive writing, objective sense of expression, skilled wordsmithing, theological insights, persistence, and profound patience are "all over" this project. May we get to work together again! Thank you, Craig.

Words cannot express my appreciation to my co-laborer Keith Wall, who was patient with me beyond words as I faced one distraction, detour, and delay after another as this book was coming together. Keith's research is thorough and systematic; his writing is paced and engaging. If you enjoy this book, the major factor will be Keith's superb contribution throughout. In all candor, without Keith this book would not have the flow, the appeal, the grace, or the charm. The really "good" writing came from him. Thank you, Keith.

I thank God for Kyle Duncan, of Bethany House, who is the consummate gentleman, with the highest integrity. Kyle knows—as any editor or publisher must—when to extend grace and when to be insistent on deadlines. Kyle is the "dream editor/publisher" for any author. This is not my first project with Kyle; I hope it is not my last. This book required not only someone to think of it—that was Kyle—but someone to shepherd it—that was Kyle again—to its bumpy but glorious completion. Thank you, Kyle.

I am thankful for the people of Skyline Church who were gracious to listen to a sermon series—not once but twice—on the topic of this book, and who heard incalculable sermon illustrations that eventually became part of the book. They endured much in the writing and completion of this project. In addition, I am so grateful for their prayers that this book would, in fact, finally be written. Thank you, church.

The board of Skyline Church has always attempted to "fan the flame" of any gifting they have seen in me. I am grateful for their consistent encouragement during this elongated experience. Thank you, church board.

I am so blessed to be able to serve with the most wonderful group of pastors at Skyline Church, who never once complained when they heard me groan in my attempts to meet various writing deadlines. They always encouraged. They were my cheerleaders. Thank you, pastoral staff.

I owe a debt of thanks to family members—my wife, children, grandchildren, mother, brother, sister, in-laws, extended family—that tolerated my "hiding away" in an attempt to finish what became a rather lengthy journey. Thank you, family.

I praise God that in his infinite wisdom he came up with a place called *heaven*. Thank you, God.

I am thankful for the sacrificial death of Jesus that provides me—in fact, all of us—the way to this glorious place. Thank you, Jesus.

A most grateful,

Jim Garlow
San Diego, CA
April 2009

A thousand thank-yous to Alan Wartes for his insights, research, and editorial expertise—a truly skilled and steadfast partner in this project. Jenny Mertes and Karen Linamen also made valuable contributions to the manuscript, talented word wizards both. Christopher Soderstrom of Bethany House employed a deft hand and cool head under less-than-ideal circumstances.

We owe a debt of gratitude to those who shared their stories—those who appear in the final manuscript and those who don't. The openness of everyone who talked about their experiences is genuinely appreciated.

Many thanks to my family—Robin, Juliana, and Logan—for patience and perseverance above and beyond the call of duty.

Keith Wall

Notes

Chapter 1: The Undiscovered Country

1. This true story is factually told except for Vernon's name. Today, Dee Ring Martz is a respected psychotherapist and sought-after grief expert in Colorado Springs.

2. Alan F. Segal, *Life After Death: A History of the Afterlife in Western Religion* (New York: Doubleday, 2004), 36.

3. Jennifer Harper, "Majority in U.S. Believe in God," in *The Washington Times* (25 Dec. 2005).

4. Chen Zhiyong, "New Light on Near-Death Experience," in *China Daily* (14 Nov. 2006).

5. "Poll: One Out of Three Believes in Ghosts," in *Associated Press/AP Online* (26 Oct. 2007).

6. Norman Cousins, *The Healing Heart* (New York: Avon, 1984).

7. Raymond Moody, *Reunions: Visionary Encounters with Departed Loved Ones* (New York: Ballantine, 1993), viii.

8. Elizabeth Kübler-Ross, *On Death and Dying* (New York: Touchstone, 1969), 150.

9. John 3:16

10. 1 John 4:18

Chapter 2: There . . . and Back Again

1. Edna St. Vincent Millay, "Passer Mortuus Est," in *Second April* (New York: M. Kennerley, 1921).

2. Melvin Morse, in Raymond A. Moody, *Life After Life* (New York: Harper-Collins, 1975), x.

3. Ibid., xiii.

4. Elizabeth Kübler-Ross, in Moody, *Life After Life*, xxii.

5. Emma Young, "No Medical Explanation for Near-Death Experiences," in *New Scientist* (14 Dec. 2001).

6. Hans Küng, *Eternal Life? Life After Death as a Medical, Philosophical, and Theological Problem* (New York: Doubleday, 1984), 20.

7. Moody, *Life After Life*, 164.

8. Hebrews 11:1

Chapter 3: Hints at the Hereafter

1. Robert McKee, *Story: Substance, Structure, Style, and the Principles of Screenwriting* (New York: Regan, 1997), 11–12.

2. Michael Shimanovsky, "Who Let the Grim Reaper Get His Hands on the Remote Control?" in *Journal of Evolutionary Psychology* (1 Apr. 2006).

3. Kenneth Ring and Evelyn Elsaesser Valarino, *Lessons from the Light: What We Can Learn from the Near-Death Experience* (New York: Insight, 1998), 28.

4. Moody, *Life After Life, 25th Anniversary Edition* (San Francisco: HarperCollins, 2001), 18–19.

5. Ring and Valarino, *Lessons from the Light,* 34.

6. Melvin Morse and Paul Perry, *Closer to the Light* (New York: Villard, 1990), 27.

7. 1 Corinthians 15:54–55

8. Melvin Morse and Paul Perry, *Transformed by the Light* (New York: Villard, 1992), 110.

9. Moody, *Life After Life,* 46.

10. Maurice Rawlings, *Beyond Death's Door* (Nashville: Thomas Nelson, 1978), 72.

11. Trudy Harris, *Glimpses of Heaven* (Grand Rapids: Revell, 2008), 38.

12. Ibid., 51.

13. Hebrews 13:5; Deuteronomy 31:6

14. Don Piper with Cecil Murphey, *90 Minutes in Heaven* (Grand Rapids: Revell, 2004), 31–32.

15. Morse and Perry, *Transformed by the Light,* 78.

16. Betty Eadie, *Embraced by the Light* (New York: Bantam, 2002, reprint), 51–52.

17. 1 Corinthians 13:12

18. Mark 14:36

19. John 1:4–5

Chapter 4: A Taste of Torment

1. Mark 9:48; cf., Isaiah 66:24

2. Maurice Rawlings, *Beyond Death's Door* (Nashville: Thomas Nelson, 1978), 19.

3. Ibid., 21.

4. Howard Storm, *My Descent Into Death: A Second Chance at Life* (New York: Doubleday, 2005), 23.

5. Ibid., 17.

6. Ibid., 24.

7. Ibid.

8. Angie Fenimore, *Beyond the Darkness: My Near-Death Journey to the Edge of Hell and Back* (New York: Bantam, 1995), 94.

9. Ibid., 95.

10. Ibid.

11. Ibid., 104.

12. Ronald Reagan, *To Hell and Back*, host Maurice Rawlings. TBN Films (documentary transcript).

13. See John 1:29.

14. Reagan, *To Hell and Back.*

Chapter 5: Things That Go Bump in the Night

1. Brian Righi, *Ghosts, Apparitions, and Poltergeists: An Exploration of the Supernatural Through History* (Woodbury, MN: Llewellyn, 2008), 3–4.

2. *www.scarystories.ca/GhostStory/The--Wesley-Ghost-2.html*

3. Matthew 14:25–26

4. Geddes MacGregor, *Images of Afterlife: Beliefs from Antiquity to Modern Times* (New York: Paragon, 1992), 11.

5. Melvin Morse, *Where God Lives* (New York: Cliff Street, 2000), 1–2.

6. Ibid., 85.

7. Righi, *Ghosts, Apparitions, and Poltergeists*, 12.

8. Adapted from ibid., 5–13.

9. M. Scott Peck, *Glimpses of the Devil* (New York: Free, 2005), 238.

10. See Mark 5:1–20.

11. Walter Martin, Jill Martin Rische, and Kurt Van Gorden, *The Kingdom of the Occult* (Nashville: Thomas Nelson, 2008), 244.

12. C. S. Lewis, "Christianity and Culture," in *Christian Reflections* (Grand Rapids: Eerdmans, 1967), 33.

13. Romans 8:38–39

Chapter 6: Grace-Filled Guests

1. Dianne Arcangel, *Afterlife Encounters: Ordinary People, Extraordinary Experiences* (Charlottesville, VA: Hampton Roads, 2005), 277–300.

2. Louis E. LaGrand, *Messages and Miracles: Extraordinary Experiences of the Bereaved* (Woodbury, MN: Llewellyn, 1999), 96.

3. Ibid., 20.

4. Ibid., 51–52.

5. Arcangel, *Encounters*, 26.

6. Ibid., 8–9.

7. LaGrand, *Messages*, 124.

8. Elizabeth Kübler-Ross, *On Grief and Grieving* (New York: Scribner, 2005), 57–58.

9. LaGrand, *Messages*, 152.

10. Joel Martin and Patricia Romanowski, *Love Beyond Life: The Healing Power of Afterdeath Communication* (New York: Harper, 1997), 12.

11. LeGrand, *Messages*, 59–60.

12. See Matthew 28:10; Mark 16:6; Luke 24:36, 38.

Chapter 7: Calling Long Distance

1. Barbara Weisberg, *Talking to the Dead: Kate and Maggie Fox and the Rise of Spiritualism* (San Francisco: Harper, 2004), 17.

2. Ibid., 19.

3. See 1 Samuel 28:3–11.

4. 1 Samuel 28:12–15

5. *http://en.wikipedia.org/wiki/Necromanteion*

6. Brian Righi, *Ghosts, Apparitions, and Poltergeists: An Explanation of the Supernatural Through History* (Woodbury, MN: Llewellyn, 2008), 44.

7. Ed Warren and Lorraine Warren, *Graveyard* (New York: Macmillan, 1993), 137–38.

8. Robert T. Carroll, "Cold Reading" (see at *www.skepdic.com/coldread.html*).

9. Gary E. Schwartz, *The Afterlife Experiments: Breakthrough Scientific Evidence of Life After Death* (New York: Pocket Books, 2002), 123–24.

10. Deuteronomy 18:10–11

11. Isaiah 8:19–20

Chapter 8: Angels Among Us

1. Doreen Virtue, *How to Hear Your Angels* (Carlsbad: Hay, 2007). Virtue has many other New Age books about angels and related topics; e.g., number sequences, oracle cards, and crystal therapy.

2. See, e.g., Matthew 4:11; 18:10; 22:29–30; 25:41; Mark 1:13; 16:1–6; Luke 2:8–15; 20:35–36.

3. See Matthew 22:28–30; Luke 20:35–36.

4. A mineral that's sometimes transparent and commonly olive-green or yellowish.

5. See Daniel 10:5–6.

6. Revelation 5:11

7. Revelation 19:10

8. Luke 16:22

9. Hebrews 1:14

10. See Psalm 148:2–5.

11. Psalm 8:5. What's more, Paul says our status will change in the future: People who are righteous through relationship with Christ will become the judges of angels (1 Corinthians 6:3).

12. C. Fred Dickason, *Angels: Elect and Evil* (Chicago: Moody, 1975), 29–32. Dickason also wrote *Names of Angels* (Chicago: Press, 1997).

Angels can learn; Peter wrote that they want to know more about God's plan of redeeming humans as told by the ancient prophets (1 Peter 1:12).

Angels feel—especially joy, since they are so close to God. In the book of Job, a poetic passage describes Creation: While God was laying earth's foundation, "the morning stars sang together and all the angels shouted for joy" (38:7). Later, Jesus told a story about a shepherd who left his flock to seek out one lone sheep that had wandered away. He rejoiced when he found it, just as the angels in heaven rejoice over one sinner who repents (Luke 15:1–7).

As far as we can tell, angels loyal to God are always doing his will; presumably they could choose one action over another at a given time while not straying from doing what God expects them to do (ibid., 33). But apparently, long ago, some angels did willfully choose to rebel. Peter says some sinned, and God sent them to hell (2 Peter 2:4), a place of "eternal fire" made for them (Matthew 25:41; hell was not intended for people). The being who is now Satan (see chapter 9), who'd been a beautiful angel, called "morning star" or "son of the dawn," asserted his own will and led the rebellion (Isaiah 14:12–14).

13. Dickason says angels, as spirits, are incorporeal (without bodies). He muses that maybe they do have a body with a structure we can't understand, or one that operates on different principles than our bodies do (ibid., 34).

14. See Daniel 10; Matthew 28:3; Revelation 15:6.

15. See Revelation 4:6–8.

16. See Ezekiel 1:4–21.

17. Angels are potent but not omnipotent: David describes them as "mighty ones who do [God's] bidding, who obey his word" (Psalm 103:20); Peter says they're stronger and more powerful than men (2 Peter 2:11). Angels can control nature: in John's apocalyptic vision, four angels hold back the winds, while another angel harnesses the sun's heat (Revelation 7:1; 16:8–9). *Nothing*—death, angels, anything—is strong enough to separate us from God's love (Romans 8:38–39).

Angels may know more than we do, but they're not omniscient. When they know the future, it's because God commissions them to deliver messages about it. If angels knew everything, they wouldn't desire to learn (1 Peter 1:12). Jesus also indicates they don't know everything future; he will return to the earth with power and glory, and while angels will announce it, they do not know when it will happen (only the Father knows—Matthew 24:36).

18. Angels can go places in ways we cannot. The angel who rescued Peter from prison was able to go through walls and appear suddenly inside a heavily guarded cell. Leading Peter out, they passed two sets of guards and through an iron gate that opened on its own as they approached.

19. Angels have direct access to God (Matthew 18:10). They had the privilege of witnessing Christ's birth and praised God for his plan of salvation (see Luke 2; Hebrews 1:6). John witnessed many thousands of angels around God's throne, singing and praising (Revelation 5:11).

Angels carry out judgment and punish wicked people (e.g., Genesis 19); an angel was sent to destroy Jerusalem (and then ordered to stop—2 Samuel 24:16); an angel slew 185,000 of Sennacherib's warring Assyrians (see 2 Kings 19), and struck down Herod Agrippa I (Acts 12).

Scripturally, most often we see angels helping people (Hebrews 1:14): bringing messages, delivering from harm, guarding, guiding, and giving support and encouragement to God's servants, even assisting at death. Concerning the birth of Jesus, angels delivered messages to Daniel, Zacharias, Mary, Joseph, the shepherds, and later again to Joseph and Mary. Angels told the disciples Jesus one day would return in the same way he left (Acts 1:7–11). And when a non-Jewish man, Cornelius, explained to Peter how an angel directed him to Peter, Peter knew he had been called to deliver the good news about Jesus to Gentiles (10:1–11:18).

Angels are our Department of Defense: "He will command his angels concerning you to guard you in all your ways; they will lift you up in their hands, so that you will not strike your foot against a stone" (Psalm 91:11–12). When facing sure shipwreck, an angel appeared to Paul in a dream and told him he and everyone else on board would be saved (Acts 27:13–25).

20. Gary Kinnaman, *Angels Dark and Light* (Ann Arbor: Servant, 1994), 82–84. For example, John Chrysostom, Origen, Basil, and Bernard of Clairvaux all supported the idea of guardian angels; John Calvin was skeptical.

21. When Jesus wanted his disciples to understand the importance of children, he said *their* angels are assigned to watch out for them—again, angels with direct access to God (Matthew 18:10).

22. Angels offer messages of encouragement, as with Paul (Acts 27:13–25) and with setting free other imprisoned apostles and giving them strength to continue their work (5:18–20). In the Old Testament, for instance, God sent an angel to comfort Hagar and Ishmael and to reveal water that sustained them both (see Genesis 16); an angel baked bread and gave water to a despondent and incognito Elijah, then gave him food for strength on his journey (1 Kings 19:3–8).

23. After Jesus' trials in the desert and temptation by Satan, angels attended him (Matthew 4:11; Mark 1:13). Later in Gethsemane, when Jesus anguished in prayer as he faced execution, an angel came to strengthen him (Luke 22:43–44).

24. See Matthew 26:53.

25. See Colossians 1:16.

26. Ephesians 3:10

27. 1 Peter 3:22

28. See Jude 9.

29. Daniel 10:21; 12:1

30. See Jude 9; 1 Thessalonians 4:15–16.

31. Mortimer Adler claims the seraphim are the highest form of "metaphysical perfection" in God's kingdom (*The Angels and Us* [New York: Macmillan, 1982], 45), quoted in Kinnaman, *Angels Dark and Light,* 41–42.

32. Dickason: *They* are the "angelic beings of the highest order or class" (*Angels: Elect and Evil*, 61).

33. Saint Denis (pseudo-Dionysius the Areopagite), *The Celestial Hierarchy*, in Kinnaman, 18, 41.

34. On Aquinas and Augustine, see citations in Kinnaman, 42.

35. Billy Graham, *Angels: God's Secret Agents*, 2nd ed. (Dallas: Word, 1994), 55.

36. Dickason, *Angels: Elect and Evil*, 59.

37. See Isaiah 14:12–14; Ezekiel 28:12–17.

38. See 2 Peter 2:4; Jude 6; Revelation 12:7–9.

39. Frank Peretti has written about this battle with the dark side, often referred to as spiritual warfare, in his fascinating novels, including *This Present Darkness* (Crossway Books, 1986).

40. Hebrews 1:14
41. See survey results in Kinnaman, *Angels Dark and Light*, appendix 1 (213–20).
42. Ibid., 51.
43. cf. Matthew 22:30.
44. Kinnaman, 46–47, 51–52.
45. Ibid., 65–66, 220.
46. Hebrews 13:2
47. Kinnaman relates three such stories in *Angels Dark and Light*: 68–69, 94, 116–18.
48. See Billy Graham, *Angels: God's Secret Agents*, 99–100.
49. Several considerations may account for the higher proportion of angelic appearances to missionaries. First, they often work in less Westernized countries that are more open to the supernatural; some cultures don't even have such words as *super*natural or *para*normal in their language (see Kinnaman, 21–22). Second, as a foreigner in a sometimes-hostile environment, the missionary often needs help that only an angel is likely or able to give. Third, sometimes angels in human form are seen not by the (unaware) missionaries themselves but by would-be attackers.
50. Angels came to the shepherds at Jesus' birth, who then passed on the good news (Luke 2:17–18). An angel came to Philip, directing him to the Ethiopian eunuch, through whom the gospel spread to Ethiopia (Acts 8:26–39). An angel told Cornelius to fetch Peter; a Gentile received the gospel and it further spread (10:1–11:18). After an angel rescued Paul from death at sea, Paul went on to Rome to preach (27:13–25; 28:30–31). In each case, angels were messengers and guardians to God's workers. Billy Graham recalls many occasions when he had no more energy to preach before huge crowds. Just when he felt he couldn't go on, he would sense a supernatural renewing of his strength. He believes angels have ministered to him time and again (Graham, *Angels: God's Secret Agents*, xiv).
51. Kinnaman, *Angels Dark and Light*, 14–15.
52. Graham, *Angels: God's Secret Agents*, 166.
53. Ibid., 167–68.
54. Ibid., 105–06; see Luke 16:22.
55. Exodus 23:20

Chapter 9: More Than a Pitchfork and a Pointy Tail

1. "The Howling Man," *The Twilight Zone*, 1960. Written by Charles Beaumont; directed by Douglas Heyes; produced by Buck Houghton.
2. *www.quotesdaddy.com/tag/Satan*
3. *USA Today* Snapshots, "The Decline in Believers," *Harris* Interactive Poll (Jan. 21–27, 2003; Nov. 10–17, 2008).
4. As recounted in Augustine's autobiography, *Confessions*.
5. See John 1:1–13, 8:12, 9:5.
6. See Genesis 3:1–7; Mark 1:12–13; Matthew 4:1–11; Luke 4:1–3; Mark 14:10.
7. While the King James Version uses the name *Lucifer*, other versions translate the term differently.
8. Isaiah 14; Ezekiel 28; Revelation 12
9. Job 1:6–7 NKJV
10. See *www.thedivinecouncil.com/Introduction% 20to% 20the% 20Divine% 20Council % 20MTIT.pdf* (writings of Michael S. Heiser); these "sons" form part of a "divine council."
11. Ezekiel 28:12–15
12. Isaiah 14:12–15 KJV
13. Ezekiel 28:16–17 RSV
14. Genesis does not explain how Lucifer indwelt a serpent or say whether animals could talk before the fall. Like many biblical narratives, Genesis often engenders so many questions

in the contemporary reader's mind that he misses the entire point. Practical details were not always paramount; they were secondary to the revealed, eternal truth of God's story. The Bible is the revelation of his love for us and of his plan for our salvation. Knowing if snakes could talk doesn't compare to the greater truth that here humanity was tempted by a non-human entity and chose to disobey God rather than keep his directive.

15. Genesis 3:1 RSV
16. Matthew 10:16 RSV
17. Revelation 20:2
18. 2 Corinthians 11:3 RSV
19. Genesis 3:14–15 RSV
20. Zechariah 3:1–2 RSV
21. 1 Peter 5:8
22. Romans 8:37–39 RSV
23. Ephesians 6:12 RSV
24. *www.quotesdaddy.com/tag/Satan/5*
25. C. S. Lewis, *The Screwtape Letters* (Harper-Collins, San Francisco, 2001), ix.

Chapter 10: Demons in the Dark

1. Paul Hiebert, *Anthropological Reflections on Missiological Issues* (Grand Rapids: Baker, 1987).
2. Mark 5:1–13 RSV
3. The King James Version uses the phrase *possessed with a devil* (or *devils*) thirteen times.
4. Acts 5:16 RSV
5. Luke 6:17–18 RSV
6. New Testament examples (RSV): demoniacs (Matthew 4:24); unclean spirit (Mark 1:23; 5:2); having demons (Luke 8:27); trouble with unclean spirits (6:18); a spirit seizes (9:39); Satan entered into him (22:3; John 13:27); Satan filled him (Acts 5:3); afflicted (5:16).

Jesus and his followers always have power over unclean spirits; demons fear the power that comes from Christ. But while those who trust in him and are filled with his Spirit have no reason to fear demonic forces, there is no reason for Christians to seek out contact with them.

7. Matthew 12:43–45 RSV
8. Luke 22:3–6 RSV
9. John 13:2–4 RSV
10. This does not invalidate contemporary writings; we shouldn't assume there are no realities and truths outside the scope of Scripture. Again, as Paul wrote, "Now we see in a mirror dimly, but then face to face. Now I know in part; then I shall understand fully, even as I have been fully understood" (1 Corinthians 13:12 RSV).
11. See Isaiah 14:13–14.
12. Mark 5:7–8
13. Matthew 12:43
14. For example, with the Inquisition, and the various witch hunts.
15. See Genesis 3:1–6.
16. 1 John 4:4 RSV
17. Mark 1:23–26 RSV
18. James 2:19 RSV
19. Luke 10:18–20

Chapter 11: A Delightful Detour

1. *Field of Dreams*, Universal Studios, 1989. Written by W. P. Kinsella (book); screenplay by Phil Robinson. Directed by Phil Robinson; produced by Lawrence Gordon and Charles Gordon.

2. John Gilmore, *Probing Heaven: Key Questions on the Hereafter* (Grand Rapids: Baker, 1989), 16, 21.

3. Ibid., 67.

4. See Genesis 1:1.

5. See 2 Corinthians 12:2.

6. Luke 23:43

7. Philippians 1:23–24

8. Luke 16:23–28

9. Randy Alcorn, *Heaven* (Wheaton, IL: Tyndale, 2004), 55–63.

10. See Genesis 5:24.

11. See Luke 9:30–32.

12. 2 Corinthians 5:1–2

13. N. T. Wright, *Surprised by Hope, Rethinking Heaven: The Resurrection and the Mission of the Church* (New York: Harper One, 2008), 147.

14. See 1 Thessalonians 4:16–17.

15. See 1 Corinthians 15:12–23.

16. 1 Corinthians 15:37, 42–44

17. See Matthew 27:50–53.

18. See Luke 24:13–32.

19. Luke 24:39–40

20. Luke 24:41

Chapter 12: A Rewarding Experience

1. A minority contends there are *three* judgments, citing Matthew 25:31–36 as a third. Here we will focus on two: rewards for those who are "in Christ" and punishment for those who are not.

2. 2 Corinthians 5:10

3. 1 Corinthians 3:12–15

4. See also Romans 14:10.

5. 1 Corinthians 9:24–25

6. See Revelation 20.

7. For this section I am indebted to Mark Hitchcock, *55 Answers to Questions About Life After Death* (Sisters, OR: Mult-nomah, 2005), 146–49.

8. Daniel 12:3

9. Hebrews 6:10

10. Matthew 10:41–42

11. See Matthew 25:31–46.

12. Luke 14:12–14

13. James 1:12

14. Matthew 5:11–12

15. See, e.g., Matthew 5:44.

16. See Matthew 25:14–30.

17. Once again, Mark Hitchcock's insights (especially from pp. 150–53 of his book *55 Answers to Questions About Life After Death*) were helpful in developing this section.

18. Revelation 2:10

19. James 1:12

20. 1 Peter 5:2–4

21. 1 Thessalonians 2:19 NKJV

22. 2 Timothy 4:8

23. 1 Corinthians 9:24–25 NKJV

24. Revelation 4:10–11

25. Frederick Buechner, *Wishful Thinking: A Seeker's ABC* (San Francisco: Harper Collins, 1993), 58.

26. John 5:24

Chapter 13: Beyond Halos, Harps, and Hymns

1. John Eldredge, *The Journey of Desire* (Nashville: Thomas Nelson, 2000), 111.

2. C. S. Lewis, *Words to Live By*, Paul F. Ford, ed. (San Francisco: Harper SanFrancisco, 2007), 34–35.

3. Rather than endnote everything from Randy Alcorn's writings that has influenced my thinking, I will give sweeping credit to this brilliant writer. Many concepts I share about what we will do in heaven are adapted from *Heaven* (Wheaton, IL: Tyndale, 2004), especially chapters 23–44 (233–435). If you want a thorough and intriguing discussion of heaven, this book is an excellent place to start.

4. See Ephesians 5:19–20; Colossians 3:16.

5. A most breathtaking view of this is portrayed in Paul Billheimer's masterful *Destined for the Throne* (Minneapolis: Bethany House, 2005).

6. 2 Timothy 2:12

7. Revelation 2:26

8. Revelation 3:21

9. See, e.g., John 21:10–14.

10. Revelation 22:2

11. See Genesis 3:17–19.

12. Revelation 15:2–3

13. See Revelation 5:7–8.

14. Revelation 5:11

15. See Psalm 8:4–5.

16. Hebrews 1:13–14 KJV

17. See Matthew 25:41.

18. See Hebrews 2:14–17.

19. See Hebrews 2:5–8; Revelation 21:7.

20. See 1 Corinthians 6:2–3.

21. See Matthew 24:30.

22. See Matthew 17:3–5.

23. Genesis 1:1

24. See Genesis 1:31.

25. Isaiah 65:17

26. 2 Peter 3:11-13

27. Revelation 21:1

28. Matthew 5:5

29. Psalm 37:22

30. Romans 4:13

31. Revelation 5:10

32. John 14:1–3 KJV

33. Paul Marshall, *Heaven Is Not My Home* (Nashville: Word, 1998), 11.

34. See Luke 15:10.

35. Revelation 6:10–11

36. Hebrews 12:1

37. See, e.g., Isaiah 8:19–22.

38. Revelation 8:1

39. See Matthew 22:30.

40. Genesis 1:27

41. See, e.g., Revelation 21:4.
42. Psalm 16:11

Chapter 14: Going From Bad to Worse

1. *Bridge to Terabithia,* Walt Disney/Walden 2007. Written by Katherine Paterson (book); screenplay by Jeff Stockwell and David Paterson. Directed by Gabor Csupo; produced by David Paterson, Lauren Levine, and Hal Lieberman.
2. See Hebrews 5:14.
3. Some churches do not use any creedal statements. They don't necessarily reject the contents of the Apostles' Creed but rather the practice of creedal rituals. The Protestant Reformation challenged the Roman Catholic Church's elaborate traditions and rejected the doctrine that holds church tradition as equal to scriptural authority. While some such churches developed their own reformed creeds, others completely rejected creeds so as to avoid the perceived Catholic error. The United Methodist Church uses the Apostles' Creed but has removed the phrase *descendit ad inferos* ("he descended to hell").
4. In John H. Leith, ed., *Creeds of the Churches: A Reader in Christian Doctrine from the Bible to the Present* (Louisville: John Knox: 1963), 25.
5. Some early contrasting Gnostic teachings: *Manichaeism:* the spiritual realm is good while the material world is evil (leading to the belief that Jesus could not have had a real body, that his appearance was an illusion); *Apollinarianism:* the Word, or *Logos,* entered into the human Jesus (so Jesus had a soul and body but not a human spirit); *Nestorianism:* the Word, or *Logos,* inhabited the body of Jesus (Jesus was a "god-bearer," and there was no union of the human and divine natures).
6. See Luke 23:43.
7. Acts 2:33
8. 1 Peter 3:18–20; 4:5–6 RSV
9. "A wonderful text is this, and a more obscure passage perhaps than any other in the New Testament, so that I do not know for a certainty just what Peter means." *www.biac. org.uk/galanswer15.htm*
10. Although we do not know the certain interpretation, I personally hold to the "victory lap" theory.
11. See 1 Peter 4:6.
12. See on "the sheep and the goats" in Matthew 25:31–46.
13. Leo F. Steleten, *Dictionary of Ecclesiastical Latin* (Massachusetts: Hendrickson, 1995), 131.
14. Psalm 49:7–15 RSV
15. Psalm 16:9–11 RSV
16. An example of progressive revelation: Ancient cultures were accustomed to the practice of slavery. The treatment of slaves is addressed in both Old and New Testament writings (e.g., Genesis 21:10; Colossians 4:1; Ephesians 6:5). However, Jesus taught that meekness, humility, and love are the traits of those who will inherent God's kingdom and commands all followers to "love your neighbor as yourself" (Matthew 22:39 RSV). As people began to better understand Christ's teachings, behavior changed so as to uphold his directives. Eventually Christians understood that "there is neither Jew nor Greek, there is neither slave nor free, there is neither male nor female; for you are all one in Christ Jesus" (Galatians 3:28 RSV). The revealed truth did not change; rather, the human understanding of the revelation matured.
17. Genesis 37:35 RSV
18. See Job 14:11–13 RSV.
19. Job 26:5–6 RSV
20. Psalm 88:4–6 RSV

21. John 16:12–13 RSV

22. Mark Hitchcock, *55 Answers to Questions About Life After Death* (Eugene, OR: Multnomah, 2005), 100.

23. Ibid., 100–101.

24. Luke 16:23 ESV

25. Luke 16:27–31

Chapter 15: Called to Account

1. Hebrews 9:27 RSV

2. Revelation 20:11–12, 14–15

3. See Revelation 20.

4. Matthew 25:31–33

5. These possible judgments include (1) The judgment of the cross, which includes the judgment of the believer's sins; (2) The self-judgment of the believer, whereby we avoid God's judgment for sins (1 Corinthians 11:31); (3) The judgment seat of Christ, in which the quality of a Christian's life is evaluated and rewarded (2 Corinthians 5:10); (4) The "sheep and goats" judgment (start of the millennium, determining which Gentiles will enter the kingdom); (5) Israel's judgment (beginning of the millennium; Ezekiel 20:33–44); (6) The judgment of fallen angels (Jude 6; 1 Corinthians 6:3); (7) The great white throne judgment ("last judgment") of those who don't believe in Christ.

6. Revelation 20:13

7. Revelation 20:12

8. Revelation 21:27

9. Aired December 8, 2008.

10. Matthew 12:36–37

11. See, e.g., Exodus 32:31–33; Deuteronomy 9:14; 25:19; 29:20–21; 32:26; 2 Kings 14:27; Nehemiah 13:14; Psalm 9:5; 69:28; Revelation 3:5.

12. Revelation 3:5

Chapter 16: The Heat Is On

1. See William Crockett, ed., *Four Views on Hell* (Grand Rapids: Zondervan, 1992), chapters 1–2.

2. See Luke 16:19–31.

3. 2 Thessalonians 1:9

4. Jerry L. Walls, *Hell: The Logic of Damnation* (South Bend: University of Notre Dame Press, 1992), 150.

5. See, e.g., Romans 6:23.

6. See, e.g., John 1:9.

7. Romans 1:19–20

8. See Revelation 20.

9. See Revelation 9:1–2, 11; 11:7; 17:8; 20:1–3.

10. 2 Peter 2:4

11. See Jude 6.

12. See Ephesians 4:9.

13. See Philippians 2:10.

14. Henry Blamires, *Knowing the Truth About Heaven and Hell* (Ann Arbor: Servant, 1998), 64.

15. Bill Wiese, *23 Minutes in Hell* (Lake Mary, FL: Charisma, 2006), 104.

16. Walls, *Hell,* 150–51.

17. Pope John Paul II, "General Audience" (7/28/99), Vatican News Service, in Albert Mohler Jr., ibid., 27.

18. Walls, *Hell,* 151.
19. We'll later discuss the conditional view and the purgatorial view.
20. See chapter 19.
21. See chapter 18.
22. John F. Walvoord, in Crocket, *Four Views on Hell,* 28.
23. Jude 13
24. Walvoord, in Crocket, *Four Views on Hell,* 51.
25. See Matthew 7:5; Luke 9:60.
26. Walvoord, in Crocket, 53.
27. Walls, *Hell,* 152.
28. We'll look more at this in following chapters.
29. Gerry Beauchemin, *Hope Beyond Hell: The Righteous Purpose of God's Judgment* (Olmito, TX: Malista, 2007), 4.
30. Ibid., 33.
31. Randy Klassen, *What Does the Bible Really Say About Hell?* (Telford, PA: Pandora, 2001), 87.
32. Matthew 25:46
33. Revelation 20:10

Chapter 17: The Ultimate Escape Hatch

1. See Larry Dixon, *The Other Side of the Good News* (Bridgepoint, 1992), 106–107.
2. Jonathan Edwards, "Sinners in the Hands of an Angry God," in Elizabeth Winslow, ed., *Jonathan Edwards: Basic Writings* (New York: New American Library, 1966; Meridian, 1978), 153.
3. Winslow, foreword to ibid., xx.
4. See Albert Mohler Jr., "Modern Theology: the Disappearance of Hell," in Christopher W. Morgan and Robert A. Peterson, eds., *Hell Under Fire: Modern Scholarship Reinvents Eternal Punishment* (Grand Rapids: Zondervan, 2004), 19–20.
5. Frederick Denison Maurice, "Eternal Life and Eternal Death," in *Theological Essays* (London: Macmillan, 1892), 377–407, in ibid., 23.
6. Mohler, in *Hell Under Fire,* 23.
7. Ibid., 22.
8. Charles H. Spurgeon, "The Resurrection of the Dead," quoted in Mohler, 28.
9. Discussion adapted from Mohler, 36–40.
10. John Wenham, *Facing Hell: An Autobiography 1913–1996* (London: Paternoster, 1998).
11. *The Mystery of Salvation, the Story of God's Gift: A Report by the Doctrine Commission of the General Synod of the Church of England* (London: Church House, 1995), 180, in Mohler, *Modern Theology,* 32.
12. Clark H. Pinnock, "The Conditional View," in *Four Views on Hell,* William Crocket, ed., (Grand Rapids: Zondervan, 1992), 135; he references "Hell's Sober Comeback," *U.S. News & World Report* (3/25/91).
13. Mohler, *Modern Theology,* 35; he cites Pinnock and Robert C. Brow, *Unbounded Love: A Good News Theology for the 21st Century* (Downers Grove, IL: InterVarsity, 1994).
14. Ibid.
15. Pinnock, in Crocket, ed., *Four Views on Hell,* 165–66.
16. We'll focus on eternal punishment in the next chapter.
17. Karl Menninger, *Whatever Became of Sin?* (New York: Hawthorne, 1973).
18. See, e.g., Bill Hybels, *Just Walk Across the Room: Simple Steps Pointing People to Faith* (Grand Rapids: Zondervan, 2006).
19. See *www.inclusion.ws/*

20. See *http://en.wikipedia.org/wiki/-Carlton_Pearson#Early_career*

21. See *www.inclusion.ws/faq1.htm*

22. J. I. Packer, "Universalism: Will Everyone Ultimately Be Saved?" in Morgan and Peterson, *Hell Under Fire*, 179–81.

23. See Dixon, *The Other Side of the Good News*, 49.

24. Pinnock, "The Conditional View," in *Four Views on Hell*, 142.

Encountering Heaven
and the
Afterlife

Contents

Your Personal Invitation to . . .
Adventures in the Afterlife

L et's take a hypothetical excursion: Suppose you and your spouse completed the paperwork for a new life insurance policy—but health care being what it is these days, the company requires more than just a stack of signed forms and an at-home blood draw from a visiting nurse. So this morning you are scheduled for a physical at your doctor's office.

Once there, you find yourself being poked and prodded by your physician. She presses a stethoscope to your chest, wraps a blood-pressure cuff around your bicep, and asks about your family history and other potentially embarrassing questions. So far, so good. But this kind of physical requires something more: You've got to complete a brisk walk on a treadmill, with electrodes taped to your chest and attached to a nearby monitor.

Okay, you can do this. You consider yourself to be in reasonably good shape. What's a little uphill climb on a moving conveyor belt?

But twenty minutes into the test, with the treadmill's speed increasing as quickly as your drops of perspiration, something seems wrong. You feel pressure in your chest. Tightness. Like someone has put a bigger version of the blood-pressure cuff around your upper torso and started to inflate it. Then you notice a tingling sensation in your left arm. Suddenly lightheaded and nauseous, you stumble off the treadmill and collapse on the cold tile floor.

Fade to black.

The next thing you know, you are in a different place. It's not your doctor's office, but it still feels *medical*—stark walls, antiseptic odor, chrome-plated instruments, fluorescent lights, and lots of scurrying, unfamiliar people wearing white and green. They're also wearing concerned expressions. Furrowed brows, narrowed eyes, clenched teeth.

It's you they are concerned about. You realize you've been taken to an emergency room. A tall woman with graying hair utters the words *myocardial infarction*. Huh? Someone else says, "heart attack." Oh, that.

You notice that you're lying on a gurney, metal guardrails at your sides, a spider web of tubes and wires tangled around your limp body. Strangers frantically turn knobs, push buttons, jab needles into your flesh. Then you hear it . . .

You've heard the sound in movies and lots of those hospital dramas on TV. It's the EKG machine that suddenly spews out a shrill, high-pitched blaring noise, reminiscent of your smoke detector at home. You look over just in time to see the once-jumping, squiggly line go flat.

Fade to black once more.

Now the questions begin. Assuming the above scenario really happened to you (and it's certainly a possibility for any one of us), what do you think comes next? The physicians and other medical personnel swarming around you, despite their best efforts, declare you dead. Now what? You're going to have the adventure of your life, that's for sure.

Yes, some people are lucky enough to get resuscitated. But what if you weren't among the fortunate who "died" and lived to tell the tale?

Researcher Dinesh D'Souza asks the question that has been on the minds of human beings for millennia:

> Is death the end, or is there something more? This is the ultimate question. It has been the defining issue for entire cultures from the ancient Egyptians to the present. And in truth, there is no more important question that any of us will face. It is the issue that makes every other issue trivial. If you have doubts about its significance, go to a hospital or a funeral or talk to a parent who has recently lost a child. You will discover very quickly that the apparent normalcy of everyday life is a sham.[1]

What happens the moment you die? Where will you end up? How will you get there? When you arrive, will you know people? Will angels escort you to your next destination? What are heaven and hell really like?

The scene described above is not far off from a real-life drama that unfolded in the life of Earl Foster, pastor of Faith Community Church in Shady Hills, Florida. For him, the prospect of flatlining on a gurney was anything but hypothetical. On March 16, 2006, Earl, age sixty-three, lay on a table at New Port Richey Hospital while medical personnel began a blood transfusion. Suffering from diabetes and a condition that causes low blood counts, Earl had accepted this procedure as a necessary requirement to keep him well.

But something went wrong. Terribly wrong.

A few minutes into the procedure, his heart stopped, and in an instant he found himself up in a corner of the room watching as physicians tried to shock him back to life with a defibrillator. From his hovering position, Earl felt a vague sense of disappointment at their attempt to revive him, and he wasn't sure why exactly.

A split-second later, he discovered himself no longer in the hospital room, but somewhere indescribably beautiful. An overwhelming sense of peace swept over him. He knelt beside a stream to drink the cool, clear water from his cupped hands. Across a lush meadow, he saw his old dog, Ram, running as fast as he ever did and leaping over the meandering brook to greet his owner. Earl's long-lost cat, Puff, came scurrying up behind. As Earl reached out to meet them, he spotted his sister, Margie, with both legs perfectly okay and working fine—even though she had died with only one leg.

Following her down the grassy hill were his mother and father, happy and healthy, with no signs of the heart attacks that had ended their lives on earth. Soon Earl was surrounded by his grandparents, looking much younger than he'd ever seen them, and a welcoming horde of aunts, uncles, cousins, and friends. Everyone appeared so robust and full of unmistakable joy.

"Right then I realized that complete healing lies ahead for every child of God," Earl said. "The blind will see exquisite vistas, the deaf will hear blissful music, cancer will disappear, and the illnesses and ailments of old age will vanish."

It suddenly occurred to him why he felt disappointed that the medical personnel were trying to jump-start his heart. He didn't want to return to his earthly life. Now he knew he never wanted to leave this place. But soon enough, he woke up to find himself back on the hospital table. Thanks to the miracles of modern medical technology, Earl had no other choice but to conclude: Heaven can wait.

Earl's near-death experience (NDE) and glimpse of paradise echo thousands of similar stories. His vivid recollections—as clear in his mind as yesterday's golf game or trip to the coffee shop—give us all a foretaste of things to come.

For most people, one NDE would be astounding. A life-changing event, to be sure. For Earl, though, a repeat performance lay ahead, only with a different encounter on the other side.

A year and a half later, on August 26, 2007, Earl was back in the same hospital for another "routine" blood transfusion. Apparently for Earl such commonplace procedures are anything but routine. Once again his heart stopped and, as he was later told, he had no measurable signs of life for two minutes. This time, he immediately felt surrounded by light and propelled forward.

Suddenly he was stopped by someone who stepped in front of him. Earl recognized his brother, Robert, who had died the previous year of cancer. He put up his hand and said to Earl, "It's not your time. You have to go back. You have to endure. You must continue on with your life."

Disappointed, Earl asked, "Why do I have to continue on? You didn't."

"You still have work to do, and I squandered much of my time," Robert said. "You still have work to finish. You have to keep on."

Then Earl asked him, "How will I know when I am finished? Will it be soon?"

Robert said simply, "You will know!"

Earl desperately wanted to ask what it was he had left to finish, but he abruptly regained consciousness on the treatment table. A physician stood over him, paddles in hand, while nurses bustled about. He had—once again—been shocked back to life.

In the pages ahead, we'll present to you more than thirty stories like Earl's, and not only about near-death experiences leading to a glimpse of heaven (or hell). We'll also tell of deathbed scenes where the final visions of dying people open a window, ever so briefly, into the next world. We'll share the experiences of men and women certain they were visited by deceased loved ones. We'll highlight the unexpected visions and spiritual insights that offer unique perspectives on the afterlife. We'll show that angels and demons travel from the spiritual world to our physical world, either to help or harass human beings. We'll even share tales of ghost appearances.

This isn't a book filled with comprehensive explanations, convincing elucidations, or cogent expositions from the Bible. Rather it is an eclectic collection, offering an intriguing look into the lives of ordinary people who have had extraordinary spiritual encounters. But you'll find much more than poignant and gripping tales: You'll gain a peek into the (usually) invisible world that surrounds us every second of every day. Gathering insights from a wide-ranging compilation like this is akin to working a jigsaw puzzle. Most people complete the flat-edged border and then go about fitting together piece after painstaking piece—until at last the picture is whole. When you read a single story in this book, you'll hold a puzzle piece in your hand, a small but vivid portion of a much larger picture. By the time you've read all the stories, you'll have a fairly well-rounded understanding of the afterlife.

We'll be right up front with you: Some of the topics covered here will bolster your beliefs and fortify your faith—but others will challenge and stretch your thinking. Who knows—some may make you angry. We acknowledge that some of the issues presented are controversial and may elicit incredulity. The Bible, our ultimate source of spiritual wisdom, is clear and explicit on many areas, but vague or silent on others. It is up to each of us individually, with God's help, to seek the truth. Our hope is to open a helpful dialogue, not a heated debate. More so, we hope to open minds and hearts to the reality that the spiritual world is real, buzzing and swirling all around us. (The last book we wrote together, *Heaven and the Afterlife,* covers a wide range of topics and is jam-packed with explanations, theories, and theological perspectives to help guide you through confusing or controversial issues. It would be a useful companion to the book in your hands.)

In addition to stimulating discussion and thought, our purposes for presenting these fascinating narratives are to demonstrate that:

The division or distance between the physical world and the spiritual world is incredibly thin—like tissue paper. It's probably more accurate to say there really is no distance. Beings with bodies and beings without occupy the same space, just on different planes. Sometimes there's sufficient overlap—or a door thrust open between worlds—to offer the opportunity for physical and spiritual entities to meet face-to-face. Further, there's much more two-way traffic between this world and the next than most people realize. The accounts in Part One of this book provide anecdotal evidence that people regularly do make a round trip from earth to heaven (or hell) and back again. According to the Bible, and supported by eyewitness testimony, angels and demons frequently leave their domains and interact with humans.

The more we learn about life beyond the here and now, the less likely we are to be unnecessarily fearful. We know the majority of people fear death—and many are downright terrified of it. When we understand that dying really is a matter of "crossing over" to another place, we're empowered to face our own death, or even the death of a loved one, with courage and peace. The spiritual encounters of reliable individuals supply us with valuable insights into what lies ahead. For those who have placed their trust in God, an amazing new place awaits us. Scripture assures us that "God is love" and "love casts out fear."[2]

The mystery and magnificence of God make life (this one and the one to come) an amazing adventure. There will always be skeptics among us, those who come up with rational, scientific explanations for spiritual phenomena. But those who have spiritual faith—those who acknowledge there's much more than what we can see, taste, smell, hear, and feel—should remain open to the possibilities that God works in our world in surprising and unexpected ways. Why should we limit the vast, creative, and unpredictable God who created heaven and earth and everything in between? Solomon wrote, "As you do not know the path of the wind, or how the body is formed in a mother's womb, so you cannot understand the work of God, the Maker of all things."[3] Through stories we gain hints, glean clues, gather inferences that help form our beliefs about the afterlife. But there will always be mystery and intrigue about the supernatural world—at least so long as we reside on *terra firma*. This is a book that embraces the unknowable mysteries of God and his creation, even as we explore what is knowable through the real experiences of reliable people.

Most of all, we hope these stories point readers to the living and loving God who desires a close relationship with every person on earth. As the apostle John wrote in his New Testament gospel account: "For God so loved the world that he gave his one and only Son, that whoever believes in him shall not perish but have eternal life. For God did not send his Son into the world to condemn the world, but to save the world through him."[4] That is the very essence of any discussion or dialogue we have about the afterlife—God has prepared an indescribably wonderful place for you to spend eternity, and he wants to enjoy it with you.

Doubter . . . or Questioner?

Jim Garlow

I have a confession to make: I am an unlikely candidate to write this book. I have never had a near-death experience. I have never had a glimpse of heaven. I have never, thankfully, had an up close look at hell. Further, I have never seen an angel (as far as I'm aware of). I have only once seen a *fully* demonized man. Only one time have I been attacked by a demon, or at least that is what I think occurred.

Unlike the people in the pages that follow, I have never had an unusual "visitation" of any kind. Although I have been a pastor for decades, I have no personal deathbed scenes about which I can write. I have never seen a ghost. The one opportunity I had to witness one, I promptly and cowardly passed up.[1]

And what about dreams and visions? Only three, frankly. I have had thousands of dreams—all of them jumbled, generally wacky, and largely forgotten by the time both feet hit the floor. But I have had only three experiences that would qualify as *bona fide* dreams or visions in so many years of ministry, all of them long ago.

Thus, I am an unlikely candidate to publish a book on these topics. And the experience of my coauthor, Keith Wall, is not totally unlike my own. He has had several "strange coincidences" that point to dramatic spiritual involvement in his life—but, like me, nothing that has been in-your-face obvious and apparent.

There is another reason I am an unlikely candidate to coauthor this book. My greatest struggle in my Christian faith is not the "normal" temptations I have observed in others. Instead, for as long as I can remember, I have privately battled an internal and persistent question, "What if all I believe is wrong?"

I don't consider myself an intellectual, but my Christian struggles have been primarily in the intellectual arena, as opposed to the "temptations of the flesh" that seem to plague others. In fact, truth be known, the likely reason I continued on an academic journey that included three master's degrees and a doctorate of philosophy in historical theology was because of the nagging thought, *What if all I believe is wrong?* I wanted to make sure I knew truth.

Flowing out of that question emerged a favorite biblical personality: Thomas. While preachers railed on Thomas for being the "doubter," I identified with him. He was my hero! And still is.

As you might recall, Thomas was not present when Jesus first appeared to his close circle of friends. When they announced to Thomas that Jesus had in fact been resurrected, Thomas responded with an understandable, "Unless I see [for myself] . . . I will not believe it."[2] Others call that doubt. I call it smart! I would have said the same thing. Thomas was not a doubter. He was a questioner. And as such, he wanted the facts.

In contrast to the wonderful Scripture passages to which many tend to gravitate, the one that remains among my favorites is: "I do believe; help me overcome my unbelief!"[3] I have lived with the tension of those two seemingly conflicting claims from age nine to the present.

In the end, the evidence for Christ and the Bible was and is so breathtakingly convincing: The Bible is true. God is God. Jesus was born of a virgin, lived a sinless life, was crucified, died, was buried, and rose on the third day, and is coming back to rule this world. And, yes, there is a heaven and a hell, and everyone is going to one place or the other.

There is another reason that I am not a likely candidate to write a book on the ethereal realm. I am an amateur historian. My last two academic diplomas were in the area of history, which is something quite tangible. History pertains to events that have occurred within time and space. But some of the accounts you are about to read seem to defy both, at least at times. I feel quite comfortable with time and space. "Heaven and the afterlife" sometimes seem—how do I say this?—intimidating, daunting, and nebulous topics.

It is important to distinguish between being rational and *rationalism*. Being rational is a good thing, as the mind is one of the greatest of God's creations. *Rationalism*, in contrast, is arrogance in assuming that *only* what I can know (see, taste, measure, quantify, and so on) and understand is real.

In summary, I approached this project with a healthy dose of well-founded skepticism. Along the way, Keith and I used reasonable and consistent vetting techniques. To accept stories as valid, one of us either needed to know the people personally—with firsthand knowledge of their integrity and credibility—or we had to know someone with a high degree of reliability who could vouch for the person being profiled. In those rare cases where we did not have such knowledge (which was only one or two instances), contact was made with a credible pastor or person in leadership to discern the character of the storyteller. Furthermore, the other criterion was that the individual had to be still living. We did not want to rely on secondhand information, even from people we knew to be trustworthy.

We admit we are not social scientists—we are, in a real sense, reporters. In contrast to our previous book, *Heaven and the Afterlife*, in which we presented in-depth explanations and scriptural discourses, we offer few theological or practical assertions regarding what you are about to read. We are following the proverbial "we report, you decide" approach.

In fact, we concede that we do not know how to explain many of these accounts. And we feel no compulsion to do so. Our response to some of the stories, perhaps like yours, is "Could this really have happened? How is that possible?" But we felt it was not our place to tamper with the stories, to somehow fit them into our constructs or preconceptions.

We do have deep convictions and make no attempt to hide them. We believe the Bible to be absolutely true, in everything it says and affirms. We believe the Bible is a reliable guide for every aspect of life, particularly as it pertains to the pathway to heaven. We believe the Bible is the Word of God. In fact, you will see that we affirm scriptural warnings—in both our books on this topic—when we make the case that a person should never attempt to communicate with the dead, as that is clearly and strictly forbidden in Scripture.

Keith and I approached our first book on heaven, hell, and related topics with great inquisitiveness, not fully certain of all the pathways we might take therein. We approached our second book with a low-grade skepticism, a sort of maybe-but-maybe-not mental framework, uncertain of what we might encounter.

The process involved a division of labor. I threw out the net to gather stories, followed up with hundreds of contacts, prodded for details and nudged for information, and vetted individuals we wanted to profile. I then classified and codified the nearly four hundred accounts that came in. Using a team of wonderful assistants, we developed a system of categorizing and rating for completeness. It was at this point that my enthusiasm for the project really grew. What we were uncovering was a gold mine. With hundreds of credible accounts emerging, we began to see consistent patterns. People, unrelated by time and geography, were reporting remarkably similar experiences.

I cannot tell you the number of times someone said or wrote to me, "I have never told anyone this, but . . ." Or "I know people might think I am crazy, so I have told very few people."

Once the stories were collected, Keith began the challenging task of selecting which ones to include. Then he began the process of interviewing and writing that resulted in the book you now hold in your hand.

Remarkably, only three featured individuals chose to use pseudonyms. One did so to protect another person in the story. Two others preferred to remain anonymous because they know that the rationalism and skepticism of their colleagues would jeopardize their professional calling. It is sad—but probably not surprising—that their co-workers might believe that nothing could possibly exist that they cannot scientifically measure.

I have close personal connections to many of the individuals featured in these pages. But the account to which I am most personally tied is a story we debated including—the death of my nephew Christopher Garlow in a fiery and truly freak car catastrophe (see the story "Never Far Away"). This occurred only one day after the official release of *Heaven and the Afterlife* and a short time before I began work on its follow-up, *Encountering Heaven and the Afterlife*. The devastating experience brought all of these issues into vivid—and tragic—clarity for me.

As you will learn, I had sent advance copies of *Heaven and the Afterlife* to my brother and his family. After Christopher's passing, I learned that he and his family had read our book and discussed heaven at some length.

As I write this new book on the afterlife, emotions are still raw for me as an uncle who performed the funeral. But they are especially so for my brother's still-traumatized family. It is for that reason that I dedicate this book to Christopher Garlow who, on July 16, 2009, at age twenty-one, encountered heaven and the afterlife.

Part One

Eyewitness Accounts

People who have had near-death experiences bring back vivid descriptions of the pathway to paradise and descent into darkness.

If you were to travel back in time a hundred years and ask your great, great grandmother what she knew about NDEs (near-death experiences), she'd probably give you a blank stare. Question her about flat-lined EKG readouts, "clinical" death, and heroic emergency-room resuscitations—and she would think you'd been nipping at the mulberry wine again.

But if you were to ask her to tell you the stories she's heard about people who'd had a brush with death—the ones who saw beautiful bright lights, visited with long-dead relatives, or felt a sense of overwhelming peace and love, Granny would most likely smile and say, "Oh, *that*! Why didn't you say so?"

Although modern medical technology has made it possible for *more* people to "die" and return with tales of incredible out-of-body journeys, the truth is, it's been happening throughout human history. Literature records variations on the experience from nearly every culture on every continent. It is only in our time of mass communication that such accounts have entered the mainstream of our collective conversation about death and dying.

That trend picked up speed in 1975, the year Dr. Raymond Moody put his professional reputation as a psychiatrist on the line and published a little book called *Life After Life*. In its pages, he attempted to tackle a question that most serious scientists wouldn't touch with a ten-foot pole—though it has haunted human beings for millennia:

What happens when we die?

After studying the firsthand accounts of hundreds of people who had "crossed over" and returned—that is, people who had survived a life-threatening crisis, sometimes after a complete loss of measurable vital signs—Moody coined the phrase *near-death experience* to describe the phenomenon. Most intriguing was the fact that the stories he gathered were remarkably similar to each other. He found that while no two NDEs are identical, most had one or more core elements in common: a feeling of being out of one's body, moving through a tunnel toward a bright light, and encounters with angelic figures or deceased loved ones.

Other far less frequently reported stories reveal decidedly dark and hellish experiences. Dr. Maurice Rawlings, author of *To Hell and Back*, believes such traumatic NDEs are vastly underrepresented in literature, giving the impression that death is always a doorway into bliss. In his view, the mind quickly walls off painful memories, so that hellish experiences fade from conscious awareness much faster than positive ones. Furthermore, he says, "Hell cases also remain unreported because of personal ego and the embarrassment of it all. Patients don't want to discuss a matter that confirms ultimate failure in life, an overwhelming defeat, a slap in the face."[1]

Early research by Rawlings, Moody, and a few other pioneers in the field triggered a veritable avalanche of interest in examining such stories for clues as to what lies on the other side of death. Since then, dozens of studies have documented thousands of NDEs among people from various religious traditions, demographic groups, and cultural backgrounds. Scientifically minded researchers have looked for purely chemical or biological explanations for the extraordinary experiences survivors describe. They've analyzed oxygen deficiency, blood pressure, drug-induced hallucinations, and even the final, frantic firings of synapses in the brain—just to name a few possible culprits—in search of a mechanistic cause for the NDE.

That thinking dominates the medical profession as well. Doctors are trained from day one to purge their practice of anything that isn't scientifically verifiable—an unfortunate attitude that has done more than anything else to suppress open-minded NDE research.

In his book *Evidence of the Afterlife: The Science of Near-Death Experiences*, Dr. Jeffrey Long, an oncologist and NDE researcher, writes:

> I heard far too many stories of the problems NDErs encountered when they tried to tell their near-death experiences to the medical staff. One of the classic stories was a patient who told his doctor about his NDE in front of several nurses. When the patient finished telling his story, the doctor looked up from his clipboard and said, "Don't think too much about it. It was just fantasy."
>
> When the doctor left the room, the nurses closed in around the crushed patient and said, "It's not fantasy. We hear about these events all the time from patients. Doctors like him live in fantasy. They never hear these because they don't listen to their patients."[2]

Still, in spite of so much highly motivated reductionist research, science has failed to identify a smoking gun to disprove what NDE stories strongly suggest: that human consciousness—what theologians call the soul or sometimes refer to as the spirit—survives beyond bodily death. In fact, as you will see in the following pages, people who have been there often report a heightened and enhanced quality to existence that is far beyond mere "survival." Most speak of feeling *more alive* while out of their bodies than they ever have before. They experience tremendous freedom, unconditional love, and indescribable peace on the other side. They commonly want, more than anything, to remain there—and they only come back out of a sense of compassion for their families, unfinished business on earth, or simply because they are given no choice by loving beings who turn them back with the words, "It's not your time yet. You have more to do."

If nothing else, NDE survivors have convincingly challenged the popular nihilistic notion that *nothing* awaits us when we die but a permanent "lights out." Not true, they say. Every single person who has crossed over and returned—and thousands of these accounts are available—would say emphatically that there is absolutely, definitely, unquestionably a world beyond this one.

We collected the stories that follow to offer glimpses into the afterlife. Like single drops of rain that become part of a mighty river, each story contributes something vital to our understanding.

Jesus said, "In my Father's house are many rooms; if it were not so, I would have told you. I am going there to prepare a place for you."[3] NDE stories may not give us a detailed floor plan of the place he has prepared for us, but they at least offer a tantalizing peek through the window. They teach us important things about how to live in *this* life, how to grieve the loss of someone we love, and what to expect when the moment of our own death arrives—as it will for each of us, without fail.

1

Heaven on Wheels

A Harley-Davidson motorcycle, a tragic accident, and a trip to the afterlife that changed Abby Cleghorn's life forever.

Six feet tall, with a salt-and-pepper goatee and boyish smile, Win treated Abby like a queen. He told her he loved her with all his heart, and indeed she'd never felt as loved in her entire life. Win gave her strength, helping her move past the painful memories of the abusive marriage she'd once been in. They got engaged in November and made plans to marry after the New Year.

One Saturday morning in December, they took Win's truck over to the Applebee's restaurant in their hometown of Aiken, South Carolina, meeting up with friends for the annual Make-A-Wish Foundation Christmas party. Win and Abby brought toys and visited with the kids. It was a wonderful morning.

That evening, it was back on the motorcycle and a short ride into Augusta for the Harley-Davidson Christmas party. As Win steered his bike up the highway, Abby wrapped her arms tightly around his waist and smiled.

Unexpectedly, Abby saw her mother first, and then her sister. She wasn't on the motorcycle anymore, but standing beside two women. Abby shouldn't have recognized her sister at all, since Patty Lynn had been stillborn two years before Abby was born. But there she was, a woman who looked to be in her thirties; and Abby, forty-four, knew immediately who she was.

Abby's mother was the first to speak. "Abigail," she said, "It's not your time. You need to go back to be with your kids and your grandbabies."

Abby said, "Yes, ma'am." But she didn't move. Go back? How in the world was she supposed to do that?

Her sister said gently, "Abigail, did you hear what Mama said?"

"I did," Abby replied, "but I can only go so fast."

Patty Lynn urged, "You need to quit talking and get going."

Abby turned and saw a field of the greenest grass she'd ever seen. Walking toward her, arms outstretched, was Win.

"C'mon, baby," he said in the playful drawl that had always melted her heart. "We're going to be late."

"But I can't go with you, Win," she responded. "Mama told me to go back."

"I don't think you want to go back, Abby," he said. "You don't know how hard it's gonna be for you. If you go back, you're going to have to be very strong."

"I can do it," she insisted. "I'll have the Lord with me, helping me along the way."

Win paused and said, "If you do go back, I want you to do something for me."

"What is it, Win?"

"I want you to remember that I love you with all my heart."

The next thing Abby remembered was lying in a hospital bed, hooked up to monitors and beepers. Sitting in a chair next to the bed was Tabi, one of Abby's stepdaughters from her previous marriage.

Tabi seemed overjoyed. "Mama, I'm so glad you're awake! I wanted so badly to tell you the news."

Abby blinked. "News?"

"While you were asleep," Tabi enthused, "I found out that I'm pregnant!"

"Abigail, it's not your time," Abby's mother had told her. *"You need to go back to be with your kids and your grandbabies."*

276

Abby, still groggy, struggled to form the words. "You found out last night? Who finds out they're pregnant in the middle of the night?"

"I didn't find out in the middle of the night. Mama, you've been asleep for five weeks."

What Abby didn't know was that on the evening of the Christmas party, she and Win had been just three blocks from home when a car driven by a teenager veered into their lane and hit Win and Abby head-on. Win died at the scene of the accident. Abby was thrown fifty feet and had to be airlifted to a hospital. In the helicopter, she died three different times and was resuscitated. She suffered severe injuries to her brain and throughout her body. She'd spent the next five weeks in a coma, surrounded by friends and family.

Two visitors practically lived at the hospital while Abby was in her coma—a woman and a young girl Abby had never met before.

The pair was the mother and sister of the young man whose car had killed Win, and they visited Abby's family almost daily.

Shortly after Abby awoke from her coma and learned that Win had died, one of the nurses said, "Abby, someone is here to see you. The boy who was driving the car that hit you is here with his family. What should I tell him?"

Most of Abby's memories of life before the accident were gone. She could barely remember the man she had promised to marry. In fact, her clearest memory of Win was standing with him in heaven as he'd said, *"I want you to remember that I love you with all my heart."* She was trying to remember that he loved her, but it was a tall order when she could barely remember their life together at all.

Her brain injury had also affected her emotions. Abby couldn't seem to muster any feelings, including sadness or even loss. She didn't remember how to cry. Even so, the thought of meeting the young man who had been driving the car that had taken so much from her evoked a strong wave of . . . something. Anger? Regret? Resolve? Unable to put a name to it, Abby looked at the nurse, who was still waiting for her answer.

"Tell him no," Abby said. "I can't see him. Not today. Maybe not ever."

Abby spent the next two months living with her daughter Beth, who was devoted in taking care of her mother, and five more months living with Tabi. Abby was in a wheelchair, and her left hand had been paralyzed. She had lost all depth perception. The greatest injury had been dealt to her brain. In addition to losing all her emotions as well as memories, she couldn't remember to do simple things like take her medicine or eat.

Even recollections of things Abby had done or known most of her life were gone. One day she and her stepmother, Pearline, were driving home from one of Abby's frequent doctor appointments when Pearline suggested grabbing something to eat from McDonalds. Car idling, they sat at the drive-through window. Abby was silent.

"Sweetheart," Pearline said, "you need to tell me what you want so I can order for you."

Abby looked blankly at her stepmom. "But I have no idea what kind of food they serve here."

Recovery was slow as Abby relearned how to walk. Because of the brain injury, she had to focus on one thing at a time. Even breathing took conscious effort, and sometimes Abby forgot. Family and close friends knew to remind her, especially if she called them on the phone in a silent panic.

Her most meaningful victories came as she began to reclaim some of her memories and eventually some of her emotions as well. One day Abby opened up the file on her computer containing all her photos. Looking at pictures she'd taken of Win and the many places they had visited, she felt a few of her own memories starting to stir. Her emotions, however, took longer to heal.

For two years Abby felt nothing. Looking back, she says now that it was as if she didn't know how to have a feeling. On the two-year anniversary of the accident, she sat in her living room, looking at the wall where she'd hung a photo of Win. Suddenly she felt a lump in her throat. The next thing she knew, she was crying. It was a major breakthrough. After several minutes, though, Abby realized something was wrong. She could feel it in her chest. Tears still forming small rivulets on her cheeks, she picked up the phone in a panic and called one of her girlfriends. As soon as the woman saw Abby's name on caller-ID and heard the silence on the other end of the phone line, she knew what to do. "Breathe, Abby!" she said firmly. "Breathe!"

Some days Abby thought about her last conversation with Win. He had told her, *"I don't think you want to go back, Abby. You don't know how hard it's gonna be for you."* As she struggled to reclaim her life, there were days she wished she had listened to Win and stayed right where she was.

One Sunday morning, Abby was watching the television program *Hour of Power*. On that show, a woman shared how she had been driving on the freeway when someone on a bridge threw a bottle of acid at her car. It not only broke her windshield, but the acid also splashed all over her, leaving her disfigured. She talked about how, in time and with God's help, she had found freedom from bitterness, even finding it in her heart to forgive the assailant.

Abby often attended church and prayed, but she'd never been one to feel any consistent direction from God. At that moment, though, it was as if God gave her a nudge. She went to her phone. With a few calls, she obtained the number of the family of the boy whose car had changed the trajectory of her life forever. Speaking to his parents, Abby said, "I'd like him to know that I forgive him. Can you give him that message for me?"

One evening soon after that, Abby was in a restaurant. As the waiter refilled her water glass, he commented on how the best part of his job was getting to meet interesting people who had done unusual things.

Abby laughed. "You haven't heard anything yet! I died after a head-on collision and have been to heaven!"

The young man stared. "Tell me more."

Abby told him her story. As she finished, tears filled his eyes. "My brother died six months ago," he said. "I've been so worried about him, but you've given me comfort and hope. I can't tell you how much that means to me."

Abby left the restaurant convinced that she had just experienced a divine appointment.

On another occasion Abby was at her doctor's office, when she found herself in a conversation with a technician. After hearing about Abby's visit to heaven, the woman said, "I know you were meant to be here today and to tell me your story. My dad died about eight months ago, and my mom has been so upset she hasn't even been able to go into their bedroom. I needed to hear your story so I could tell it to her."

Before long, Abby noticed that almost everywhere she went—doctors' offices, restaurants, coffee shops, hardware stores—she met people who had questions about death or about God. Time and time again, they found comfort in Abby's story of what she had experienced.

One day Abby told a friend, "Before the accident, I was close to the Lord, but I can't say I took the time to really listen to anything he was saying to me. Now I hear him on a regular basis, telling me to share my story with the folks he brings across my path."

Today Abby walks with a limp. She still has limited memories of her life before the accident and continues to have to relearn the most unexpected things. "I wasn't feeling well recently and went to my doctor. He said, 'Are you feeling nauseated?' I told him, 'I have no idea what that word means or what it's supposed to feel like.'" She laughed. "It wasn't until I threw up in his office that we figured out that, yep, I'd been feeling nauseated!"

Win is buried in Williston, twenty miles from where Abby lives today. She has never visited his grave and says she probably never will. "I don't need to see dirt," she explains. "I can see dirt anywhere. I know where Win is. I've seen him there."

Abby continues, "What Win told me in heaven came true. Coming back was harder than I ever thought it would be, and I needed to be strong. Without my experience in heaven, I don't think I would have been strong enough for what was ahead of me, what lies ahead of me still. But what I told him in heaven was true too: *I can do it. I'll have the Lord with me, helping me along the way.*"

After she saw Win in heaven, Abby got a tiger-paw design tattooed on her ankle. Win graduated from Clemson University, and the paw print is the logo of their mascot, the Clemson tiger.

It's a symbol of strength, to be sure. It's also a reminder of the man who once gave her the courage to love and whose parting words gave her the courage to live. Abby says it's in honor of someone waiting for her on a field of the greenest grass she's ever seen—someone who loved her with all of his heart and, she believes, loves her still.

2

"An Angel Picked Me Up and We Flew"

Four-year-old Kennedy Buettner was dead at the bottom of a swimming pool for nearly fifteen minutes. Or was he?

On June 15, 2000, the Buettner family—Craig and Amy and their five small children—had just one thing on their minds: *baseball*. Little League baseball, to be exact. The oldest of the kids, ten-year-old Jacob, was a member of the top-seeded team in that year's championship series. Craig, a Tuscaloosa family physician and the University of Alabama football team doctor, was serving as assistant coach. As they prepared for the first game that afternoon, expectations were high. The adults decided to give the boys extra incentive by promising to throw a swim party that evening—*if* they won.

They lost.

When Craig and Brad, the head coach, saw how disappointed everyone was after the game, they quickly decided to have the party anyway.

"When we told them that, the boys were so happy," Craig said. "Turns out they were more upset about not getting the swim party than about losing the game."

Forty people, most of them children, crowded into the backyard of one of the team families that evening. The father, George, grilled hot dogs and hamburgers while the rest of the parents supervised the kids in the pool. When it was time for dinner, everyone was herded out of the water and into the yard, where they sat on towels and blankets.

Craig settled his kids down with plates of food. Four-year-old Kennedy, in his baggy red swimsuit, sat on a nearby towel with other children. Amy focused her attention on their five-week-old baby, Mark. Craig brought Amy a hamburger and finally sat down himself to enjoy a few moments' relaxation before the party moved back to the pool.

"I took one bite and felt like God gently tapped me on the shoulder and told me to find Kennedy," Amy recalled. "Somehow I knew before I ever turned around and looked that he was not on that towel with his brother anymore."

She was not terribly alarmed at first. As the mother of five small kids, she had learned long ago not to panic every time one of them wandered out of her sight. Still, Amy felt an unusually strong sense of purpose as she got up from her place and began searching for her son.

Her first stop was the pool. Kennedy had taken swim lessons and was at ease in the water. He might have somehow slipped back inside the fence while no one was looking. She searched all around the pool. No Kennedy. She walked to the front yard, calling his name as she went.

Still, no luck. Amy returned to the backyard and told Craig about the situation. He joined the search. Like Amy, he searched around the pool first for a glimpse of a little red swimsuit. Seeing nothing, he went inside to where Kennedy might have gone to play with toys. Outside again, he got distracted when one of the other children was run into by a tricycle and needed his attention.

Then Craig experienced the kind of horrific moment that haunts a parent's nightmares. He heard Jacob screaming, and ran to find him:

"Daddy, Daddy, we found Kennedy! He was at the bottom of the pool!"

Fear seized Craig. As a doctor, he was well prepared to deal with emergency situations. But he also knew the horrible implications of Jacob's words. He expected to have to jump in the water to bring Kennedy to the surface. When he arrived, he was surprised to see his son lying on the concrete at the pool's edge. Jacob and two other young boys had already dived in and retrieved him from beneath nine feet of water in the deep end. Kennedy was out of the pool—but the sight of him added to Craig's growing alarm.

His son had been underwater for more than twelve minutes.

The boy's body was deep blue. His skin was bloated and his belly looked like he was "nine months pregnant." He wasn't breathing and had no pain response. His pupils were dilated and unresponsive.

"Those are all the things I look for when I pronounce somebody dead at the hospital," Craig said. "Why I didn't want to just sit there and hold my child in my arms and cry right then, I don't know. Somehow the Holy Spirit gave me the power to ignore what my eyes saw and believe that my son wasn't really gone."

While others around him got on their knees and started praying or quoting passages from the Bible, Craig immediately began to administer CPR. After two and a half minutes, Kennedy still had not responded. At five minutes, he began taking erratic breaths on his own. Between five and ten minutes, the boy began to thrash around and exhibit behavior that doctors call "abnormal posturing," a kind of muscle seizure that indicates severe brain damage—and usually precedes death.

At eleven minutes, paramedics arrived.

Amy Buettner knew Kennedy was gone the moment she saw him. His leg felt like "cold rubber" to her touch.

But that didn't stop her from praying for a miracle.

"I fell on my knees and cried out to God, *'Please don't take him; I'll have him any way you'll give him to me.'* I didn't stop praying for an instant."

After a few minutes her hope revived, as she saw Kennedy start to breathe and move. But when she observed him posturing, she knew what it meant. She had seen that before.

Six months earlier, Amy had been at the bedside of her brother, Mark, when he died of brain cancer. For many months, she had watched him slowly succumb to the disease, which left him horribly scarred and incapacitated. Just before he died, at age thirty-five, Mark was seized by posturing spasms that she later learned resulted from a loss of brain function when someone is near death.

Mark had been the Buettner kids' favorite uncle. A Louisiana native, he was an avid deer hunter and outdoorsman. The kids called him "Uncle Buckmaster." His loss had been a severe blow to the whole family.

Still Amy prayed, "Lord, I know you are the true physician. I know you can heal my son."

Several hours later, Craig and Amy arrived at the intensive care unit of Children's Hospital in Birmingham, Alabama. While Kennedy had been transported from Tuscaloosa in a Lifesaver helicopter, they traveled the fifty miles by car—a trip that seemed to take, Craig said, "about five years."

Kennedy was now on a ventilator and attached to an array of IVs and instruments. He was restrained and paralyzed with special drugs to keep him from thrashing around in the bed and injuring himself further.

The doctor in charge did not sugarcoat the assessment he gave the Buettners that night. Based on clinical measurements of Kennedy's condition, he estimated the boy had only a 15 percent chance of survival. If he lived, there was only a 1 percent chance he'd recover to lead a normal life. In the bed next to Kennedy lay a girl who'd also drowned. She was still in a coma after three weeks.

"At that time the guilt and fear absolutely overtook my body," Amy said. "Why didn't I see him go to the pool? I felt like such a horrible mother. I accused myself of not giving him enough attention as the middle child, of not reading to him as much as I did the older kids when they were young, all those kinds of things. It felt like Satan had his claws sunk into my shoulder."

For her, the next forty-eight hours were a blur: meetings with doctors; nursing the baby, Mark; and fighting desperately to hang on to hope. On the third day, Amy was alone in the room with Kennedy, her Bible open on the bed. She asked God what she should read, and the answer came to her: "Today is the eighteenth of June—read Psalm 18."

As she read, one verse leapt from the page as if it were lit up in neon: "He reached down from on high and took hold of me; he drew me out of deep waters. . . . He brought me out into a spacious place; he rescued me because he delighted in me."[1]

"It was like a switch turned on," she said, "and I just knew that God was going to draw Kennedy out of 'deep waters' and rescue him."

That day doctors discontinued Kennedy's pain medication and removed his restraints.

Craig's faith "switch" was flipped the next day. He had noticed that ten-year-old Jacob was withdrawing deeper and deeper into himself as time went on. The boy blamed himself for what happened to Kennedy. "What kind of a big brother am I not to protect him?" he asked his father in despair. "It's my fault."

Craig escorted him to Kennedy's bedside. In spite of his critical condition, he looked much better than he had the last time Jacob had seen him—at the side of the pool. He was conscious, but just barely.

"There we were, crying and talking about ordinary stuff. I was explaining to Jacob what all the machines were for. Then I said to Kennedy, 'Little buddy, let Jacob know you're going to be all right, will you?' And even though he was still being artificially paralyzed, his left arm lifted up, reached across his body, and gave us a thumbs up. It was like electricity passing through our bodies when we saw that little thumb go up in the air. We knew God had told us Kennedy was going to be okay."

A while later, as Craig was sharing with Amy what had happened, he looked down at the plastic hospital bracelet both he and Amy wore while Kennedy was in the ICU. What he saw stopped him mid-sentence. The name of the doctor who had been there when Kennedy first arrived, but whom the family hadn't seen since, was *Mark Buckmaster.*

"To me it was one more sign that God was in charge and that everything would be okay. From then on, he got better and better."

Later that day doctors took Kennedy off the medication keeping him immobile. He still had a ventilation tube down his throat but was responding with nods and head shakes to questions. The attending neurologist was at a loss to explain what he was seeing.

"Are you scared?" Craig asked his son.

He shook his head. *No.*

On Tuesday doctors reluctantly took him off the ventilator. He coughed and sputtered as the tube came out of his throat. His voice was hoarse, but he was in good spirits. Amy held him in her arms for the first time. She could finally ask him the question that had haunted her for five days:

"Baby, what happened?"

His answer was not what she expected to hear.

"I was in a whirlpool, then an angel picked me up and we flew," he said, in his quiet, gravelly voice. "We flew through walls, and I flew through *you,* Mommy."

On Thursday—one week after arriving at the hospital with a 99 percent chance of being paralyzed and severely impaired cognitively for the rest of his life—Kennedy Buettner went home. That afternoon he played baseball, gingerly, with his brothers and sister.

Over the next few days, Kennedy talked more about things he had experienced after he went into the water.

"I was very, very careful not to put words in his mouth," Amy said. "I just let him tell me about things in his own way and in his own time."

Craig added, "As he told us where he went and what he saw, he would look to the left and right and even point, like he was remembering physical places he'd been."

The following conversation is compressed, having taken place over several days:

When the angel picked you up, where did you go?
I went to heaven.
What did you see?
I saw Jesus. I saw lots of people and angels. They were very happy.
Did you see Uncle Mark?
Yes. He looked just like Jesus. All his boo-boos were gone. He was happy. I saw a door with jewels on it. There was snow on the other side when they opened it.

"When he talked about what happened next, Kennedy got very quiet," Craig said. "He spoke in a whisper."

I saw a volcano, and there was a Pokémon[1] in it. No, it wasn't really a Pokémon, I've never seen that one. It was a dragon.
Was the dragon happy or sad?
He was happy. He looked at me and growled.
Were you scared?
No, I was with Jesus and Uncle Mark. I was standing on glass and I was invisible.
Was the volcano part of heaven?
No. (His tone seemed to imply, No, silly . . .) It's not part of heaven. There were lots of people in the volcano. They were very sad.
How did you get back?
Uncle Mark pushed me down, and an angel brought me back. You know, Mommy, Jesus is coming back here.

"I'll never forget how his little finger pointed down at the ground when he said, 'Jesus is coming back *here*,'" Amy said. "And, no, he didn't say when," she added with a smile.

Kennedy made a full recovery without ever suffering a setback. Ten years later, he has no negative residual effects from his brush with death. He is physically and academically normal—he's especially good at math. He plays on his school basketball team and enjoys tennis.

As a medical doctor, Craig admitted, "There is no science behind his recovery. I saw the X rays and the test results myself. The neurologist on his case can't explain it. This experience taught me vividly that life is so very fragile, but God is totally sovereign. In my practice I don't act like I have all the answers anymore. Now I know anything is possible."

For Amy, there is solace in knowing her brother, Mark, is healed and happy in heaven. She also takes comfort from the fact that, even in the grip of a potentially frightening death, Kennedy didn't suffer and wasn't afraid.

"There was no sting of death for him," she said. "All Kennedy remembers was he was in a whirlpool—which might have been the sensation of water swirling around him—and an angel picked him up. There was no struggle and no pain. He went straight to heaven."

The Buettners share their story every chance they get, but they stress there is nothing special about their family. Their purpose is to reveal what God did for them.

"We are the least qualified people in the world to talk in front of people," Craig said. "But it's not about us; it's about the plan God has for every one of us. It is about asking people, 'If you die today, do you know what comes next? Do you know where you will spend eternity?'"

3

To the Edge of Hell

When Ron DeVera "died" during open-heart surgery, he woke up to his worst nightmare.

Ron DeVera stepped carefully to keep his footing on the last patches of packed snow at the edge of his driveway, the crusty remnants of a storm that had blanketed Cleveland in early November 2008. He was loading luggage into the back of his car and looking forward to celebrating Thanksgiving in two days with his mother, Helen, and step-father, Richard, at their home in Columbus, a two-and-a-half-hour drive away. He always welcomed the chance to be with family—and was also glad for a break from his government job at the Defense Finance and Accounting Service.

Ron's wife, Julia, buckled their two children into the back seat of the car, a boy and a girl, five and two. Julia grew up in the former Soviet Union where she had become a licensed physician before emigrating to the United States. Here, her education qualified her to pursue a career as a registered nurse.

The sun was shining that day, and the air was crisp—chilly, but not bitterly cold. Ron started the car, pulled onto the street, and drove away without a backward glance. He had no reason to suspect he was heading toward a date with eternity, no clue it would be weeks—not days—before he returned home. There were no signs warning him that this journey would take him *much* farther than he planned.

He was about to go to the edge of hell and back.

The road trip itself was uneventful. Traffic was light, and the kids weren't as restless in their seats as usual. The family arrived at their destination and spent a relaxing evening of engaging conversation over a good meal. Finally, the kids were tucked in and the adults were getting ready to call it a day as well. Julia had already retired to the guest room. Ron was on his way to join her when he felt a twinge of discomfort in his chest.

The sensation wasn't dramatic, not like a full-blown heart attack that strikes with sudden, excruciating pain. Even so, the mounting pressure Ron felt in his chest summoned his undivided attention. He stopped in his tracks in the hallway as the tightening continued to build into a dull ache. He held his breath for what seemed a long time, then exhaled in deep relief when the pain began to subside and the pressure disappeared.

He continued on to the bedroom, where he told Julia about the incident. She sat up in bed like she'd received an electric shock, suddenly wide awake. As a medical professional, she knew all too well the implications of what her husband described.

"She didn't hesitate," Ron remembered. "She said, 'You need to get to the hospital. Right *now.*'"

Her urgency might seem like an overreaction, until one knows something about Ron's history with heart disease. Beginning in 2002, he had received medical treatment for significant blockages in his arteries almost like clockwork, every two years. He'd undergone multiple angioplasty surgeries, in which doctors inserted a balloon-like device into the clogged artery and inflated it to stretch the tissue. They'd left stents behind to hold open the passages. To make matters worse, heart disease was common among the men in Ron's family. His father died of a heart attack at age forty-two, along with two of his brothers—Ron's uncles—at forty-two and forty-three.

"It was simple chemistry with me," Ron said. "By this time I was eating healthier than ever, less of the bad meat and more vegetables and fruits. But there was no denying I was high risk."

His first thought when the pressure struck: *Not again!*

289

Still, by the time he told Julia what had happened, he felt much better. The pain and pressure were gone. He promised to go to the hospital in the morning if the discomfort returned. She reluctantly relented.

But at breakfast, the pain *did* return.

Richard drove Ron to the emergency room at a nearby hospital. Once aware of Ron's history, the ER physicians wasted no time admitting him for tests and observation. They quickly came to a troubling conclusion: Angioplasty was no longer an option. Ron had blockages of at least 70 and 80 percent in two arteries—in one instance in spite of a stent put there to prevent such a recurrence. The only remaining course of action was open-heart surgery to perform a quadruple-bypass operation.

Surgery was scheduled for the following Wednesday. Ron would spend Thanksgiving in the hospital.

Over the next several days of waiting, Ron pondered what might happen if he didn't make it through the surgery. He asked the hospital administration about executing a power of attorney and making out a will. They set him up with a staff lawyer who helped complete the necessary paperwork. He talked with Julia about whether the kids should come to visit him in the hospital. Though he wanted to see them, Ron decided against it—not wanting to be seen in his vulnerable and weakened state. He worried about insurance policies and mortgages and whether Julia and the kids would be taken care of if he died.

The one thing he never considered was what dying might mean for his soul. He never took inventory of his relationship with God.

Ron had gone to church regularly as a young man, but had stopped after disagreeing with some of the hypocritical practices he observed. After many years, he had recently found a congregation near his home and was attending services again—"once in a while." The whole issue of religion and salvation lay on the periphery of his life. So much so that, even lying in the hospital awaiting major heart surgery, Ron didn't stop to consider what might await him on the other side should something go wrong.

"It never really crossed my mind to talk to God," Ron admitted. "I figured, what was there to worry about? I didn't do evil things. I wasn't thinking about all the sins I had committed. I thought being basically a good person was enough. I was wrong."

The morning of the operation loomed cold and cloudy. The time for Ron's surgery came and went, since the patient on the table before him was in the operating room longer than expected. The minutes ticked by. Julia was there, along with Helen and Richard. Finally, Ron's turn came. Nurses put him on a narrow gurney and wheeled him through labyrinthine hallways to a set of double doors leading to the OR—a boundary his family couldn't cross. They said their good-byes and expressed love for each other. When his family had gone, the nurse briefed Ron about what to expect on the other side of the double doors. The next thing he knew, he was looking up into bright surgical lights. The process of getting prepped for surgery is a blur in his memory. He remembers voices, towels, IV needles, and then . . . darkness.

When Ron woke up, he was confused. Something wasn't right. He remembered where he was *supposed* to be—in the hospital recovery room. He looked around expecting to see familiar faces and feel a comforting touch. What he saw instead filled him with horror and stone-cold dread. He was in the middle of a dark forest. In every direction there were dead, barren trees against an ashen sky. A sticky "black gook" hung like moss from the ends of the twisted branches. He knew instinctively he would suffer great harm if the stuff ever touched his skin.

But that was not all he saw. Among the trees—reaching to the horizon all around him—lurked a virtual army of grotesque demons. Hundreds of them. Disbelief and confusion gave way to raw terror.

"Some of the demons were small, like gargoyles, with horns and claws," Ron recounted. "Others looked more like humans, except they were terribly misshapen. One close to me had something growing out of its back and sides—something like bones, but twisted and deformed."

Ron couldn't hear a single sound, but he saw the demons' lips moving and knew they were communicating with each other. Those nearest him suddenly fixed their attention on him and started moving slowly in his direction. One of the human-sort sat down beside him, and Ron immediately experienced a stabbing pain in his right hand. He couldn't see his own body, but clearly felt the demon press its claws into his flesh, torturing him just for the pleasure of witnessing the pain.

"I felt such panic," Ron said. "I thought, *This is it. I'm going to be tortured for the rest of my existence, and there is nothing I can do about it.* I knew if I didn't get out of there, they would keep me forever."

Then he had another thought: "*I don't belong here. I'm a good person.*"

Unable to move or flee, Ron called out to God for help. He barely recalls the words he prayed in pure desperation, but his plea was a heartfelt cry for deliverance from his tormentors. He asked God to lift him out of there and to make the demons go away.

The moment he prayed, they began to disappear. The small horned ones were the first to go. The taller human-looking variety seemed stronger and required all his focus and attention to resist. For what seemed like hours and hours—maybe days—he prayed. He still couldn't hear any sounds, but was intensely aware of the hatred the demons felt for him. Some of them would disappear when he prayed, only to be replaced by others. He fought on, continuously pleading with God for deliverance.

"There were so many," Ron said. "After a while I got extremely tired, just fighting to stay awake. Eventually, I couldn't do it anymore, and I fell asleep."

When he awoke again, the demon-filled forest had vanished. Instead, he found himself in a small, dark cave, the walls and ceiling pressing in on him. And he was not alone. Five or six demons lay on top of him in the cramped space, their weight pressing down on his chest with suffocating intensity. These creatures were different in appearance from the others he had battled for so long. They looked human but were translucent and ghostly white in color. The most striking feature of each of the demons was a pair of hideous, bright red eyes looking at Ron. Some of them were male in form and others looked female.

"My first thought when I woke up was that I'd failed," he recalled. "I thought in terror that these would be my tormentors forever. Those horrible eyes were redder than anything I'd ever seen. They were doing disgusting things to each other. I knew if I didn't escape somehow, they would start doing them to me too."

Once more, Ron refused to give up, clinging to the thought that he didn't belong there. He began to pray again, asking God to save him from the demons. He prayed with all his might and, as before, they started to disappear. Yet even as they were fading from sight, the weight of their bodies seemed to grow heavier and heavier until Ron feared he would be crushed. He cried out to God more fiercely than ever.

Suddenly a bright light broke into the darkened cave. He heard ordinary human voices around him—the first sounds he'd heard since he awoke in hell. The demons were completely gone now, and Ron was filled with assurance, at last, that he would recover. God had answered his prayers.

Ron DeVera's surgery was supposed to take only four hours. After twelve, his exhausted doctors were finally satisfied they had accomplished what they set out to do. But as soon as they began to close him up, Ron flatlined.

"I died on the table, and they had to open me back up," Ron said. "They shocked me three times to restart my heart."

Afterward, he was unconscious for ten days. During the first five, doctors kept his chest open, ready for emergency intervention. Later, Ron learned from Julia that nurses had to tie him down at one point because he kept struggling to get out of bed. He had no difficulty imagining what could make him do that.

After he woke up, Ron had only one thing to say to the medical staff: "I want to be baptized—*now*."

"When they saw I was serious, they said I was crazy," he said. "They told me about the risk of infection and all that, but I didn't care. All I could think about was getting things straight with God."

The physicians' arguments prevailed, and baptism had to wait. But not for long. Once he was released from the hospital, Ron arranged to be baptized by sprinkling at his mother's Methodist church on the Tuesday before Christmas. The pastor insisted on meeting beforehand to be sure Ron understood what he was doing and why. It was a formality that, in Ron's case, was hardly necessary. He knew exactly what was at stake. Hell was no longer an abstract concept to him. It was a vivid and harrowing reality.

After the ceremony, Ron told his story to the group of twenty or so people in attendance. He's told it many times since then.

"You can see in their eyes that most people don't really believe it," he said. "But that doesn't matter. I now know that heaven and hell exist. I have to warn people to change how they live and how they think, or they will end up where I was. If I can help one person avoid that, then I've done what God asked me to do."

Since spending time in hell, Ron has become committed to his faith and more involved at his church. He reads his Bible with enthusiasm. He tells his story often to anyone who will listen. Ron doesn't worry about the small stuff the way he once did. He confesses that he used to struggle with lust, but his old habits are simply gone now. He is less judgmental and less uptight about money. He knows God will provide.

After his close call with an eternity of torment, Ron's theology is very simple:

> It matters how we live, but just being a good person is not enough.
> We must confess our sinfulness to God and ask for forgiveness.
> We are expected to pass on to others the love and forgiveness we have received.

"I know now my life on this planet is very short, but I'm not afraid of death anymore," he said. "I know God is real and that Jesus died so I don't have to go back to hell ever again."

4

Road Trip to Redemption

A serious accident gave Peter Bower a glimpse of the afterlife—and the desire not to leave.

The shadows were starting to lengthen across Alton, Illinois, as a hot, sticky afternoon in the summer of 1994 began its metamorphosis into a pleasantly warm evening. Alton sprawls eastward from the banks of the Mississippi River, just a stone's throw from where it is joined by the Missouri in the long journey to the Gulf of Mexico.

The town is home to Southern Illinois University, where twenty-six-year-old Peter Bower had just completed his second year of dental school. As sunset approached that day, he had every reason to think his life was *very* good. He had successfully completed national board exams a few days earlier—a major milestone on the road to realizing his dream of becoming a dentist. He had managed to get that far without relying on his family for financial support, an accomplishment he was proud of. And he was heading home to spend an entire month with his parents at their home in Downs, a small town on the outskirts of Bloomington, Illinois. Life was good.

As Peter slid into the driver's seat of his tiny white and black Honda CRX for the trip, he especially looked forward to spending time working beside his dad, who was presently up to his ears in renovating the family home. The thought of hanging drywall or working on the roof for a few weeks was an appealing contrast to the stressful intellectual demands of school.

Nearly two and a half hours later, Peter exited Interstate 55 onto a two-lane county highway for the last leg of his journey—a route he'd traveled many times before. The road cut through gently rolling farmland that was covered in every direction by fields of shoulder-high corn. The sun had set at last, and away from the glare of the busy interstate the night was dark. Cool, moist air settled in the newly irrigated fields. Peter accelerated to feel the refreshing wind on his face through the open window—and to reach his destination a little sooner. Signs warned of road construction ahead, but he wasn't worried; he knew the road like the back of his hand. Besides, work was surely finished for the day. The posted speed limit was forty-five. He was doing fifty, maybe a little more.

About a mile from home, Peter crested the top of a gentle rise in the road. What he saw in his headlights on the other side made him instinctively cry out:

"Lord, help me!"

Peter Bower grew up in a Christian home. He was the youngest of five boys, with one sister, Becky, a year younger than Peter.

"We were a very close family," Peter recalled. "For most of my childhood, we lived in a small rural community in New York. We were poor but happy. My brothers and I would spend hours and hours in the woods pretty much doing whatever we wanted. There was always food on the table, but sometimes it came only from the garden because we had no money."

The family attended the Alliance Bible Church. At age three, Peter knew he wanted to become a believer too, and as he grew older, his faith became the focal point of his life. He was baptized during his senior year of high school.

In college, Peter helped establish a chapter of InterVarsity Christian Fellowship on campus. He developed a reputation as the guy who would openly speak up anytime the subject of evolution arose—which it frequently did in his many biology and anatomy classes. All a professor had to do was mention Darwinism, and his classmates would roll their eyes, put down their pens, and turn their attention toward Peter, knowing he would not pass up an opportunity to debate God's role as the sole Creator of the universe.

"I seemed to be going against the grain most of the time," Peter said. "I would go home almost every weekend, because nearly all my classmates were getting drunk or hanging out doing the things I wasn't interested in doing."

The words flew out of his mouth faster than thought: "Lord, help me!"

In the road, not more than a hundred feet ahead, stood a mound of dirt and sand left by the road construction crew. It was at least fifteen feet high and spilled into both lanes. Peter was driving too fast to avoid a collision. His car struck the shoulder of the pile and began to roll.

Not that Peter really noticed.

"As soon as those words passed my lips, a feeling came over me that is nearly impossible to describe," Peter remembered. "As my car rolled, it all seemed like a distant dream. In fact, I don't remember the events at all. What I do recall was the *feeling*—like being wrapped in a blanket of peace and love. I could not have cared less what was happening around me."

Peter had grown up hearing about the peace of God that "transcends understanding."[1] He even thought he had felt it once or twice in his life. Now as he flew through the air not wearing a seatbelt—and only vaguely aware of any danger—he experienced real peace for the first time.

"I think the reason I don't remember everything is because it didn't matter," Peter said. "Something far greater was happening—being held in that pervasive peace. I knew I wanted to stay right there forever, like it was the thing I'd been looking for all my life and didn't even know it. I was now complete."

Peter didn't feel his car come to rest. He has no memory of being ejected from the car as it rolled or of crawling from the wreckage. The next thing he knew, however, he was lying in the dirt in a cornfield beside the road. He felt no pain. His eyes were closed, yet he had a vivid sense of clarity and awareness. Peter has no idea how long he lay there, as time seemed to disappear. In that state, he felt an overwhelming sense of joy and peace.

"I was suddenly part of a vast culture of knowing, where nothing is hidden and everything is clear, so that fear and worry just vanish.

Communication was naturally forming in my mind all the time. Words were completely irrelevant."

In this altered state of awareness, Peter intuitively knew two things. First, he didn't *ever* want to leave. Having arrived in such an indescribably beautiful place—far beyond anything he'd ever experienced on earth—he was determined to stay forever.

Second, he knew he *had* to leave. His glimpse of existence beyond this life was only temporary.

"I knew I had to go back, but I was putting up a fight," Peter said. "I didn't want to go. Then, for the first time I felt an actual being coming near me. I sensed it was an angel—a messenger—and it was there because I was resisting going back."

Peter could not see the being, but clearly perceived his powerful presence. When he spoke, Peter heard the words plainly—and audibly: "Your work isn't finished."

"He spoke with such undeniable authority," Peter recalled. "I knew I had to comply."

Becky Bower, age twenty-five, was alone in her parents' home that evening. She expected her brother Peter to arrive from school at any moment. Outside, the family dogs were frantically barking. In fact, Becky suddenly realized that they had been riled up for a while—at least half an hour. It was not like them to bark for so long. She stopped what she was doing and went to the window to investigate. Looking out, she wasn't really surprised to see Peter's car in front of the house.

But something was wrong. Even in the dark she could see the windshield was shattered and pushed in to within a few inches of the steering wheel. The roof was bent and buckled. Becky ran outside and found her brother lying on the ground beside the car. He seemed stunned and confused. She led him into the house, then called her parents on the phone and told them to come right away.

"I have no idea how I got home that night," Peter said. "One minute I was in the cornfield, the next minute Becky was helping me up off the ground in front of the house. I was really confused about where I was, but not *who* I was or what had just happened to me. It's part of the miracle how I got from one place to the other—I just don't know."

As Peter lay down on the couch in the living room, the incredible envelope of peace and love that surrounded him began to fade. Waiting for his parents to arrive, he felt increasingly disoriented and distressed.

"As that beautiful, peaceful feeling left me, another feeling took its place," Peter said. "But this time, it was a feeling of horrible guilt. I felt keenly aware of my own sin, and I felt shame and horror. My sins surrounded me now, instead of the peace I had felt only minutes earlier."

When his father arrived, Peter told him what had just happened—and of his feelings of deep unworthiness.

"He did what we always did in our family when a crisis came along," Peter recounted. "He prayed with me. I had been living a Christian life, but right then I asked Jesus to forgive me and to be my Lord. That made me feel better."

Apart from the mild concussion Peter suffered that night, there was not a scratch or a bruise anywhere on his body. But he was not the same man as before. He now knows firsthand what the "peace that transcends understanding" really feels like, and that it awaits him again someday. He also gained personal insight into how the prophet Isaiah felt when he saw God in a vision: "Woe to me! . . . I am ruined! For I am a man of unclean lips, and I live among a people of unclean lips."[2]

"I've lost all fear of death," said Peter, who has been a dentist for more than ten years and lives in Phoenix, Arizona. "I know for a fact that what lies on the other side is absolutely astounding. I know who I am and what's going to happen to me when I die. Most of all, I know we are truly saved by divine grace, and nothing else."

5

Upward and Onward

Having questions about God, Marisa Vallbona found answers through a near-fatal accident.

Nineteen-year-old Marisa Vallbona waited impatiently for her sister, Maria, in the living room of their parents' home in Houston, Texas. The two girls had plans to go for a run together, and Marisa was eager to get started. The noontime summer heat outside grew more intense by the minute. Marisa leaned over and retied the laces of her running shoes. She methodically stretched her hamstrings and other leg muscles—again. She put a cassette in her Walkman and placed the headphones over her ears.

Marisa wasn't a very tolerant person, and she didn't like to be kept waiting.

When Maria finally appeared, Marisa threw open the front door and charged into the glaring sunlight. The Gulf Coast heat swept over her like a molten avalanche. It would be a tough run today, but Marisa remained undeterred. It was in her nature—and a part of her upbringing—never to quit or take no for an answer. Besides, running time was Marisa's prayer time—and she had a *lot* on her mind that day. Since starting college a year ago, her life had been one long chain of vexing questions. Today she planned to talk to God until he came through with some solid answers.

She cranked the volume on her Walkman and ran. After only a couple of blocks, her white shorts and shirt were already soaked, and her blond hair was slick with sweat. She labored to breathe in the dense, humid air. Still, she pressed forward. Ten minutes later, Maria signaled that she'd had enough and was turning back. Marisa nodded—and went on without her. Her prayerful purpose that day was too important to abandon so soon.

Marisa was raised in the Catholic Church, but she'd been a misfit and a rebel from the very beginning. Her Spanish father, a renowned physician and sought-after lecturer, took her with him on his many business trips abroad.

"Everywhere we went, he'd drag me to Mass," Marisa said.

And she didn't like it. She was not drawn in by the pomp and ceremony and liturgies.

When it came time for Marisa, at age seven, to receive her First Communion in the church, she dutifully attended catechism classes. She met every requirement put before her—except one: She refused to go to confession. Marisa told the nuns in charge of her education that she didn't believe it was right to confess her sins to a mere person. She would confess directly to God or not at all.

Full of spunk even then, she challenged the nuns to read their Bibles more closely if they didn't believe her. Eventually they conceded and allowed her to take Communion without going to confession.

At age twelve, Marisa attended a Baptist summer camp. The Protestant emphasis on an intimate, personal relationship with God, based on grace, was different from the Catholic approach she'd been taught—and it appealed to her immensely. Back at school, she became actively involved in Young Life, a campus ministry that reaches out to teenagers. Throughout high school, Marisa's relationship with God continued to mature and deepen. Her faith had become unshakable.

Or so she thought.

After her graduation in 1982, Marisa enrolled in a prominent liberal university, where she was immersed in an entirely different philosophical worldview than the one she had known. On campus, God seemed to have been banished from every classroom and dormitory. Everywhere she turned, she was confronted by Darwinistic thinking and a deeply entrenched belief in science and reason as the only possible source of ultimate truth.

Predictably, she began to question her faith in the face of so much competing and contradictory "evidence."

As if that weren't enough, nearly all her newfound friends seemed to be having a great time—drinking, doing drugs, and having sex. Aside from trying alcohol like nearly everyone, Marisa didn't follow along with the "party" crowd. She and her boyfriend decided to avoid sex and even attended church together. But being surrounded by so many contradictory influences was enough to make her question her own view of right and wrong.

"I'd always tried to walk straight," she said, "but the way these people were living suddenly looked like so much *fun*. I asked God, 'Am I wrong to be tempted? Why do I feel like I'm growing apart from you? What's the right thing to do?'"

These were the questions swirling through Marisa's mind as she ran that day, the sticky asphalt radiating heat like a hot griddle beneath her pounding feet. She turned onto a street that led past the neighborhood swimming pool, where she had spent many hours as a teenager. The cool, refreshing water had never looked more inviting—but she would not stop. She was driven by a single question forming in her mind, one that summed up all the others that troubled her:

"God, are you truly real?"

According to those who witnessed what happened next, Marisa should not be alive today. She should have died—and not come back.

A huge early 1980s-model Cadillac rounded the corner behind Marisa. A big-boned blonde in her forties named Diane was at the wheel. It remains a mystery why she didn't see Marisa running on the road ahead, a few feet from the curb. Maybe her eyes were drawn toward the swimming pool that was packed with people that day. Maybe she was adjusting the car's air-conditioner, or switching channels on the radio. Maybe Marisa wandered into her path, distracted by the music playing in her ears and the questions troubling her mind. Whatever the reason, Diane hit Marisa directly from behind.

Wham!

The impact tossed the girl's body into the air like a rag doll. She came down hard on the hood of the car, with the sickening *whump* of buckling

302

metal. Reflexively, Diane slammed on the brakes. Marisa rolled off the hood and fell limply to the pavement beside the car. It finally came to a stop, with the rear wheel pinning Marisa's right leg to the ground.

The whole catastrophe unfolded in less than two seconds.

The on-duty lifeguard across the street watched it all in horrifying slow motion from his umbrella-covered perch overlooking the pool. He was Marisa's age, a former high school classmate of hers named Smokey Mountain. He ran faster than he'd ever run to the scene of the accident and performed mouth-to-mouth resuscitation. Marisa was unconscious and blood poured from a cut on her head. He ran back to the pool office and dialed 9-1-1.

Mercifully, Marisa—that is, the part of her that was conscious and aware—was not present for any of the above. She never realized she was about to be hit by a car. She didn't feel it strike the back of her legs. She had no sensation of being hurled into the air, landing on the hood of the car, or falling to the asphalt.

"I immediately left my body," she recalled. "One minute I was running, the next minute I felt like I was on the outside of everyday life. It was dark. I don't mean creepy dark, just dark like having your eyes closed. I couldn't see anything, but I knew God was very, very present. I felt really, really good."

Marisa struggles, like so many people who've had similar experiences, to find the right words to describe what happened to her. Language, she says, can only crudely approximate the ineffable quality of the sensations she felt and the radically altered state of awareness she enjoyed while outside of her body.

"To have some idea, get in the deep end of a swimming pool," Marisa said. "Go under the water and hear how quiet it is—experience how peaceful you feel just floating there. Open your eyes and you can see all these other bodies swimming along beside you. You are suddenly aware of things you couldn't see a moment ago, because they were hidden underwater. Your movements are effortless. Nothing hurts. You don't even feel gravity or the weight of your body. You have no wants, no needs, no fears."

As soon as she left her body, Marisa was filled with a deep, indescribable feeling of peace and well-being. She knew she had died and wondered why she had ever been so afraid of something so wonderful. Knowledge and communication were fundamentally different from anything she'd ever experienced in life. Nothing was hidden from her mind. She had only to think a question to know its answer.

Marisa became aware of other beings all around her on a "spiritual plane." She doesn't know if they were angels or human spirits. But they were each made of a beautiful, radiant light. None were threatening or frightening in appearance. She remembers feeling astonished to realize that living people are surrounded by such a rich spiritual reality all the time—and are completely oblivious to it. She had been a Christian for several years but had never been taught just how close the spiritual plane really is.

"I felt perfectly safe and at home," Marisa said. "And I had the sensation of moving upward through the darkness toward something; I never saw what. I didn't go toward a bright light like some people describe. But I definitely felt like I was moving up."

As she traveled, Marisa began to think that she wasn't ready to die.

"I thought, *I'm only nineteen. I'd like to see how my life turns out, to see if I succeed in life and if I have kids.* Right then, I felt that I was a participant in the decision, like it was my choice."

Then Marisa had a conversation with God.

"I said to him, 'Now that I know what death is all about and that it is totally cool, send me back and let's see what kind of a difference I can make. I'm going to sing your praises and spread the Word. Put me to work!'"

God told Marisa, "I will send you back, and you will make a difference—now that you know I am *real.*"

Then Marisa stopped moving upward and away from her earthly life. She was suddenly hovering in the air above the scene of her accident. She could see what was happening below with startling clarity. She saw her body on the ground covered in blood. Paramedics had arrived and were preparing to place her in an ambulance. Her mother and sister stood at the back of the ambulance, sobbing and screaming. A large crowd of onlookers from the swimming pool stood in a wide circle in the street around her lifeless body. Marisa felt no fear or pain at what she saw, but took it all in as if it were happening to someone else.

In a flash, that feeling of detachment came to an abrupt halt.

"I was right back in my body," she said. "The pain was instantly excruciating. Even worse was the feeling of not belonging here anymore."

Marisa suffered a concussion that day and a nasty gash on her head. She was bruised and scratched up, but no bones were broken—not even the leg that wound up under the car's wheel. However, to this day she suffers from severe migraine headaches that began after the accident.

But Marisa was undoubtedly changed dramatically by her near-death experience. She became much less judgmental and more focused on looking for the good in people. Though she has enjoyed a successful career, achievement and accolades in life took a backseat to serving God. She has never felt the slightest fear of death. On the contrary, she looks forward to it when her time does come. Most important of all, she has never again questioned her faith—and she isn't shy about sharing it with others.

"I know with absolute certainty that God exists," she said. "We are accountable to him, and we would be crazy not to believe in him and have a relationship with him. Now I know we can die at any given moment. You don't have until tomorrow. When it comes to getting your faith in order, *right now* is all you've got."

On some days, Marisa, who now lives in La Jolla, California, wishes she had not asked to come back to earth. Then she thinks of her two wonderful sons and she remembers why she did: to "make a difference" for them—and anyone else willing to listen to her story.

Part Two

Someone to Watch Over Me

Angels, wearing halos or Harley jackets, regularly intervene in the lives of ordinary people.

Have you noticed the increase in angel sightings over the past decade? We're not talking about *actual* angelic encounters—though we can't rule that out. We mean our society's fascination with these heaven-sent beings. They seem to be everywhere these days: blogs and bumper stickers, trinkets and TV shows, music videos, and coffee mugs.

Not that long ago, the popularity of angels saw a dramatic spike around Christmastime. We would all sing familiar carols such as "Angels We Have Heard on High" and "Hark! the Herald Angels Sing." Millions tuned in annually to watch the holiday film classic *It's a Wonderful Life*, with George Bailey and his kind but clumsy guardian angel, Clarence Odbody. And many of us grew up listening to Mom or Dad read the nativity story from the New Testament, in which angels played a starring role: "Greetings, you who are highly favored!" an angel tells Mary. "You will be with child and give birth to a son, and you are to give him the name Jesus" (Luke 1:28, 31).

More recently, the interest in angels has gained momentum and is not only the domain of holiday hoopla. Who can forget the popular TV show *Touched by an Angel* that aired from 1994 to 2003? It was a feel-good series that featured a group of angels sent by God to help humans mired in a mess of one sort or another.

And today your search for angelic insights will reap a bounty of material, some genuinely helpful, most of it not so much. There are thousands of CDs, videos, Web sites, novels, seminars, and retreats ready to aid your quest for angelic intervention. More than a few books promise to show you how to "activate" angels in your life.

All of this interest in angels is good in the sense that it opens people's hearts and minds to the awareness of the spiritual world and the participation of God's emissaries in our daily lives. The downside is that much of the information being dispensed is based not on fact but on fantasy and fabrication (much of which we discussed in *Heaven and the Afterlife*). With that in mind, here's a biblically based version of "Angels 101"[1]:

The term itself comes from the Greek *angelos*, which means "messenger." In ancient times, when travel was slow and communication limited, personally delivered messages were coveted and critical; battles could be won or lost due to a courier's expedience or delay. It's not surprising that Greek mythology has a winged messenger as one of its gods: Hermes—also known as Mercury in later Roman times. Other cultures and religions included the idea of messenger gods. And then there is Hebrew literature, which contains many accounts of angelic messengers with names like Michael and Gabriel.

Scripture provides these angelic insights for us:

First, angels, like humans, are creatures, meaning "God-*created*." They are not equal to God, but exist to carry out his missions and accomplish his will.

Second, they have personality—intellect (thought), emotion (feeling), and will (choice). They are creatures with distinct and unique abilities, purposes, and personalities.

Third, they exist in time and space. They're limited by these dimensions, although they have much more freedom than we do. The writer of the book of Psalms says the angels should praise God because he created them.[2] Another song of praise says humans were made "a little lower than the heavenly beings."[3] Like us, angels are personal creatures: responsible, accountable, and dependent upon God.

Though existing in time and space, angels seem able to appear and disappear suddenly or travel from one place to another very quickly. They often appear in some kind of glorified humanlike form—with unusual brightness resembling fire, lightning, polished metal or precious stones, and/or shining white linen clothing.[4] Other angels, not resembling humans at all, are likened to unusual beasts.[5]

There's no question angels are superhuman. The angel encountered by the Old Testament prophet Daniel was stronger, smarter, and faster than any human. He could fight heavenly battles, see into the future, and even though it took time, go between Persia and Babylon without breaking a sweat. But they aren't all-powerful or all-knowing, and they cannot be everywhere at once. Only God has these qualities.

With that basic knowledge in mind, it's also safe to say that we don't know when angels might appear and, if they do, in what form. As protectors, they are unpredictable. As messengers, they are mysterious. They do God's bidding, and frankly, we don't always understand what God's bidding is. Theologian F. Forrester Church wrote:

> If angels came in packages, we'd almost always pick the wrong one. Even as the devil is evil disguised as good, angels are goodness disguised. They show up in foolscap, calico, gingham, and brown paper bags. Jesus discovered the realm of God in a mustard seed, the smallest and least portentous of all seeds. Mustards seeds and angels have this in common. They are little epiphanies of the divine amidst the ordinary.[6]

Despite what we don't know about angels, surely there's one thing we do know: they are at this moment actively engaged in the affairs of our world and our individual lives. They are helping, guiding, protecting— usually unseen.

When we share stories of angelic encounters—like ones in the pages ahead—many people wonder, "Why didn't angels come to my rescue when I needed them? Where were they in my time of trouble?" The obvious answer is: God only knows. But there's another answer, just as true: It's highly likely that angels have swooped into your life at various times unnoticed or unrecognized. Who knows how many times you've been shielded from evil forces? Who knows how many times you've been saved from a fatal accident by a hairsbreadth? Who knows how many times a blessing has dropped in your lap "coincidentally"? You'll never know—this side of heaven.

Yet another thing is true: We probably rub shoulders with angels much more than we realize. As the writer of Hebrews advised: "Do not forget to entertain strangers, for by so doing some people have entertained angels without knowing it."[7] If you doubt for a moment that angels show up at unexpected times, in unexpected ways, just read the stories to follow and see if your faith in God's messengers isn't bolstered.

6

Angels All Around

On the brink of death, Ryan Heer brought home a message from beyond.

The medical student stood for several minutes studying the face of the little boy in the bed in front of her. Turning to his mother, she asked, "Do you have a picture of him?"

Cheryl Heer glanced over at her five-year-old son. He was unconscious, his neck, face, and head swollen to twice its normal size. She couldn't see his eyes or, for that matter, any other features that made him recognizable as the vivacious little boy he was. Cheryl walked numbly to her purse and pulled a school photo from her wallet.

An ICU nurse herself, Cheryl knew exactly what the med student was thinking and why she needed the photo. The nurse was thinking, *I can't see a kid in there.*

Cheryl had done the same thing at times, asking families for photographs of her patients. Caregivers asked for photos when patients were so ill or wounded they were barely recognizable as human beings. It helped the nursing staff reconnect and remember that this was a real person they were treating.

That's when Cheryl realized the gravity of the situation.

It was hard to believe that one week earlier Ryan was at home with his younger brother, Jordan, watching cartoons and eating popsicles while the two boys recovered from routine cases of chicken pox. When one large pock behind Ryan's ear turned red and began to swell, Cheryl and her husband, Jeff, weren't too worried. But as the swelling continued, they realized something was terribly wrong. Within hours, Ryan's neck had swollen so much that it pushed his head over against his left shoulder. What's more, his temperature shot up to 105 degrees.

Rushed by ambulance to Riley Hospital for Children in Indianapolis, Ryan's condition only worsened. His head, swollen to twice its normal size, had been pushed upright again because the massive swelling had spread now to both sides of his neck. His temperature remained elevated, and his torso grew inflamed and red. As infection raged throughout his body, he was put on oxygen and a heart monitor in anticipation of pneumonia or cardiac arrest.

The infection was being caused by streptococcus bacteria that had invaded one of Ryan's chicken pox. At that point, the swelling had so severely twisted Ryan's neck that doctors were afraid it would break and damage his spinal column. Believing the infection had entered Ryan's bones, doctors wanted to operate so they could scrape the infection from Ryan's vertebrae and insert pins to hold everything together. Still, they were certain Ryan would not survive the surgery. They also knew he would not survive without surgery. Concluding there was nothing left to do but wait, they fully expected Ryan to die from a broken neck.

On a Sunday evening ten days after their ordeal began, Jeff was at home with two-year-old Jordan. Alone with Ryan in his hospital room, Cheryl wept over the realization that her son was dying.

There had been another Ryan, years ago, but he'd died too. Ryan Updyke wasn't actually Cheryl's brother, but he might as well have been. The little boy had been just three years old—and Cheryl seven—when he became part of her family. The son of Cheryl's mother's best friend—a single mom who worked evenings—Ryan spent most afternoons and evenings at Cheryl's home. When he was sixteen, Ryan was diagnosed with bone cancer. He died eighteen months later. When Cheryl and Jeff married and had their first baby, they named him after the "little brother" Cheryl had loved and lost.

Cheryl's son didn't know about the young man whose name he shared. She had been looking forward to telling him about the older Ryan one day. Now it seemed that day would never come. As Cheryl looked around Ryan's room—overflowing with hundreds of cards, stuffed animals, and flowers—she knew that people in churches all over the country were praying for Ryan. And yet it felt like hope was draining away with every passing hour.

Cheryl saw Jeff's devotional Bible lying open on a nearby table. Picking it up, she read a reflection written by Billy Graham about Psalm 91:11: "For he will command his angels concerning you to guard you in all your ways."

Could God send angels to guard Ryan? Where would he put them? Cheryl looked around Ryan's room again. It was definitely standing-room only. Too many stuffed animals and balloons, not to mention all the medical equipment. The only empty places in the room were the corners. Sobbing, she began to pray.

Through her tears, she prayed, "Lord, send four of your angels to guard the four corners of this room. Watch over my son, protect him, comfort him if he's in any pain, and guide him home to you if he's not going to stay here with us."

Cheryl soon fell into a troubled sleep, waking every few minutes to the sounds of beepers and monitors, and the bustle of nurses coming and going throughout the night.

At the Heer family home, Jeff was praying a different kind of prayer. Having finally gotten Jordan to bed, Jeff paced the house. Finally, in his bathrobe, he went into the backyard and looked up at the stars. Raising his arms, he yelled toward the heavens, "What's going to happen? God, help us!"

The following night, it was Cheryl's turn to stay home with Jordan while Jeff spent the night by Ryan's side.

The last thing Cheryl did before falling into an exhausted sleep was to phone the room and speak with Jeff.

"How is he?" she asked, then listened as he told her there was no change and that Ryan was still unconscious but appeared to be resting well.

Cheryl went to sleep. Ever since she'd read Billy Graham's devotional, she'd had a sense of peace. No matter what happened, God was going to see them through this devastating trial.

The next morning, Cheryl phoned Jeff again. She could hardly utter the words "Good morning" before her husband said, "You need to get down here right away."

Cheryl's heart dropped into her heels. In a panic, she choked out the words, "Why? What's happened?"

"Because Ryan woke up around four this morning and started crawling around his bed, rearranging all his pillows. He said they weren't comfortable enough!" Jeff laughed. "Just get here as quick as you can!"

When Cheryl walked into Ryan's hospital room, he opened his eyes—mere slits in his still-swollen face—and called out, "Hi, Mommy!"

An influx of doctors and nurses kept Ryan busy for hours. At one point, Ryan's doctor turned to Jeff and Cheryl and said, "Well, things are turning around. Thank God we didn't take him into surgery! Let's just see how he does."

Ryan's swelling continued to subside by the hour.

Later that day, Ryan's grandmother pulled him in a little red wagon to the hospital library to watch a movie. The following day, he colored Easter eggs and got to sit in the wagon again while Cheryl pulled him to the nurse's station so he could tell her where to hide the eggs.

Two days later, he was home.

Ryan spent the next several days lying on the couch and watching cartoons and movies. He was still weak, but recovering quickly.

One day when he'd been home about a week, Cheryl was sitting at her dressing table putting on makeup while Ryan sat on a little bench next to her table and watched and played, as he often did.

Cheryl said, "Ryan, you were so, so sick!"

They talked about his stay in the hospital. She was thankful he remembered nothing from the first ten days when he was either in excruciating pain or unconscious.

"I remember the wagon," Ryan told her as he played with some string he'd pulled out of his pocket. "And seeing a movie. And coloring eggs."

"I prayed for you, Ryan," his mother said. "I prayed for angels to watch over you and help you not feel bad."

"Yeah, I know," he answered.

She looked at him quizzically. "What do you mean, *you know*?"

"I know," he said. "I saw the angels."

Cheryl glanced at her son. Now he was playing with her makeup brushes. "Really? Where were the angels, Ryan? What did they look like?"

Ryan said matter-of-factly, "They were standing in the corners of the room. And flying around too. There were mommy and daddy ones, and baby ones and grandma and grandpa ones. They were yellow and white and really pretty."

Cheryl didn't know what to think. She half-believed him. Then again, maybe through his coma he'd heard her praying.

"I had a dream too," Ryan said as he hopped around the table. "About Jesus. We were planting stuff in a garden. He said I was a good boy and that he loved me."

She looked at her son in wonder. "That's interesting. Anything else?"

Ryan was getting fidgety now. He'd sat for too long and was ready to play. He started skipping toward the door. Cheryl turned back to her mirror.

But he stopped and said over his shoulder, "Oh, yeah. Ryan says '*Hi*.'"

Something pierced Cheryl's heart. She turned toward him. "Wait. Come back here. What did you say?"

Ryan skipped back to the dressing table.

Cheryl stared at her son. "What did you say?"

"Ryan said to tell you '*Hi*.'"

"Anything else?"

"Nope." And he skipped off.

Cheryl sat there for a long time, crying. So it was true. Everything her son had seen and told her was true. God had answered Jeff's prayer for help, and Cheryl's prayers for angels, then sent her a message from the older Ryan too, so she would believe. Her heart overflowed with gratitude.

A week later the phone rang. It was one of the coaches with the T-ball league at the local YMCA saying that Ryan would be on his team. Jeff and Cheryl had signed Ryan up to play T-ball months ago, before his razor-thin brush with death. Cheryl explained everything to the coach, adding, "He's still getting his strength back, but I know he really wants to play. Why don't we bring him to practices and see how he does?"

Ryan did great, playing first base all spring and summer—and the next summer, and the summer after that—eventually playing baseball through junior high.

Not that it should have come as any surprise considering the name of Ryan's very first T-ball team: the Angels.

7

Divine Defenders

Martha Cabot and her granddaughter, Abby, know from firsthand experience that angels are real—and ready to lend a hand when we need them most.

In late June 2004, Martha Cabot and her seven-year-old granddaughter, Abby, stepped out of an air-conditioned movie theater in Fort Worth, Texas, into a hot and muggy summer evening. The sun had just disappeared below the horizon, and a murky dusk was quickly turning to night. The two were laughing and discussing the animated film they'd just seen. To Martha, the sound of Abby's laughter was like sweet music; it had been some time since she'd heard it.

Abby's father, Robert—Martha's son—had been called to active duty, along with the rest of his National Guard field hospital unit, and sent to Iraq for fifteen months. He'd been gone for five months already, but to everyone in the family it felt more like five years. In addition to the emotional burden of constant worry for Robert's safety, the family was under heavy financial pressure, since his military paycheck did not fully cover monthly expenses. Abby's mother, Rachel, had been forced to take a second job. Most of all, the strain of Robert's absence was taking a toll on Abby. With every passing day she grew more withdrawn and sullen.

Martha had recently decided she wasn't going to let fear and uncertainty defeat her family without a fight. She had just emerged from a lengthy battle with depression after the sudden death of her husband in a car crash two years earlier. The turning point in her own recovery had arrived when she resolved to keep busy with things she enjoyed, no matter how bad she might feel on any given day. Martha would invoke the same wisdom to help Abby—with tickets to the ballet, regular ice-cream dates to try out new flavors, trips to the zoo or the children's museum—anything to remind them both that the world was still a safe, fun place to be, even when hardships arise.

It had been an especially hard week for everyone, and Martha found herself looking forward to a little childlike frivolity. Today, Abby had chosen to go see the latest Disney film—just the thing they needed: a good dose of singing and silliness. After the movie was over, the theater emptied out quickly, but Martha and Abby lingered until the credits ended. By the time they gathered their things and emerged through the exit into the parking lot, the rest of the moviegoers had already found their cars and driven away.

"Holding Abby's hand as we walked and laughed together felt really, really good," Martha said later. "It was like we were the only two people in the world that day, and nothing could possibly harm us. Our troubles seemed very far away."

But that feeling didn't last long. They had walked half the distance to the car when Martha sensed movement in her peripheral vision. She looked and saw four young men walking across the nearly empty parking lot—on a course to intercept them. The man leading the others was tall and slender. He wore an oversized sports jersey and baggy pants that were barely held up by a belt that rode beneath his hips. A ball cap sat sideways on his head. As he walked, he never took his eyes off of Martha. The others behind him stole furtive glances at her as well, when they weren't scanning the parking lot for signs that someone might be watching.

Martha knew instantly they were in trouble. She glanced back toward the theater, judging how long it would take to reach the safety of the lobby. An icy panic flooded her body when she saw a fifth young man following them—and blocking their retreat. Martha tightened her grip on Abby's hand and quickened her step toward the car. The leader of the gang matched her accelerated pace and stepped between her and the driver-side door just before she reached it. Up close, Martha saw that he wasn't a man at all, but a teenage boy of about seventeen. His arms were covered in menacing tattoos, and his eyes were hard and determined.

His body may be young, Martha realized, but that doesn't make him less dangerous.

"What do you want?" she asked, with more confidence than she felt.

The young man grinned. "We're taking donations for our college fund today," he said. "You want to help us get a head start in life, don't you?"

The rest of the gang now stood in a loose circle around Martha and Abby. Someone snickered at the dark humor.

"I'd love to help you," Martha said, her voice trembling with tension, "but threatening an old woman and a little girl is hardly what I'd call a head start in life."

"Thanks for the tip," he said, his face hardening with malice. "Now give me your purse." He looked at Abby, clutching her grandmother's arm with one hand and the child's purse she'd received for her last birthday in the other. "You too, runt."

Martha scanned the area, desperately hoping to see someone who might hear a call for help. Night had deepened now, so that all she saw were cones of light thrown by street lamps onto the now empty parking lot. Traffic streamed by on an adjacent road—too far away to offer any hope. She knew they were on their own.

"Do it now!" the young man shouted and stepped closer to Martha, towering above her menacingly. The others moved inward as well.

Martha's split-second reaction surprised her. Instead of feeling frightened and helpless—as the gang clearly intended—she was flooded with courage she couldn't explain. She thought of her son serving in the desert halfway around the world, doing his part to rid the world of terrorism. She wasn't about to give in to it so easily here at home. And alongside that resolve, she felt a deep, inexplicable compassion for these boys who had lost their way so completely.

Martha tightened her grip on her purse and on Abby's hand.

"No," she said, firmly. "We won't give you anything."

The young man's face twisted into a mask of anger. He spat out a string of vicious expletives and grabbed hold of Abby's purse. He yanked it so hard that she fell to the ground—still holding on to the purse strap. He drew back his foot to kick at her.

"Don't you dare!" Martha cried and reflexively bent down to shield her granddaughter.

One of the other men shoved her violently from behind. As she fell, someone ripped her purse from her shoulder. Martha braced herself on the pavement with both arms to keep from landing hard on Abby. She sat up with her back against the car door. She knew there was nothing else she could do to prevent the gang from finishing what they had started. The leader was ranting now about giving them "what they deserved."

"Dear God, have mercy," she said aloud and gathered Abby in her arms. "Lord, protect us."

"Ma'am, are you all right?"

The words rang out from several yards away in a deep, resonant voice. Martha strained to see who it was, but her view was blocked by the car.

"Help us!" she cried.

The gang leader, now fully enraged, shouted some more expletives then yelled back at the man, "It's none of your business! Get out of here!"

"No, I don't think we can do that," he said, stepping from behind the rear of the car. He was joined by a second man who stood calmly beside him. "Return what you've taken and leave. *Now.*"

"I was looking right at them," Martha recalled later, "but I couldn't see their features very well. All I can say is that they were big and gave off an incredibly comforting sense of power and confidence. It's like they were instantly in control of the situation."

Martha heard receding footsteps as some of the gang members ran away without a word. The leader hesitated. His back was turned to her, but Martha imagined him glaring at the two men, calculating his chances against them. A tense silence lasted a few seconds, and then he suddenly dropped Martha's purse and took off running as fast as he could go.

"Oh, thank you, God!" Martha said in deep relief. "Thank you! Thank you!" She got to her feet and helped Abby up.

Martha called out loudly to the men, "If you hadn't come along, I don't know what would have happened!"

But as Martha looked around, she was suddenly confused.

"Where did those men go?" Abby asked.

Martha saw no trace of their rescuers in any direction. She did see the gang leader disappear into the darkness at the edge of the lighted parking lot, still running as if his life depended on it—but no one was pursuing him. She and Abby were completely alone.

It was a mystery, but she wasn't going to stand around trying to solve it. Martha hurriedly loaded Abby in the car and drove straight home.

Later, however, after reflecting on the evening's events, she came to an inescapable conclusion: God had sent his angels to protect Abby and her from certain harm. From the moment the two "bodyguards" arrived, she had felt safe and secure, enveloped in a comforting presence that she could only describe as supernatural. It had been a wide, open area where they had been confronted by the thugs—and where the protectors had appeared—and surely she would've seen them walking away. In an instant, they had simply vanished from sight.

"When I tell this story, a lot of people want to speculate about what might have happened had the angels not intervened," Martha said. "But all I can think about is that they *did* help us, and what that means about our ability to trust in God's merciful protection."

Paradoxically, the incident served to strengthen the family's faith that Robert was being cared for too. At prayer times, Abby took to asking the angels, with unshakable conviction, to please watch over her daddy. Martha understood where the girl's new ability to trust had come from: She had seen God's angels with her own eyes. And indeed, Robert remained safe throughout his tour of duty.

8

Friends of the Family

Stricken with cancer, teenager Carly Kilander drew comfort from frequent visitors not of this world.

O n the fifth anniversary of her daughter's death, Kim Kilander worked late. Earlier in the week, co-workers had covered Kim's desk with so many cards and balloons that the day before a young woman from another department had stopped to ask Kim if it was her birthday.

After Kim explained that the flowers were to honor her daughter Carly, a flash of recognition crossed the face of the twenty-something woman standing before her.

"Your husband wrote a book about your daughter, didn't he?" she asked. "I've wanted to read it."

They chatted for a few minutes, and as her visitor walked away, Kim couldn't help but notice she was about Carly's age. Or, to be more precise, the age Carly would have been if she were still alive.

It had lifted Kim's spirits being able to talk about her daughter with the young woman. But today, on the anniversary of Carly's death, Kim felt melancholy. Her daughter's passing had been as extraordinary as her life, but what difference did it make now, five years after the fact? Her family and friends had been through so much. Had it all been in vain?

The last two months of Carly's life had been filled with pain—but with miracles as well. Take, for example, the angels.

The first time they had showed up was on a Sunday. The day began oddly anyway because from the moment Carly woke up she was her old self. She felt bright and lucid, not groggy and pain-addled like she'd been for several weeks.

Carly was no stranger to pain. When she was just eighteen months old, she'd been diagnosed with neurofibromatosis, a disorder that causes large, benign tumors to grow in the nervous system. Other symptoms of the disorder include abnormal development of the spine, skull, and shin bone. Indeed, by the time Carly was thirteen, she'd undergone a dozen operations. One stubborn problem had been a severe bow in her ankle bones. Doctors had tried everything to remedy the problem, implanting bone chips from Carly's hip, a battery pack to stimulate growth, and finally a metal rod. But nothing seemed to help. Almost every night, Carly would ask her mom or dad to rub her foot, finding relief in their touch.

In December of her senior year in high school, Carly complained that she wasn't feeling well. One day in early February, she came home from school embarrassed because she had lost control of her bladder while in class. When a CT scan revealed a large tumor, doctors operated to remove it—plus her uterus, both ovaries, and four inches of colon. Unlike Carly's previous tumors, this one was not benign, and Carly underwent a second surgery in May, and began chemotherapy in June.

Before the end of the year, she had received five rounds of chemotherapy and was hospitalized five times.

In January hospice was called.

A few weeks later, the Kilanders' pastor visited Carly and prayed that angels would surround her. Perhaps his prayer brought the angels, or maybe the angels had been there all along. Either way, about a week after he prayed, they started showing up.

Carly woke up that Sunday morning "bright-eyed and bushy-tailed," as her dad, Scott, liked to call it. After Scott and Adam, Carly's fifteen-year-old brother, left for church, Kim carried her daughter from her bedroom to the family room. It wasn't all that daunting a task—at that point Carly weighed a hundred pounds, despite being five-feet-nine-inches tall.

After getting Carly settled comfortably in her favorite chair overlooking their sunny backyard, Kim asked, "Do you need anything? What can I get you?"

Carly shook her head happily. "Nothing. I'm good."

Kim headed to the bathroom. Two minutes later she heard Carly yell. "Mom! Come quick!"

Kim ran back into the family room.

Carly beamed. "Mom, you missed it!"

Kim looked around. "What, sweetheart? What did I miss?"

"Sit down," her daughter instructed. When Kim complied, Carly took her hand and held it. "Mom, you missed the most beautiful light. For just a second, I thought the TV had come on by itself, but that wasn't it at all. I could *feel* the light. And I was looking at it, studying it, and then . . ."

Carly began to rub her mother's hand.

She continued breathlessly, "And then, Mom, I felt this—like I'm rubbing your hand. But on my foot. A soft hand rubbed the top of my foot. Just like this. Then a wave went through my body from my toes to my head. It was the most wonderful sensation, Mom. And it wasn't the meds. I know it wasn't the meds."

Kim asked, "Carly, do you know what it was?"

Carly smiled.

Kim answered her own question: "It was an angel."

"I know, Mom," Carly said.

When her dad walked in the door from church a couple of hours later, Carly made him sit down in front of her and then repeated the entire story.

Scott looked at Carly's right leg, riddled with scars of every size from so many surgeries. His eyes welled up.

"Which foot was it?" he asked, even though he was certain he already knew.

Carly said, "My right one."

The angels showed up regularly after that. Carly referred to them as her friends. They seemed to be of every age, many of them children.

One afternoon, Kim walked into Carly's bedroom and found her crying softly. Kim reached for her hand. "Sweetheart, why are you so sad?"

"The little boy was just here," Carly answered, "and he was packing up my things to go. Where am I going, Mom?"

Kim—knowing that her daughter was in pain and hated traveling anywhere—assured Carly there were no errands or doctors' visits planned that day. They would be staying home.

Later, when Kim told her best friend Carol about what Carly had seen, Carol said simply, "Kim, don't you realize what's happening? The Lord is preparing Carly to leave this world. He sent an angel to help her pack. He's preparing her mentally."

Tears filled Kim's eyes. "You're right, Carol." It was a bittersweet realization.

Carly often made comments like, "My friends are here," or "I saw my friends today."

Then one evening, she had an experience of a different kind—apparently, a visit from a deceased relative.

Carly looked at her mom and asked matter-of-factly, "Mom, did one of your aunts just die?"

Kim said, "No, why?"

The girl motioned with her eyes toward the kitchen. "She looks kind of like you, Mom, like she might be related to us."

Kim looked toward the kitchen, which appeared empty but apparently was not. "Are you sure it's not Great-Grammy?"

Carly rolled her eyes as only a teenager can do and said, "C'mon, Mom. I know what Great-Grammy looks like, and that's not her."

So it wasn't Scott's grandmother. Who else could it be? Kim thought for a moment, and then said, "You know what? I'll bet it's *my* grandmother. She died in a car accident when she was about my age."

"I think you're right, Mom," Carly answered.

Kim breathed a small sigh and felt comforted. Could it really be her grandmother watching over Carly? God had apparently given her permission to visit her descendants on earth.

That night Scott came home from his job at a nearby construction site. He spent time with Carly and helped Adam with schoolwork. Around nine-thirty or ten, as the household began to wind down toward bedtime, he went to the computer in the living room.

When Carly's battle with cancer began the previous year, Scott hardly knew how to turn on a computer. But with so many family members and friends praying for Carly, it had been important to keep everyone informed. Carly had started keeping a journal at a Web site called *caringbridge.com*, where families facing health crises can post updates and communicate with friends and family. As Carly weakened, Scott started logging regular updates, always typing with two fingers. Carly's bedroom was around the corner from the computer desk, and she would answer her dad's questions so he could share her thoughts in their online journal. Sometimes, as Scott wrote, Kim would be lying on the couch next to him, crying softly into the cushions.

Indeed, Carly's suffering was immense. Her bowels would clog several times a day, and the bile would churn in her stomach until she threw up. She dwindled to ninety pounds. She was smart, and she knew what was happening to her, but she never got mad. Just gracious and grateful— grateful for her family, friends, and the gift of her angels.

One day Kim told Scott, "I wish I could see what Carly sees. At the same time, it feels like such a personal, intimate thing between Carly and God. So whether I see Carly's friends or not, I'm just thankful God is taking care of her."

Scott understood. As a young man, he'd had the amazing experience of seeing angels surrounding the pulpit at his church. Another time, he'd picked up a hitchhiker who had disappeared suddenly after asking to be dropped off in an empty parking lot. Scott was pretty sure the young man had been an angel.

For Scott, Carly's angels were more than a window into the afterlife. He told a friend, "Carly's angels have given me a trust in God that nothing can take away. Nothing worse than what I've gone through can happen to me. Watching my little girl suffer the way she did took me to the bottom, to the pit, to hell and back. And God was with us even there."

Carly died on March 16, 2004, surrounded by Kim, Scott, Adam, her aunt Chris, and of course, her angel friends.

And yet her story didn't end with her death.

For a year after Carly died, Scott continued writing every night in their online journal. He shared many of the journal entries in a self-published book called *Carly_Bugg03: A Journey of Faith*, titled after Carly's online nickname.

For months and even years, people across the country responded to Carly's story. Carly's life—and her death—resonated not only with people who had loved her but with complete strangers as well. For a long time, e-mails and letters arrived weekly if not daily. For Scott and Kim, it helped knowing that even though Carly was gone, her influence on others continued.

Five years after Carly's death, working late in her office and thinking about the rich and painful journey they had all traveled, Kim wondered if it was finally done, if Carly's life—and her story—had run its course. Carly's angel friends, if they were still around, were invisible once again. Was it time to say good-bye to her daughter and all that her extraordinary life had signified?

Kim gathered her purse and sweater to leave the office. On her way out the door, she stopped by the copy machine to do one last thing. She was still standing there, lost in sad thoughts, when she heard someone calling her name. She looked up.

Someone was waving and hurrying up the hallway toward Kim. It was the young woman who'd thought the balloons and flowers on Kim's desk had signified her birthday.

By the time she got to Kim, she was practically out of breath. She said, "I had to tell you. I got the book about Carly yesterday and read the whole thing last night. It changed my life. I've always believed in God but had walked away from my faith long ago. But not anymore. I'm going to rededicate my life and my son's life to God. Reading Carly's story inspired me so much. It's such a reminder that there really is something more to life, and to death too."

Brimming with gratitude and joy, Kim couldn't wait to get to her car and call Scott on her cell phone.

"Scott, it's still happening!" she blurted, "Carly's story isn't over after all. . . ."

9

Mountaintop Miracle

Trapped on a remote Arizona mountain, Leroy and Fran Lane found unexpected help.

Leroy Lane felt uncomfortable, but he kept driving—higher and higher up a mountain road east of Phoenix, Arizona. Leroy and his family had recently moved to the Phoenix area so he could recover from the allergies that plagued him in their native Michigan. Now on this sunny, ninety-degree Saturday in May 1981, he was taking his family on an adventure—an exploration of the country surrounding their new home.

For a self-described flatlander, however, driving a big blue Chevy van to an elevation past fifteen hundred feet on a narrow, rock-strewn road was nerve-wracking. Leroy had to concentrate hard on every switchback as the Chevy climbed. Just twelve inches past the edge of the asphalt, sometimes on both sides, the road fell away sharply, revealing deep canyons far below. They were so close to the sky Leroy almost felt he could reach out and shake hands with God.

"This is so weird," said thirteen-year-old Mike, looking out the back-seat window at the brown, treeless mountain and barren landscape below.

"It's ugly," said his brother, nine-year-old Matt.

Fran, Leroy's supportive wife, didn't comment from her viewpoint in the front passenger seat. But Leroy could tell from the expression on her

327

face that she was equally unimpressed. Their outing was off to a less-than-stellar start.

A moment later, Leroy saw a chance to salvage the situation. Up ahead was a small metal sign pointing left. It read, MORMON FLAT DAM.

Leroy took the turn.

"What are we doing?" Fran asked.

"We're going to see Mormon Flat Dam," Leroy answered. "It's an adventure!"

The adventure included one of the roughest roads Leroy had ever seen. Rocks the size of footballs littered the trail. He slowed to a crawl, but the Chevy still bounced around like a ball in a pinball game.

Finally, the Lanes reached a flat area about fifty feet long and fifteen feet wide that marked the end of the trail. Sheer rock walls bordered the deserted "parking lot" on the right and straight ahead. To the left was a narrow ramp that dropped to another flat area twenty-five feet below. On both sides of the ramp and beyond the lower flat area was a drop-off of hundreds of feet.

The Lanes got out of the van to look around. They discovered another couple that had driven to the lower level in a small station wagon. They also heard the sound of rushing water, but there was no sign of the dam.

"We must have missed a turnoff someplace," Leroy surmised.

"Dad, let's go home," Mike said. "There's nothing here."

Leroy took a last look at their forlorn spot. There was no trail, no marker pointing a way to the dam. He had to admit defeat.

"Okay," he finally said. "Back in the van."

Leroy realized the "parking lot" didn't offer enough room to turn the van around. But he could see the ramp in his rearview mirror. If he could back down the ramp a few feet, it would provide the extra space he needed to maneuver the van and point it toward the direction they had come.

After turning the steering wheel, Leroy inched the Chevy back toward the ramp. He felt the rear wheels descend. But he still needed more room to complete the turn. He backed up some more.

Suddenly, Leroy felt the van's front left side slump.

Uh-oh.

He rolled down his window and peered down.

The Chevy's left front tire was dangling over open space. Leroy cracked the door open to make sure he wasn't seeing things. Sure enough, the view down went on and on. Suddenly, the Lanes were in an extremely precarious position.

"Everybody stay calm," he said—as much to himself as to his family.

He considered the predicament a moment. They were more than fifty miles from home. They were in mostly deserted mountains. His Chevy now blocked the couple in the station wagon below. And since this was long before the advent of cell phones, there was no way to call for help.

No doubt about it—they were in big trouble.

"Okay, everybody get out on the right side," Leroy said in a quiet, firm voice. "Get clear of the van." His family quickly obeyed.

Leroy hadn't been wearing his seatbelt. Now he strapped it on and slowly straightened his wheels. He shifted into drive and attempted to inch forward.

The Chevy had rear-wheel drive, but the back wheels couldn't find traction on the ramp's slippery rock surface. They were stuck.

Leroy climbed out the right passenger door to take a closer look. Fran and the couple with the station wagon joined him.

Leroy shook his head. "How are we going to get this thing out of here?"

"Well, we could push," the other man offered. "We can help you."

"Thanks," Leroy said. "I guess it's worth a try."

Leroy crawled through the right doorway and back into the driver's seat. Fran and the other couple took positions at the back of the van. Leroy put his foot on the gas pedal. But on every attempt, the rear tires simply spun in place. The Chevy didn't move.

"I think you need to give it more gas!" the man called from the ramp.

"Yeah, I think you're right," Leroy answered. "We need more horsepower."

The two boys joined the team at the back of the van. When they were ready, Leroy floored it. He stopped when he heard a *thud*.

Wondering what had happened, Leroy scrambled out the right door again. Everyone was gathered around Fran, who stood there gritting her teeth and examining her leg. Leroy looked, too, and saw a large area on her thigh quickly growing black and blue. When he'd punched the gas, the spinning right rear tire had found just enough traction to grab one of the football-sized stones and hurl it into Fran's leg.

"Fran, I am so sorry," Leroy told her. He felt terrible. He was also more worried than ever. Fran was able to stand but was clearly in pain. Her leg didn't seem broken, but what if her injury was more serious than it appeared? How were they going to get medical attention?

Their adventure was turning into a nightmare.

Leroy didn't know what to do, but he didn't want his family to know that. He got back into the driver's seat as if he had a plan in mind. Then he closed his eyes and bowed his head.

"Lord," he prayed aloud, "I need your help *now*!"

Leroy opened his eyes—and was shocked to see an old Buick LeSabre rattling toward him. It moved within a few feet of the van's front bumper and stopped.

Both front doors flew open, and out stepped two characters that Leroy would have avoided on any other occasion. They were big men, with un-shaven faces and dark, scruffy hair that fell to their shoulders. Both wore blue jeans, sleeveless T-shirts, and red bandanas on their heads. They looked like they belonged on Harleys instead of inside a Buick.

"You guys need help," the driver said. It was a statement, not a question.

Leroy wasn't sure if he trusted these men. Their expressions weren't menacing, but they weren't smiling either. Their look was businesslike—they were there to do a job.

No matter their intentions, Leroy couldn't deny the dire circumstances. "We certainly do," he responded.

The Buick's driver positioned himself at the front of the van on Leroy's side while the other man moved to the Chevy's rear.

"Turn your wheel to the right," the driver instructed.

That didn't make sense to Leroy. But even as he doubted, he felt a sense of calm and assurance wash over him. He somehow understood that these men knew what they were doing and would help.

"Okay, back down slowly," the driver said. "Easy now."

Leroy did as he was told.

"Brake!" called the man in back a moment later.

For the next few minutes, the men gave Leroy instructions on how to maneuver the van. They spoke in quiet, confident voices, never con-tradicting each other. Leroy had the sense they'd done this many times before.

Soon Leroy had all four wheels on the ramp and was backing all the way down to the flat area below. As soon as he was on level ground, he turned his head behind him to make sure his family and the other couple were safe and accounted for.

A second later, Leroy turned his head forward again. He wanted to thank the two men who had appeared out of nowhere and saved him from a frightening scenario.

But the men were gone.

Leroy blinked.

Where did those guys go? he thought. *How did they do that?*

Leroy's mind raced. The two men had been standing close to the van. Even if they'd somehow scampered up the ramp and out of sight in the moment Leroy turned his head, where was the Buick? It would have taken the same maneuvering down the ramp that Leroy had just completed for them to turn around. Even if they had backed out the way they came in—which would have been dangerous and foolhardy—Leroy would have heard them bumping over the rocks through his open window.

Leroy ran up the ramp, his eyes scanning the area for clues, but there were none. The men and the LeSabre had vanished.

Leroy returned to his family. No one had seen the men leave. It was a mystery—but not to Leroy. He'd never seen angels before. Yet there was no other explanation. After all, hadn't they appeared the instant after his prayer?

God sent them, he thought. *He sent helpers at just the right moment to keep the four of us from harm. I have just witnessed heaven's angels coming to the rescue of human beings.*

Leroy's plan for an adventure, which had come so close to disaster, had instead turned into an adventure of faith.

"Thank you, Lord," he said aloud. "Thank you. Thank you. Thank you."

Leroy has talked about what happened at Mormon Flat Dam many times since. "Some people, after I tell the story, still doubt the presence of actual angels. You can see their expressions turn skeptical, and I can almost see their minds coming up with rational explanations," he reflected. "But I don't care! Those men—or rather, those angels—gave me such a strong feeling of the presence of God that I will never doubt. I will always remember and give thanks to Him."

Part Three

Mischief-Makers

The devil's minions seek to harass, confuse, and distract people from the truth.

My dear Wormwood . . ."

If you recognize that salutation, chances are you've read *The Screwtape Letters*, the classic epistolary novel by C. S. Lewis. First begun as a series of short pieces for a magazine, then gathered into book form in 1942, this little volume tackles big issues about demons and, moreover, the way human beings think, act, and are led astray.

The story is a collection of letters from a senior demon, Screwtape, to his nephew, a junior tempter named Wormwood. The mentor schools his apprentice in the ways to deceive, delude, and discourage his assigned human, a British man known only as "The Patient." Those of us who deplore bureaucracy, administrative minutia, and the endless red tape of modern life will be amused to find that Lewis, even in the 1940s, portrays hell as a hierarchy (actually called a "Lowerarchy") with rules, procedures, a devilish corporate ladder to climb, and even a House of Correction for

Incompetent Tempters. Throughout, Lewis sprinkles in thought-provoking gems about human nature, including:

- "The safest road to hell is the gradual one—the gentle slope, soft underfoot, without sudden turnings, without milestones, without signposts."[1]
- "The humans live in time but our Enemy [God] destines them to eternity."[2]
- "All mortals tend to turn into the thing they are pretending to be."[3]

In the end, it is revealed that the Patient has been killed during a World War II air raid and has been transferred from earth to heaven. Wormwood is punished for letting a soul "slip through [his] fingers."[4]

Since one of Lewis's most popular books featured demons (which he referred to as devils), what was his counsel to people in dealing with these dark and devious entities? In short, acknowledge their presence and afford them due respect, but don't confer too much power on them. He said:

> There are two equal and opposite errors into which our race can fall about the devils. One is to disbelieve in their existence. The other is to believe, and to feel an excessive and unhealthy interest in them. They themselves are equally pleased by both errors and hail a materialist or a magician with the same delight.[5]

In the pages that follow, we describe several encounters with demons—in contrast to Lewis's fictional account, the ones we present really happened. The intent is not to perpetuate Hollywood-style sensationalism, but to portray how Satan's minions seek to mislead and misinform people. A few foundational thoughts should be kept in mind:

If you believe the Bible is true, you ought to believe that demons are real. Nearly everyone believes in angels—probably because they are bright, helpful, and full of goodness. Many people don't believe in demons—probably because they are dark, harmful, and full of badness. Nevertheless, the Bible contains so many references to demons, demon possession, unclean spirits, exorcisms, healing, and the casting out of evil spirits that we must allow for the reality that the universe is more complex and mysterious than it may appear to our senses. If Jesus encountered demons and evil spirits during his lifetime on earth, his followers likewise may face them.

Demons have less power than Satan, who has far less power than God.
Again, Lewis's insights are helpful: "I believe in angels, and I believe that some of these, by the abuse of their free will, have become enemies to God and, as a corollary, to us. . . . They do not differ in nature from good angels, but their nature is depraved. *Devil* is the opposite of *angel* only as Bad Man is the opposite of Good Man. Satan, the leader or dictator of devils, is the opposite not of God, but of Michael [the archangel]."[6] Why is this important? Because Christians—children of the Living God—can rely on God's power and provision. God is the Creator of all things, including demons, and he holds all authority.

Harassment of humans falls on a continuum—and possession is rare.
Most people these days form their perception of demons from hyped-up Hollywood fare. They walk away from films such as *The Exorcist, The Exorcism of Emily Rose,* and even cheesy horror flicks like *Night of the Demons,* thinking demons take possession of people all the time and cause them to behave like feral animals. Such wild, demonically induced behavior does happen—but rarely.

There is a huge difference between demon affliction (being bothered, harassed, troubled) and demon possession (being inhabited).

Affliction can be explained as a spectrum that ranges from demonic influence *on* a person to the extreme of a demon actually *in* a person's body. One way to understand this concept is to consider the way alcohol makes a person drunk. We know that the first sips cause changes and reactions, gradually going from relatively mild to more pronounced. As more and more is consumed, the body's responses become more noticeable (bloodshot eyes, slurred speech, loss of coordination). It is a progression of *levels* of inebriation: sober . . . tipsy . . . drunk.

This analogy describes the continuum from demons *on* to a demon *in* a person. This continuum is demonstrated as a gradual progression of influence—from low-grade affliction to eventual possession (complete bodily possession generally is rare, despite what we see on the big screen).

Demonic possession and various stages of demonization have been documented for thousands of years in cultures worldwide. The anthropologists, psychologists, sociologists, ministers and priests, and dedicated laypersons who have devoted their lives to studying such supernatural activity report an amazing consistency in the encountered cases.

Are demons real? We believe they are—just as real as angels. But those who believe in God and recognize his power need not tremble at the thought of a demon appearing. Yes, they are malevolent mischief-makers, not to be trifled with or toyed with. And, yes, they have spiritual abilities greater than humans . . . but much weaker than our ultimate protector and provider, God.[7]

10

Dueling in the Dark

For Ross Purdy, an out-of-the-blue phone call led to an intense spiritual battle.

Sitting in his book-lined church study on a Friday afternoon in late February 2000, Ross Purdy was prepping Sunday's sermon when his secretary put a call through, saying it sounded urgent.

When he picked up the phone, the voice on the other end said almost breathlessly: "I've got a problem. But I need to tell you first, pastor, that I'm not crazy. My name is Kent, and I'm a sheriff's deputy. I'm not some kook."

"I understand," Ross assured the man. "I'll be happy to help if I can."

"What do you think about ghosts?" Kent blurted. "Really, I'm not crazy. But I want to hear what you know about ghosts and spirits. Do you believe in poltergeists?"

Ross, pastor of Lake Arrowhead Community Presbyterian Church in Lake Arrowhead, California, was respected in the picturesque small town nestled in the mountains above San Bernardino Valley. The friendly, gracious thirty-five-year-old talked with community members regularly and sometimes took out-of-the-blue calls—but this one was surely more out-of-the-blue than most.

His first thought was, *Why didn't you call the Roman Catholic Church or a denomination that emphasizes supernatural activity more? Why not talk to a priest or pastor better versed in the spirit world?* Nevertheless, he launched into an explanation about angels and demons and how they fit into the spiritual hierarchy described in the Bible.

Ross realized he was dispensing far more theological background than Kent probably wanted. He stopped and asked, "Tell me, what's going on? What's the real reason for the call?"

Kent exhaled loudly. "I've never believed in this stuff before, but my wife and I don't know what to do. We've got strange things going on in our house. Unexplainable things. The kinds of things you see in movies."

Asked to elaborate, Kent told of objects moving without being touched. Plates scooted across the kitchen counter while he and his wife, Dana, cooked. Utensils fell to the floor even though no one stood within ten feet.

Then he mentioned his three-year-old son, Dylan, who regularly played in the basement. Recently he had been speaking to someone, or something, he called Frankenstein. The boy's parents initially chalked it up to his active imagination, just playtime fun and games. But when other inexplicable phenomena began occurring, they wondered if everything might be connected.

He ended by saying again, "I'm a sheriff's deputy, and I don't know if all this is real or not. But when our son talks about seeing a man walking around in the basement, it's definitely time to do something."

Ross could hear the desperation in the man's voice. "I'll certainly try to help—and soon—but let me ask you one thing: Why did you call *me*?"

"Yours was the first name I came across in the phone book," he answered. "We don't go to church and don't know any ministers. So I'm grateful for your help."

Checking his calendar, Ross suggested he go to their house the following afternoon. He asked that they find a place to take their son so he wouldn't be frightened. And he said he'd like to bring along another pastor.

"Good thinking," Kent said. "It's always smart to bring backup."

The next day at one o'clock, Ross met a fellow pastor named Dale who led the Community Bible Church in town. A tall man with an ample midsection, Dale had relocated to the area from Austin, Texas, and people in the lakeside town were drawn to his gentle drawl, quick laugh, and corny, cowpoke humor. In the four years he'd been at Lake Arrowhead, he had become a respected and recognizable leader.

The two men hopped into Dale's Ford pickup and rumbled down Rim of the World Highway along the lake. It was a cold and gray day with low-hanging clouds hovering overhead. As they drove, the pastors discussed their approach to the meeting ahead: Their main purpose, they agreed, was to share biblical truths for whatever the situation turned out to be. They concurred that the family needed to have a foundation of faith and belief in Jesus Christ.

A few minutes later, Ross said, "Dale, I seem to recall your mentioning you've had experiences with the occult and spiritual warfare, right?"

"Yep, I sure have—more than a couple," he answered. "You never know what'll happen, but we'll hope and pray for the best."

"That reminds me," Ross said, pointing to a pullout on the road, "let's stop and pray before we get to the house."

Crunching over remnants of the last snowfall on the ground, Dale maneuvered his pickup to stop a safe distance from passing cars. Over the sound of the heater warming them against the chill outside, both men took turns praying. Ross prayed that if they were about to encounter malicious spirits, their hearts would be pure and any evil would be revealed. Dale focused on seeking God's protection from any harm.

After they said their *amens*, Dale declared, "All right, then, I think we're covered. Let's go."

Ten minutes later, Ross and Dale strode up to the door of the house—a neighborhood home built on a hillside with a lodge motif. Kent and Dana welcomed the pastors, mentioning that a neighbor was watching their son. As Dana hung up their jackets on a coatrack, she told them how grateful she was that two clergymen were there to help "stop all this weirdness."

Kent, with his muscular build and clean-cut appearance, looked very much like a sheriff's deputy, as he had been so determined to let Ross know he was. He and his petite brown-haired wife exchanged glances, and he said to Dale, "I know it sounds crazy, but really, we're just normal people."

"We believe you. You've got some concerns about things going on here," Dale said, his faint lilt taking the edge off a tense situation. "We're going to see if we can bring peace back to your home."

Ross mentioned that anything shared or revealed during their time would be held in strict confidence. Then they all sat down in the living room, the couple taking seats on the couch, and the two pastors opposite them in cushioned chairs. Ross and Dale shared what the Bible has to say about the spiritual world and gave an overview of Christian belief. Ross mentioned that he didn't believe in ghosts per se, but certainly believed in evil spirits. And while evil spirits are real, God is the ultimate authority over everything. His Son Jesus is the power, and his very name makes demons tremble. After nearly an hour of discussion, Kent and Dana said they would like to become Christians, and the two pastors led them in a simple prayer of salvation.

Then the couple took Dale and Ross on a tour of the house. They all moved into the kitchen, and Kent pointed to the counter where dishes had slid several feet on their own. He pointed to a clock that had seemed to jump off the wall. He told of hearing objects fall to the ground in rooms that were unoccupied.

They proceeded to Dylan's bedroom, where he had spoken to shadows in the corner. Dana explained that at times he seemed to be engaging in discussions with them and answering questions.

Next the couple showed the two pastors a stairway that led to a large basement, which was used as a family room and their son's play area. Kent and Dana decided they would wait upstairs.

As the two guests descended the stairs, Ross felt a sudden chill in the air—an extremely cold space. But he told himself not to get too worked up about a drafty spot in the house. The two began walking and praying, and after several minutes Dale stepped into a laundry room around the corner from the stairs. Ross wandered around, noticing a small, dark alcove apparently used for storage.

Soon Ross went to rejoin his colleague. As he turned the corner, he was stunned.

Dale had stepped out of the laundry room and was crouched down with his back against the wall. He was huddled in an almost fetal position, and his face wore an expression of pain and fear.

Ross hurried toward him. "Dale, what happened? Are you okay?"

He stayed near the floor, silent. Finally he said in a near whisper, "I'm okay. Just give me a few minutes. I'll be all right."

Ross couldn't help but notice how visibly shaken Dale appeared. "I'm going to keep praying—for this house and also for you."

As he paced around the room, Ross felt a strong impression that he should pray while walking up the stairway. Halfway up the stairs, still praying for Dale and against any evil in the house, he suddenly felt himself thrown back against the wall. *Wham!* It was as if an invisible wrestler had body-slammed him.

Up against the wall, he felt a large pair of hands choking his throat.

He continued praying—more frantically and now silently since he could not speak or breathe for the next several seconds.

Heavenly Father, help me. I rebuke this evil in the name of Jesus Christ!

Immediately, the pressure ceased from around his neck, and he gulped in air.

Then, adrenaline coursing through his body, he sensed something moving, something he couldn't see. Though he couldn't visibly detect it, he had no doubt something was there. He followed the being or entity as it entered the dark storage area. It was as if this evil thing had retreated to its shadowy hole for safety. Still praying, Ross asked Jesus to remove all evil.

He descended the stairs and walked around the corner again, finding Dale on his feet but breathing hard and perspiring. "Are you okay?"

"Yes," he replied. "I think I was being spiritually oppressed. I'm okay now."

After another ten minutes in the basement, they walked back upstairs and said a prayer for Kent and Dana. Ross told them what had happened and that they had prayed over the entire house.

"I think our prayers have taken care of the situation," Ross said. "Besides, you are now followers of Jesus, and he doesn't share his holy presence with darkness." Ross assured them he would follow up soon.

Dale said very little in parting. His usual jovial demeanor had vanished.

As soon as they left, Ross again asked Dale what had happened.

"I felt spiritually attacked." He didn't seem to want to say more.

Arriving back at the church parking lot, Ross suggested they pray together before going their separate ways—since obviously something powerful had just transpired. They uttered a short prayer and left, saying few words as they went.

The following Monday, as Ross sat in his church office, a phone call came from a friend in the community.

"Did you hear what happened to Pastor Dale?"

Ross immediately felt a gnawing irritation that his partner in Saturday's ordeal had told someone about what occurred—against their confidentiality agreement.

But the person on the phone continued. "I can't believe it. It's just come out that Dale has been having an affair. Apparently it's been going on for months and involves a teacher at the high school. It's so sad. I hate to tell you—I just thought you needed to know."

Ross would later learn that a parishioner at Dale's church had begun to suspect immoral behavior and felt God's urging to confront him. When she did—the day after the encounter with an evil spirit—the pastor dropped to his knees and confessed everything.

But at the moment, Ross sat at his desk in stunned silence, thoughts and feelings swirling and churning.

How awful for Dale and his family.

That sure explains a lot about Saturday's events.

What a dangerous position to put himself—and me—in.

That demonic encounter may not be over after all.

Later that night, while he was still at church, Ross's wife, Kathy, called and asked him to come home immediately. She sounded panicky. It turns out that as Kathy and their five-year-old daughter, Katy, sat on the living room couch, they both heard a deep growl as if an animal were behind them. Katy screamed and held tightly to her mom. Kathy looked over her shoulder; nothing was there. But then she felt a hand hit the back of her head and watched as Katy's hair was ruffled from behind.

When Ross arrived, he found them in a different part of the house, holding on to each another. They all prayed together and no other incidents occurred.

Two days later, Ross called four friends from other churches whom he knew to be people of integrity and prayer. He scheduled an appointment to return to Kent and Dana's house for follow-up prayer. The couple told him nothing had changed since the pastors' visit a few days earlier—the strange occurrences had continued. Ross thought he knew the reason why.

With Dylan again staying with neighbors, the five guests, along with Kent and Dana, walked around the house and prayed. They decided to keep their prayer simple, asking Jesus to make this his home and to drive out all darkness. The group moved steadily through the house, feeling unified and confident.

But the drama wasn't over yet. Ross felt a strong urging to stay in the boy's bedroom to pray after the group left for the next room. He felt led to open the closet door and pray inside it. When he opened the door, he saw two little boys sitting inside clinging to each other, trembling, with fear on their faces. Then, fading away slowly, they disappeared.

Ross called for the others. Without mentioning what he had just witnessed, he asked Dana what she knew about the house's previous owners.

"All I know," she said, "is that two boys used to live in this house with their father. He was a drug addict and used to abuse them. We heard that they used to hide all over the house from their dad."

There's no way this could all be a coincidence, Ross thought. He revealed what he'd seen and the group prayed some more.

After two hours of prayer at the house, the team left, all reporting a deep sense of peace and serenity. Ross kept in touch with Kent and Dana, and they did not have another incident of anything "weird." They went on to join a church in the area and to grow in their newfound faith.

And what became of Pastor Dale? He revealed his affair to the congregation a week after he was confronted, and he resigned from pastoral ministry. He and his wife moved to another part of California, worked through the painful ordeal, and stayed together. Some time later, Dale took an administrative position for a Christian ministry.

Reflecting on his experience, Ross says: "It certainly made the reality of Scripture come alive in a vivid and powerful way. The New Testament tells us, 'For our struggle is not against flesh and blood, but against the rulers, against the authorities, against the powers of this dark world and against the spiritual forces of evil in the heavenly realms.'[1] Ministry, as with faith in general, is about living the kingdom, not just talking about it. If we preach Christ, we will find opposition, especially spiritual opposition. But the great news is that Jesus has power over all things."

One more thing, he adds: "Angels are real, and so are fallen angels—evil spirits. If you're going to tangle with dark forces, you had better be filled with the light."

343

11

Evil Comes Home to Roost

When Dorothy Hedin encountered a demon, she found a unique solution to removing the menace.

It had been an especially long and tiring day. Summer was always a busy time around the Hedin place—a two-story country home that lay at the edge of the dense Pacific Northwest rainforest near Eugene, Oregon. Dorothy lived there with her husband, Rusty, and two teenage sons, Carl and Garth.

Late one evening in the summer of 1978, the day's chores were finally done, and the sun had set at last. Some days it seemed the work would never end. Dorothy and Rusty, an insurance agent by day, kept a variety of farm animals on the property surrounding the house—chickens, rabbits, sheep, geese, turkeys, and a couple of pigs. On top of the routine care and feeding of the animals, Dorothy fought a running battle with wild predators from the nearby forest that were determined to take their share of the family's livestock. That night, Dorothy finished cleaning up in the kitchen, turned out the lights, and headed gratefully toward her bedroom for what she hoped would be a good night's sleep.

But peaceful slumber was *not* what lay ahead.

To reach the door to her ground-floor bedroom, Dorothy had to pass by the bottom of the sweeping circular staircase that ascended to the second floor. The house was quiet and the light in the hallway was dim.

Seventeen-year-old Carl was in his room at the top of the stairs, doing homework or getting ready for bed himself.

"Carl was a good young man, trying to live a Christian life," Dorothy said of her younger son. She worried at the time that his Christian values might be making things hard on him at school, but he never gave her reason to fear he was in danger of losing his faith or getting into serious trouble. He was a source of comfort and joy to her.

As she walked toward her room that night, Dorothy happened to glance up the staircase. What she saw sent a chill through her body and stopped her in her tracks.

"The best way I can describe what I saw is to call it a 'heat wave,'" she said. "It looked like the shimmering air you see rising off hot pavement at a distance in the summertime."

The disturbance in the air was limited in size—as wide as the staircase, but only three or four feet high—and was advancing slowly but steadily up the stairs toward the door to Carl's room. It made no sound and gave off no heat or odors. Instead, it emanated a different kind of energy—a blast of menacing hatred that Dorothy recognized immediately.

"I felt an intense wave of evil coming from the thing on the stairway," she said. "It felt very dangerous. All of a sudden, I just *knew* it was a demon and that it was headed toward Carl to do him harm. I can't explain how I knew; I just did, without stopping to think about it."

Dorothy was not the sort of person who is obsessed with evil spirits or prone to seeing demons around every corner. In fact, she gave them no thought at all, having never encountered one before. The Nazarene church she attended placed more emphasis on serving a loving God than on fearing Satan and his minions. Even so, she was no stranger to the idea of spiritual warfare.

"During those years, I did feel like the devil was after my family," she confided. "We'd had some really hard times. The devil never let us alone. It seemed like there was always something negative going on."

Her sole thought as she stood looking up at the demonic presence advancing toward her son's room, however, was desperation and determination that she had to do *something* to protect him. She instinctively understood that if she didn't, the demon would "enter Carl's body." She sensed the evil spirit was strong and very determined to reach its goal.

Dorothy instantly began to plead with Jesus to protect Carl and to force the demon back down the stairs away from her son. It was an anguished prayer of such intensity that it immediately drained her physically and emotionally. She cannot say how long she stood there fervently begging God to intervene—a few minutes at most—but the "heat wave" stopped ascending the stairs and started back down.

"Even when the demon began moving down toward me, I never felt afraid for myself, only for Carl," Dorothy recalled.

Although God appeared to have answered her prayers by forcing the demon to turn away from Carl, Dorothy felt it was not enough. She remembered something her pastor had once said on the subject of spiritual warfare. It was his belief that when casting out a demon, one should ask God to send it into another living creature—just as Jesus did when he freed two men from a multitude of demons by sending them into a herd of pigs.[1]

Intent on preventing the demon's return, Dorothy raced to think of a way she could follow that advice. What came instantly to her mind was the image of a young rooster in her chicken yard named Le Le. He was a red-and-black bantam with a long plume of shiny dark tail feathers.

"We had other animals, but Le Le was all I could think of," Dorothy said. "I begged God to send the demon, which was still moving toward me, into that rooster."

All at once the evil, shimmering heat wave disappeared. Dorothy didn't see it leave the house or enter the rooster, but she had no doubt it was gone. She collapsed onto the stairs in exhaustion and gave thanks to God for hearing her prayer. She felt confident that he had done exactly as she asked and had sent the demon into Le Le.

"I felt so tired, like I had worked hard since sunup," she said. "But it wasn't the kind of tired where you can go right to sleep. I can't put into words how shaken up I was. It stayed with me for hours. But the Lord assured me that it would be okay, that he had taken care of matters. I was so relieved that Carl was safe."

The next day, Dorothy confided the details of her harrowing experience to her pastor's wife, Faye, in spite of her fear of ridicule. To her relief, Faye shared stories of her own experiences with spiritual warfare, confirming Dorothy's conviction that the incident was real, and that her response—to call on God for help—was the only correct one.

In more than thirty years since then, Dorothy has never again been called upon to do battle with a demon. Though she still wondered many times if she had imagined the whole thing, God always gently reassured her that it really did happen.

Dorothy still lives in her forest home in Oregon with her husband, Rusty. Eventually, her family got through the hard times they'd suffered back then. Today, Carl is a successful Christian businessman and the father of two kids of his own.

As for Le Le, he was never the same.

"I know roosters can be really mean without having a demon in them," Dorothy joked. "But after that night I couldn't go anywhere near the chicken yard without him jumping on me."

Though Le Le had never threatened anyone in the family before, he began to attack Dorothy every time she came near, flapping his wings menacingly and pecking and clawing her with his sharp spurs.

"More than once he made me bleed," she said. "A few times he even jumped up on the back of my neck when I bent down for the eggs. It was scary, but I always figured it was a small price to pay for keeping Carl safe."

Ever since the night of Dorothy's prayer, the rooster seemed intent on vengeance. Indeed, Le Le's barnyard battle with Dorothy persisted until he died of old age several years later.

What advice does Dorothy have for those who might one day find themselves in her shoes?

"Demons are real—believe that," she said. "I've experienced it firsthand. But all you have to do is pray. Call out to God and believe that you will be protected. And you will be."

12

Kitchen Table Conflict

Pastor Ross Purdy unexpectedly confronted two determined spirits.

Ross Purdy smiled, stood at the doors exiting the sanctuary, and waited. The lead pastor of Burbank Presbyterian Church in Burbank, California, he'd already delivered his sermon and was now prepared to greet people leaving the service. His work for the day was nearly done, and he was ready to go home and enjoy some family time on this warm Sunday in the summer of 2009.

While the parishioners filed out of the sanctuary, a handful of people lingered to ask questions about the sermon or to offer thanks for the message. Ross was finishing one such conversation when he noticed a fortyish woman with shoulder-length blond hair and brown eyes making her way toward him.

Uh oh, he thought. *I bet I know what this is about.*

In a moment, the woman was beside him. Julia was the single mother of two daughters. She smiled, but behind the pleasant expression was a look of concern.

Ross could guess why. Though he hadn't been there, he'd been told about the church-sponsored youth retreat the weekend before. Julia's fifteen-year-old daughter, Marissa, had smuggled in an Ouija board. She'd apparently used it to try to contact spirits of the dead and had encouraged other girls

348

on the retreat to try it too. The retreat leaders eventually found out and took the board away.

Ross wondered if Julia was unhappy about the way the church staff had handled the situation.

"Hi, Ross," Julia said. "I'm wondering if we could talk. It's about my daughter."

Ross thought this might require more than a quick and casual conversation. "Sure," he said. "The best thing is to send me an e-mail, and we can set up an appointment for later this week. How's that sound?"

A strange look—was it fear?—flashed across Julia's face. But she quickly recovered her composure. "All right," she said. "I'll do that."

Ross forgot about the conversation until later that afternoon, when he mentioned it to his wife, Kathy.

"You know, Ross, I think you should call her," Kathy said. "She spoke to me this morning when she picked up her kids after Sunday school. She sounded really concerned, almost panicked."

Ross made the call and was surprised at Julia's story. Marissa, it seemed, had moved past the Ouija board. Now she was calling on spirits directly. What had seemed like innocent teenage game-playing had taken a much darker turn.

The night before, Marissa had been awakened in her bedroom by the feeling of something clutching her ankle. She looked up and in the shadows saw a man standing there, a smile on his face, his hand wrapped around her leg.

Marissa repeatedly tried to jerk away, but the man wouldn't let go. When Marissa tried to crawl off the bed, the man yanked her back. He never stopped smiling.

Marissa screamed.

The sound woke up Julia. She raced down the hall and threw open her daughter's bedroom door. She saw Marissa writhing in bed, but there was no sign of the man. The intruder had vanished.

Ross wasn't sure what to make of the story. Most likely, he figured, it was the case of a teenager with an active imagination. Or too many hormones, too many scary movies, excessively graphic video games—who knows? But he also believed in the reality of the spirit world, both good and evil. After all, he'd had encounters with dark forces in the past (see the earlier story "Dueling in the Dark"). He told Julia that he and Kathy would come over that evening.

The night was getting dark but staying warm when Ross and Kathy arrived at the front door of Julia's home. The one-story house was actually a converted garage with a small living room and kitchen. Marissa slept in the single bedroom, while Julia and her younger daughter converted the front room into a shared bedroom each night.

Ross thought of himself as a typical guy in most ways, not nearly as intuitive about his environment as his wife. But when he walked through Julia's front door, something got his attention.

Whoa, something's not right, he thought. *There's darkness here. This feels wrong.*

Kathy took Julia's younger daughter outside to play while Ross, Julia, and Marissa went on a quick tour of the house. Marissa had long, dark hair, a round face, and large, expressive brown eyes. She told Ross about other strange things that had happened, especially in the bathroom, where objects that had been on the counter mysteriously ended up on the floor.

While they were in the bathroom doorway, Julia interrupted with her own story. "I'm not crazy," she said. "I was in here a few days ago and a ceramic angel that used to hang on the wall, right there, suddenly flew across the room and smashed against the other wall. It was like someone had thrown it at me."

Ross could sense the fear in both of their voices. *What's going on here?* he wondered. *Is this just their imaginations, or Marissa wanting attention, or is it something more?*

The three of them sat down at the kitchen table, where Marissa explained further about her recent attempts to converse with the dead. She'd been speaking with two "spirits," a boy named Daniel and an adult named Isaac. She believed that Isaac was the man in her bedroom the night before. She wanted Ross to make Isaac go away, but she wanted Daniel to stay because he was a "good spirit."

Ross asked Marissa how she spent her time when she was alone. She said she was fascinated by the idea of demonic possession. She watched shows about it on TV and researched it on the Internet. She'd been freaked out by the movie *The Exorcism of Emily Rose.*

Ross thought, *No wonder she's frightened and panicked.*

"You know, Marissa, you really shouldn't be messing around in that world," Ross said. "It's not good for your mind. The Bible actually forbids talking to spirits this way. You're opening your life up to things that are forbidden by God."

Marissa seemed to think about this for a moment. In a quiet voice, she asked, "Am I in danger?"

Ross took a breath. "Let me ask you something first: Have you given your life to Jesus Christ?"

Marissa shook her head.

"Then you need to make a decision. I think you need to accept Jesus as your Lord and Savior. With him you have nothing to fear. Without him you have everything to fear."

Ross leaned forward, resting his elbows on the table, and locked in on Marissa's big eyes. "Marissa, would you like to invite Jesus Christ into your life?"

Ross couldn't believe what happened next. The moment he finished his question, the chair beneath him—a typical wooden kitchen chair, from which he'd just taken his weight off—slid back with an audible scrape.

He turned quickly. No one was there.

The chair had moved more than two feet.

Oh boy, he thought. *I did not do anything to move that chair. Someone does not want to let her go.*

Ross turned back to face Marissa and Julia. Their eyes were open wide.

"Okay," he said. "You both saw what just happened, right?"

The women nodded.

"I'm not going to let that distract me from what I was just asking you," Ross said. "Marissa, would you like to invite Jesus Christ into your life?"

"Yes," she said. "Yes, I would."

"Then I think we should pray," Ross said. He bowed his head. "Marissa, we're all sinners, saved by the grace of God and the blood of Jesus Christ. Will you now invite him into your life?"

"Yes," Marissa said. "Jesus, I want you to come into my life."

Ross knew Marissa didn't understand everything that had just happened. They continued to talk. Marissa asked, "Can I still talk to spirits? I'd still like to talk to Daniel."

Ross shook his head. "I think you need to make a choice here," he said. "These spirits are generally from the Evil One. Remember, someone was just in your bedroom pulling on your ankle. Jesus comes to bring peace, not fear. If you're communicating with spirits that bring fear, I can promise you they're not of God. So let's pray about that now too."

Again, Ross lowered his head and began a prayer. "Lord," he said, "I ask that you would protect Marissa, Julia, and this household from any spirits that are not of you. I ask that any other spirits would leave right now."

Marissa suddenly interrupted: "Did you hear that?"

"I didn't hear anything," Ross said.

"Neither did I," Julia agreed.

"I just heard this shriek right next to me," Marissa said. "Then it got fainter, like it was moving away."

When Ross and his wife left the house, he encountered a very different feeling than when he'd arrived. He felt peace and calm.

A few days later, Ross returned to the house with a team from his church. They again prayed for the home and family. Neither Marissa nor Julia has been visited by spirits since.

Ross isn't ready to embark on a new career as an exorcist. But the experience has been a reminder to him that the spirit world is real. It calls to mind the words from the apostle John: "Every spirit that does not acknowledge Jesus is not from God. This is the spirit of the antichrist, which you have heard is coming and even now is already in the world. You, dear children, are from God and have overcome them, because the one who is in you is greater than the one who is in the world."[1]

Ross added, "It's easy to go to church, hear the sermon and the teaching, and forget that things haven't changed since those words were written two thousand years ago. We're still in a fight with darkness—but we still have the power to overcome. It's the power of God."

Part Four

Fond Farewells

A window between this life and the next opens routinely—in the eyes of the dying.

The Hall of Hewn Stones was packed with angry men that day. Their voices reverberated off the walls in a loud rumble of righteous indignation, all aimed at one man who stood alone before them. He had been dragged off the street to face charges of blasphemy against the Law of Moses. Death hovered above him, because a verdict of guilty—a likely outcome—would be swiftly followed by execution.

Built into the north wall of the temple in Jerusalem, half inside the sanctuary and half outside, the hall was the meeting place of the Sanhedrin, the "supreme court" of ancient Israel. The Romans ruled the streets outside, but within these walls seventy-one religious judges retained full authority over the hearts and minds of the people.

The accused, a man named Stephen, was a follower of Jesus, the troublemaker these men thought they'd seen the last of after they arranged his crucifixion at the hands of the Romans. But no! Apparently, his infectious message lived stubbornly on.

"All who were sitting in the Sanhedrin looked intently at Stephen, and they saw that his face was like the face of an angel."[1] Perhaps this new rebel now stood in precisely the same spot as his Master before him. But where Jesus had remained mostly silent as he faced his accusers, Stephen had plenty to say. He pulled no punches as he gave this learned assembly a history lesson in the long line of God's prophets who were persecuted and murdered by their ancestors for speaking the truth. In summary, Stephen condemned those present for killing the very Messiah about whom the prophets spoke.

That was the last straw. The hall erupted in noise and fury. Stephen had just sealed his fate, and his death was imminent.

> But Stephen, full of the Holy Spirit, looked up to heaven and saw the glory of God, and Jesus standing at the right hand of God. "Look," he said, "I see heaven open and the Son of Man standing at the right hand of God."
>
> At this they covered their ears and, yelling at the top of their voices, they all rushed at him, dragged him out of the city and began to stone him.[2]

You may read this story and think that moment-of-death visions like Stephen's are the rare privilege of exceptionally holy saints and mystics. That's an understandable conclusion. You might also think that such glimpses of glory only occurred in the early church times—the period when the book of Acts was written, when miracles of all sorts seemed to be as numerous as the new disciples joining the Christian church. Based on the stories we have heard, including those we are about to relay, we would like to challenge those assumptions.

As the stories in this section reveal, deathbed glimpses of what awaits us are remarkably commonplace. People who approach death slowly, and with awareness, often report that the ordinarily impenetrable barriers between worlds become see-through and porous well before our final crossing. They see angels in the room or deceased loved ones waiting for them on the other side. They hear music or voices telling them there is no need to be afraid. They see bright and beautiful scenes displayed before them.

We personally believe that the benefit of these visions can be summed up in one word: *comfort*. For the living and for the dying. For those about to cross over, the experience offers reassurance that death is not the end of existence, but only a doorway to another realm—perhaps even one populated with angelic beings and familiar faces.

Some doubt whether we'll recognize each other when we get to heaven. But in Scripture David speaks of a future reunion with his son who had died.[3] There is biblical support for heavenly rendezvous with our loved ones.

Indeed, many of these experiences are a source of encouragement years after the fact and are passed down like family heirlooms. For instance, there's the story of Tunzel Gilliland, who lost her first husband and first child in a flu epidemic in Texas during the early 1900s. Throughout her life, she recalled the heartrending sorrow of looking out her bedroom window and watching family members bury her deceased infant in the field by the farmhouse where she lived. She hadn't even been allowed to hold her baby.

In 1978, decades after the loss of her child, Tunzel approached death at Bethany Hospital in Bethany, Oklahoma. Her granddaughter Lin sat by her bedside when the elderly woman suddenly looked up toward heaven, raised her hands, and exclaimed, "There's my baby! There's my baby! Oh, I'm finally going to get to hold my baby." Shortly thereafter, she passed from this life into the next—no doubt to be reunited with the child she had lost so many years before.

Another encouraging account features Coral Butcher, who steadily moved toward death through a battle with cancer. She stayed in the parsonage of Skyline Wesleyan Church in San Diego to be cared for by her son, Orval, the founding pastor of the church, and other family members. As it became apparent that her time on earth was drawing to a close, Coral's husband, children, and grandchildren gathered around her bed. Since she had always loved music, Orval sat at the piano in the room and everyone began singing "My Home, Sweet Home." As they all sang the last verse from Coral's favorite hymn—"Life's day is short—I soon shall go, to be with Him who loved me so"—she abruptly sat up, looked upward, and smiled brightly. Her granddaughter Sharon remembers how she called out the names of family members who had gone before. As she breathed her last, her family continued singing: "My beautiful, beautiful home. Home, sweet home. . . . I see the light of that city so bright—my home, sweet home." Years later, this sacred scene bolsters the faith of Coral's descendants and friends.

Deathbed visions like these are a great source of consolation for those who are left behind. Grief after a loss is often dominated by the need to know that our loved ones are not simply "gone," but continue to live on in another plane. Having heard from their own lips what the dying have seen on the other side—and that it is *good*—goes a long way toward helping us let them go and get on with living our own lives. Furthermore, we gain confidence that our present separation is only temporary. One day it will be our turn to be welcomed by those who've gone before us.

William Winter wrote, "As much of heaven is visible as we have eyes to see." The stories that follow are an invitation to gather at heaven's window and have a look for yourself.

13

Welcome Home

On his deathbed, Charles Kimbrough saw his beloved wife and knew he would be reunited with the love of his life.

I sure love those kids of yours, Shari. They've brought so much joy to my life. Remember that time we juggled milk containers in Shelbi's school cafeteria? And when Patrick and I marched down the street playing those trumpets I bought, pretending to be a parade band? What a hoot!"

Charles Kimbrough chuckled as he said the words, clearly relishing the memories. His two grown children, Shari and Denise, stood by his bedside in the dark Oklahoma City hospital room and laughed too. But there was sorrow behind the laughter and smiles. Their father was dying.

It had been a difficult five years for the close-knit Kimbrough family. In 2000, Judie Kimbrough—Charles' wife and Shari and Denise's mother—was diagnosed with multiple myeloma. Judie struggled and suffered with the cancer for a year before succumbing in March 2001 at age sixty-two.

For Judie's daughters, grandchildren, and especially Charles, it had been a devastating loss. Charles and Judie met when they were in eighth grade, wed when he was nineteen and she was eighteen, and shared forty-three years of married life together. Partners in every sense of the word, they enjoyed a rare and radiant love, as if the innocent and passionate blush of teenage romance had never faded. Charles, handsome and athletic, pursued a professional baseball career before earning a bachelor's degree in science education and a master's degree in microbiology. He taught for years in high schools and junior colleges, and then became an assistant school district superintendent.

In her work life, Judie was secretary to a pastor and a counselor. But her most important role was as Charles' strength behind the scenes. She supported and encouraged him through all the joys and trials that come with being a father, educator, and community leader.

A compassionate and godly woman, Judie also encouraged her husband in his faith. Charles believed in God, but the scientist in him wanted empirical evidence to rely on. They often talked about it at the kitchen table after church.

"Judie, how can you just believe?" he'd ask.

Patting his hand, Judie would answer, "Charles, I don't know. It's all in God's Word and I believe it. It's as simple as that."

"Well, honey, I need to *see* a miracle," he'd respond. "If I saw a miracle, I'd believe without any question too."

For Charles, his wife's excruciating illness and death was not only an emotional blow, but a spiritual one as well. After a visit with Judie at the hospital, he talked about it with Shari while sitting in their car in the parking lot.

"How can a loving God let a precious woman like your mother go through something like this?" he asked, tears of anger and frustration stinging his eyes.

Shari tried to find the right words. "Dad, I understand what you're feeling, because I feel it too," she said through her own tears. "But here's the thing: Suppose she's right about God and the Bible and heaven. Why take the chance of not being with her again? That's the bottom line."

Despite words of reassurance to their father, Shari and Denise also struggled after their mother's death. Shari felt angry and bitter toward God. Her trust in him wavered. At a low point, she thought, *I could do just as well without this.* Denise's faith was stronger, yet she also felt empty and sank into a depression that plagued her for years.

It was Valentine's Day 2005 when the Kimbrough family learned from doctors that Charles, age sixty-six, had pancreatic cancer. Shari and Denise, who were just beginning to heal from their mother's death, were stunned. The shock wave to their family, and their faith, was doubly devastating.

How could the God I've heard about since I was little allow something like this to happen? Shari thought. One cherished parent ripped away prematurely because of cancer and then the other likely to follow? It was all too much. Where was this loving, compassionate God?

Charles, on the other hand, discovered an unexpected strength. It was as if he realized that the time for questions was past. He finally knew in his heart what he believed. Though he was deeply concerned about leaving his daughters and two grandchildren behind, he did not fear death.

"I've got to tell you girls something," he said to his daughters. "I certainly don't want to go through cancer and all the treatments after seeing what it did to your mother. But think of it this way: The worst possible outcome would mean that I'll get to go and be with your mom—and in that case, the worst thing would be the best thing. If I die, I'll get to be with the person who was my partner, lover, and best friend nearly all my life."

For several months, treatments kept the cancer at bay. Charles continued to work and play golf as before. But on December 9, he entered the hospital to examine a buildup of fluid in his belly. The cancer, they all learned, had metastasized to his abdomen.

Shari and Denise rearranged their schedules so they could be with their father around the clock at the hospital. Charles' health declined quickly, and he drifted in and out of sleep.

It was during the wee hours of Wednesday night and Thursday morning, December 14 and 15, that Charles and his daughters reminisced about better times. Shari stood at one side of the bed and Denise at the other. It was agonizing for them to watch their dad, once a proud and strapping athlete, wither away. The unspoken anger toward the Lord still gnawed at their souls.

When awake and alert, Charles continued to reflect. He told Shari and Denise how proud he was of them and how much he loved being their father. He talked about how blessed they all were to be in a family so close and connected.

Suddenly, in the middle of a conversation, Charles's eyes shifted from his daughters toward the ceiling.

"What's that smoke?" he asked.

Denise's eyes darted back and forth. "What smoke, Dad?"

"Up there," he responded. "And why did that tile move?"

Shari and Denise, following their father's gaze, stared at the ceiling. Nothing had changed.

"It's not moving, Dad," Shari said.

"Yes, it is," he declared. "Right there."

The daughters exchanged glances, their eyebrows raised.

"Well, I don't know, Dad," Denise finally replied. "Maybe they're doing some work on the hospital." She didn't know what else to say.

Charles continued to stare intently at the ceiling. Suddenly he gasped. "*Judie,*" he whispered.

Shari and Denise looked again at the ceiling. They still saw nothing unusual. Yet Charles, his eyes wide, his mouth smiling, remained fixed on the vision only he could see.

"I've missed you so much," he said in a gentle voice. Then he raised his arms and wrapped them around himself, as if giving someone a tight and loving embrace.

"You're so beautiful," Charles whispered again. "It's so good to see you."

Shari and Denise stood in shocked stillness. What was happening here?

In the middle of his conversation, Charles turned to Shari. "How's my breath?" he asked. "How's my breath?" Shari was too stunned to reply.

The dialogue—one-way from Shari and Denise's perspective—continued for a couple more minutes.

"Judie, it's just so good to see you," Charles repeated.

Then he glanced away from the ceiling, the meeting apparently over.

After a moment, Charles, beaming and bright-eyed, reached out a large hand to each of his daughters.

"Girls," he said, "I want you to tell everyone you know that it's there. It's really there."

Shari knew exactly what he was referring to—heaven. She found her voice. "Dad, we will," she replied.

"You've got to," Charles said. "You've got to tell everyone. There's no doubt it's there."

Charles then closed his eyes and fell asleep.

Shari and Denise were amazed. Their father was a practical man, never prone to theatrics. He was on very little pain medication. To claim that he'd just glimpsed his wife in heaven was completely out of character.

They could conclude only one thing: The encounter was real.

As the rest of Thursday unfolded, Shari and Denise continued to be amazed. Word of Charles's dire condition had gotten out. Friends, colleagues, and former students streamed into his room to pay a final visit to the man who had touched their lives in so many ways over the years. Yet rather than acting like he was on his deathbed, Charles seemed energized.

"Hey, how are you doing?" he greeted each person who walked in the door. "Guess who I saw yesterday?"

"Who's that?" the guest would ask.

"Judie and Jesus," Charles answered.

Usually, the person would look over at Shari or Denise.

"Yes, he did," they said with a smile.

That night, after all the visitors had gone, Charles stopped communicating and slipped into semi-consciousness. By early evening of the next day, he labored to breathe. Shari and Denise, along with a cousin and friend, were at his side. Soon they were joined by their pastor.

After a few words of Scripture and comfort, the pastor said, "Girls, let's see if we can sing him into heaven." They chose the hymn "Amazing Grace."

Their gentle voices filled the room: "Amazing grace, how sweet the sound . . ." Charles's breathing relaxed. By the start of the second stanza, he was no longer in his earthly body.

Shari and Denise clung to each other and sobbed. It was another heart-rending loss. Yet they also felt great peace. They knew without a doubt that Charles had joined his wife and his Savior in heaven.

"Being there when he saw Mom and reached out for her, I have no doubt it really happened," Denise said. "It's an extra boost for my belief and faith."

Shari added, "It was such a comfort and gift to us. I miss them both tremendously, but I have the assurance that we'll see them again. My anger at the Lord and my mistrust—that's all gone. I have no questions now about heaven, and I never will."

Both daughters agree that a grand reunion took place the day Charles joined Judie in heaven . . . and another homecoming is yet to happen when it's their turn to be embraced by open, eager arms.

14

The Final Ascent

After a rock-climbing accident, Bobby Mason passed on—but not
before sharing a glimpse of heaven with his best friend.

Bobby Mason died on a beautiful spring day in May 2008. He left
this world as he might have chosen to, if he'd had time to give it
any thought—outside in the open air, with the sun on his face and
the earth at his back.

Forty-one-year-old Bobby spent the last morning of his life—indeed, the
last few moments—in the company of his best friend, Alex, doing what
they loved more than anything: rock climbing. Bobby died slowly, and with
no apparent pain, at the base of his favorite route on the vertical wall of
the Black Canyon in western Colorado.

But his death was far from a silent slide into oblivion. In fact, normally
a man of few words, Bobby had plenty to say about what he saw in the
moments before he departed for good.

It had been an unusually cold and snowy winter. Bobby lived in a small
corn-farming town called Delta, where the Gunnison River emerged from
the steep and narrow Black Canyon, just a few miles from its confluence
with the Colorado River. He worked at an auto parts store most of the
year, saving enough money to spend his summers on the rocks. While some

in the sport sought after product endorsements as a way to pay the bills, Bobby preferred to stay clear of the distractions that came with corporate money—and to just climb.

The day he died was the first opportunity of the year to make his favorite ascent. It had become a tradition for him to start the season on this particular route. For one thing, the hardest part of the whole climb—the crux—occurred within the first one hundred feet, a challenge that appealed to Bobby's sense of adventure. After a rather routine beginning up to about thirty feet, the route's difficulty level rose dramatically.

"We had done this climb together many times," said Alex, a science teacher at the local high school and two years younger than his friend. "It was almost a ritual with us. That day we flipped a coin to see who would climb and who would be on belay. Bobby won the toss."

For all but the most adventurous, climbing is a two-person sport. The person on belay remains on the ground to take up the slack in the climber's rope with a special belaying device clipped to a harness. Should the climber fall, the person on belay must respond instantly, using the device to apply enough friction to the rope to keep his or her partner from falling very far—usually only as far as the previously placed anchor in the rock. To be on belay is to have another person's life—literally—in your hands. Over the years, Bobby and Alex had learned to trust each other completely, and they rarely climbed with anyone else.

That day Bobby was especially excited as Alex double-checked his rigging. He'd been away from the rocks longer than usual, waiting for the last of the snow and ice to melt. Sure, he could travel to other locations where conditions improved sooner, but he preferred to start the year off right.

"I'd never seen him so eager to get going," Alex remembered. "I joked with him about having a date at the top, but I knew that for him reaching the top wasn't the point. He enjoyed every reach and every hold along the way."

Finally harnessed and ready, Bobby took a deep breath and placed his hands on the base of the wall.

"On belay?" he asked Alex.

"Belay on," came the expected reply.

Climbers—safe ones, at least—take nothing for granted and communicate thoroughly before making a move.

"Climbing."

"Climb on," said Alex. He was ready to assume his duty.

Bobby let out a whoop and began his ascent. He was a traditional climber, not a sport climber. That meant he always placed his own anchors in the rock rather than relying on equipment left behind by others. He preferred it that way for safety reasons—he trusted himself to do it right—but also because it gave him a greater sense of conquest and accomplishment, knowing he might have been the very first person in history to do the climb in precisely that way. Instead of pitons, which must be hammered into the rock, Bobby's tool of choice was an invention called a cam. Once inserted into a wider gap in the rock face, it is designed to expand outward and hold tight when the force of a climber's weight is applied.

That day, Bobby rose quickly through the first section and reached the crux of the climb in no time. He placed another cam into the rock before proceeding.

"Here we go," he called out to Alex below, who tested his own footing on the ground, alert and ready. Alex knew the next fifty feet of rock face was smooth and relatively featureless. It took great skill and strength to find and exploit the tiny fissures and ledges that were present. Sometimes a climber chose well and found an invisible pathway forward, one miniscule hold leading to another. Sometimes every choice seemed to lead to a dead end.

"At first Bobby was tearing it up," Alex said. "Everything was going right. Then he came to a standstill and decided to backtrack a step or two. That's when it happened."

When Bobby changed direction, his right foot slipped from the half-inch lip of rock where he'd placed it. It was enough to unbalance him.

"Falling!" he called out, alerting Alex to be ready to catch him.

Bobby let go of the rock, expecting to drop only a few feet before being stopped by the rope threaded through the last cam he'd placed. Such falls happen all the time and typically pose little danger. They are jarring, perhaps, but nothing more. Usually the worst part is knowing that you are giving back territory you'd already climbed.

Not this time. Alex quickly and skillfully took up slack in the rope as Bobby fell, but when the rope went taut against the anchor, the metal cams broke free from the wall as they expanded. The winter ice had weakened the rock enough that it gave way under Bobby's weight. It was a climber's worst nightmare.

Alex moved backward as fast as he could over the loose rock at the bottom where he stood, trying to take up the sudden slack, but it was too late. There was nothing he could do to stop Bobby from falling all the way to the ground.

"I watched him drop like it was happening in slow motion," Alex said later. "I wanted to believe he'd be okay, but part of me knew better."

Alex ran to the spot where Bobby lay. Miraculously, he'd barely missed a large and jagged boulder. Instead he landed on a flat, muddy patch of earth just a few feet wide. Still, the impact was enough to cause severe injury. Bobby lay on his back, conscious, but unable to move.

"I was terrified," Alex recalled. "We were miles away from anyone or anything, and I knew I'd have to leave him there to go for help. I told him that and was blubbering on about how sorry I was that I'd let him fall. But he smiled at me. There didn't seem to be any pain in his expression, just this warm, peaceful smile."

"Don't go," Bobby said. "It'll be all right."

Alex was about to argue, but the look on Bobby's face stopped him. His friend looked upward past him. His eyes went wide with wonder.

"Oh man, you've got to see this," he said. "Unbelievable."

"What is it?" Alex asked, captivated by the air of calm that had come over his friend.

"A beautiful green field," Bobby said haltingly. He was having difficulty breathing but didn't seem to notice or care. "I've never seen flowers like that. So many. So *bright*. The light is in the flowers and grass, like that's what they are made of. And music. Unreal! Can you hear that?"

Alex thought he almost *could* hear it, seeing the powerful effect it had on his friend. Bobby's face lit up and tears filled his eyes—tears of joy.

"They're all there!" Bobby said. "Waiting for me!"

"Who?"

"My grandma and grandpa. Uncle Daniel! He looks so good."

Alex knew Bobby's grandparents had died when he was a boy. His uncle Daniel passed away only the previous year, after a long battle with cancer. He was barely more than a skeleton by the time the disease had taken him.

Bobby strained to get the next words out, but he spoke of seeing friends he'd known welcoming him and urging him forward. He talked more of brightness, vivid colors, and how people looked so happy.

Alex sat quietly beside his friend, knowing the end was near.

"Okay," Bobby said. "They say it's time to go, brother. I need to go. Don't worry. Please don't worry. I'm okay."

Bobby died six minutes after his fall, but for Alex time had stood still. For those few moments, eternity seemed to wrap its arms around them both. He felt as if he'd been to heaven and back himself, in spite of his overwhelming pain at losing his best friend. Alex cried all the way into town. And all the way he heard Bobby's voice in his mind repeating again and again: "Don't worry. I'm okay. It's so incredibly beautiful."

And Alex believed it.

15

A Time for Letting Go

Could Pam Burton's determination keep her severely injured son from crossing into the next life?

M om!"

Through the phone line, Pam could hear the panic in her youngest son's voice.

"Someone called and said Kevin was in a crash on a bridge!" Chris blurted. "They're transferring him by helicopter from Winnsboro to the hospital in Tyler right now!"

Pam had been running errands in Tyler, Texas, all morning. At that moment, she happened to be fifteen minutes from the hospital where her eighteen-year-old son, Kevin, was being flown, instead of at her home in Alba almost an hour away.

She drove as fast as she could. As she pulled into the parking lot, a helicopter was hovering noisily above the landing pad in front of the hospital.

A glass blockade kept Pam from rushing onto the helicopter pad. From a distance, she watched as paramedics slid open the doors and pulled out an emergency gurney laden with a shrouded figure. Pam ran alongside the glass, staying parallel with the paramedics as they wheeled the gurney toward the hospital entrance. Near the entrance, the blockade ended, and Pam ran to her son.

Kevin was unconscious and bleeding from his nose and ears, his head and face swollen and still swelling. Shocked, Pam fell back as the paramedics pushed Kevin through the emergency doors and disappeared.

Frantic, Pam began to pray.

Lord, if Kevin dies, I'll kill myself! I couldn't take it. I couldn't go on without him. You've got to let him live, please God . . .

Forty minutes later, Pam was still standing outside pleading with God when several cars pulled into the parking lot. In moments, she was surrounded by half a dozen family members, including her ex-husband, Charles, and sixteen-year-old Chris, the son who had called Pam nearly an hour earlier with the news. A few minutes later, Kevin's fiancée, Gae, arrived with her mother.

Charles wrapped his arms around Pam. They were both crying.

"I got to the hospital in Winnsboro just as they were putting him on the helicopter," Charles said.

"Charles . . . what happened?"

The words tumbled from his mouth. "He was in a speedboat on the lake with three friends. Going under a bridge, the boat hit a concrete piling, and Kevin was thrown from the boat into the piling."

Pam closed her eyes. "I can't believe this is happening. Will he be all right?"

A doctor came outside and approached the family. After a brief introduction, he said, "I have bad news. Kevin has massive brain damage. He's not going to make it through the night. I'm sorry."

Suddenly, his voice sounded farther and farther away. Pam remembers crying. She remembers sliding to the ground. And then everything went black.

Pam awoke on a bed in a small room where the nursing staff had placed her until she could regain consciousness. Her mom and sister were with her and, when she felt strong enough, the three women joined a growing number of family and friends in the waiting room. Charles was describing Kevin's condition to several newcomers.

"Kevin's on life support right now, but it doesn't look good," he was saying with a pained voice. "The doctor says he's never seen anyone with that much brain damage make it."

Gae's eyes were still red from crying. A pretty girl with auburn hair, she was a year older than Kevin and had just started college to become a veterinarian. She enjoyed everything her fiancée enjoyed—animals and hunting and fishing—although she hadn't tried bull roping yet, which Kevin was learning to do and loved.

As everyone continued talking and processing the news, Gae began to hyperventilate, then shake. Someone called for a nurse as Gae went into a full-blown seizure brought on by shock. Several nurses helped her into a wheelchair and took her to a private room for sedatives and observation.

All through the night, Pam prayed like she'd never prayed before, always pleading for Kevin's life. "Take me instead," she begged. "He's too young to die. I can't live with this, Lord. I'll take my own life if anything happens to him. I can't bear the thought of going on without him."

The next morning, Kevin remained in a coma. But he was still alive.

Over the next several days, Pam refused to leave and refused to sleep. Her greatest fear was that if she left the hospital for even a few minutes, Kevin would die while she was gone. So she stayed. And prayed.

One afternoon Pam asked Kevin's doctor, "Is there any hope? You said he wouldn't make it through the night, but he's made it this far. Can you give me a percentage of his chances?"

The doctor shook his head. "I don't like percentages."

"I'm not asking you to put it in concrete," Pam persisted. "Just give me a percentage."

"All right, Pam," the doctor said with a frown. "Maybe 10 percent."

Pam breathed a sigh of relief. "OK. Thank you. At least that's something. At least you're not saying there's no chance."

The doctor looked pained. "Look, Pam, Kevin is still on life support because he still has some brain activity, but not much. I don't know why he's still alive. That's why I'm saying 10 percent. It's not because I've seen anyone with his injuries ever survive. It's just because Kevin's still hanging on, and none of us can figure out why."

Every few hours, the ICU nurses allowed three visitors at a time to sit with Kevin. Visiting times were brief, about thirty minutes. Knowing how much Gae and Kevin loved each other, Pam often let Gae stay with Kevin the full half hour while other family members rotated in and out.

One night during visitation, Chris and Pam found themselves alone at Kevin's side. Chris turned to his mom and said, "Do you think he's going to make it?"

"I hope so, Chris. He's lived this long . . . maybe he'll make it."

Chris and Kevin had always been close. Now the sixteen-year-old just nodded, wanting desperately to have hope.

"Chris," Pam admitted softly, "ever since the accident, I keep hearing Kevin's voice. Over and over. He keeps telling me to let him go, that everything will be okay and I need to let him go. But I can't do it."

Chris looked up, alarmed. "We can't let him go, Mom."

"No, we can't," Pam agreed solemnly. "And we won't."

Five days after the accident, Kevin's doctor met with the family. "Kevin is fading. He won't last till morning, and there are some decisions we need to talk about."

When he asked Pam and Charles about organ donation, Pam exploded.

"You're not going to touch him!" she yelled. "We're not donating any organs! He's going to be fine!"

After the doctor left, Charles and other family members began planning Kevin's funeral, talking about who would officiate at the service, who would serve as pallbearers, and what music Kevin would want.

As she had many times since the accident, Pam heard Kevin's voice. Once again, she heard him clearly say, "Mom, let me go. It's going to be okay." Once again, the answer formed in her thoughts. *I can't let you go, Kevin. I can't.*

The next morning, Kevin was still alive.

Mid-morning, one of Pam's girlfriends arrived at the hospital. "Pam," Janice said. "I feel like the Lord wants me to pray for Kevin."

Pam got permission to take Janice with her into the ICU to see Kevin. As Janice prayed for healing and peace, a feeling of calm came over Pam. After a few minutes, Janice excused herself and left the room.

Pam stayed with Kevin through the afternoon. She studied her son. He had jet-black hair, just like hers. His striking green eyes were swollen shut, and Pam wondered if she'd ever look into those beautiful eyes again.

Walking to the window and staring into the now dusky sky, she suddenly felt her son's presence very strongly in the room. She felt that he was awake and present in spirit even though he remained in a deep coma. At the same time, she felt a second presence, one she felt certain was Jesus.

Then she heard someone speak, as clearly as if that person were standing next to her in the room.

"Pam," the voice said, "I want you to go to the hotel across the street and get a good night's sleep. Tomorrow morning at ten o'clock, I'm going to take Kevin home with me."

Greater peace than she had ever known flooded over Pam. When she returned to the waiting room, several family members saw the calm on her face and jumped to their feet.

"What happened?" someone asked. "Did he come out of the coma?"

"No," she said, "everything's the same."

Except that it wasn't. At least not for Pam. For the first time in six days, she had peace.

She left the hospital and checked into the hotel across the street. Accompanied by one of her sisters, Pam slept soundly all night long. She awoke the next morning and, still peaceful, walked back to the hospital, where the rest of the family were still keeping vigil.

"The doctor said they were taking him for another MRI," Charles told her. Pam just nodded.

At ten o'clock, the doctor appeared and asked Pam and Charles to come with him into the hall where he told them simply, "I'm sorry. He's gone."

Pam didn't cry. Instead, she said, "Thank you. I know you did everything you could."

Back in the waiting room, Chris told his mom, "I know you didn't want to talk to the doctor about donating organs, but Kevin signed the permission form on the back of his driver's license. It's what he wanted."

Pam looked at Chris, then at Charles. "Really?"

They nodded.

"If that's what Kevin wanted," she said, "then that's what we'll do."

Kevin's heart was donated to a man who later wrote to Pam, letting her know that, as a result of Kevin's decision, he had been given more time with his grandchildren. Two women had their lives extended after each received one of Kevin's kidneys.

Several months after Kevin died, Charles and Pam were together in Kevin's room, sorting through books and photos, hats and boots and roping gear.

Pam sat on Kevin's blue-striped bedspread, holding his pillow to her face. "It still smells like him," she said.

Charles stood near the bedroom doorway. "I knew Kevin was going to die."

Pam nodded. Charles had eventually told her that when he saw Kevin in Winnsboro shortly after the accident, a doctor told him the injuries were so severe that recovery was all but impossible. Charles had known from that moment that there was very little hope. From the day of the accident, he'd understood what Pam had been unable to grasp until God gave her a supernatural peace, six days later.

Now Charles looked at Pam, still holding Kevin's pillow. He said, "But even though I knew he was going to die, I also knew everything was going to be okay."

"How did you know?" she asked.

"The whole time we were there, I kept hearing Kevin's voice. He kept saying 'Let go, Dad, just let me go.'"

Pam stared at Charles. With awe in her voice, she said, "He kept telling me the same thing."

Charles said through tears, "He knew. He knew he couldn't be saved. His spirit was there and wanted to leave, but he couldn't. Not until he knew we would be okay."

Following Kevin's death, Pam went on to create a ministry home for troubled girls. More than a thousand girls have come through the ministry, which Pam calls Holy Highway. Some stay for a year, others for just a few months. They attend school, get counseling, and find a fresh start away from the drugs or other influences that have wreaked havoc in their lives. Pam says that helping other parents and kids who, for whatever reason, can't be together for a while has helped her find a measure of healing.

Pam keeps Kevin's picture on her desk in her office at Holy Highway. Kevin would be a man by now with children of his own, but there are never any new photos to update the old. To Pam, her son is still eighteen and always will be, and the girls often ask about the handsome dark-haired boy with the beautiful green eyes.

Part Five

Many Happy
Returns

If a deceased loved one pays you a visit, should you . . . Rub your
eyes? Run? Or rejoice?

The beloved author and minister Frederick Buechner recounts a
dream involving a friend who had recently died—a "very undream-
like dream." The deceased friend stood in his room, and Buechner
said, "How nice to see you. I've missed you."

"Yes, I know," the man responded.

"Are you really here?" Buechner asked.

The friend replied, "You bet I'm really here."

Seeking tangible reassurance, Buechner asked, "Can you prove it?"

"Of course I can prove it." And the friend threw Buechner a piece of
blue string, which he caught.

"It was so real that I woke up," he recalled.

The next morning over breakfast, Buechner reported the incident to his
wife and the friend's widow, who happened to be visiting.

When he mentioned the blue string, his wife called out, "I saw it on the rug this morning!"

Buechner hurried to the place his wife had seen the bit of blue string and, sure enough, there it was. "I knew it wasn't there last night," he said.

He concludes: "Either that's nothing—coincidence—or else it's a little glimpse of the fact that maybe when we talk about the resurrection of the body, there's something to it."[1]

When you hear a story like this—or more dramatic cases of deceased loved ones appearing and even interacting with those still living—you likely have one of three responses:

You don't believe it. "Sure, lots of strange things happen," you protest, "but seeing dead people and that kind of thing is all in the imagination—or just an odd coincidence of circumstances. Great stuff for scary movies, but not for real life."

You're skeptical but open-minded. "Some of those stories sound pretty far-fetched," you might say, "but anything's possible, especially with the mysterious world of the afterlife."

You are convinced these experiences do indeed occur. "Why doubt phenomena we can't fully understand from our time-bound, earthly perspective?" you might be asking. "Since we live in a spiritual world among spiritual beings, we shouldn't be surprised when supernatural events happen."

Should you find yourself among the dubious and doubtful, it's possible that you fear the interference and influence of psychics, mediums, clairvoyants, and the like. You've heard too many spurious stories, seen too many 1-800-PSYCHIC ads on TV, and perhaps even known people duped by charlatan palm readers. That is a legitimate and justified concern.

Let us say clearly and emphatically: Seeking out communication with the dead is a boundary that must not be crossed. Under no circumstance should someone *solicit* communication with or *summon up* the presence of the deceased. Why? Doing so would expose ourselves to deception on the part of unscrupulous purveyors or, worse, open our lives to the darkness of evil spirits. Most of all, God gave explicit instructions on the matter: "Let no one be found among you who . . . practices divination or sorcery, interprets omens, engages in witchcraft, or casts spells, or who is a medium or spiritist or who consults the dead."[2] And again, "Someone may say to you, 'Let's ask the mediums and those who consult the spirits of the dead.

With their whisperings and mutterings, they will tell us what to do.' But shouldn't people ask God for guidance? Should the living seek guidance from the dead? Look to God's instructions and teachings! People who contradict his word are completely in the dark."[3]

Having said that, let us point out that there is a vast difference between *asking for* a dead person's appearance and *acknowledging* it when it comes without solicitation. What we are talking about here are when deceased family members or friends appear to you unbidden and unrequested—when they come looking for you, not vice versa.

We should mention our personal views on this topic, which we agree upon. When we wrote our previous book, *Heaven and the Afterlife*, we were in the second category mentioned above: open to the possibility that such visitations happen but fairly skeptical and suspicious. Our opinions began to change during the writing of that book, as we came across plenty of research that revealed this phenomenon is quite common. One study found that 64 percent of bereaved people who responded had an afterlife encounter of some kind following the death of someone close, and 98 percent of those said the experience had given them great comfort.[4]

But we became thoroughly convinced when we started researching the book in your hands. That's because we talked with or corresponded with scores of people who reported the appearance of a dearly departed loved one. Frankly, we were shocked at how many of these accounts came to us. And these people we heard from are not wacky, out-on-a-limb types—they are credible and reliable men and women, many of whom we know personally. These are professors, pastors, business owners, attorneys, military personnel, and the like—folks typically regarded as sensible and down to earth.

For those who remain dubious, you might consider that there is precedent for after-death visits found in the Bible. For instance:

The appearance of Moses and Elijah. One time Jesus took his disciples Peter, James, and John up on a high mountain. "There [Jesus] was transfigured before them. His face shone like the sun, and his clothes became as white as the light. Just then there appeared before them Moses and Elijah, talking with Jesus." Peter was so awestruck that he said, "Lord, it is good for us to be here. If you wish, I will put up three shelters—one for you, one for Moses and one for Elijah."[5]

375

After the resurrection of Christ. The New Testament writers record Jesus' appearance to his disciples and a gathering of five hundred people following his death and resurrection.

Then there is the intriguing reference made by the writer of Hebrews: "Since we are surrounded by such a great cloud of witnesses, let us throw off everything that hinders and the sin that so easily entangles, and let us run with perseverance the race marked out for us."[6] It seems that deceased saints can observe what is going on here—is it possible they could do more than observe? We don't know.

That calls to mind the words of respected university professor and theologian Gerard Reed, who was in deep grief from the loss of his beloved wife following a battle with cancer. This man, not given to displays of emotion, said with tear-filled eyes, "I believe in the communion of the saints." He meant that even though his wife had gone on to heaven, he was still enjoying meaningful communion with her. Following scriptural directives, he was not seeking out contact with her; he simply was aware of her periodic presence.

In our quest to be open and honest about our exploration of "supernatural" events, we will acknowledge that the idea of dead people appearing to the living is highly controversial. Skeptics often say, "What grief-stricken person, overwhelmed by emotion and perhaps sleep deprived, wouldn't *want* to see their deceased family member or friend in a happy state? It's a matter of *projection* or *wish fulfillment*, a handy trick played by the mind." In some cases, that is probably true. And some events may simply be coincidences rather than supernatural events. But it isn't so easy to explain away the hundreds of reported visitation experiences that occur each year—often by people who were themselves skeptical at one point.

It is not our intent here to sway your opinion, but simply to present the experiences of several people as honestly and accurately as possible. We encourage you to discern the truth with God's guidance.

16

Never Far Away

After her brother's heartbreaking death, Megan Garlow drew strength from a surprising source—her brother.

"Max!" Chris said in his best Jim Carrey-Grinch voice, "Grab a bag and we'll come back for the rest. Of course, when I say 'we,' I mean 'you.'"

From behind the steering wheel of her brother's car, Megan laughed. Of course Megan had heard the line before—probably a hundred times—but she never tired of hearing Chris's rendition of his favorite movie lines.

Which was a good thing. It was the second weekend of July 2009 and the siblings had embarked on a road trip, driving five hundred miles from Kansas to Colorado for a friend's wedding, then driving home again the next day. Over the course of the weekend, Megan would hear many funny quips from her entertaining brother.

The day after the wedding, while driving home, their banter took a deeper turn. On a whim, Megan turned to Chris and said, "Let's plan your wedding! Tell me who you'd pick for your groomsmen."

It was Chris's turn behind the wheel and, as he drove, he began spouting off the names of nearly a dozen men, a combination of brothers, cousins, and close friends.

"Wow! I'm impressed!" Megan said, then teased, "You've got this all figured out. You're not sweet on anyone, are you?"

Chris, twenty-one, grinned and shook his head. "Nope. But it's easy to know who I'd choose to stand with me at my wedding. Each of these guys has had a huge impact on my life."

Megan and Chris had always been close. Best friends really. But this was a new side to her brother. She was fascinated. "Tell me more," she prompted.

Chris told her the things he most appreciated about his brother-in-law Caleb, brother Nathan, cousins Jimmie, Wes, and Josh, and friends Wes, Jameson, Jack, Scott, and Matt.

When she got home, Megan told her parents, Bill and Laurie Garlow, about her conversation with Chris. Looking forward to Chris's wedding one day, they wrote down the names of his future groomsmen.

Two weeks later, these men would serve as pallbearers at Chris's funeral.

On July 16, Chris's charred car was discovered in a supermarket parking lot with someone inside, burned beyond recognition. Authorities were still trying to identify the body, but there seemed little reason to believe the young man who had perished was anyone other than Chris Garlow.

If any accident could be called "freak," it was this one. Parking lot security cameras showed Chris's car pulling into the lot around 4:45 in the morning and stopping at the far end of the lot. The video showed that no one approached or got out of the car. A little later, smoke could be seen coming from the hood of the car, then flames engulfed the engine and spread rapidly.

The best explanation the authorities and the family have been able to piece together is this: Chris was on his way home early that morning after being with friends. His frequent struggles with insomnia meant he was normally awake past 3:00 a.m., at which time he would become profoundly tired. In addition, he had just begun taking new medication to assist with his allergies, and it might have affected his alertness. Extremely sleepy, and not wanting to get pulled over for weaving, he turned into the parking lot.

It was a warm night. Chris turned off the headlights but left the car running, along with the air-conditioner. He pushed his seat back and closed his eyes. He just needed a short nap and he'd be good to go. When the car overheated and the fire started in the engine block, Chris didn't wake up. He was overcome by fumes and later by flames. He probably never stirred at all.

Looking back, Megan and her family realized Chris's death might explain something that had happened years earlier. Chris and Megan's older brother, Robbie, who has Down syndrome, became very ill with altitude sickness during a family visit to Colorado. The situation became so serious that he had to be hospitalized. While there, he was sedated after having a tracheotomy tube inserted in his throat. At one point, he suddenly became agitated, then nearly hysterical. Over and over, he cried out, "Fire! Fire! Chris! Chris out! Fire!" Robbie kept pointing and yelling until Chris was brought to him so he could see that his little brother, then ten, was safe.

It seemed that Robbie had a premonition of his brother's death more than ten years before it happened.

In the months following Chris's funeral—officiated by his uncle Jim Garlow and attended by hundreds of grieving but grateful loved ones—his family continued trying to cope with their profound sadness. For Megan, preserving precious memories of Chris became extremely important. She spent most of the summer making photo collages of Chris and writing letters to his closest friends—the men he'd identified for groomsmen, the same ones who had carried his casket—recounting for them the wonderful things Chris had told her about each of them days before his death.

One of Megan's most enjoyable memories of Chris was the road trip they took together to Colorado. Her most poignant memory, however, was of the final evening of a Fourth of July family camping trip shortly before Chris died.

Bill and Laurie had taken all six kids RV camping and one night around the campfire, as often happens, the enveloping darkness and mesmerizing flames inspired meaningful conversation. Someone brought up the book their uncle Jim had just written with coauthor Keith Wall titled *Heaven and the Afterlife,* and the discussion turned to many provocative subjects. As various family members shared their thoughts and feelings about a range of topics—including near-death experiences, angels, demons, heaven, and hell—it was a bittersweet reminder that their precious years together on earth were temporary. It was also a reminder that, because of their

Christian faith, the separation would be temporary, and one day the family would be reunited for eternity in heaven. Looking around the circle of fire-lit faces of people she loved, Megan couldn't imagine life without any of them. And yet eleven days later Chris would be gone.

That fall, Megan moved to Colorado to begin a career as a high school teacher. The start of the school year kept her busier than she could have imagined. Still, the ache was there, and she missed Chris more than she could express.

And Megan still had a pressing question. She wanted to know what Chris's life was like *now*. Over and over again, she wrote in her journal, "Chris, where are you? What's it like where you are now? What's heaven *really* like?"

One night she dreamed about her brother.

It wasn't the same dream she'd been having for weeks, where Chris was hanging out with her family and then suddenly disappeared. Every time she had that dream, Megan awoke with the heart-sickening realization that, yes, Chris was truly gone forever.

This time she dreamed she was with her mother and her sisters Brooke and Amanda. The four women were laughing and reminiscing about the things they loved most about Chris.

"Remember how he always quoted funny movie lines?" Brooke said.

Amanda added, "Remember how Dad would always say to him, 'How can you remember *that* stuff and you can't remember the stuff you need to know for your tests at school?'"

The other women smiled fondly.

Suddenly, just to the right of where her mother sat, Megan saw her brother's face begin to materialize, and then his body. He was laughing right along with them, as if he'd been listening in and just now decided to make his presence known. He looked just like, well . . . Chris. He was tall and tan with brown hair and mischievous brown eyes.

"Chris!" Megan cried out.

He assured the women it was really him and, when Megan wasn't so sure, he took her hand and placed it on his arm. Despite the fact that he was still somewhat transparent, Chris's arm felt solid to the touch.

Megan realized this was her chance. "Chris," she said breathlessly, "tell me about heaven."

His faced glowed. "It's awesome and beautiful beyond words. And people are themselves. They still look like themselves, and they have their same personalities."

Megan and her sisters exchanged glances. "So Brooke will still be Brooke? And Amanda will still be Amanda?"

"Exactly!" Chris said. "And everyone has jobs. Not like the jobs here, where people are often bored or unhappy. Everyone loves their jobs there. In some ways it's like earth, but everyone is happier."

One of the sisters asked, "What's your job, Chris?"

"Oh, I haven't found one yet."

The women laughed. Apparently, heaven really *was* just like earth for their happy-go-lucky brother.

Chris caught their drift and grinned, "Now, hold on a minute. It's not like that. The reason I don't have a job yet is because right now I'm staying pretty busy looking out for my friends and family. And there are a lot of you guys, so it takes up most of my time. Plus I guess I'm not ready to leave you all behind quite yet and be fully committed there—"

And that's when Megan woke up. But for the first time since the accident, she awakened with an overwhelming feeling of peace.

A few months later, in January, Megan sat in a plane, flying home to Kansas to visit her family. After the crew had made their announcements and everyone had settled in for the flight, Megan reached for a book she'd just purchased titled *Heaven*. The author, Randy Alcorn, had based his findings on twenty-five years of research. As she began to read, Megan discovered that Alcorn's portrait of heaven included none of the stereotypical images of clouds and harps. Instead, she read about a place much like earth, only perfected . . . a place where beauty abounded and people had personalities and even purpose.

Suddenly she was struck by the thought that nothing she read sounded new to her at all.

Heaven, as Alcorn portrayed it, is exactly the way Chris had described it to Megan in her dream two months after he died.

Megan put the book down. She looked out the window, overcome with peace and something else too. What she felt was gratitude.

381

Staring out over the magical landscape of clouds, she thanked God for Chris, for the life Chris was experiencing even now in heaven . . . and for the answers and comfort Chris had been allowed to give her.

Chris's family will be the first to admit that on the bad days it feels like Chris is gone forever. It's an overwhelming sense of loss. But on the good days it's a little easier to remember what they've come to understand with all their hearts: Chris hasn't stopped existing, but is merely someplace else. The separation—although painful—is temporary. And most of all, one day the Garlow family reunion in heaven will be worth the wait.

17

A Bond Between Brothers

After his brother drowned, Juan Valdivia was given extra time to say good-bye.

On a particularly beautiful spring day—May 12, 1992—Juan Valdivia could see blue sky and bright sun outside the window of his Sacramento office. He'd recently finished the classroom portion of his training to become a legal clerk and had landed a promising job at a local law firm. His wife, Cindy, and their three kids were healthy and happy. Life was good.

Then he got the phone call. Cindy was on the other end of the line.

"Joe is missing," she said. "The prison called to say he never showed up for work this morning."

Time stood still in Juan's tiny office when he heard those words. The spring sunshine pouring through the glass suddenly lost its warmth, and a chill went through his body. Joe was his older brother—though, in truth, Juan thought of him as more of a father. As a teenager, he had even lived with Joe in Germany for a time, while his brother was in the military and stationed there.

These days, Joe worked as a prison inspector at the Mule Creek State Prison in Ione, California, an hour-long commute from his home in Sacramento. Joe left home every workday between four and five o'clock in the morning.

383

"You have to understand something about Joe," Juan said. "He was the kind of guy who'd show up for work early, leave late, and not take a lunch break. He was regular and reliable like a clock. So for him not to show up for work was a big deal. We knew immediately that something was not right."

Juan headed straight home when he hung up the phone, while another brother, Eddie, and Joseph, Joe's son, began retracing Joe's probable route to work that morning. At home, Juan sat helplessly on the couch in his living room with a cold feeling of dread whipping around him like a winter wind. Though it wasn't like him to feel chilly, that day he wrapped himself in a blanket and waited for news.

It didn't take long for the phone to ring again. Eddie and Joseph had found Joe's cream-colored Chevy Blazer beside a wide, concrete-lined aqueduct where it crossed Florin Road in southeast Sacramento. The hood stood open, and the cap was off the radiator. The engine was running—just as it had been for at least ten hours. Police were on the scene now and had begun to search the water, which was ten feet deep and flowing rapidly southward to the farmland of the San Joaquin Valley.

"I wanted to jump in my car right then and drive out to the canal and help look for my brother," Juan said. "I felt useless doing anything else. But we decided to go to my mom's house instead and wait there, in case the worst had happened."

The entire family bristled with anxious energy—and dread. It had already been a hard year for Joe and his wife and kids. A few months earlier, he'd been shot in the legs by a stranger, for no better reason than the fact that the man wanted the San Francisco 49ers jacket Joe wore. After massive surgery and lengthy physical therapy, Joe was left with several pins and rods in his legs that caused him constant pain.

And now this. Juan could hardly believe it was really happening.

The phone rang once more, and their last sliver of hope was shattered. Authorities found Joe's body—a quarter mile from where his truck sat—pinned by the rushing water to a metal grate designed to catch brush and other debris. He'd been dead since early that morning.

After the funeral, Juan was plagued by a swarm of conflicting feelings. He was confused by the many unanswered questions concerning Joe's death. He felt betrayed and abandoned by his brother—and then felt guilty for his selfishness. Juan endured devastating grief along with the overwhelming sense of responsibility to care for the family Joe left behind—his wife and four kids. Most of all, he was angry at God.

"I had only been a Christian a couple of years, and I didn't know anything about going to heaven or hell," he said. "Like lots of people, I had questions, but no answers. I didn't really give the afterlife that much thought."

Exactly one week after burying Joe, Juan was seized by the urge to drive out to the canal where Joe had died. He hadn't been there yet, not fully trusting his fragile emotions to hold up. But that day he was compelled to go, as if he had no choice in the matter. He went to remember and reflect—and grieve the father figure he had lost.

He parked his car beside the canal fence, which was newly patched and secured so no one else could climb down to the water. He got out, crossed to the passenger side, and sat on the hood. The afternoon sun was headed toward the horizon, bathing the wide-open fields all around him in a golden glow. He looked out over the aqueduct, his mind a torrent of motion, like the water below, full of painful questions. A deep silence settled around him.

"Hey, Johnny, what are you doing here?"

Joe's voice came from the direction of the setting sun. There was no mistaking it for someone else. When alive, Joe always called Juan "Johnny."

Juan glanced toward the sound and saw his brother's silhouette, backlit by the sunlight, coming toward him. At first, Joe looked indistinct, like a shadow. But the closer he came, the more real and solid he appeared. By the time he came to a stop just a few feet from Juan's car, Joe looked as substantial as any living person. Juan heard his voice just as clearly too.

"It sounds strange now," Juan recalled, "but I wasn't scared or surprised at all to see him there. I hadn't gone out there expecting anything like that to happen. But once he was standing there, it all seemed so natural."

Joe was wearing the formal Department of Corrections dress uniform he'd been buried in. Juan's eyes were drawn to the flash of a gold pin in the shape of the letter "J" on the lapel of his jacket—right where Juan had put it when he leaned over his brother's casket a week earlier to say one last good-bye. It had been a Christmas gift from Joe the previous year.

His brother looked good—healthy and alive. His skin was clear and fairer than it had been. There was a soft angelic light around him.

"Johnny, what are you doing here?" he asked.

Juan calmly explained that he just needed some answers. He wanted to see where Joe had gone into the water and find out what had happened.

Juan looked at the figure standing before him. "Did you suffer?"

"No, I didn't suffer," Joe answered. "When the truck overheated I tried to get some water from the aqueduct. I slipped on the algae at the edge of the water and hit my head. It knocked me out, but I didn't feel anything."

Then Juan's brother explained: Pulled immediately under the surface, Joe then saw a hand and arm reach down and take hold of him. It pulled him upward out of the water. Joe glanced back down and saw his body drift away in the murky current. When he looked around for the person who'd lifted him up, there was no one to be seen.

He knew then that he was dead—and felt an amazing sense of peace and well-being. He told Juan he visited everyone in the family after that, to say good-bye—though without being seen by anyone. He attended the funeral and was proud of the way the family came together and supported each other, even in their pain and grief.

"He repeated to me parts of conversations I'd had with the family that day," Juan said. "He described what our mother was wearing—and laughed because she'd had on two different shoes. Nobody else noticed that."

Joe knew that Juan had been upset on the day of the funeral because his mother had invited a troupe of Aztec dancers in native dress to perform during the ceremonies—without consulting the rest of the family. He advised Juan to let it go and accept it as a necessary part of their mother's grieving process.

Joe talked about how long they'd had to wait at the cemetery for the last cars in the funeral procession to finally arrive.

"He thanked me for not taking the freeway," Juan remembered with a smile. "That was something he always hated when he was alive. We took the back roads, and even though we had twenty-two motorcycle escorts, it still wasn't enough."

Joe asked Juan to watch over his kids and keep them out of trouble.

Then Juan broke down and revealed how he felt about being abandoned by the brother he depended on for so much. Everything Juan knew about being a father and a man, he'd learned from Joe—and there was so much more to know.

"How could you leave me?" he asked.

"It was my time," Joe replied matter-of-factly. "I had no choice. But things are amazing here. And I don't have any more pain."

Suddenly, Joe said it was time for Juan to go home, before Cindy got worried. He began to walk away in the direction from which he had come. Juan slid off the hood of the car and walked to the driver's side door. By the time he got there, Joe was gone. Forty-five minutes had gone by.

Shortly after this encounter, Juan made a major change in his life. He left the legal profession and became a mortician.

"What I went through with Joe made me intensely curious about the whole death process," he said. "I wanted to know what happens to bodies when we die, how an autopsy works, and so on. It definitely gave me a huge amount of compassion for people who have suffered a loss. Even after eighteen years in this business, it is more than just a job to me. I still get emotional when helping a family who has just lost someone."

And the experience has matured and strengthened Juan's faith in God.

"I know for sure that God's angels are watching over us and that death is not an end. It's a beginning," he said. "I believe Joe is about the Father's business now, just like Jesus said."

Weeks after his visit with Joe, Juan sat looking through the photos taken at the funeral. In one, Joe's wife, Erlinda, is seated next to his mother at the graveside. Since Joe was a veteran of the armed forces, Erlinda is reaching out to receive a folded flag from a uniformed member of the honor guard. But that's not what caught Juan's attention. Instead, his eyes were drawn to his mother's feet.

He grinned when he saw that she wore two shoes, both of the same style—but one brown and the other black.

18

"You've Come Back!"

After the death of her husband, Norma Knudson's sagging spirits
were lifted when she was visited by his spirit.

Late one evening, Norma Knudson reclined on the sofa in the living
room of her comfortable San Diego home. An open book lay in her
hands. Her eyes moved as if reading the words, and she turned the
page at appropriate intervals—but her mind was elsewhere. Or perhaps it
was simply nowhere, a foggy place where all her senses had gone numb,
where time seemed to inch along like a mountain glacier. Some nights she
turned on the TV and stared blankly at the screen, watching the images,
but never really seeing them.

She was an old woman, about to turn eighty—on April Fool's Day.
Anyone who saw her sitting there, staring vacantly at her book, might
have chalked up her lethargy to simple fatigue or a mind gone slack with
age. But that would have been incorrect. Her problem wasn't old age or
slipping mental faculties—it was deep depression.

Norma suffered from *grief*.

Just two months earlier, Curt, her husband and devoted partner of
fifty years, had died in the bedroom just a few steps from the sofa where
she rested. After an exhausting and emotionally trying year, Curt suc-
cumbed to a rare condition called Lewy body disease, a little-known cousin
to Alzheimer's and Parkinson's diseases. Lewy bodies (named for their

discoverer, Frederick Lewy) are microscopic protein deposits that form in nerve cells in the brain, disrupting normal function. There is presently no cure, and the debilitating symptoms—increasing dementia, loss of motor control, and a progressive inability to communicate—all advance rapidly after they first appear.

"I am a strong person; I know that," Norma recalled. "I cared for both my aunt and my father for years toward the end of their lives. But this was almost more than I could take. I cared for Curt almost by myself. My daughter helped, of course, but she was busy running her own business. He couldn't swallow well and wouldn't eat what I made for him. Worse, he couldn't tell me what he did want. I loved him dearly, but I have to admit I got angry and frustrated at times."

Being suddenly unable to communicate with Curt was the hardest part for Norma. They had been best friends for all those years together. Talking and laughing with each other and Hanna, their only daughter, was as much a vital part of their lives as the food they ate and the air they breathed. Before he died, Curt could no longer express his most basic needs, much less carry on the sort of conversation Norma had so enjoyed. He looked blankly back at her when she tried to tell him how she felt or what the doctors said when they finally diagnosed his condition correctly.

For months, Norma had done nothing but care for Curt. Gone were the frequent strolls down Grand Avenue to the stretch of Pacific beach they had marveled at together for years. Also gone was time to spend on her work as an artist. Tending to her beloved husband had consumed her life and depleted her energy.

After the funeral, her physical and emotional exhaustion caught up with her—and she withdrew even more deeply behind the drawn shades and closed doors of her house.

"I cried a lot," she said. "Everything in the house reminded me of him. Nothing seemed worthwhile without him there to share it."

So that night, when she lay on the sofa attempting to read a book, it was just another evening in the flat landscape her life had become. The gray house cat, Boogie—an abused stray Curt had rescued from a life on the streets two years earlier—climbed onto Norma's chest and settled in for a nap. Soon, Norma fell asleep as well, too tired to move to the bedroom. The only sounds in the house were the hum of the refrigerator in the kitchen and Boogie's soft purring.

A short time later, a sharp pain piercing her chest jolted Norma awake. Boogie had suddenly jumped up and scratched her as he darted away down the hall toward the bathroom. Norma's first thought as she rubbed her clawed skin was one of irritation at the cat. But it took only a second to forget about that and to realize something was very, very different.

She heard a sound coming from down the hall. Water was running loudly in the bathroom shower.

Then she smelled the floral scent of soap and shampoo.

And then . . . could it be? Curt's booming, beautiful singing voice filled the house, just the way it used to whenever he took a shower.

"Oh my, you've come back!" Norma cried, as waves of relief and comfort washed over her. Time not only seemed to stand still, it practically vanished altogether. "I am so glad you are home!"

Boogie returned from the bathroom and began running around the house, frantically excited, his raccoon-like black-and-gray ringed tail waving like a flag.

"Oh, I am so glad you are home!"

But wait, Norma thought as she remembered the events of the past several months. *I must be dreaming. He couldn't have come home. This is not real.*

She looked toward the bathroom. The sound of water splashing seemed real enough. Curt, a professional musician and music teacher in his younger days, was belting out a song he'd sung so often while living—Tennessee Ernie Ford's classic tune:

> You load sixteen tons what do you get
> Another day older and deeper in debt
> Saint Peter don't you call me 'cause I can't go
> I owe my soul to the company store

"I know what I heard, and I certainly *felt* wide awake," Norma recalled later. "I had the red, stinging cat scratches to prove it. But I still didn't believe it."

She went to the kitchen to put on a pot of coffee and "straighten herself out." The comforting aroma helped settle her mind. When she returned to the living room, the shower was still running. Her deceased husband was still singing. She sat down gingerly on the sofa to collect herself.

Then suddenly the sound of cascading water stopped—and Curt strode into the room, beaming with energy and presence. He sat down beside Norma in his favorite chair, smiling and laughing. The achingly familiar scent of the cologne he wore when alive—*Allure Homme* by Chanel—filled the air. Though he died at age seventy-nine, Norma was astonished to see him as he had looked when he was a handsome "youngster" of thirty-five. His skin was young and supple, his hair curly and brown. Curt wore clothes Norma had never seen before—a crisp white shirt with blue stripes under a tan jacket. He had on tan trousers and shiny brown loafers.

"He looked *great*," Norma said later. "He looked like a million bucks!"

The disbelief she had felt moments ago evaporated and she said to him again and again, "You're home! I'm so glad you came home!"

"Yes," Curt said to her warmly. "I'm fine, I'm good! Don't worry."

The sound of his voice was pure music to Norma's ears. Weeks before he died, Curt had lost the ability to speak. It was devastating to soul mates like them who talked to each other all the time about everything. They conversed on long walks, during dinner, before sleep at night. They had no secrets and indulged in no brooding silences. Now there he was talking to her, after she'd given up on ever hearing his voice again.

"You look wonderful," she said.

"I am!" he replied with a smile that seemed to stretch from ear to ear. "Everything is wonderful."

"I can see you, but I know I can't touch you," Norma said, thinking that *must* be one of the rules when you are visited by your deceased husband, no matter how strongly his cologne fills the room.

His smile broadened. "Oh yes, you can," he said, playfully.

He held out his hand to her. Without hesitation, she took it. His skin was soft and alive—and very real.

"His hand was warm, almost hot," Norma remembered. "We held hands like that for quite some time and just looked at each other. He smiled, and looked so wonderful and healthy. I couldn't believe my eyes."

"Don't worry," Curt said again. "Everything is fine."

Then he slowly disappeared from sight, like a movie that gradually fades at the end. After a few moments, Boogie jumped into the chair where Curt had been seated and, at last, sat still.

What in the world just happened to me? Norma thought, without a trace of fear. On the contrary, she felt like shouting and dancing. She went to the kitchen and poured a cup of coffee, glad to have something familiar to do with her shaking hands. Even there, his scent was still powerfully present. An idea suddenly crossed her mind, and she practically ran to the bathroom to see if the shower was wet.

It was dry.

She checked the medicine cabinet in case the last bottle of Curt's cologne had fallen over and spilled.

No, it hadn't.

"I drank coffee the rest of the night," she said with a laugh. "I couldn't possibly sleep. I know he came back to tell me that everything was okay, that I should stop worrying and grieving so much."

And that's exactly what she did.

"Since my husband came to visit, my life has turned around completely," she said. "I still walk around the house and I see things that remind me of him, but now it's okay. I've seen for myself that he is well where he is, and I'm not afraid. I know we'll see each other again."

Norma no longer spends her evenings in a fog of depression, staring blankly at the television, or at books she can't remember reading. She's painting again—creating lovely portraits, her specialty. She's cooking once more, enjoying the flavors she had all but forgotten during Curt's illness and after his death. And every morning she takes a long walk on the beach.

Occasionally, Norma's house still fills with the scent of *Allure Homme*, but she no longer checks the bathroom medicine chest for a spill. She just smiles and thanks God for the comfort it brings.

"Now I have absolutely no fear of death," she said. "It's just a continuation of living."

19

1127

After her dad died, Hanna Sheldon found comfort in an unexpected place.

Hanna Sheldon turned out the lights in her office at the Pine Hills Lodge and was surprised at how feeble the late-afternoon light was that fell through the window. The rain that threatened to spill from low-hanging clouds all day had finally followed through, coloring the surrounding Cuyamaca Mountains a heavy, foreboding shade of gray. The lodge—Hanna's labor of love for the past several years—was a rustic but elegant resort in the historic mining town of Julian, California.

Today as she ran through the storm to her car for the ninety-minute trip home to San Diego, Hanna felt as dark and dull on the inside as the world looked outside. In truth, a deluge of tears had been steadily gathering throughout the day along with the rain. She shut the car door behind her, looked at her drenched appearance in the rearview mirror, and knew it was going to be a long ride home.

In all the years she'd been making the trip to the lodge, she had never grown tired of the beautiful scenery—rolling mountains, lush apple orchards, and forests of oak, cedar, and pine. But three months ago, all that changed. Something happened to drain the joy out of Hanna's life and wrap her in a suffocating depression.

Her father died.

After a year of progressively losing his ability to walk, eat, and communicate, Curt Knudson died of Lewy body disease, a rare brain ailment akin to Parkinson's and Alzheimer's (see Norma Knudson's story in the previous chapter). He had been a wonderful father to Hanna—involved, fun-loving, and caring. Letting go of him had been the hardest thing she had ever been called upon to do. She'd begun to doubt whether her life would ever regain its luster.

As she pulled her car onto the winding highway and headed toward home, Hanna began to cry. She let loose and gave up on trying to be brave and controlled. She cried and cried. And she verbalized all of her feelings, as if her father were seated in the seat beside her.

"I'm sure I looked like a crazy woman, crying and talking out loud to nobody," she recalled. "But I didn't care who saw me. There weren't many people on the road that day anyway, though it wouldn't have mattered. After carrying so much emotion, I was ready to unload."

And she did. She "opened a vein," as creative types say, and let her blood and guts spill out. She had no typical unfinished business with her dad—no confessions to make, no forgiveness to ask or give. Mostly she wanted to express how sorry she was that his condition had been misdiagnosed for so long during the year he was in decline. Improper medication had contributed to his dramatic loss of normal mental and physical function.

She poured out all the things she'd been unable to say to him in the last weeks and months of his life, as his ability to communicate became more sporadic and impaired. Though she was uttering words in a car occupied only by herself, she sensed she wasn't alone. She thanked her father for the recent miraculous after-death visit he'd made to her mother and told him how much that had meant to both of them.

She remembered something then, something very significant: the number 1127. And she wondered if this sign would appear again. On that day, when her emotions were raw and her tears ran, she earnestly hoped so.

Why 1127? A few weeks before anyone in the family knew Curt's gradually failing health was serious, Hanna began to wake up unexpectedly at night. She would glance at the digital clock across the room. Each time it would display exactly the same time—11:27.

It happened during the day as well.

"I'm not a person who is obsessed with the time," Hanna explained. "I rarely look at clocks. But something suddenly started happening a lot: when I did look at a clock, it would say 11:27. That really got my attention. It made me think I needed to spend more time with my parents and to more actively help find out what was wrong with Dad."

How could four simple numbers communicate all that to Hanna? The answer lies in the address of the home where her parents had lived for many decades: 1127 Grand Avenue, San Diego, California.

As unorthodox as the experience was, Hanna decided she must act on the message she was receiving. Running Pine Hills Lodge had kept her from seeing Curt and Norma as often as she once did. But over the following year, she became much more involved in helping them cope with her father's encroaching illness. When he could no longer drive, she took him to doctor appointments and on other errands. She spent hours helping her mother deal with Curt's daily care. Throughout this time, it became a common occurrence for her to see 11:27 on clocks everywhere she went—sometimes at random times of the day when the clock *shouldn't* say 11:27.

Hanna was present when Curt died in his own bed. His passing was peaceful, his daughter holding one of his hands and his wife holding the other.

The very next night she woke up—at 11:27. In the weeks after her father's funeral, she saw 11:27 even more often. It was on the microwave, on the clock on her computer, just about anywhere there was a digital time display.

"I tried to tell myself it was all in my head," she said. "But it really did feel like my dad was trying to comfort me."

Then came the tearful day she drove from Julian to San Diego, months after her dad's death, when she found herself talking out loud to her empty car as she navigated rain-slicked streets. She had so hoped for another sign that he was okay. By the time she arrived home, she felt strangely refreshed after crying so hard and pouring out her heart.

Several days later, around 3:30 in the afternoon, Hanna was busy checking the empty cabins at the lodge before heading home for the day. She was making sure the heaters and lights were off, no water was left running, and the doors were securely locked. Toward the end of her rounds, she stepped into "Pine Cone One," a cozy 1920s-era cabin—the only one her parents ever stayed in when they visited Pine Hills.

The room was dark—the curtains were drawn and the lights were off. In the shadows, a flashing yellow light caught Hanna's attention. She turned toward it and saw the digital clock on the table blinking on and off, the way they do after a power outage, a common occurrence in the mountains. That day, the tiny display might as well have been a neon billboard at Times Square as it repeatedly flashed:

11:27 . . . 11:27 . . . 11:27 . . .

"First, I laughed out loud," Hanna recalled. "Then I sat down on the bed and cried. It is hard to describe, but the whole atmosphere in the room changed. The air felt warmer and heavier somehow. Everything seemed to be moving in slow motion. I was certain he was right there with me, and I sat there for what seemed like a very long time just saying, 'Thank you, Daddy' over and over. It was such a beautiful, comforting feeling."

Then the flashing numbers on the clock changed to 11:28, and the moment passed. She had received the message she had hoped for. And it became the turning point in her process of grief and healing.

"Now when I think of him, I have such a grateful, happy feeling," she said. "I'm not so sad anymore. This is exactly the sort of thing he would do, so fun and playful and creative."

Hanna still sees 1127 appearing at odd times every now and then—and it always brings a smile to her face and comfort to her heart.

20

A Gift Like No Other

With an illness more serious than physicians thought, Miranda Zorn's life was likely saved—by a deceased friend.

M om, we should see ourselves in a mirror!" Miranda said with a laugh. "We're covered in powdered sugar."

It was December 18, 2004, and Miranda Zorn was home from college on winter break. Decorating cookies with her mom, Phyllis Zorn, in the sunny kitchen in their home, in Ellis, Kansas, Miranda felt like Christmas had finally arrived.

The banter between the two women was lively and warm as the cookies took shape. A few days earlier, a neighbor had given them a hand-painted Christmas plate piled high with home-baked goodies, and Miranda and Phyllis were making cookies so they could reciprocate.

Sliding another batch of snowballs out of the oven, Miranda's thoughts flew back in time ten years as she found herself remembering another neighbor who had been a cherished part of her life. In fact, Mary had been much more than a neighbor. The mother of Miranda's best friend, Mary was like a second mom to Miranda and her brother, and like a sister to Phyllis. The two families had done everything together. And while it was hard not to think of Mary at Christmastime, it was impossible today—the anniversary of her death.

On this day nine years earlier, Mary had died unexpectedly after a brief illness, leaving behind four of her own devastated children, plus Miranda and her brother, Ben, as well.

Arranging the cooled cookies on a plate, Miranda turned to her mother. "I remember how Mary always doubled the recipes so we could bake one batch of cookies and eat the other batch raw," she said. "And remember when the car broke down? She made sure we had groceries, drove us to school, then drove you all around town to shop for another car."

Phyllis smiled wistfully. "She always did take good care of us."

It was impossible to talk about Mary Frederick without feeling a sense of delight. At 6' 3" with long red hair and freckles, Mary stood out in a crowd. But the most memorable feature had been her vivacious spirit. When she died of a staph infection, it had been a huge blow to everyone who loved her. To make matters worse, there had been little warning. A case of pneumonia had gone awry and within thirty-six hours Mary was dead at age thirty-four.

A few days after making cookies with her mom, Miranda developed a cold, then a sore throat. On Christmas morning, despite waking up to the smell of cinnamon rolls and coffee, she groaned and pulled the covers up tight around her neck. Her throat still felt raw, and pressure still filled her sinuses. But now her ears hurt too.

The next day, when Miranda began feeling nauseous in addition to everything else, Phyllis bundled her daughter into the car and drove her to the ER. Miranda was diagnosed with a virus, given a steroid shot to boost her immune system, and sent home to recuperate.

Instead of feeling better, however, Miranda felt increasingly fatigued. Two days later, she complained that the spot on her hip where she'd gotten the shot was not only tender, but red and inflamed as well.

"The nurse said it might get sore," Phyllis reminded her daughter. "But let's keep an eye on it."

On New Year's Eve, while getting dressed for a party, Miranda again complained about the tender place where she had received the shot. When Phyllis went to inspect, she let out a gasp.

The spot on Miranda's hip was no longer a pinkish nodule about the size of a dime. Now several inches in diameter, the mark looked angry and inflamed, dark red, and obviously very painful.

Alarmed, Phyllis snapped a picture of the affected skin on her cell phone and emailed it to their family doctor.

The next day, all Miranda could do was sleep. Exhausted and achy, she felt constantly nauseated. The injection site burned. By midafternoon, she was ready for her third nap of the day. Pulling on a T-shirt and a pair of pajama bottoms, she climbed into bed, pulled the covers up to her chest, closed her eyes, and began to pray.

Lord, I don't know what's wrong with me, but I'm scared that it's a lot more serious than any of us realize. Please help me. Please. . . .

While still praying, she felt the mattress shift as someone—probably her mother or brother—sat down on the bed beside her. Miranda opened her eyes. She blinked and stared.

The woman sitting on the bed with her was Mary.

She'd aged a little, the laugh lines on her face a little deeper, the hair at her temples starting to go gray, the rest of her red mane pulled up and back into a ponytail. Reaching over, she stroked Miranda's hair, tucking a wayward lock behind her ear.

"It's going to get worse before it gets better," she told Miranda. "But it's going to be okay. You're going to be all right."

Mary patted Miranda's face. Miranda closed her eyes and smiled. She felt a wave of warmth wash over her body. Feeling relaxed and at peace, she fell sound asleep.

She woke up a couple of hours later. Usually a restless sleeper, Miranda thought it odd that she woke up in the exact position she'd been in when she fell asleep, on her back with the covers pulled up to her chest. The only difference? A lock of Miranda's hair was tucked behind her ear, and there was still an indentation in the covers where Mary had sat.

Miranda climbed gingerly out of bed and hurried down the hall to find her mother. She found Phyllis at the kitchen table, drinking tea and reading a book.

"Mom!" she called out. "I just saw Mary!"

Phyllis looked up, startled.

Phyllis listened intently as Miranda told her what had happened. Mary's message had been clear: Miranda would get worse before she would get better. And yet Miranda's doctors weren't treating her illness very seriously. Realizing her daughter was in danger, Phyllis placed another call to the emergency room. It was time to get aggressive about finding Miranda the help she needed.

Back in the ER, Dr. Alan Adams examined Miranda. "It might be an acute allergic reaction, but it could also be an infection—possibly from receiving an injection with a dirty needle. I'm putting you on 2000 milligrams of antibiotics, and I want you to use hot compresses for the pain."

When Phyllis asked the doctor to take a culture to see exactly what the problem was, Dr. Adams advised doing the procedure at the right time, when the wound opened. Miranda's regular physician, meanwhile, continually resisted getting a culture, saying it was unnecessary.

The following weekend, the abscess on Miranda's hip burst open and began to drain. Phyllis called the ER and spoke with the doctor on call. She demanded he run a culture on the infected site, and this time she wouldn't take no for an answer.

Three days later, Phyllis and Miranda returned to the doctor's office to hear the results of the tests. But instead of being led into one of the exam rooms, they were ushered quickly down the hall into the office of an infectious-disease specialist.

The new doctor entered the room and greeted the two women. "What can I do for you today?" he asked with a smile.

Miranda sighed, in too much pain to bring the new guy up to speed. Phyllis filled him in and explained that they'd come for the results of Miranda's culture.

The doctor went to his computer and looked up Miranda's file. As he read the test results aloud, Phyllis's blood ran cold. Miranda's problem wasn't because of an allergic reaction after all. Miranda had an infection due to staphylococcus aureus. The doctor said he was going to operate and clean out the infected site immediately.

Miranda winced. "Do you have to? Can't I just take stronger antibiotics?"

Phyllis turned toward her daughter. "Miranda—" There was a sobering tone in her voice that drew Miranda's attention immediately. Phyllis said, "We don't have a choice. We can't have the same thing happen to you that happened to Mary."

As Phyllis looked on, understanding slowly dawned in Miranda's eyes. Understanding, and then awe. "Mary?"

Her mother nodded.

"It's the same kind of infection that killed Mary?"

Her mother nodded again.

At that moment, both women knew. The ever-protective second mom, Mary had visited Miranda in order to keep her from dying from the same illness that had claimed her own life nearly ten years earlier.

That afternoon, the doctor applied local anesthetic and made his incision to clean out the infection. He was shocked to realize the extent of the damage wreaked on Miranda's body by the bacteria. Staphylococcus aureas, when trapped under the surface of the skin, releases a toxin that destroys surrounding tissue, turning it into liquid. The amount of liquefied tissue that needed to be removed created a wound the width of a person's hand and several inches deep. Other than the local anesthetic, the surgery had been performed without anything to numb the pain. To make matters worse, the resulting wound had to be cleaned and repacked with gauze every day for weeks—another painful process.

In the ensuing days, Miranda was too consumed with healing to think much about her visit from Mary. Then one morning, several weeks into her recovery, she was eating breakfast and flipping channels on the TV when she came across a documentary on ghosts. She paused, TV remote in hand, as a wave of emotions came crashing in on her.

"I've always believed we wouldn't go through what we go through here on earth if there wasn't an afterlife, and Mary's visit is proof," she reflected. "Now I know there's more to life than just what we can see here on earth. God often sends help in ways we would never expect—sometimes in truly miraculous ways."

Three years later, Miranda had lunch with Leslie, one of Mary's four daughters. Before Mary visited Miranda, it had been years since the girls had even seen each other. Since Mary's visit, the girls—who live three hours apart—had been making the effort to meet halfway for an occasional late-afternoon lunch at Cinnamon's Deli.

Halfway through the meal, Miranda took a deep breath and said, "Leslie, I know I've shared with you about the time, three years ago, when I got really sick. But there's a part of the story I've never told you, because I didn't know how it would impact you."

Leslie raised her brows. "Impact *me*?"

"Yes, you or even your sisters," Miranda said. "Because . . . because it has to do with your mom."

Miranda shared her story again, except this time she told the whole story, leaving nothing out. By the time she was finished, Leslie's cheeks were streaked with tears.

"I was ten when she died," Leslie said. "I've missed her so much. If she can come to you like that, why not me? Why hasn't she come to see me?" A wave of conflicting emotions crossed Leslie's face. Then, almost as quickly as it came, it was gone. She softened. "I'm glad she's all right. I've wondered so many times how she's doing. Now I don't have to worry that she's stuck in limbo or something. Now I know she's okay and that she can still watch over us sometimes."

Miranda had tears in her eyes as well. "Honey, I don't know why she came to me and not you. Maybe she knows it would be too hard for you or for her. Or maybe I was so close to dying myself she knew she had to intervene. I don't know. But I do know that she sees you, Leslie, and your sisters too. I also know I couldn't have gone through what I did without her words to hang onto."

Mary's visit was a gift of life for Miranda and a gift of hope for others who loved her and miss her still. Nearly ten years after her death, a woman known for being protective and generous found a way, yet again, to impact the lives of those she loved.

21

When Grandpa Said Good-bye

For Jennifer Mizicko's family, the final farewell wasn't so final.

Jennifer turned in the cushioned chair and tried to find a more comfortable position. As hospital waiting rooms went, this one wasn't bad—furnished more like a living room than the cold, sterile rooms in some medical facilities. But still, she and her family had spent many long hours here, sitting, praying, holding vigil, and waiting for the heartbreaking news that Ron was really gone.

Ron Wallace was Jennifer's stepfather, and at fifty-three he seemed a young candidate for myelodysplastic syndrome, the rare bone marrow disorder that would soon claim his life. Four months earlier, he had begun the tedious and lengthy process of receiving a bone marrow transplant in the hope of staving off the disease. But when a freak infection spread to his brain, he was transferred from the cancer ward to ICU. His family was notified: It wouldn't be much longer now.

It was night, and Jennifer wished she could find a way to fall asleep in the waiting room. She was so tired. She closed her eyes. She actually began to drift into a restless sleep.

Suddenly she was awakened by flickering lights. She opened her eyes. The bright overhead lights were glowing solidly, without a flicker in sight. She thought to herself, *Maybe I'm seeing angels.*

403

She tried to fall asleep several more times, but every time she got close to crossing over into slumber, she was aroused by flickering lights before her eyes. Finally she sat up and looked at her sister, Laura, who was also wide awake.

"You can't sleep either, huh?" Jennifer asked.

Laura said, "Every time I fall asleep I see angels flying around the room and lights flashing."

Jennifer stared at her sister a full minute before responding. "Really? That's strange. And you know what's even stranger? I keep seeing the same thing."

Ron had come into their lives nineteen years earlier when he married their mother. He had been a good stepfather to Carol's four daughters. He had been an even more amazing grandfather to his fifteen grandchildren. He was the kind of grandpa who was forever taking one of the kids fishing, to the park, or out for ice cream.

The night passed slowly. Around daybreak, a doctor approached the family and said it was just a matter of time. They took Ron off the ventilator and began allowing family members into his room to say their good-byes.

Jennifer and her sisters discussed whether or not to let their children in the room to say good-bye to their grandfather. Jennifer's eight-year-old son, Chris, and Laura's four-year-old daughter, Kira, wanted desperately to see Grandpa Ron one more time before he died. But the skin on Ron's face was turning black as the tissue began to die—something that can happen in the last hours of life—plus he was unconscious, so he couldn't have said anything to the children. In the end, the sisters decided that the disease had so ravaged Ron's body that his grandchildren would be better off not seeing him in his final hours.

And so the children stayed with relatives in the waiting room. They were nearby—the waiting room happened to be adjacent to Ron's room in ICU—and that would have to do.

In the final hours of her stepdad's life, Jennifer thought about the flickering lights she and Laura had seen each time they'd started to doze. She looked into the space above the bed where her stepfather lay dying. The air seemed empty, but was it really? Were angels there? Angels that could be glimpsed in the twilight between consciousness and sleep? Angels that had congregated in the thin space between life and death?

Ron died around four o'clock that afternoon. The girls cried and tried to comfort their mother, Carol.

About ten minutes later, Jennifer headed toward the waiting room to let Ron's grandkids know that he was gone.

As she walked into the room, Chris jumped up and ran to his mother. "Mom, Grandpa just died," he blurted.

Jennifer nodded. "He did. How did you know?"

"A few minutes ago I was getting tired so I sat down and started falling asleep, and just as I did, Grandpa came to me in a dream and told me he loved me and would miss me, but it was time for him to go to heaven. And, Mom, there were angels all around Grandpa, and they were singing this really amazing song. Then Grandpa waved to me, and I woke up."

Jennifer's husband, Mike, joined them as Chris finished telling his mom about his dream. No one else knew about Chris's experience. So when another grandchild had the same dream that night, the family took note.

It was four-year-old Kira this time. She awoke on the morning after Ron's death singing a song. When her mother asked what she was singing, Kira said simply, "Grandpa was in my dream. He told me he loved me, but he was going to live in heaven and he would see me again one day. And there were angels everywhere and they were singing this song." Kira began to sing again and, indeed, sang that song for several weeks.

Kira and Chris had begged to be in the room with their grandpa when he died. Instead, they'd been in the waiting room. Is that why Ron appeared to them? To comfort them in their grief and disappointment at being so close yet not being allowed into the ICU? Or perhaps their senses had been sharpened as they waited in the same room where Jennifer and Laura had already sensed the presence of angels.

A third child had taken Ron's death particularly hard. Five-year-old Ashlee lived with her mother in a house they had shared with Grandpa Ron. She had loved her grandpa so much she had shaved her head during his illness out of solidarity and support. One night, about a week after Ron had died, Ashlee got out of bed to go to the bathroom, which was next to the room that had belonged to her grandfather when he was alive. Still aching at his absence, Ashlee walked slowly down the hallway and past his room. The hallway was dimly lit, the only light coming from a night-light in the bathroom. So Ashlee walked gingerly with her head down, watching her feet to avoid stumbling. Suddenly she walked into someone and fell backward, landing in a sitting position on the floor. Looking up, she saw her grandpa.

"Ashlee, what are you doing up?"

"Grandpa! What are you doing here? They said you died!"

Her grandpa squatted down so he could look her in the eyes. "I just came to check on you, and tell you that I love you." He smiled and nodded toward Ashlee's room. "Now get on back to bed." And with that, he was gone.

One thing the experience taught Jennifer Mizicko and the rest of her family members: Death is never final, and good-bye is not forever.

"All of the amazing events surrounding my stepdad's death showed us that the dividing line between life on earth and life beyond hardly exists," she said. "We are spiritual creatures living in physical bodies. One day, each of us will shed our bodies, but our spirits will go right on living."

Part Six

Do You Believe in Ghosts?

In spite of our best efforts at denial, mysterious encounters with otherworldly entities seem as common as ever.

L et's face it: In our culture, claiming to see ghosts is generally not taken as a positive sign. It may be good for a few laughs with friends around the campfire on a dark night deep in the woods, or at a teenage slumber party, with a flashlight pressed to your chin throwing ghoulish shadows on your face.

But that's all just for fun. If someone you know—maybe your spouse, or your sister, or a co-worker in an adjacent cubicle—suddenly starts talking seriously about seeing apparitions, you would probably back away a step or two and begin thinking about psychiatric intervention. We all know ghosts aren't real, right? Anyone who says otherwise is crazy, right?

Yet at the same time, we as a society spend millions of dollars every year on the latest spooky books and movies—the scarier, the better. What do we want from those darkly imaginative filmmakers and storytellers? Goosebumps, and lots of them. We feel disappointed if we aren't a little apprehensive about turning off the lights at bedtime. How do we expect them to deliver that? By making us believe—truly believe, even if only for a few hours—things that go bump in the night are real.

In other words, we can't make up our minds whether to scoff at the experience or seek it out.

Well, what if there is an explanation for that? For a variety of reasons—fear of ridicule, fear of nightmares, fear of attracting evil entities into our lives—we don't often let the subject of unseen spirits see the light of day. Out of sight, out of mind. But what if we are drawn to realistic and convincing ghost stories because we intuitively sense there is more to reality than our eyes normally perceive? What if we just want to know more about something we wonder about? Ghost stories offer a way to examine our feelings about that while keeping one foot on the fire escape—in case things get too uncomfortable. "That's just make-believe," we can say, and walk away.

If that describes you, then the stories in this section may push you outside your comfort zone. Why? Because the tales that follow didn't come from the pen of a playwright, novelist, or screenwriter. They often seem as improbable as fiction, but that's where the similarity ends. These experiences actually happened to ordinary people who aren't selling anything—and who are most definitely *not* crazy. They have come forward at the risk of sounding like they've come unglued to share with us events and encounters they can't explain. What's more, most of these people—and the many others we spoke to whose stories don't appear here—were firmly in the "skeptics" camp . . . before they encountered an apparition for themselves. "I never believed in ghosts and used to scoff at people who did," almost all of them said. "That is, until I saw one myself—and I *know* I saw one."

They aren't alone. Recent surveys reveal that nearly one in four Americans claims to have encountered an apparition. Even the other 75 percent would probably relate to the spooky scene Mark Twain describes in *The Adventures of Tom Sawyer*: "Out of the stillness, little, scarcely perceptible noises began to emphasize themselves. The ticking of the clock began to bring itself into notice. Old beams began to crack mysteriously. The stairs creaked faintly. Evidently spirits were abroad."[1]

Many have experienced moments like that—walking alone on a dark night, sensing a presence in an otherwise unoccupied room, or waking suddenly to the spine-tingling feeling we are not alone. But we've been trained by our scientific worldview to ignore the messy spiritual implications and blame our overactive imagination for making things up. Researcher Brian Righi writes:

> Not that long ago, to suggest that what lurked about lonely crossroads or in dark attics was anything *other* than a ghost would have sounded ridiculous, and might have even gotten you stoned out of the village.
>
> Contrary to this, Western science finds the belief in ghosts a hard pill to swallow. After all, science measures the world around it in observable, quantifiable facts and outcomes that can be consistently reproduced, while ghosts, on the other hand, have continually given a rather poor performance under such conditions. Ghosts don't seem willing to squeeze under a microscope or into a test tube for science to dissect and examine, but to say that a lack of willingness on the part of ghosts to be examined proves they do not exist would be erroneous also.[2]

We know that a handful of stories won't answer all the questions and settle any debates. But our purpose in presenting them here is to raise a question: How did we ever come to believe that the only real things in life are those we can see, touch, taste, hear, and smell? For people of faith, the existence of an ethereal spiritual reality is not a foreign concept—it is *central* to our beliefs.

With that in mind, read on and listen to the experiences of average people who offer a glimpse into the world we can't see with our everyday eyes. Admittedly, some of the stories will raise questions for you—and maybe raise hairs on the back of your neck. In our first book, *Heaven and the Afterlife*, we discussed possible explanations for these kinds of experiences. They include overactive imaginations, disembodied spirits, and evil spirits. We make no attempt to draw firm conclusions about these accounts. But in our ongoing conversation about the afterlife, these tales represent an important and intriguing piece of the puzzle.[3]

22

The Room With a Bay Window

As a young lawyer, Martin Herrera learned not to discount eyewitness testimony about things unseen.

By the time Martin Herrera was a junior in high school, he knew he wanted to become a lawyer. That's what the guidance counselor's questionnaire recommended and what his siblings predicted every time he won an argument on a technicality. He also knew he would come back home after law school at prestigious Tulane University in New Orleans to practice in the small southern town he loved. There was more money to be had in a big-city corporate law firm, but he wanted to spend his career serving the community that had given him so much.

On trips home from college, Martin often strolled the square around the county courthouse wondering which of the historic buildings he would eventually settle in with his own firm. The exercise was halfhearted, though, since he had long ago picked out his first choice: an old brick house on the corner. The yard was dominated by sprawling live oak trees draped with Spanish moss. A black wrought-iron fence lined the sidewalk in front. But for as long as he could remember, the place had been home to a music conservatory and was unlikely to be available anytime soon.

No one was more pleasantly surprised than Martin when Lydia, the elderly music teacher who owned the school, abruptly closed up shop and put the building on the market—two months before he passed his bar exam. The day she handed him the keys was one of the happiest of his life.

"I must give you one warning, however," she said to him with sudden gravity as they stood out front. "The building is haunted. That room there in particular," she pointed a thin finger at a bay window on the second floor overlooking the street.

Martin snickered to himself, sure the old woman was either crazy or playing a joke at his expense. He'd accepted years ago that the South had a long and rich tradition in both possibilities, particularly among the old-timers.

"She was pretty insistent, I must admit," he said. "But the idea of ghosts didn't fit anywhere in my Christian upbringing. Besides, I'd just spent several years and a lot of money getting a law degree that said to the world I could be trusted to be level-headed and rational. I wasn't about to start my legal career by letting it get around that I was indulging in superstitious nonsense."

Martin busied himself moving into his new building and forgot all about Lydia's spooky warning. His offices and a reception area were downstairs. The second floor held a conference room and a smaller library for filing cabinets and law books. Being a native son, it was not difficult for him to land work, and he quickly found he needed a clerk to help with the paperwork, in addition to his appointments secretary, Helen. He hired a young woman named Rachel, who aspired to become an attorney herself one day. Her desk was in the library—right in front of a broad bay window with a view of the street.

"Rachel was perfect for the job," Martin said. "She was bright and eager and energetic. And she didn't seem to mind how tedious it was to keep track of all that paperwork. Nothing seemed to faze her."

The first sign of trouble appeared about a month after Rachel started work.

"Who was that little girl I saw this afternoon?" she asked at quitting time one day. "One of your nieces? You should introduce me."

Martin looked at her quizzically. "What girl?"

Rachel described how that afternoon she'd seen a small girl walk out of the library, across the second-floor landing, and down the stairs. She was about seven or eight years old, wearing a plain brown dress. She seemed to be headed somewhere, so Rachel didn't bother to introduce herself.

Martin and Helen wore puzzled looks as they told Rachel there had been no children in the building that day. They were sure of it.

"After an awkward moment, we all just shrugged it off," Martin said. "She admitted she'd just caught a glimpse of the girl out of her peripheral vision, so it could have been her eyes playing tricks on her. We laughed about her becoming cross-eyed or blind from looking at too many legal documents."

Always one to tease, Martin bought Rachel a pair of plastic super-vision glasses at a novelty shop and left them on her desk the next day. She took it well and said nothing more about seeing things.

But from that day on, a gradual change came over Rachel. Where she had been bright and cheerful, she began to be more quiet and withdrawn. She paid less attention to her personal appearance. And over the following weeks, the efficiency of her work slowly slipped. She became more forgetful and sometimes misplaced important documents.

"It's not like the changes took place overnight," Martin recalled.

"The best way to describe it is that she seemed increasingly depressed and withdrawn."

One day Martin felt the time had come to approach her and find out what was causing her distress. He walked up the stairs and into the library. Though it was a hot day in late summer, Martin noticed for the first time that the library was remarkably cooler than the rest of the building, where the aging air-conditioner seemed incapable of keeping up. He commented on the fact to Rachel, who was there at her desk with an open file in front of her. She agreed and said it was always cold in there.

Setting aside that mystery, Martin told Rachel his concerns about her demeanor and disposition and asked if there was anything he could do to help.

"It was as if a dam broke," he said. "She told me in a flood that she had decided to quit her job. She said she was going crazy and that she couldn't get a grip on her feelings anymore. She felt so *sad* all the time, for no apparent reason."

Martin didn't know what to say. He was not equipped to be a counselor. And since he hadn't grown up with any sisters, he'd always felt awkward in handling women's moods. But when he saw the joke glasses he'd given Rachel lying on the desk, intuition prompted him to ask if this had anything to do with the little girl she thought she saw weeks ago.

Rachel hesitated before answering. "Yes," she said at last.

There ensued a long pause, as if Rachel were debating saying more. Finally, she explained that the little girl had begun appearing to Rachel every few days and not just in fleeting glimpses, but in sustained moments as well. At random times, she would be sitting on the hallway floor beside the staircase, or standing at the window gazing out—long enough for Rachel to see her in more detail. The girl looked solid, like a living person, though with less color in her skin and clothes. She wore old-fashioned shoes and stockings, and always had on the same plain dress. Her dark hair was cut short, and she was thin to the point of looking unhealthy. Rachel had tried to speak to her or make eye contact, but the girl acted as if she were oblivious to her presence. There was sadness in her expression.

"And no, my eyes have not been playing tricks on me," she concluded. "And yes, I know it sounds crazy—and it sounds like *I'm* crazy. But those are the facts."

Martin stood there dumbfounded. "I didn't know what to say. I couldn't deny that Rachel really believed what she was telling me, but I wasn't ready to start thinking seriously about ghosts in the attic, much less right in our office. I was marshalling all the usual arguments about the power of the subconscious mind and all that Freudian stuff I'd learned in college—when I suddenly felt the hair on my neck stand up. You know, like when you're a kid and you're out walking at night and you're just *sure* somebody is right behind you? *That* feeling."

He turned to look, but no one was there. Still the feeling persisted, like there was something just outside his vision he couldn't quite discern.

"It didn't feel evil or threatening," he said, "just very unhappy. I suddenly felt inexplicably lonely."

That afternoon, Martin did two decisive things: He moved Rachel's desk downstairs into Helen's office, and he called Lydia on the phone.

"She didn't seem too surprised to hear from me," he recalled. "She repeated her claim that the building is haunted. I asked if she'd ever actually seen a ghost. She replied that *she* never did, but several of her students reported sightings over the years, mostly of a young girl. As for Lydia, she'd never been able to use that room for anything other than storage. 'There was too much bad memory in there,' she told me."

"Memories of what?" Martin asked her.

Lydia didn't know for sure, but said she always assumed it had something to do with the orphanage that once occupied the building.

That sent Martin to the public library and the county courthouse in search of records to substantiate Lydia's improbable claim. Sure enough, the house had been built by one of the town's founders in the 1830s. In 1899, the family patriarch died and left the building to a privately owned orphanage. It served in that capacity until the early years of the Great Depression.

One news story from 1918 preserved on microfiche in the county library caught Martin's attention. It reported on the severe toll the Spanish Flu had taken that year on residents of the town. Perhaps some of the dead were children, Martin thought. Perhaps one of them had died in the room with the bay window.

"All of this was way over my head," he said later. "I'd been taught as a child by my parents that whenever you find yourself in a circumstance like that there is only one thing to do—*pray*. So I gathered some people from my church that I trusted not to laugh me out of town, and we went upstairs to the library and prayed. I felt silly at first—and I thought these people would think this lawyer had lost his marbles—but we asked God to either banish it if it was a demon or help it home if it was a human spirit that somehow got stuck here. And apparently he answered."

Rachel kept her job and since then has returned to her former self. And the room with the bay window is the hottest one in the whole building.

23

Attention-Starved Spirits

An early nineteenth-century colonial house in Connecticut wasn't as empty as Patrick and Donna Harrigan assumed when they bought it.

In December 1991, Donna and Patrick Harrigan were ecstatic—and relieved. It was the day they finalized the deal to buy a historic house on Main Street in Newtown, Connecticut. They had spent their last nickel to make it happen and had driven to the closing meeting in a moving truck packed with all their worldly belongings.

It was a bold gamble, but one that symbolized the new life they were creating together. After enduring a painful divorce, Donna was eager to make a home with her new husband, Patrick—the *right* man for her and a good father to her young daughter, Sarah. God was giving her a second chance, and she wasn't about to miss it.

Newtown is steeped in early American history. Purchased from the Pohtatuck Indians in 1705, the town was incorporated in 1711. French General Rochambeau's army encamped in the area in 1781, on their way to the fateful battle at Yorktown—and the end of the Revolutionary War. French soldiers used the weather vane atop the town hall—just a block away from the Harrigans' new home—for target practice.

Their house was built in 1810 by Matthew Curtiss Jr. as a home for his daughter. It stood right next door to his place, a classic colonial-era saltbox-style house built in 1750. The Matthew Curtiss House, as it is known today, is a museum operated by the Newtown Historical Society. Upon moving in next door, Donna and Patrick learned from society volunteers that their house actually replaced an older one that had burned to the ground.

"The house was grand, with high ceilings and a great front porch," Donna recalled. "It had a rustic stone foundation on a dirt floor in the basement. The walls down there were made of stones piled on top of each other. You could see the hand-hewn beams and floor joists throughout the basement and attic. There was a sense of the passage of time everywhere you looked."

The new family got busy settling in. During their first winter, the ancient oil stove in the basement called it quits, but that didn't dampen their enthusiasm. They heated the place with two wood-burning stoves—one on the ground floor that warmed the kitchen, breakfast area, dining room, and large living room; and one upstairs to heat the three bedrooms, bath, and landing.

All was well.

Yet almost immediately, Donna began to smell the sweet fragrance of flowers in bloom and to feel cold breezes inside the house that she couldn't account for—especially on the upstairs landing by the master bedroom. Like most rational people, at first she shrugged it off. As Patrick pointed out to her, the house was more than a hundred eighty years old, with single-pane windows and practically no insulation. The old girl could be forgiven a chilly draft or two.

But when the sensations persisted, Donna began to feel something more was going on. The cold, flowing air was more than a draft. It was a *breeze*, even when all the windows in the house were tightly closed. And the scent of flowers in the air was not just a hint of perfume—it was a powerful aroma.

One day, Donna and Patrick were standing in the kitchen talking about the oddities she'd been experiencing upstairs. Since moving in, they had learned that nearly every house on the street was rumored to be haunted, often backed up by spine-tingling stories of strange happenings. Upon hearing which house the Harrigans had purchased, locals frequently asked if they'd had contact with any ghosts yet.

"I never took that sort of thing very seriously, but with all that had been happening, it suddenly seemed more possible to me," Donna said. "One night in the kitchen, I rather sheepishly told Patrick I thought these experiences might be supernatural."

Patrick, however, was adamant: Ghosts don't exist.

"I was 100 percent skeptical," he explained. "I am a touch-it-and-see-it kind of guy. I told Donna there was no need for exotic or spooky explanations. Everything she described was the natural result of living in a drafty old house."

He said as much to his wife that night in the kitchen: "Be reasonable. Ghosts exist in the imagination and on the big screen—not in houses, even old ones."

At that moment, as if on cue from a theatrical director backstage, water suddenly poured full force from the kitchen sink faucet just a few feet from where the couple stood. *Steaming-hot* water. Patrick rushed to turn it off.

"It had certainly never done that before and never did it again," Donna said. "In fact, ordinarily you had to stand there with the water running for a couple of minutes, waiting for it to heat up. This time the water came on full blast and was piping hot all at once."

Donna just laughed at the eerie coincidence, because the thought of sharing the house with a ghost didn't frighten her. She hadn't sensed the presence of anything evil or menacing, and didn't mind the occasional benign manifestation. But Patrick was not ready to let go of his belief that everything in the world—no matter how mysterious it might appear at first glance—had a logical, rational explanation.

"He was determined to prove that it was just an old faucet that had been left on and that was forced open by some pressure build-up," Donna remembered. "He spent a long time, what seemed like hours, standing at the sink trying to make it happen again. After all that time, he was only able to get the faucet to drip with cold water."

According to Patrick, it was *three* hours—without success. "I'll admit it spooked me a little for the water to just turn itself on like that. But I still wasn't about to say there were ghosts in the house. Just because I couldn't figure it out didn't mean there wasn't a perfectly reasonable explanation."

A couple of months after the family moved in, they invited an insurance agent to come over one evening to discuss the policies his company had to offer. When the young man arrived, they decided to meet where they would not be disturbed by Sarah and the family dog, Tex, who were playing upstairs. The dining room was ideal, since it had three doors they could close for privacy. One opened inward from the entryway; the other two opened outward—to the kitchen and the living room.

"The agent's pitch took about half an hour," Patrick said. "The time had come for him to sign us up and sell us something—and he had us on the hook, by the way. We were sold."

Before getting down to business, the friendly young man casually asked—like so many others had—whether Donna and Patrick had seen any weird things in the house to make them think it was haunted. The couple looked at each other, silently trying to decide how much to share with their visitor.

"But before we could say anything, all three doors in the room flew open at the same time and smacked into the walls—*wham!*" Patrick said. "It was like a gust of wind caught them and threw them open."

Without a word, the insurance salesman quickly gathered up all the pamphlets and brochures spread out on the table, stuffed them into his satchel, and scurried from the house. He never looked back and never contacted the Harrigans again, giving up a sure sale.

"After seeing where we lived, I guess he figured we were too high-risk," Donna said with a chuckle.

Still, Patrick looked for mundane answers.

"I thought it could have been caused by a difference in temperature in the house," he explained. "Our only heat came from the woodstove on the other side of the closed doors. They weren't really latched, so maybe the air flow pushed them open. Of course, there is the fact that only one of the doors opened *into* the room. The other two swung outward. I admit I could never come up with a plausible reason for that."

One night that summer Donna woke up from a deep sleep, startled. What was that sound? She looked at the clock on her bedside table—*2:11*.

Then it happened again—a series of three perfectly rhythmic *bang*s that shook the entire house. Her heart pounding, she nudged Patrick awake. Before he was fully conscious, the three bangs repeated. Again the whole house trembled.

Patrick was wide awake now, having heard—and felt—the last round of loud percussive noises for himself. They repeated once more.

"My first thought was that someone was ramming a car into the side of the house," he said. "I was trying to get dressed and downstairs before the whole thing came down. I've never been in an earthquake, but I imagine that's what it feels like."

Patrick ran outside and around the house, frightened by what he might find. But he never expected to see—*nothing at all*. There was no car, no people, no tree fallen on the roof. He inspected the entire house, inside and out. Being summertime, the new boiler they'd installed was turned off. The hot water heater was functioning normally. There was no sign of teenagers playing a prank. And Newtown was not experiencing an earthquake.

"I stayed up the rest of the night trying to find some explanation for what Donna and I both heard and felt," Patrick recalled. "But I never did. There was no damage to the house, no physical evidence at all. To this day I have no idea what that was. It rattled me, no doubt about it."

All these years later, Patrick still describes himself as a skeptic—though, perhaps no longer 100 percent.

"It was interesting and makes for great conversation," he said. "My opinion, after all that, is that if there are ghosts, they are not going to harm you. My faith in God leads me to believe we had nothing to fear. Our experiences never really felt menacing, even when we were freaking out. That said, if the walls had started oozing blood or something like that, I'd have had the family out of there in a flash."

Donna thinks there really were ghosts present in the house, and that they were simply trying to be recognized. "Those strange occurrences nearly always happened right when we were talking about the possibility that the house was haunted," she said. "It's like they were acting out to get our attention and saying, 'Yeah, we're here!'"

The Harrigans left their house on Main Street two years later when Donna got a new job in another city. They've encountered no attention-grabbing "spirits" since then.

"Even the Bible talks about spirits," Patrick said. "So I believe it's possible for ghosts to be around. But I'll probably never know for sure if that's what caused all those odd things at our house. Something definitely happened—I just can't say what."

24

Treasure on Earth

While house-sitting for a friend's mother, Alex and Leah Nagel apparently looked like trespassers to the woman's dead husband.

After finishing his master's degree in economics at Texas Tech University in Lubbock, in May 1996, Alex Nagel had planned to return home to Pacific Grove, California, to work in his family's printing business while he saved money to continue his education and get a doctorate. His wife, Leah, had quit her job as a graphic designer; they had taken their son, Josh, out of preschool; and they'd given the landlady notice of their intention to move. She had already rented the place to a new tenant.

But when Alex was offered a last-minute position as an adjunct professor at the university, it was an opportunity he couldn't pass up. He would teach four undergraduate courses the following fall semester. The pay wasn't great, but it was enough. And it was a step in the direction of his ultimate ambition—to become a full professor and eventually land a tenured position somewhere.

That only left one question: What to do for the summer? It was too late for Leah to get her job back, and the employment market wasn't very encouraging at the moment. After a couple of weeks, it began to look like financial necessity might overrule opportunity, and they'd wind up in California anyway.

That's when Leah received a call from her friend Jan. She knew of the couple's predicament and claimed to have the perfect solution: Would they be interested in house-sitting—or more precisely farm-sitting—for Jan's mother, Carol, for six weeks that summer while she went on a long overdue vacation cruise with her sister? Her husband had passed away the previous year. While alive, he'd always resisted spending money on such "foolishness." Alex and Leah could live in the house free of charge, and Carol would pay them to take care of the few remaining animals on the place—an aging horse, a passel of chickens, and a few cats.

"We thought about it for, oh, about sixty seconds and then agreed," Alex said. "It sounded like an answer to prayer to us—and it would be great for Josh to be around animals for a few weeks."

It was settled, and a week later Alex and Leah arrived to take temporary possession of their new home, a two-story clapboard farmhouse, about twenty miles outside the city. Carol and her husband, William, had grown mostly cotton there for nearly all their married life. Lubbock, located in the Texas panhandle on the high plains, has a geography that can be summed up in one word: flat. You can see for miles in any direction. The evening the family moved in, thunderclouds began gathering in the west and the wind kicked up.

"At first glance, the place appeared to have real country charm," Leah said. "But the closer you looked, it became obvious that it was tired and run-down. I guess that's what happens when a farmer gets old and his kids move off to an easier life somewhere else."

Even so, the house was comfortable and would be a perfectly fine place to spend part of the summer. They got acquainted with the layout and unpacked their things. Before she left, Carol had insisted they sleep in the master bedroom because the others had been taken over by storage and would be too difficult to make ready for them. Josh would sleep on a roll-away bed beside theirs. Alex thought it odd that there was a night-light plugged in to every outlet along the bedroom walls—three in all—but he just shrugged it off.

By nightfall, the line of thunderstorms that had been approaching all evening finally arrived. Rain fell in buckets, and the house groaned in the wind. Loud claps of thunder rattled the windowpanes. Alex expected Josh to be terrified, but the four-year-old giggled and squealed with every new flash and boom.

"When we were getting ready for bed, I went around the room and turned off all the night-lights," Alex recalled. "Josh had outgrown his at home, and I had trouble sleeping unless it was good and dark."

Alex was the last to get in bed. After reading for a few minutes, he turned off the lamp on the nightstand.

"As soon as that light went off," Alex said, "the hair on my head stood straight up. You know how you can sense when someone comes up behind you? I had that feeling, but times ten. And instead of being behind me, I would have sworn there was somebody right in front of my face."

Alex fumbled awkwardly with the unfamiliar lamp to turn it back on. He sat up, half expecting someone to actually be present in the room. Josh and Leah were already asleep. Alex sat there long enough to chastise himself for acting like a spooked kid again. He'd been terribly afraid of the dark as a child, but had long since gotten over that. He decided to lie down and try again.

He switched off the light and instantly felt the same presence again. And this time he knew that whatever it was didn't seem happy.

"I had that light back on real quick," he said. "I looked at the cheap plastic night-lights I'd turned off earlier and suddenly had an idea why they were there in the first place."

He got up and turned each one back on. Then he climbed back in bed and turned off the lamp—his eyes wide open. He was acutely aware of the sound of rain dripping off the roof outside and of every creak in the whole house. But this time, Alex did not feel the menacing presence as he had a few moments before.

Soon he fell asleep.

At breakfast the next morning, the sunshine through the windows looked brighter than usual. Leah said she had slept like a rock. Josh was watching cartoons on TV in the living room. By the time Alex finished his oatmeal, he was convinced the spooky incident from the night before had been no more than a weird dream. He laughed at himself and blamed it on the microwave Chinese food they'd had for dinner.

"I was getting ready to go out and play farmer and feed the animals when Josh came into the kitchen," Alex said. "I'll never forget it. He said, 'Daddy, the man by the TV said he'll be mad if you take his coins.'"

Leah looked quizzically at Josh. "You mean the man *on* the TV?"

"No!" the boy insisted. "The man *by* the TV."

Alex and Leah both headed for the living room, but it was empty. They questioned Josh further about what he had seen—a man standing beside the TV trying to get his attention away from cartoons.

What did he look like?

An old man in a blue shirt.

What did he say?

He'll be mad if you take his coins.

Did he scare you?

No. I think he's the one who is scared.

"I didn't know what to make of *that*," Alex said. "But it certainly made me think again about what had happened the night before. I was ready to start thinking we had a ghost on our hands. I was about to tell Leah my story, when I noticed she suddenly looked distracted and a little pale."

Leah, it turned out, had a story of her own. That morning she woke up early. The sun seemed especially warm and bright after last night's storm, so she decided to have coffee outside. The chickens were already scratching in the grass for bugs beside the driveway. Songbirds filled a drooping peach tree nearby. Leah sat on a rusting water tank turned upside down to enjoy the moment of peace.

"Right then I thought I saw movement near the barn door out of the corner of my eye," she said. "I looked and was startled to see a man standing there, about twenty or thirty feet away. He was looking past me at the house. I stood up and shielded my eyes from the sun to get a better look, but then he was gone. I don't mean he walked away or anything. He was just *gone*."

Initially, she concluded her eyes were playing tricks on her and dismissed the incident. But when Josh described the man by the TV, she wasn't so sure anymore. The man at the barn was old and wore a blue shirt.

Alex and Leah concluded something very strange was going on. It wasn't their imagination—at least they were pretty sure it wasn't. What to do about it was another matter. They couldn't very well pack up and leave, since they had agreed to take care of animals for another five weeks and six days. Besides, where would they go? They decided the best course of action, as always, was to ask for God's help and protection. If a little night-light could make things better, surely prayer could do a whole lot more. They spent considerable time praying throughout the house and the property, requesting that God remove any spiritual darkness and replace it with his light.

Leah said, "We also decided that if there was a ghost in the house, and if he was worried about our stealing his coins, whatever that meant, it couldn't hurt to tell him we had no such intention."

Along with Josh, Alex and Leah made a game out of playfully saying out loud in every room, "We don't want your coins."

After that, there were no more encounters with an angry spirit in the dark or an old man in a blue shirt. The family enjoyed a nice country holiday of their own until Carol returned.

They never fully solved the riddle of the experience, but months later they received another clue from Jan. She casually mentioned that her step-father, William, had been an avid coin enthusiast. In fact, he had amassed quite a valuable collection over the years. But being perpetually worried about thieves, he hid his prize in increasingly clever places—so clever that a year after his death, Carol had still not found it.

Part Seven

An Eye Toward Eternity

Visions and divine signs provide a peek into the afterlife.

Candice Tully, just shy of her fifth birthday, sat down on a park bench next to her mother, Tina, in their Fort Walton Beach, Florida, neighborhood.

"Mommy," the little girl said earnestly, "do you remember the lady and her little boy we went trick-or-treating with when we lived in Texas?"

"Yes, I sure do, sweetheart," Tina replied. "You're talking about Tricia and her son, Justin."

Candice nodded solemnly. "The mommy died in a car accident. The boy and a friend of his were also in the car, but they're okay."

Tina didn't know what to think. She hadn't heard of any tragic accident involving their old friends.

That was as far as the conversation went, since Tina couldn't figure out what her daughter meant, and Candice didn't seem upset.

The next morning, September 25, 2009, Tina received a call from a friend in Texas who informed her that Tricia had been killed in a car wreck the day before. Thankfully, the caller said, Justin and another boy riding in the vehicle survived.

Deeply shaken, Tina wasn't sure how to interpret her daughter's comment in light of the terrible news. She decided to probe gently and matter-of-factly to avoid upsetting or frightening the girl.

"Candice, how did you know this happened?" she asked. "Did you see the accident or did someone tell you about it?"

"Oh, I saw the accident, Mommy," the girl explained. "I was the only one who saw it. The crash happened with a blue truck, and the man driving had brown hair."

Tina asked her daughter how she knew the woman was dead.

Candice pointed to the toes her mother had recently broken. The girl said, "All her bones were broken, Mommy, just like the ones in your foot."

You might call them visions, divine signs, or extraordinary spiritual insights. Sometimes for brief moments, the curtain between this world and the next is pulled back to allow a fresh glimpse or new awareness.

Of course lots of people in our rational, scientifically oriented society call such experiences coincidences, flukes, or chance occurrences. To get an idea of our cultural bias against treating visions as valid and valuable clues to the nature of the afterlife, we need look no further than the dictionary. *Webster's* defines a vision as "some product of the fancy or imagination; an imaginary or unreal thing."

A few entries later we read that a *visionary*—one who has visions—is a "dreamer; an impractical schemer."

Hmm. Imaginary? Unreal? Impractical?

We doubt the apostle Paul would have used those words to describe his experience on the road to Damascus. Called Saul at the time, he was on his way to persecute and imprison followers of Jesus.

> As he neared Damascus on his journey, suddenly a light from heaven flashed around him. He fell to the ground and heard a voice say to him, "Saul, Saul, why do you persecute me?"
>
> "Who are you, Lord?" Saul asked.
>
> "I am Jesus, whom you are persecuting," he replied. "Now get up and go into the city, and you will be told what you must do."

The men traveling with Saul stood there speechless; they heard the sound but did not see anyone. Saul got up from the ground, but when he opened his eyes he could see nothing.[1]

The episode—for Paul and the men with him—was as real as it gets. For three days, he was blind and refused to eat or drink anything. And the experience had vast practical implications. As a direct result, he not only ceased his efforts to stamp out nascent Christianity, but he also became its leading advocate and promoter around the Roman Empire. The effects of his vision and transformation are still being felt today.

Obviously, the experiences of a first-century saint and a twenty-first-century girl are quite different. These examples—and many more throughout the intervening centuries—show that the spiritual world sometimes interrupts our lives at times and in ways that can be dramatic, inspiring, and perhaps plain old mysterious.

The stories that follow serve to demonstrate that visions still occur today among quite ordinary people. They represent a revealing source of information in our quest to better understand the afterlife. In fact, in some cases, such visions are practically identical to near-death experiences—only without the physical trauma that brings about a brush with death. They are just as vividly real—and just as life changing. Some of the visions feature divine signs—God's way of bringing comfort during anguished times. The effects of such incidents are powerful, and most of the people we spoke with were overcome with emotion in the telling, even years later.

Read on and discover for yourself the very *modern* power of visions to illuminate what happens after death and confirm that God is still very much involved in the world.

25

"Tonight I'm Going to Take You to Heaven."

Grieving the loss of his son, Trevor Yaxley didn't have to die to go to heaven for a visit.

A few days before Christmas 1986, the residents of northern New Zealand got what they'd been praying for—an end to the punishing drought that had left the island's normally verdant landscape parched and brown.

But they didn't expect the first rain in months to arrive on the powerful and destructive winds of Cyclone Raja, which was currently making its way northward in the Pacific toward Fiji.

On the evening the storm arrived, Trevor and Jan Yaxley had just finished leading an evangelical rally for several hundred local teenagers at a meeting hall not far from their home. Darkness had fallen by the time they left the building and headed into the torrential rain and lashing wind. They were soaked the moment they stepped out the door.

Trevor pulled the car onto SH 1 for the short drive home. He hadn't gone far when a fierce gust of wind pushed the car effortlessly across the pavement into the oncoming lane. He steered back to the proper side of the road and commented to Jan how fortunate they'd been that no cars were coming toward them just then.

"It was absolutely blowing a gale," Trevor said. "Really terrible weather and very dangerous driving conditions."

As they carefully made their way through the storm, they thought of their two children who had left the rally an hour earlier and headed home along the same route. Sixteen-year-old David was driving, his sister Rebecca in the car with him. The concerned parents said a prayer—and tried not to worry about the hazardous stretch of road ahead.

The Yaxleys were quite familiar with highway accidents. As well-known Christian ministers in the area, they often accompanied emergency responders to accident scenes to provide spiritual assistance as needed. Only a week ago they'd been present when a young person died in a terrible wreck. In other words, they knew better than most people what was at stake on a night like this one.

"By the time we reached Dome Valley, just a few miles from home, we saw that the road ahead was completely blocked by an accident," Trevor said. "It was a horrendous sight, with flares burning on the road and lights flashing everywhere. A helicopter was trying to land to assist."

There were no other cars ahead of Trevor and Jan, and he pulled right up to the police barricade in the road.

"I turned to Jan and said, 'Honey, brace yourself, I think something terrible has happened.' I told her to stay in the car and I would go see."

Jan said, "It's David! It's David! I know it's David!"

Although Rebecca was also in the vehicle, their hearts told them that something awful had happened to David.

As Trevor crossed the barricade and walked into the scene, he saw immediately that the cars involved were "totally wrecked and torn apart." The rain continued to pour, drenching him to the skin, but his only thought was the growing stone-cold awareness that one of the cars belonged to David. Just then a teenage boy named Andrew, a member of David's youth group who had been traveling safely in another car, approached and fell into Trevor's arms, sobbing and unable to speak. His presence confirmed what Trevor already suspected. Pain and dread flooded his body. He raised his hands to God.

"Somehow I said to him, 'Though you slay me, yet will I trust you.'"[1] "Even at that time I felt God clearly speaking to me. 'You just watch what takes place now, and you will see what I can do in a person's life.'"

Trevor and Jan buried David on Christmas Eve 1986. To attend the funeral, they had to leave thirteen-year-old Rebecca in the intensive care unit of the hospital being treated for injuries she sustained in the crash. She eventually recovered.

And life went on. Sort of.

The couple decided to continue their work with Lifeway Ministries, the organization they founded when Trevor left a lucrative career in business to realign priorities to his family and community. The calendar was already packed with speaking engagements and evangelical rallies.

But nearly two years after David's death, the pain was still fresh for Trevor. The joy and light had still not returned to his life. Trevor and Jan had seen many thousands of people touched by God in their ministry, but Trevor's heart was still wounded and raw.

In 1988, the Yaxleys embarked on a major ministry trip to the South Island. After twelve days of leading as many as three meetings a day, Trevor and Jan arrived in the city of Invercargill for the final rally of the tour. They were physically and emotionally exhausted. That night, waiting to begin, Trevor looked out over the packed auditorium. Every seat was filled—except for one. It was in the front row, right where David always sat when he accompanied his parents to meetings like this one.

"David was a very hip kid, very cool," Trevor recalled. "The other kids loved having him around. He was also a Christian leader. He was my chief cheerleader at these engagements. When I saw that empty seat that night, I felt his absence very strongly. Then the devil said to me, 'See, he's gone. Everything will be a shambles. Nothing will happen tonight, because you don't have anything to say.'"

It didn't work. Trevor told Satan to stand aside. And the evening was a tremendous success.

That night, Trevor fell into bed worn out, body and soul. He missed David as much as ever. He began to pray. In spite of all he could see the Lord doing through their ministry, he asked God for reassurance that he and Jan were in the right place, doing the right thing.

God answered: "*Yes, you are. And, by the way, tonight I'm going to take you to heaven.*"

What was that? Trevor had learned to trust the sound of God's voice when he spoke in times like this. But had he heard correctly? Was God really promising to take him to heaven?

"Somehow I knew that didn't mean I was going to die," he said. "But I was amazed at the possibility it might really happen. I tried to go to sleep. But when God has said he's going to take you to heaven, you can't go to sleep!"

Trevor tossed and turned most of the night.

"At about six o'clock, it was still dark outside. I was lying on my back, and I said to God, 'You haven't got much time left, only a couple of hours.' As the words left my mouth, an absolutely incredible thing happened."

Suddenly Trevor felt as if he were flying upward so fast he could barely breathe. He felt pressure on his body, like the wind resistance one feels riding a motorcycle very fast—only greater. The tremendous speed he was traveling made it difficult to open his eyes. He had the impression that he was moving past many bright lights.

All at once, he felt an enormous "thump" as his feet landed on solid ground.

"At first, I felt really wobbly," he said. "As I opened my eyes, the sights and sounds and scents just flooded my senses. All of them were instantly heightened beyond anything I had ever experienced. I was especially aware of the most amazing fragrance. It is completely impossible to explain how wonderful it was. You don't just smell it. You *experience* it. It affects your whole body. It affects *you*."

Trevor immediately felt an overwhelming sense of well-being. His body was flooded with an intense feeling of acceptance, love, and understanding, like he was the only person in the world.

He looked to his left and beheld an immense, beautiful tree.

"I immediately noticed some incredible differences between this tree and the ones we have on earth," Trevor said. "It was emitting its own light. Light didn't shine on things there, it came out of everything. I was surrounded by light."

As he was trying to cope with his heightened emotions, Trevor noticed he was standing on a path that wound its way downward away from the tree. Just then he sensed there was someone standing behind him. He turned and saw a person who emitted light in the same way as the tree. Trevor didn't notice anything about him except his radiant face that exuded love and kindness—and the fact that he was speaking without moving his lips. Communication was forming in Trevor's mind without the need for sound.

"Hey, how are you doing?" the man asked, very matter-of-factly. "How long have you been here?"

"I said that I had just arrived," Trevor recalled. "But I was stunned, because it was like he was speaking with two voices. Underlying what he'd said was this stream of affirmation that continuously kept telling me what an amazing person I am and what wonderful qualities I have. I will never be able to express the joy I felt at this."

As the person was speaking these things, Trevor noticed a building nearby that looked like a child's playhouse. The man beckoned him to follow inside. He did, ducking his head to get through the low doorway. Once inside he saw a spacious room filled with equally radiant people.

"As I looked at all these people, I saw an expression come on the face of the one who had been speaking to me," he recounted. "Everybody inside looked up at me and smiled. Suddenly I just knew that everything had been prearranged. You just know, you don't have to ask. I knew God had set this up for me as a father. I knew my son was behind me. I turned around, and there he was on the path."

Just as he had often done in life, David smiled at his father and enticed him to play a game of chase. "See if you can catch me!" he called, turning and running down the path past the tree.

"My son looked so full of life!" Trevor said. "This wasn't a dream. It was utterly real."

Trevor didn't want to chase David. He wanted to *hold* him. He excused himself from the people in the playhouse and took off running. As he ran, he noticed he was not expending energy at all the way he would have on earth. He didn't grow winded or tired. He felt as if all the energy of heaven was *one*—and it was all fused into himself.

"As I was following David, I noticed I was standing on these unbelievable flowers. They were transparent, with incredible colors like you can't imagine—and they were *humming*. I know how crazy that sounds, but they were humming praise to God. Nothing was broken. I felt guilty about even standing on them, but they would just stand straight back up again."

Trevor continued running after David. The path led through a stand of trees where leaves were falling to the ground in a carpet of light. Again

Trevor was struck that there was light everywhere, coming from everything. Then he caught up with David, and they embraced.

"I could feel the muscles on his back and could smell him again," Trevor said. "The look on his face was one of absolute delight and peace. His eyes were so clear, and he was so pure it was almost scary. There was nothing in him other than purity. He was changed, and yet he was still himself. He was perfect."

David said, "How is Mom's garden going? I'm glad to see you are still growing things."

Just before he died, David had helped Trevor plant a garden in the yard for Jan.

"I said it was doing great, but I didn't want to talk about Mom's garden. I asked him, 'How are *you*?'"

"Wonderful! Let me show you around."

David took his father's hand and led him through a field covered in what looked like "freshly mown velvet." Everything was arranged with a "random perfection." There were houses spread across the field that Trevor knew were waiting to be occupied by God's people. He was overcome by the beauty of what he was seeing and the joy of being with David. He began to cry.

"Don't cry, Dad," David said tenderly. "Nobody cries here."

"I'm just so happy, I can't help it!"

"But there is no *need* to cry."

As they were speaking, David's voice suddenly began to fade, and things felt to Trevor as if they were "going in reverse." He felt himself moving again—backward this time—at incredible speed. He felt his body hit the motel bed where he'd spent the night back on earth. It landed with a jolt and a thump. He immediately burst into tears, and Jan jumped out of bed and ran to his side. For a long time he only sobbed while Jan comforted him.

"I couldn't talk about my experience to anybody but Jan for a long time," Trevor said. "Everybody told me, 'You're different, what's happened?' But I couldn't tell the story. It was too close. Even so, from that day on I truly was a totally different man. My grief had gone and my joy had returned. I was able to smile and laugh and play again."

Trevor's trip to heaven that night energized his desire to tell others about God's grace and salvation—something he and Jan have continued to do through various ministry opportunities. Having seen firsthand the wondrous eternity people give up in exchange for a few years of earthly pleasure, he is determined to spend his life helping them make a different choice.

"God loves us so much and has put so much effort into what he's prepared for us," he said. "I see now that I'm living my life for future generations and for heaven as well. I want heaven to be proud of my life. That is a profound responsibility."

26

The Scars to Prove It

After being electrocuted and pronounced dead, Art Walters returned to life—but the miracles didn't stop there.

On the morning of September 18, 1971, Art Walters rolled out of bed as he usually did—straight onto his knees. Having escaped a few years ago, with God's help, from a dead-end life of addiction to drugs and alcohol, he knew better than anyone how easy it would be to let temptation drag him back into the past. It had become his habit to avoid that possibility by dedicating each day to God right from the beginning.

He had been married for two years to Vicki, a Christian woman who shared his dream of reaching out to street people, especially those whose lives had also been ravaged by drugs and alcohol. Together they had helped create *Casa de Vida* (House of Life), a Christian halfway house in Santa Barbara, California. Its mission was to assist people who were trying to break free from the downward spiral of homelessness and addiction. As live-in counselors, Art and Vicki provided shelter, job training, and spiritual guidance to anyone who sought it.

To help make ends meet, residents often took on odd jobs around the community—landscaping, painting, or minor renovations and repairs. On that September day, Art was planning to supervise several ongoing projects.

But first, on his knees in the bedroom that morning, his former lifestyle came to mind. He thought of all his old friends still partying, ruining relationships, and living only for themselves.

"I asked God to burn bridges in my life that morning," Art said. "I asked him to get rid of everything in my life that might still tempt me to turn back. I guess it really is true you have to be careful what you pray for."

Later, Art set out on his rounds under a gorgeous, sunny blue sky. His first task: Check in with Bud, a *Casa de Vida* resident who had become a Christian just two weeks earlier. That day, Bud was tackling a variety of odd jobs at a local motel being remodeled. Art learned that the manager had offered to give an almost brand-new, fifteen-foot television antenna to the halfway house—provided they would remove it from the motel roof. After a quick assessment of the job, Art and Bud decided to take her up on the deal.

Using a stepladder, the two men climbed onto a wooden trellis covering the patio alongside the building. From there they stepped onto the clay tile roof and made their way upward to the antenna. It was attached to a long pole that fitted into an even longer one anchored in the ground below. All they had to do was lift the top portion free and lower it down. Art and Bud took positions on opposite sides of the pole, got a firm grip, and lifted. According to their plan, it came free.

But the antenna on top was heavier than they imagined. Furthermore, its weight wasn't balanced—and the pole slowly began tilting to one side. The men strained with all their might to hold it upright, but they lacked the leverage to counteract the pole's growing momentum.

"I don't have it!" Bud shouted.

Art didn't either.

As if in slow motion, the antenna toppled onto a cluster of high-voltage electrical wires that had been strung too close to the building. The force of the impact broke through the wires and sent the live ends falling to the rooftop. Two cylindrical transformers on top of the utility pole exploded, showering the roof with sparks. A ball of fire traveled down the pole and engulfed Art and Bud in flames. The repulsive force of the electricity threw them both like rag dolls onto the roof tiles.

Art was instantly knocked unconscious. And his clothes were on fire.

"The last thing I remember," Art recalled, "was holding on to the pole and watching my hands start to bend over with it. Then everything went black, like I had been shoved into a dark closet."

He believes he died at that moment. "I was still awake and aware, I just couldn't see anything," he said.

Suddenly, Art felt a cool breeze on his face, as if a fan had been turned on. He looked to his left and saw something in the distance coming toward him—or maybe *he* was moving toward *it*. He had the impression of looking through binoculars and trying to focus on the image as it drew closer. Then Art saw clearly that the object was his own body. Looking down at himself, lying on the roof, charred and burning, he *knew* he was dead.

"Then I looked to my right and saw the huge chest of a man, from the neck down to the hands. I knew right then I was in the presence of the Lord. It was like he was too big for the picture frame. His chest took up the whole sky. I watched as his hands scooped up my body, held it for a few seconds, and then set me back down. I could feel his wonderful presence in those hands and in that embrace."

When Jesus put him back down, Art awoke in his body again—and he stood up. He was surprised to see that he was now off of the roof and surrounded by members of the fire department and ambulance crew. Art looked down at his horribly burned body.

Then he passed out.

Like Art, Bud had been thrown to the tile by the force of the high-voltage shock. His first thought upon seeing Art's unconscious body was that his friend was dead. Art's clothes were in flames, and the sparking wires dancing wildly across the rooftop occasionally made contact with Bud's torso and legs. It occurred to Bud that he would also be dead soon.

Although his new relationship with God was barely two weeks old, Bud cried out, "Jesus!" He thought it would be his last word. Instead, a surge of strength passed through his body and stood him on his feet. He patted out the flames on Art's shirt and pants. Though he had severe burns over 30 percent of his body, Bud dragged his friend across the tile to the edge of the roof and the patio covering where they had climbed up. Leaving Art there, Bud descended the ladder. At the bottom, he was trying to figure out the best way to get Art off the roof.

When he looked back up, Bud was astonished to see a man standing on the roof. He held Art's limp body in his arms and was handing him down the ladder. Bud took his friend from the man and laid him on the ground. When he looked up again, the man had vanished. He later told Art he was certain it was an angel of God, sent to help.

When emergency medical technicians arrived, they quickly pronounced Art dead. They estimated he'd been dead at least ten minutes. He had second- and third-degree burns over 70 percent of his body—and no measurable signs of life.

Bud sat nearby and began to repeatedly pray, "Please, Jesus, don't let him die!"

At that moment, Art abruptly stood up from the stretcher as if someone had lifted him to his feet. He looked around, then at himself—and collapsed. The EMTs sprang to action. They packed Art's body in ice gathered from the motel ice machine. On the way to the hospital, Art's heart stopped beating five times. Each time he was revived.

Over the next three weeks, Art Walters had every reason to wish he had died that day. Once he regained consciousness at the hospital, he was in constant, excruciating pain. A renowned British plastic surgeon, Dr. John Chapple, "coincidentally" was on duty in the emergency room when Art was rushed in, so he received excellent care. But there was nothing anyone could do to diminish the agony of his deep and widespread burns.

The prognosis was not good. Doctors told Vicki and Art that he could die of fluid loss, infection, even exhaustion from his treatment. If he survived, he might be paralyzed or might have suffered heart or brain damage. There would certainly be severe scarring over his entire body, including his face. In fact, Dr. Chapple had already decided that damage to Art's face warranted immediate surgery.

"I heard that and visualized myself as a hideous monster for the rest of my life," Art said. "I cried out to God, 'What are you doing to me?'"

God answered Art's prayer with a promise—and a question. "*I can heal you completely. But would you be willing to carry these scars for my glory, as a testimony to what I can do?*"

Art agreed, though he didn't know exactly what that meant for his future.

God replied, "*As a sign to you, I will heal your face so there is no scarring.*"

The next morning Dr. Chapple took one look at Art's face and canceled the surgery.

"He came in, looked at me, and in that British accent said, 'My, how remarkably your face has healed overnight.'"

Still, the pain went on. And the rest of his body remained in critical condition.

Every day Art underwent the horror of having his bandages changed. First, nurses stood him upright using his specially designed mechanical bed frame. Then he spent half an hour stepping away from the mattress that had stuck to the seared flesh on his back. Once free, he was taken in a wheelchair to a basement whirlpool and immersed in body-temperature water. There he endured more agony as nurses pulled away the old bandages to prepare his body for new ones.

"I screamed and screamed night and day," Art said. "I couldn't eat or drink. I couldn't sleep. It was horrible. Not knowing when the pain would end was the worst part."

Doctors expected Art to be in the hospital undergoing treatments for at least three months. After four weeks, things were not going well. Infection was a constant concern, as was keeping Art's body hydrated. He was allowed no visitors except Vicki. Even then, she was dressed in full protective clothing so that only her eyes were visible to Art. On top of everything else, he battled with growing despair.

A bright spot in his day came when a Christian nurse would snatch a few fleeting moments to read to him from Scripture. One verse in particular gripped Art's heart: "No temptation has seized you except what is common to man. And God is faithful; he will not let you be tempted beyond what you can bear. But when you are tempted, he will also provide a way out so that you can stand up under it" (1 Corinthians 10:13).

A way out. That sounded good. "I knew God was telling me to keep looking for the way out he had provided and not to give up," Art said.

Several weeks into his recovery, Art spotted greenish smoke pouring into his hospital room around the door. His first panicked thought was that the building was on fire. But he quickly realized that an evil spirit had entered the room, filling it with thick, oppressive smoke.

"It was a satanic presence," he said. "I started hearing a voice in my head saying, 'Wouldn't you like to be done with this pain? It could be over in a matter of seconds. Go on, you can do it.'"

Art's right arm had been burned from his armpit to his fingertips, but he somehow managed to reach for a pair of scissors on the bedside table. He picked them up and felt an unseen force pushing his hand toward his body.

He began to pray, "But I am a Christian! I serve God. I know this isn't right."

Still something pressed on his hand, moving it closer to his chest. He continued to pray—and then felt another force take hold of his clenched fist and push in the opposite direction. He felt it was the Holy Spirit responding to his prayers.

"I was in the middle of a spiritual battle, a tug-of-war, with my life on the line," Art said. "Then all of a sudden the room was filled with light. I looked and saw the Lord Jesus standing at the foot of my bed. He was radiant and beautiful! He smiled at me and put his hand on the end of my bed. Instantly, I fell asleep—a miracle in itself, since I had been unable to sleep for at least four weeks until then."

The next day when nurses entered the room to begin the daily ordeal of changing bandages in the whirlpool downstairs, they were astonished to find him asleep. As usual, they proceeded to stand his bed up and to free his skin from the mattress.

"This time, as I stepped away from the bed, I closed my eyes and saw the face of Jesus smiling at me, just like he had done the night before," Art remembered. "He told me, 'I am the way out.' I knew he was talking about the verse in First Corinthians. I kept my eyes closed, looking at his face. It seemed like only a few seconds."

But when he opened them again, his body was already wrapped in fresh bandages—without a trip to the whirlpool. The nurses had painlessly removed all the old covering and replaced it with new.

"From that moment on, things began to turn around. Surgeries were more effective, infection reversed course, and the pain was more manageable. Contrary to the doctor's prediction, I was able to walk out of the hospital two weeks later. I looked like Frankenstein, but I was walking."

Art's road to full recovery was still arduous and lasted many months. But he did recover. As for Bud, he overcame his injuries as well. Art and

Vicki lost contact with him over the years; but they'll never forget how his remarkable faith and fervent prayer brought Art through the fire that day.

Today, not even Vicki can see a trace of scarring on Art's face. And God has used Art's remarkable story many times through the years to draw people to himself. The couple has continued in full-time service to God throughout the years—as missionaries to Central America and in various U.S. churches and ministries.

Art summed up his miraculous experiences: "I was given a gift—more time on earth to help people and serve God. Each day is an opportunity I try to use to the fullest."

27

Comfort in a Cloud

As her heart ached, Rita Hauck received reassurance from an unexpected source.

New mother Rita Hauck—exhausted yet elated as she lay in the hospital bed—cradled the precious bundle that had just been placed in her arms. She and her husband, Bob, had chosen to name their first child Erin Irene—Erin because it was a name they had always loved, and Irene to honor Rita's mother, Opal Irene Pope.

It was a sweet, tender moment for Rita, but one also tinged with longing. *Oh, I wish I could tell Mom*, she thought on that clear, sunny day in Hillsboro, Kansas, the last day of September 1971.

Rita had always enjoyed a close relationship with her mother. Opal was a godly woman who loved her family dearly and dedicated her life to being the best mother she could be. Rita dreamed of sharing the experience of motherhood with Opal. She saw what a wonderful grandmother Opal was to her brothers' children, and Rita couldn't wait to start a family of her own.

However, for the first six years of their marriage, Rita and Bob were unable to conceive. Opal, meanwhile, dealt with her own crisis. She developed sarcoma, cancer of the connective tissues, and doctors were forced to amputate her right leg. Despite the amputation, Opal spent more than six years fighting the cancer in other parts of her body.

For Rita, it was heartbreaking to watch her mother decline and suffer. She wasn't ready to say good-bye. She and the rest of her family prayed for a miracle, yet Opal's condition continued to worsen. Finally, at the end of summer 1970, Opal was admitted to a hospital in Enid, Oklahoma. The end was near.

Rita, a music professor at Hillsboro's Tabor College, rearranged her teaching schedule so she could support her father and be with her mother six days a week. Every Tuesday night, after a full day of teaching, she jumped into the car for the three-and-a-half-hour drive to Enid. As the fall season deepened, Rita watched leaves in the trees alongside the road change from green to vibrant reds, yellows, and browns. She enjoyed their beauty, but knew it was temporary. Winter was on its way, and the leaves would soon be gone. It reminded Rita that this time with her mother was still beautiful, but that this season would also end all too soon.

The pain Rita felt over the possibility of losing her mother and never sharing her own children with her was almost unbearable. One day as she sat by Opal's hospital bed, she tried putting it into words:

"Mother, I so long to tell you that I'm pregnant," Rita said, her eyes welling with tears. "I wish you could live to know our children. I've seen the impact you've had as a godly grandmother. You could pray over our child."

"Rita," Opal said gently, tears forming in her own eyes, "I know that God is going to give you a wonderful family someday. I don't know how it's going to happen, but I know he's going to. It's enough for me to know that my daughters have married wonderful Christian men."

On another night, when Opal couldn't sleep and Rita massaged her mother's back, Rita admitted how devastated she was by the idea of losing her. "I don't know if I can go on without you," she said.

Opal smiled. "My precious girl, all you have to do is think about what I would say or what advice I would give, and you'll know what to do."

Rita laughed. She knew it was true. Her mother was so open about her beliefs on parenting, how to love a husband, how to serve God, and so much more that Rita felt she would always understand her feelings about any topic.

Opal continued to decline. In the last days of November, doctors said she might have only three weeks left. On November 30, at the hospital, Rita's dad said to her and her sister, Connie, "We've been praying that

Mother would be home for Christmas. Well, the Lord has just spoken to me. He said, 'She's going to be home.'" Then their father burst into tears.

Opal went home to the Lord the next afternoon.

Over the following weeks and months, Rita wrestled with heartbreaking grief. Though she trusted God's love and sovereignty and had moments of peace, waves of sadness continued to overwhelm her. At Christmastime, Rita again joined in the family tradition of gathering around the piano and organ at her parents' house to sing Christmas carols. Yet even as she sang, tears flowed down Rita's face. Her beloved mother would never again be part of this usually joyful scene.

In early February, Rita and Bob decided to drive to Los Angeles to attend graduation ceremonies at USC, where Bob had earned a doctorate in musical arts. It was a bittersweet time. Just two weeks before, they'd learned of a miracle: At long last Rita was pregnant. She'd conceived in the same month that Opal died. Equally amazing, Connie was also pregnant for the first time—with the same due date as Rita's.

Rita was thrilled, yet in some ways the incredible timing intensified her grief over her mother.

On the trip west, after a lunch stop in Albuquerque, Rita was behind the wheel of their white Chevy Bel Air as Bob slept in the backseat. The miles rolled past as they traveled through New Mexico's red hills on Route 66. A light dusting of snow covered the desert on both sides of the highway. The skies were mostly blue and sunny, though a cloud bank stretched across the horizon and a group of puffy clouds loomed closer.

Rita didn't pay much attention to the weather as she drove, however. Instead, she cried and prayed.

Lord, I'm asking you to help me. I don't want to be constantly grieving. I don't want to be constantly feeling the pain of Mother's death. Please give me a way to have victory in this.

Rita wiped her eyes and glanced upward. To her astonishment, the cloud directly ahead had formed the shape of the upper half of an angel, complete with a face, arms, and wings.

Time seemed frozen. Rita stared at the cloud, though whether it was for seconds or ten minutes, she didn't know.

Suddenly, Rita gasped. She recognized the angel's face.

It was her mother.

The angel in the cloud looked directly at Rita in the car. Her expression was one of sorrow.

Oh, she's sad because I'm weeping, Rita thought.

Then the angel spoke in what to Rita seemed an audible voice, though she appeared to be addressing someone else: "I wish there was some way I could communicate to my family how wonderful everything is for me here. Then they wouldn't grieve for me so much."

Out of shock and gratitude, Rita began to sob. She knew that her mother wasn't literally an angel, but she believed that this was a gift from the Lord to show her that her mom was in heaven.

The next sound to reach Rita's ears was the singing of a heavenly choir. They sang a beautiful tune she'd never heard before. The words were "Holy, Holy, Holy. Holy is the Lord God of Hosts. Heaven and earth are full of His glory."

Even as she drove and wept, Rita continued to focus on the angel cloud in the image of her mother. As she watched, the angel's arms lifted up. At the same time, two new clouds in the shape of mighty arms reached down, connected with the angel's arms, and lifted them into the bank of clouds above until no more shapes were visible.

Overcome, Rita pulled to the side of the road and stopped. She put her arms and head onto the steering wheel and let the tears flow.

Bob awoke and climbed into the front seat. He didn't say a word, but simply put his arms around Rita and waited.

Eventually, Rita collected herself enough to speak. "I've had a vision of Mother," she said. Then she smiled. She realized all her sorrow, pain, and grief were gone. Rita knew her mother was happy and whole, that she wasn't sad about the separation from her family. Indescribable relief and comfort swept over her.

Suddenly, thanks to God's love and the appearance of an angel in the clouds, Rita was at peace.

The months passed, with Rita becoming more and more excited about her soon-to-expand family. After Erin Irene was born, Rita looked out her hospital room window at the colorful changing leaves. It reminded her of the drives to Enid a year earlier and the beauty of her mother's soul and spirit, now in heaven.

She so wished she could let her mother know about Erin. Then she felt the Lord's spirit speak to her: "She already knows all about your baby. I told her. We are rejoicing together with you in heaven."

Ten days later, Connie's daughter was born. Her name was Melyna Irene. Connie and her husband hadn't yet heard Rita and Bob's choice of a middle name for Erin. Both daughters chose to honor their mother in the same way.

Three more children joined Rita's family in the following years. The family went through the usual heartaches and struggles. Yet when Rita wished for her mother's presence and advice, she realized Opal had been right—she always knew just what her mother would say.

Rita and her family experienced many joyous events as well: birthdays, high school and college graduations, weddings, and the birth of grandchildren. For Rita, each one brought back fond memories of her mother and of the angel in the clouds.

"How grateful I am for the vision God gave me that day," Rita reflected, years after the event. "It has been a healing balm, a close presence that has supported me, cheered me on, and encouraged me through the trials of life."

She continued: "I know that some people would doubt what I saw. They would probably say that if you look at a cloud's changing form long enough, you can see whatever you want to see. That doesn't matter to me—I am absolutely certain about what I witnessed. It is a testimony of God's creativity and grace. When I think about how he heard and answered my cries to him, I feel totally loved. I understand his kindness and mercy. He has blessed me over and over."

28

Eternally Anonymous

In a few short moments, David Rutherford saw enough of the nature of hell to last a lifetime.

David Rutherford could not afford to be sick—literally.

In the fall of his sophomore year at Ozark Christian College in Joplin, Missouri, David would have been an ideal poster boy for every flat-broke college student in the country. An expensive visit to the doctor's office was no more within his budget than a week's vacation in Monte Carlo.

Not only that, he couldn't afford the *time* it took to be sick. He had papers to write and tests to study for. He had ministry duties at the tiny farm-country church in nearby Alba, where he volunteered. Spending time with Suanne—who had recently become his fiancée—was definitely non-negotiable. To top it all off, David was a member of the college basketball team—presently at the height of the season. Practice, travel, and games allowed no time to think, much less take a day off.

Nevertheless, David *was* sick and had been for weeks. What started as a simple cold had grown progressively worse. He had survived on willpower and perpetual motion for weeks. But when he developed pleurisy—a painful inflammation of the lining around his lungs—something had to give.

"It felt like having a broken rib," David said. "Every time I moved, I felt a sharp pain in my chest. I couldn't get a deep breath. Playing basketball like that was no fun. I didn't know where to turn."

Fortunately, the answer was nearer than he thought, and it had a name: Bonnie Oney. Bonnie, in her seventies at the time, was the organ player and general pillar of the church in Alba, where David ministered. She was far more than a member of the congregation to him; Bonnie was his best friend, mentor, and surrogate grandmother. She was aware of his declining health and wasn't about to stand by while he ran himself *all* the way into the ground.

"Somebody once told me there is a Bonnie in every church in America," David said. "I don't know for sure, but I have my doubts. She was such a dear saint of a woman. I have to think she was one of a kind."

Bonnie arranged for David to be seen by a local doctor, a Christian man who routinely provided care to people in exchange for whatever they could afford to pay. In his fifties, he spent a month out of every year on mission trips abroad, treating people with limited regular access to medical care.

The day David went to the clinic, the low-level fever he'd been living with for days had begun to climb. He felt exceptionally drained and lethargic. It seemed his appointment had come at an opportune time. Suanne accompanied him into the waiting area. Moments later, he left her there to follow a nurse to an examining room.

Right away, the gray-bearded doctor bustled into the room and confirmed the diagnosis: David had pleurisy. But there was no need to worry, he said reassuringly. A shot of medicine—along with a little rest—would quickly have David back on his feet.

"I would have done anything at that point to get better," David said. "I did as he said and dropped my drawers. Then I felt the needle going into my hip."

David can't say what happened next—because he doesn't remember.

He must have passed out and collapsed to the floor, since that's where he woke up moments later.

He can't recall falling or hitting the hard tile.

Perhaps the doctor was startled when David collapsed.

Maybe he opened the door and called for help from his nurses.

When they arrived, the doctor may have instructed them to help revive the stricken young man. One on each side of him, they bent down to roll him over and try to sit him up.

The doctor must have left the room.

David will never know for sure.

He was only out a few moments. His first memory after waking is of hearing a blood-curdling scream—only to realize it was coming from his own mouth. Thrashing about in terror, his fingernails were dug into the arms of the two women trying to revive him and calm him down. He heard their voices reassuring him, telling him everything was okay.

Slowly, David remembered where he was and began to settle down.

"The nurses didn't seem concerned at all, like this kind of reaction happened all the time," David said. "They said it was nothing. I wanted to scream at them, 'Nothing? You just missed *everything*. The whole world just changed.'"

What David *does* remember, once the needle entered his skin, is finding himself in a white, featureless room. It was blindingly bright. There was no discernable beginning to the room, and no end. Even so, David had the impression he was standing in a corridor of some kind—or more precisely, at the intersection of two corridors—that stretched away from him farther than he could see.

"I didn't feel any pain, or fear, or anything at first," David said. "Mostly, I was curious about that place and about what would happen next."

Suddenly, something appeared in the distance down one of the corridors. It approached David slowly, and, as it drew nearer, he could see that it was a human face—only a face, with no body. Then another appeared at the end of the second corridor. It too moved toward David. Soon, others began to follow them in a kind of parade with two processions crossing where he stood. The faces looked like they belonged to ordinary people, though he didn't recognize any of them.

"Some were male and some female. They didn't look dead, but none of them smiled or showed any emotion," David said. "I remember thinking, *Good, now I can talk to someone and get to the bottom of this. I can find out where I am and what's going on.*"

He attempted to stop one of the faces to get some answers, but he received no response. He tried again and again, but none of the faces would even look his way, much less stop and listen to him. Now they were coming faster and faster, from both directions, until they became a blur.

Hundreds of dull, blank faces poured past him, each seemingly oblivious to his existence. The more the faces raced indifferently past him, the more desperate he felt for some recognition, some connection or reassurance that he was not alone. Horrible panic rose within him.

"I know that doesn't sound so bad now," David said, "but it was the most agonizing experience of my life. I felt incredibly isolated and alone, like there was not the slightest chance of belonging or ever being cared for again. It was absolutely excruciating."

David woke up on the floor of the doctor's office, a long, loud wail coming from deep within himself. He was drenched in sweat and screaming for somebody—anybody—to acknowledge or recognize him. His heart pounded wildly in his chest. Gradually he became aware of his surroundings—the examining table where he'd leaned to steady himself for the shot, the cabinet with glass doors that held medical supplies, two young nurses bending over him to help him to his feet.

His immediate sense of terror began to subside, but not the memory of that terrible loneliness. He felt it in his whole body. Embarrassed by the episode, he buttoned his trousers, joined Suanne in the lobby, and quickly left.

David struggled over the next few days to understand why his experience had been so terrifying. Slowly, he realized that God had given him a vision—a miniscule snapshot—of what hell is really like. He now knows firsthand that it is a place of absolute and complete loneliness, a desperate isolation that no one ever experiences here on earth, no matter how alone they think they are. David didn't just feel separated from God—a state many people might associate with being in hell. He was cut off from *everyone and everything* familiar and comforting. Of the hundreds of faces racing past him, not one offered him the slightest morsel of connection or contact.

"A lot of people joke about preferring to go to hell because that's where all their friends will be, or that's where the party is," David said. "What I saw made me realize it isn't like that at all. No matter where you go on earth, you have something in common with people. Even without knowing the language, it is possible to connect and communicate on a basic level. Not in hell. And it is a horrible, horrible feeling."

David went on to become a full-time pastor and now leads a dynamic church in Fresno, California. From that day on, his ministry was shaped by an extraordinary empathy with people who feel alone in the world. He considers his experience to be a gift from God, not a punishment.

"Because of the snapshot I was shown, I know that the search for connection to each other drives people far more than theology," he said. "We want to belong and be seen for who we really are. In heaven we will feel complete acceptance, and we'll know each other in full and be known. But not in hell. There will be no comfort there, not even in the company of others who share your fate. That's why my whole life mission boils down to helping people avoid hell and instead spend eternity in heaven."

29

A Helping Hand

For Yvonne Clark, a premature labor seemed headed toward tragedy until a surprising vision changed everything.

Yvonne Clark smiled as she stood at the kitchen sink in her one-bedroom Seattle home. Though her hands kept washing dishes, her mind was elsewhere. She looked down at her protruding belly and wondered again at the miracle of birth. Would she have a boy or a girl? What would her baby be like? She was twenty-two years old, excited, and full of questions.

It was April 25, 1975. Yvonne's baby was due in three months. Yvonne and her husband didn't have much in the way of possessions, so earlier in the day she and her mother-in-law had shopped for a TV set. A couple of times, Yvonne had stopped to bend over after a strange and sudden pain. But the discomfort had subsided, and now she was in the kitchen with her husband and in-laws.

Yvonne turned her attention back to the dishes. It was time to think about getting something for dinner.

That was the moment when her world turned upside down.

"Oh no!" Yvonne called out. She turned to face everyone. "My water just broke!"

Everyone stared at each other, too shocked to speak. Yvonne began to cry. She realized it was much too soon. Her precious baby was suddenly in big trouble.

The family moved into action, speeding Yvonne to the hospital. She was given a room with another woman who was due in a month and at the hospital for a test. Concerned nurses and doctors hovered and hurried around Yvonne, creating such a stir that her roommate panicked and also went into labor.

At first, the hospital staff hoped they could delay Yvonne's labor, but the lack of fluid and Yvonne's body determined otherwise. She was in labor, and there was nothing anyone could do to change it.

Anxious hours passed. Yvonne was told she shouldn't bear down because her baby was too fragile and tiny. She wasn't given pain medication for fear it would be too much for the baby.

At first, the pain and contractions were manageable. But as ten hours stretched into twenty, and then thirty, Yvonne's pain, exhaustion, and fear multiplied and converged like a pack of hungry wolves. She felt tortured by questions she couldn't answer. Would she be able to deliver her baby? Would the baby live?

Finally, a dejected nurse turned to Yvonne. "I'm sorry," she said. "The baby's not going to make it. It's going to be a dry birth. It's just too early."

Yvonne became hysterical. "No, that can't be true!" she cried, tears streaming down her cheeks. "My God, why am I going through all this if my baby's going to die?"

Despondent, she turned her head away from the medical staff to look out the window. The scene did not match her mood—it was a beautiful, sunny morning. Yvonne could see another structure, probably an office building, through the glass.

And then, suddenly, there was something else. It wasn't close to the window or near the other building. It was somewhere in between, and it was huge.

Impossibly, it was a giant hand.

The open hand faced Yvonne and moved gently forward and back, the universal gesture to slow down, to be calm.

At the same time, Yvonne sensed a soothing voice speaking to her. *Everything's going to be all right,* she heard.

Somehow, Yvonne understood the voice and hand belonged to God.

Amazed, she stopped crying and turned back to the nurses. "The baby's going to be fine," she said. "It's not going to die."

The nurses didn't know what to make of Yvonne's sudden change of attitude. They had trouble finding a heartbeat for the baby and remained pessimistic. But a doctor decided to allow Yvonne's labor to continue.

Then they heard a hiccup. The baby was still alive.

Nurses wheeled Yvonne into another room. A doctor came in with forceps. Everything moved quickly. The doctor used the instrument as Yvonne fought the urge to push.

Soon a tiny, wonderful cry reached Yvonne's ears. It reminded her of the mew of a kitten. It was her new daughter.

Yvonne had little time to enjoy the moment. Her baby was whisked away for urgent medical attention. Yvonne, exhausted after thirty-six hours of labor, passed out.

Hours later, she was rolled in a wheelchair to the preemie ward, where she saw her baby. The tiny infant was like a Barbie doll, less than two pounds twelve ounces and under a foot long. Because she was premature, she was covered with body hair. She looked like a small monkey.

"That's my baby?" she asked, her voice a mixture of fatigue and joy. To Yvonne, she was beautiful.

Only later did Yvonne reflect on what she'd seen outside her hospital room window. She'd been so close to despair, to believing the word of the nurses about her baby and giving up. Only when God intervened to calm her spirit did she find the strength and hope to keep trying.

"It was incredible," she says, "just incredible."

A non-practicing Catholic at the time, Yvonne says her experience at the hospital did not immediately recharge her faith. But God was still reaching out to her. Two years ago, a co-worker invited her to a church service. When the speaker spoke of the need to be committed to God, Yvonne responded.

While on her knees at the front of the church, as the speaker prayed specifically for Yvonne, she felt a nudge on her forehead. Along with the nudge came a sense of incredible power.

It wasn't the speaker or any other person. Once again, after so many years, Yvonne felt touched by the presence of God.

Today, Yvonne works as a paralegal in San Diego. Her faith in God is stronger than ever. Her spiritual beliefs, she says, are the foundation of her life.

The premature baby who wasn't expected to live is now a newlywed and an executive for an artificial intelligence firm in Texas. Yvonne's miracle baby—Christine—is also "smart, beautiful, an amazing young woman," says her mother.

Yvonne still marvels at the birth of her daughter and God's surprising appearance all those years ago.

"Some people might say that I hallucinated and imagined the comforting hand out the window," Yvonne said. "But I know what I saw. It was God's hand, and it assured and comforted me. I'll never forget it. I cannot deny that there's a God. I've felt him, seen him, and heard him."

Further Glimpses of the Afterlife

When we began researching this book and put out a call for unique spiritual encounters, we were surprised—stunned, really—to receive an avalanche of stories. More evidence, if we needed any more, that God continues to work in the world today as much as ever.

Since we couldn't, unfortunately, include all of the experiences, we would at least like to present several more in brief, providing further glimpses into the world beyond this one.

"Is That What Death Is Like?"

Before working in the labor and delivery unit, I spent nine years in emergency-room work. On my shift one night in the ER, a man was checking himself in for chest pain when he collapsed in the lobby at the front desk. We got him on a gurney and rushed him into the Code Blue room. We had begun CPR because he was without a pulse or respirations. The EKG monitor showed a flat line.

After no response with the appropriate IV medications, we shocked him twice. He regained consciousness and looked up at us, saying, "Wow, I was over there, and now I'm here again. That was easy. Is that what death is like?"

But before he could say anything else, his heart stopped again and he went unconscious. We shocked him again. His heart rhythm returned, and again he looked up at us, this time smiling.

"Hey, it happened again!" he said. "I was over there, and now I'm here again—just like that. Wow! Was I dead? I think I was dead. It was so easy."

Well, he did it again. His heart stopped, and immediately we shocked him. This time it took several shocks. When he finally came back, his rhythm was unstable, and the physician said we had to calm him down or we would lose him again. So we gave him morphine, and he became fairly incoherent. By that time the internal medicine doctor had joined us, and we shipped the patient off to the ICU. That was the last I heard of him.

That man had at least three round trips between this life and the next in the span fifteen minutes!

—David Hatton, pastor and nurse, Sacramento, California

Thicker Than Blood

When my dad, Rick, died in 2009 of heart disease, I took it really hard. Frankly, I was devastated, since he was a good friend as well as a great father. But an experience in his final moments gave me tremendous comfort.

For decades, Dad enjoyed close friendships with two of his high school classmates, Drayton and Lance (I always knew them as Uncle D and Uncle L). These teenagers—who grew to be men and fathers—were actually more than close friends; they were kindred spirits and soul mates. They always said, "We aren't related by blood—it's something stronger that holds us together." Amazingly, when Uncle L got drafted into the Vietnam War, Dad and Uncle D enlisted, and they were in combat together. Years later, my dad explained matter-of-factly, "We couldn't let one of our comrades go into battle by himself, now, could we?"

Each year, these three took off for a weeklong adventure together: camping in Montana, fly-fishing in Alaska, surfing in Hawaii. They even took a cross-country RV trip together (and somehow remained friends!). And they supported each other through lots of hard times as well, such as when Uncle L's wife up and left him, when Dad went broke after a failed business venture, and when Uncle D nearly died in a work accident.

Over the years, one by one they each drifted back to the spiritual faith they'd left behind in their twenties. Uncle D was raised Catholic and later in life rejoined the church. Uncle L returned to his roots as a devout United Methodist. Dad was the lone holdout for many years, but Uncle D and

Uncle L finally wore him down, and Dad became serious about his faith in God during the last decade of his life.

And one by one, they started dying off. Uncle D, who had diabetes for years, passed away in 2004. He was followed three years later by Uncle L—a massive stroke took him in an instant. My dad was never the same after those losses.

A few years later, when it was Dad's turn to face the end, he lay in the ICU ward at University Hospital in Denver. He'd been there for several days, and my sister, Kim, and I stayed by him constantly (our mother had left the picture long ago). Unconscious and laboring to breathe, Dad was ready to go on. The hours lingered as Kim and I sat by the bedside, feeling completely helpless and distraught.

Early one morning, Dad suddenly sat straight up, looked toward the ceiling, and called out as clear as day, "There they are! It's my brothers. They're waiting for me." He sunk back into his pillows, lapsed into unconsciousness again, and an hour later breathed his last.

I know some people will say that's just what Dad *wanted* to see as he was slipping toward death. I don't believe it for a minute. These three men had such a strong bond that I have no doubt the others were there to welcome Dad as he arrived in heaven.

—Cassandra Holland, Denver, Colorado

Security With a Sword

After relocating to a new city for a job, I bought a house in a quaint neighborhood next to a large city park filled with beautiful old trees. What I didn't realize was that the neighborhood was overrun with drug traffickers. In fact, a dealer lived in the house next door, and his customers frequented the neighborhood at all hours of the night.

I called an alarm company to check the cost for a monitored security system. As I considered making the $35-a-month commitment, the thought occurred to me, "For that price, I could sponsor a third-world child through Compassion International!"

Suddenly a second thought occurred to me, this one even stronger than the first. I felt God saying, "Mayme, if you sponsor that child, I'll be your security system." I sponsored Stephen Henrique, a beautiful little boy from

Colombia. Then I went about my business, living life in my new home and trusting God to be my protection.

My job required working long hours and I often got home after dark, too late to walk safely in the park that was a stone's throw from my house. The park was a popular place for drug dealers and users, and police had been trying to clean up the illicit activity. But it was still no place for a woman walking alone after hours.

Nevertheless, determined not to live in fear—and remembering that I had the best "security system" of all—I often laced up my tennis shoes and hit the sidewalks that meandered through the tree-lined park.

One night as I was walking, a patrol car pulled up next to me. A police officer rolled down his window and asked, "Have you seen any suspicious characters in the area?"

My heart sped up. "No, officer, I haven't seen anyone."

"Let us know if you see anything," he said. "We've gotten several calls from people who report seeing a seven-foot-tall man walking around the park, wearing a white muscle shirt, and carrying a sword."

No joke! That's exactly what he said.

I assured him I'd call if I saw anyone fitting that description. As the patrol car drove away, something struck me, and I couldn't help but laugh out loud with delight and gratitude.

I'm sure the officer had just described my guardian angel.

—Mayme Shroyer, Colorado Springs, Colorado

Ready for the Family Reunion

I was pastor at the Lebanon Wesleyan Church in Lebanon, Indiana, from July 1978 to August 1995. While there, I became well acquainted with a man named Fred Welch who in the 1950s lived in Barberton, Ohio, and worked for the Salvation Army.

Fred was married, had two sons, and his wife was six months pregnant with their third child. While working one night at the Salvation Army, he was given a message that his house was on fire. He rushed home to find it completely engulfed in flames. His entire family was lost in the blaze.

Fred had a nervous breakdown. He spent six months in an institution and nearly died. When he was released, he somehow made his way to

Lebanon and found work there. He became a part of our church, experienced a changed life, and became a great encouragement to those around him.

At one point, Fred had a heart attack and had open-heart surgery at Methodist Hospital in Indianapolis. While on the table during surgery, his heart stopped, and he was without vital signs for five minutes. Later he told me the following:

"I left my body and floated toward the ceiling. I looked down on all they were doing to me on the table. I then was drawn to a strange light through what seemed to be a tunnel. When I came out of the tunnel, the great light was still there, but it was in the background. I stood on what seemed like a river, the water clear like glass and just as smooth.

"On the other side of the river were my wife and two sons. She was waving her hand for me to come across and asking me to join them. There was a marvelous feeling of peace and I wanted to go to them, but I could not cross. I suddenly was back in the operating room looking down on my body again. I saw them use the paddles to shock my heart, and the next thing I knew I was waking up in recovery with nurses and doctors all around me."

I heard Fred tell this story many times and it never changed. He was certain that his family was with God and that he was going to rejoin them again someday.

—Rev. Paul Trent, Chesterfield, Indiana

"You've Brought So Many With You!"

The devastating disease attacked Judy's body at an early age. Diagnosed with cancer at age thirty-two, this young mother lived six years beyond the initial discovery of the cancerous cells.

Three ladies from Judy's church met with her each Thursday for prayer, Scripture reading, and encouragement. They performed this act of love for more than three years, even traveling to other states when she was in medical treatment facilities.

After an extended remission period, the cancer cells resumed the process of destroying her body. In January 1996, Judy had weakened to the point that she needed continuous hospital care. She was admitted to Madigan

Army Medical Center in Fort Lewis, Washington. Judy's husband was a physician on the staff at the hospital. At the time I was a US Army chaplain assigned as the director of pastoral care at Madigan. I knew Judy through previous times she had been a patient there.

It was evident to all that Judy was dying. That is, all except her mother, who desperately wanted Judy to keep fighting the disease. Judy's brother had died a few years earlier, and it was a tremendous burden on her mother to have a second child nearing death.

The last night of Judy's time on earth was one of great pain. Her parents were in the room with Judy throughout the night. Her husband was at home with their two beautiful girls, who were eight and ten years old. During the early morning hours, as Judy was in such intense pain, her mother told her it was all right for her to pass on.

At about 7:00 A.M., Judy called her husband at their home. She said to him, "I am going home today." He asked what she meant. Judy said, "I am dying today."

Quickly her husband dressed the girls and made the short trip to the hospital. I remember that when he arrived he spruced up the room. Things were in disarray from the difficult night. He turned on softly playing worship music. Then he gently placed the girls, one on each side of their mother, in the hospital bed. By this time Judy's strength was so limited that she could only barely touch them.

After a few minutes, the children were removed from the bed, and we waited. In less than half an hour, we could tell the end was near.

Suddenly Judy mustered all her strength and raised up on her elbows. She looked toward the walls of the room. She was not looking at any of us. While still propped up, she whispered, "Oh, you've brought so many with you!" Joy and amazement were in her voice.

She settled back on the bed, and within minutes her breathing stopped.

Normally a person's body would be removed from the room rather quickly. But not Judy's. She had many friends, and they began coming to the hospital to be with her family. For the next six hours, the visitors were constant. There were three separate spontaneous celebration worship services held in her room. Two were led by pastors who knew her and one by a friend who was part of her prayer group. Songs, prayers, tears, and laughter mingled throughout those hours.

I can't say for certain what Judy saw in her final moments, but her words "You've brought so many with you!" are still clear and vibrant to me. I have a strong inkling she was ushered home by a welcoming throng.

—Lou Shirey, Centerville, Georgia

Strong Enough to Go Home

I had the privilege of being with C. L. Cummings, a great spiritual leader from Kansas, just minutes before his passing. He had been in the hospital and was then put in an extended-care center because his wife, Grace, was not able to care for him at home.

I was there visiting with both of them when C. L. suddenly stopped talking and began to stare at the corner of the room. Then he got up, put on his coat and hat, and said, "It's time to go." When asked where he was going he said, "Heaven. The angels are here to get me. Don't you see them?"

His wife convinced him to take off his coat and sit down. He did, only to repeat this again.

While I was there, his doctor came in and said, "Well, C. L., it looks like you are strong enough to go on home. I'll sign the papers, and you will be on your way this afternoon."

So I prayed with them and left. When I arrived at my next destination, about a fifteen-minute trip, I had a call telling me C. L. had passed away. He knew where he was going, and he was ready to go.

—Max Colaw, Bartlesville, Oklahoma

Angels on Guard Duty

Our family lived in Minnesota during our growing-up years. In 1946, I was ten and my brother was eight, and on one particular Sunday we were both sick with either the measles or the mumps. Our mother was needed to play the piano at church. She never left us home alone, so it must have been very important for her to be in church on that specific Sunday. She told us to stay in the bedroom and play checkers or other games.

There were two windows in the bedroom, each in different walls. As we were playing games, I looked up and suddenly saw a white being with wings walk past the window. It appeared to be an angel! It passed by the one window and then the other.

"Joe, do you see that?" I called to my brother.

He looked around. "What?"

I said, "There's an angel walking past the window."

Then it went by the other window again as if it were circling the house. We were in awe. I saw another angel following after the first. We were not frightened, but instead felt completely peaceful.

When our mother got home from church we were very excited, and we told her about it. She said, "How wonderful! I asked Jesus to send his angels to walk around the house to protect you while we were away."

We all were on cloud nine the rest of the day, knowing that God in heaven was watching out for us.

—Anna Rowell Jackson, Tucson, Arizona

Speaking With the Saints

As a student at Princeton Theological Seminary, I chose near-death experiences as a topic of study for my educational psychology course. Upon graduation and ordination, in my first pastorate in Dallas, Texas, my hard work as a student was blessed by a whopper of an account:

Bob was one of those highly motivated Bible students you both appreciate and want to avoid at the same time. He had several mail-order degrees from magazine-ad Bible colleges, none I had ever heard of—which means he was in my office twice a week to challenge me on the finer points of Scripture and doctrine. He was a devout, well-informed follower of Jesus.

Bob entered the hospital with a massive stroke and was there for months. Elders and I prayed over him, anointed him with oil, and waited. He was moved to intensive care and we awaited the phone call telling us he had gone to be with God. The phone call came, but it wasn't what we expected.

His wife pleaded with me, "Please come! Bob woke up, and I think he's been to hell. All he kept saying was, 'I don't want to go back! I don't want to go back!'"

I hurried to the hospital, knowing he'd likely had an NDE. When I walked into the room, Bob looked relieved to see me. I sat down and asked him to tell the whole story.

"I went there!" he said. "I was in heaven! Pastor, it's all just like the Bible says. Everything was gold: the streets were gold, the buildings, the statues, everything. Oh, pastor, you're going to love it. The gold there was so pure you could see through it. I wanted to see Jesus, and I could tell where he was. I went to him, but there were huge golden doors with no handles on them. So I started knocking and praying and asking to be let in. A man came up to me and asked what I was doing. I said, 'Jesus is in there, and I want to be with him.' He said, 'You can't. Jesus needs to be alone sometimes.' I didn't like that, so I said, 'Well, who are you?' He answered, 'Paul.' And I said, 'Paul who?' He responded, 'PAUL!' And I felt so embarrassed. But then others were there: Philip and Bartholomew and others. It was so wonderful being with them and you could ask them anything and they'd tell you."

I interrupted Bob to ask what they talked about and for how long. He said a long time, but he could remember nothing of the discussion.

Bob continued: "I finally got to see Jesus and, Pastor, it was so wonderful! It is what we're made for—I was on my face before him and everything was complete and perfect. Just to be there praising him was the completion of my soul. But after a while Jesus said I had to go back, and I asked why. He said I had more to do, but I didn't want to go. Finally, I said, 'Okay, Lord, whatever you want,' and I started getting pulled away from him. It was the most painful thing you can imagine. I changed my mind and pleaded, 'I don't want to go back! I don't want to go back!'"

I asked him if there was anything he could remember that Jesus had taught him or revealed. He seemed to search his mind, but then it came to him: "Oh yes, there's one thing. You know how churches are always fighting and arguing about their differences? All the splits and denominations? Jesus hates that!"

I promised Bob that he would have a chance to share his story with the congregation. He remained in the hospital several more days and was released. The stroke had caused problems, but he was sound in mind and retraining himself for public life.

He and his wife returned to church about six weeks later. I asked him if he was ready to tell his story to the congregation, and he said, "What story?" I later sat down with him and recited verbatim his account to me, and he remembered none of it. Two signs of his experience lingered: one was his solid faith in Christ, and the other was an event I observed during

Sunday school. As I walked around checking on the various classes one Sunday, I listened at the door to a discussion Bob was involved in—the subject was death. Bob, formerly so strident and argumentative, gently chimed in: "You don't have to worry about death. There's nothing to be afraid of at all."

I walked in and challenged him: "How do you know that, Bob?"

He looked at me as though I had questioned the most obvious fact in the universe. He seemed to be searching for an answer, or the source of his conviction, and then said, "It's in the Bible!"

I smiled and nodded.

—Noel Anderson, Bakersfield, California

A Cry for Help

My husband died in 1995, and left me in a bit of a mess with the bills and paperwork, all of which he had previously handled. A week after his death, I was looking everywhere in the house for our mortgage payment coupons. Frustrated, I began crying and yelling out to my dead husband, "Why did you do this to me?"

I went to bed, and for some reason I woke up in the middle of the night. I could smell my husband. I sat up in bed and then suddenly had a thought come to me: The mortgage coupons were in a folder in the bookcase behind his desk. I walked to his desk and knew exactly where to look. I had never seen the folder before. Even though he never spoke to me, I could sense him there and I could feel him directing me. I felt him touch me ever so softly, and then he was gone. After that I looked at life differently. The experience helped sustain me through my grief.

—Gunilla Pratt, Rancho Sante Fe, California

A Procession of Protectors

One night when I was five years old, my dad took me up to bed. My bedroom was at the end of the hall, facing the stairs. My bed was along the wall that faced the hallway. I remember walking into the room feeling like

I just walked into a freezer. I was afraid and asked my dad not to leave me alone because the room was scary.

My dad reassured me that everything was fine and went to get an angel night-light we had in another room. He plugged it into the wall and left despite my pleas for him to stay. I watched him walk down the hall and out of sight as he descended the stairs. Immediately I saw a fireball come up the stairs and head straight for my room. I huddled under the covers in great fear. After a few moments, I peeked out from underneath the covers. The room still felt as cold as ice to me.

Above me swirling around the ceiling was a glowing red "bodybuilder" with an angry look on this face. He was very muscular and from his waist down he was a jet stream of red light. He kept within the swirl about my head. He covered the ceiling of my room in a fury of red light and was endless energy as he darted around and around. I dared not move a muscle for fear that he would notice me. He did not seem to be interested in me, and I wanted to keep it that way. I wondered if he even knew I was there. I pinched myself very hard several times to wake myself up from this dream or to see if it was real. I wondered how I would sneak out of bed and get downstairs to get my dad. I did not want to yell and get the being's attention or get up and be noticed. I looked down the hall.

Coming up the stairs was a line of angels! They were little girls with flowing hair to their mid backs. Each carried a single candle in both hands and had a long choir dress to the floor. They glowed with a soft white light. The little girls had solemn looks on their faces and in single file marched slowly up the steps in a procession. They entered the door that led to my parents' room (halfway down the hall). Still not wanting to arouse attention, I decided not to move and to watch the angels until I fell asleep.

Years later, my mom asked me if I remembered the night I saw the angels. Like yesterday, I stated! She told me that I shared the angel story with her the next day. I do not remember doing that. She also went on to explain to me that she said nothing to me at the time because I was too young to understand. But now she wanted to tell me that she had been struggling with a deep depression and that night was the low point. She had gone to bed (earlier than me), and as she lay there, demonic faces flashed above her head. She was struggling and kept praying to the Lord. I did not understand all that as a child, but I told her the next morning that the angels were protecting her.

—Marie McWhorter, Queensbury, New York

Encouraging Encounter

In 1963, I was pastoring my first church in Yakima, Washington. My wife, Barbara, and I had just celebrated our wedding anniversary. We felt very blessed. God had given us a daughter and a son, and the church was growing. A few days after our anniversary, Barbara became ill with what appeared to be a severe case of the flu. When it didn't clear up after four days, I called the doctor and he said to bring her in to the hospital. He checked her over and said he was going to admit her. He wanted to call in a specialist because there appeared to be pressure in the cranium. The next day the specialist showed me an X ray and pointed to a dark spot. "I can't be sure," he said, "but I believe that is an inoperable tumor."

Barbara was in the hospital for two months, critical most of the time, and then the Lord called her home.

About a month after her graduation to heaven, I was downtown with our daughter, Pam, who was three at the time. She said to me, "Daddy, where were you the day Jesus came to our house?" I started to dismiss her question but realized it was not like her to ask something of that nature. So I began to quiz her.

She described the visitor as dressed in white and talking with her mom while Pam played on the floor with her toys. I asked her what her mother did, and she said, "She talked with Jesus and then she cried a little bit."

The moment Pam mentioned her mother crying, I remembered an afternoon about a month before she became ill. I had been out visiting parishioners and stopped by the house to get something. Barbara met me at the door and was wiping her eyes. I asked if she was okay or if something had happened. Her response was "No, I'm fine. I just had such a good visit with the Lord today."

Not once during her two-month illness did she despair or question why she had gotten ill. You will have to draw your own conclusion as to who came to the house that day. Maybe it was an angel or maybe it was the

Lord. I just know that someone prepared her in a supernatural way for what would transpire.

—Leonard DeWitt, Ventura, California

More Work to Do

In 1968 I was diagnosed with acoustic neuroma, a benign tumor near the auditory nerve. From my original diagnosis until a ten-hour operation, the tumor had grown from the size of a fifty-cent piece to that of a small lemon.

The prognosis was unsettling to a twenty-two-year-old in his first pastorate: facial paralysis, total loss of hearing, speech difficulties—and possible death during surgery. Thanks to the answered prayers of many across the nation, I survived the surgery—though with the fulfillment of every worst-case prediction except death.

During a routine change of bandages in the intensive care unit, I suddenly experienced cardiac arrest. My first sensation was of a halo of brilliant light. I was at first in its center and subsequently seemed to hover above. I didn't have any sense of a physical bodily presence; it was as if I was above the scene, looking through the brilliance at the activities in the ICU.

I remember being in a state of total relaxation, as if the Spirit of God was present, calming me. I could see the physicians and nurses working on the patient (me) in a hurried fashion, but I wasn't able to see their efforts in detail. Before the incident was over, I heard a voice saying, "I have more for you to do." Within a minute or two, my heartbeat was restored.

Thankfully, the Great Physician had appointed an earthly physician, a heart specialist, to be working on a patient in the bed next to mine at that exact moment.

—Jerry Brecheisen, Fishers, Indiana

Friends Calling Long Distance

My mother, Eleanor, was in a nursing home—Heritage Manor in Flint, Michigan—awaiting her time to go to heaven. Mother was eighty years old and had been failing for a couple of years. My dad, John, wanted to be near to her to help with her care, so he checked himself into the home to be there day and night.

Mom kept telling him there was a long barrel with a light at the bottom, and voices of her departed friends kept calling her name and telling her they were waiting for her. They told her she would like it when she was with them. This was repeated several times before she went to her final destination with Jesus on November 1, 1975.

—Maurice Kilmer, Alpine, California

"I See Gwamma"

I had just finished speaking at a youth camp in Westcliffe, Colorado, and was heading back to Marion, Indiana, where I served on staff at Lakeview Wesleyan Church. I'd spoken at this camp a couple of times before and decided to take the whole family out this time to enjoy the beauty of the Rocky Mountains. Besides, my mother had died three months earlier, and I dreaded being separated from my three favorite people in the world—my wife and two sons. So I took vacation time and we made that twenty-seven-hour trek together in our little Honda Accord, stopping on the way there and back to see friends, family, and a couple of tourist spots.

After the camp ended that Saturday, July 1, we drove all the way back to Topeka, Kansas, where I had been on staff at Fairlawn Heights Wesleyan Church prior to moving to Indiana. We attended Sunday services and were invited by Ed and Sharon Rotz to join their family for lunch and an afternoon at the pool of one of the parishioners.

At the pool that day, our young boys, Davey and Jono, played well with the older kids there. All of the adults had congregated down at the deep end of the pool while the kids splashed in the shallow end. Davey, at three-and-a-half years old, had already become a decent swimmer. Jono, age nineteen months, wore safety arm floats and was being carefully watched it seemed by a couple of the older girls. So we settled in comfortably to chat with friends.

Suddenly someone screamed, "Jono!" I turned to see him, facedown, in the shallow end with no movement and no pronounced ripples of water around him to indicate he'd ended up like that within the past few seconds.

All of the kids had gotten out of the pool and were snacking at the nearby picnic tables. Jono had taken his safety arm floats off for snack time. He had then slipped away from everyone, unnoticed, to follow a ball that had rolled off the edge of the pool and into the water.

Apparently in reaching to retrieve the ball he fell into the water, and no one knew exactly how long he had been there.

When I heard the scream from one of the older kids, I immediately began to swim to rescue my son. Before I could get there, Ben Rotz (about nine at the time) jumped in the water, grabbed Jono around the waist, and yanked him up the steps of the pool and out of the water. As I saw my son being dragged from the water, I was still a few yards away, trying to run through the shallow end to get there as fast as I could. His face was pale blue, and there was no sign of breathing from his limp body. Having been a lifeguard, I had only seen that look once before. My heart sank.

It was not Jono's day to leave us, though. By the time I got to the steps of the pool, I heard the glorious sounds of coughing, spitting up, and gasping for breath. Life began to come back into his face. Unknowingly, young Ben Rotz had saved Jono's life by yanking hard on his midsection as he dragged him out of the water. Needless to say, we were beyond grateful to still have our son with us.

Soon after the incident, we said our good-byes to friends and hit the road for Chicago, where we would be rendezvousing with our staff at Wrigley Field for a Fourth of July Cubs game. On the way, still rejoicing over Jono's miracle, I talked with the boys about how much fun the day was. After some chit-chat and a moment of silence, Jono piped up, "I fall down."

"Yes, you did, buddy," I said. "And you scared Mommy and Daddy."

Jono then said, "And I see Gwamma too, Daddy!"

My first reaction was surprise since, at his age, and given the long distance we lived from my parents, Jono had only seen my mom a few times in his short life. Before Mom's death, they had been living in Southern California, where Mom was the Dean of Nursing at Azusa Pacific University. The boys spoke with them at least once a week on the phone and we would exchange video clips of the boys' activities and grandparent greetings. But something told me that these were not just offhand, childish words from a kid who barely knew his grandma.

I decided to probe gently. "Who did you see, buddy?"

"I see Gwamma," he repeated.

I felt a lump in my throat and my eyes clouded over with tears. I wasn't sure if this was a conversation I even wanted to continue. Then I felt my wife, Brenda, touch my arm from the passenger seat. She gave me a reassuring smile.

I choked out the next question to Jono. "Are you sure you saw Grandma, little buddy?"

"Uh-huh."

"Where did you see Grandma?" I asked.

"When I fall down. And Gwamma was sad too."

At that moment I envisioned my mother's face with her highly expressive, pleading eyes that always emerged when a subject of urgency or pain was discussed. It was the kind of face that would make a nineteen-month-old child see hurt or sadness.

Barely able to compose myself by this time, I asked, "What did Grandma say to you, Jono?"

"She say, 'Swim now, Jono! Swim!'"

I don't know how to explain what my son saw that day. But I often wonder if his vision of his Grandma was what kept him from panicking and filling his lungs with irreversible amounts of water, thus leaving enough earthly life for Ben to yank him up and inadvertently jump-start his drowning little body. Or did he actually catch a glimpse of the other side where his Grandma encouraged him to stay on this earth a while longer?

—David Blackburn, Brevard, North Carolina

Afterword

Jim Garlow

Thank you for allowing us to be your tour guides for the past couple hundred pages. Let us share some final thoughts before this journey ends.

We do hope you will check out the detailed biblical overviews provided in our first book on this topic, *Heaven and the Afterlife*. It has a more detailed exploration of the scriptural underpinnings of our beliefs.

Following is a brief part-by-part review of the basis for this book.

Part 1: Eyewitness Accounts

We believe that God by his grace has given many people glimpses into the spectacular reality of heaven as they "passed over" and "came back." One reason this seems to happen with much greater frequency in our era is because of advances in modern technology, which allow many more people to be resuscitated than in decades and centuries past. These reports affirm what Scripture teaches about the splendors that await those who know the Lord.

But not all afterlife accounts are wonderful and beautiful. Some reveal the horrors of hell. While not as widely reported, they are just as real. Universalists—those that believe *all* will go to heaven—disbelieve these stories. One doctor's extensive research confirms that unless the stories are gathered immediately after the near-death experience, the story is most frequently lost forever, unable to be recalled a few days later.

Scripture states that the way to destruction (hell) is wide and broad while the road to life (heaven) is narrow. These verses should be taken seriously.[1]

Part 2: Someone to Watch Over Me

We believe that angels actually exist, and that some persons have seen them.

Part 3: Mischief-Makers

We believe the Scriptures teach that demons exist and that they do, on occasion, manifest their ugliness. The great news is that those who believe in Jesus have authority over them and therefore need not fear them.

Part 4: Fond Farewells

We recognize that, like Stephen in the New Testament, some are given a unique glimpse of heaven as they are exiting this earth. Those glimpses are in full alignment with what the Bible explicitly teaches regarding the afterlife.

Part 5: Many Happy Returns

As coauthors, we had many discussions about the fifth section in this book, and we readily acknowledge that the topic of "visitations" represents perhaps the most controversial aspect of any afterlife discussion. Indeed, many people struggle with, or even scoff at, the notion that some deceased persons could "cross back over" into this world.

However, if we were going to be honest with the many reports we accumulated, we could not simply ignore this challenging subject. Thus, in the end, we decided to include some of these remarkable, and at times inexplicable, accounts. We do not feel a need to explain what was reported to us. However, it might be advantageous for us to provide some framework for understanding what we ascertained.

As we've stated elsewhere, it is imperative that one never attempt to contact the dead. To do this is not merely to violate the Word of God but to invite deception, at best, and destruction, at worst. Nevertheless, there is apparently no biblically stated prohibition that blocks deceased persons from revisiting this planet they once fully occupied. Like Moses' and Elijah's post-death visit to this earth, there are reliable reports of persons unexpectedly seeing their recently deceased loved ones.

After vetting these types of accounts from credible and rational persons, we have developed a type of grid—unscientific, anecdotal-based observations. What was universally reported was that:

- The living person was surprised by the appearance or visitation of the recently deceased. In other words, they did not seek such a visitation.
- The living person was not frightened by the visit of the recently deceased. In fact, the visit brought comfort regarding the reality of an afterlife and of heaven.
- The visit vastly reduced the fear of death.
- The visit advanced the needed emotional healing among the living, in some cases bringing full and complete healing.
- The visit was typically a one-time event.

In contrast to the characteristics listed above, there are indicators when such a visitation is spiritually untrustworthy and dangerous. A demonic presence masquerading as a deceased relative is referred to as a *familiar spirit*, something to be avoided. Some possible ways to know that the visitation or apparition is demonic is when any one of the following is present:

- The living persons have pursued contact with the dead.
- The living persons were frightened or terrified by the visitation, or described it as eerie. This would be in contrast to the stories presented in previous pages, in which the living persons felt remarkable peace and calmness.
- The living persons came away from the encounter with an anti-biblical belief in Universalism—that is—*all persons* are automatically destined for heaven.
- The living persons attempt to solicit some new truth or information from the deceased. It is at this point that Satan's deceptive powers

are manifested. Truth is to be received from God's Word, not from deceased loved ones.

Neither of us began writing our two books on heaven and the afterlife with any thought that we would encounter such stories. In fact, we were originally skeptical of the accounts, until we began seeing the repeated patterns in these reports. Most convincing to us was the fact that their accounts did not violate any Scripture and that these were reported by people in whom we had strong confidence.

The same week that this book was being completed, I (Jim) was being interviewed by a major Christian network. After we went off the air, I hesitatingly ventured to reveal that our newest book contained accounts of these visitations.

I watched the facial reactions of the host and co-host as I explained our discoveries, wondering what their response might be. Before I could finish my explanation, the co-host interrupted me and said, "I know exactly what you are talking about. My father died in 1977. A short time after his death, he appeared to me."

Having heard this type of account numerous times, I responded, "And let me guess—you were not frightened when it happened and you were significantly healed emotionally due to that visit. Right?"

He looked quite surprised, as if I had taken the words right out of his mouth. "Yes. How did you know?"

"Because I have heard this so many times," I responded.

Part 6: Do You Believe in Ghosts?

Leaving this aspect of positive visitations, we do believe that many so-called "ghost" accounts involve demonic activity. The fact that they are eerie or scary—instead of comforting and reassuring—places them in the suspect column.

Part 7: An Eye Toward Eternity

Finally, like the prophets of old, we believe that visions and signs can be a method God uses to communicate with us. He will never communicate something contrary to Scripture. In fact, if a dream or vision or sign is, in any way, counter to the revealed Word of God, it should be regarded as untrustworthy. However, just as God has used visions and signs during biblical times, he can use them today.

As a final thought, we can say that gathering and presenting the stories in this collection—and thinking deeply about many aspects related to the afterlife—has bolstered our faith in and love for our heavenly Father, the Creator of heaven and earth and all things in between. Though we certainly believed in heaven before undertaking this project, we now even more enthusiastically and confidently embrace the reality of a future heaven. To put it mildly, through this experience we grew to more deeply love God and his Word. We hope and pray that this book, along with our previous one on the topic, will have the same influence on you.

Acknowledgments

We owe a debt of gratitude to the hundreds of people who responded to our request for stories of spiritual encounters. Each account represents a significant personal and spiritual event, and we deeply appreciate those men and women for having entrusted their stories to us.

Special thanks to Tracy Burger and Pam Dahl—without whose support I would not be able to do what I do.

And heartfelt gratitude to my wife, children, extended family, and my church family, all of whom patiently support me during the "birth pains" of each new book.

—Jim

This book would not have been possible without the invaluable contributions of my close friend and colleague Alan Wartes, whose enormous creative skills are matched by his integrity and devotion to truth-telling. Strategic help was also provided by Karen Linamen and Jim Lund, who invested their time and talents to see this book through.

Another close friend, Kyle Duncan with Bethany House, championed this project from the beginning and encouraged its development at each phase. Julie Smith patiently put up with pleas for additional writing time and answered endless questions. Our editor, Ellen Chalifoux, provided sound judgment and clear insights to sharpen and hone the manuscript.

Last, but far from least, a thousand thank-yous to my family—Robin, Juliana, and Logan—for enduring my crazy hours and constant stress as I wrote this manuscript. I offer you my unending love and gratitude.

—Keith

Notes

Adventures in the Afterlife

1. Dinesh D'Souza, *Life After Death* (Washington, D.C.: Regnery Publishing Inc., 2009), 3.
2. 1 John 4:16, 18 NKJV
3. Ecclesiastes 11:5
4. John 3:16–17

Doubter . . . or Questioner?

1. In 1976, as a graduate student writing my doctoral dissertation on the eighteenth-century revivalist John Wesley, I was touring England alone for a time before joining up with a group of seventy other Americans. I took the long train ride north from London, followed by a lengthy cab ride with an accompanying expensive fare—at least for a poor student—to the Lincolnshire town of Epworth. There I visited the boyhood home of the famous John Wesley, receiving a delightful privately guided tour of the two-story structure built in 1709 after the Wesley family suffered a frightening house fire.

The curator, knowing my desire for detail, enthusiastically included a full explanation regarding the house's long-term, active ghost, Old Jeffrey, the name affectionately given it by Samuel Wesley, his wife, Susanna, and their children.

As the tour ended, it was apparent that darkness was coming soon on that cold October British evening. The curator, knowing I was a long distance from any motel, graciously informed me that persons were allowed to pay a small fee and stay overnight in what would otherwise be an empty house. The fact that it was a rainy night likely only increased my apprehension. Knowing quite well the many Old Jeffrey stories, I quickly declined, fumbling for some excuse as to why I needed to get back to London. Thus I missed my *primo* opportunity for an encounter with one of the world's most documented apparitions!
2. John 20:25
3. Mark 9:24

Part One Eyewitness Accounts

1. Maurice Rawlings, *To Hell and Back* (Nashville: Thomas Nelson, 1993), 22.
2. Jeffrey Long, *Evidence of the Afterlife: The Science of Near-Death Experiences* (New York: HarperCollins, 2010), 34.
3. John 14:2

Chapter 2 "An Angel Picked Me Up and We Flew"

1. Psalm 18:16, 19
2. Pokémon is the anglicized name for a collection of Japanese anime cartoon characters popular in the United States. It is the contraction of two words, "Pocket Monster." (*Pokémon,* Wikipedia: The Free Encyclopedia, *http://en.wikipedia.org/wiki/Pokemon.*)

Chapter 4 Road Trip to Redemption

1. See Philippians 4:7.
2. Isaiah 6:5

Part Two Someone to Watch Over Me

1. Some of this is taken from our previous book, *Heaven and the Afterlife* (Minneapolis: Bethany House, 2009). For more detailed information about angels, see chapter 8 of that book.
2. Psalm 148:2–5
3. Psalm 8:5
4. See Daniel 10:5; Matthew 28:3; Revelation 15:6.
5. Revelation 4:6–8
6. F. Forrester Church, quoted in: *Leadership*, vol. 9, no. 3.
7. Hebrews 13:2

Part Three Mischief-Makers

1. C. S. Lewis, *The Screwtape Letters* (New York: Touchstone, 1942, 1961, 1996), 61.
2. Ibid., 75.
3. Ibid., 47.
4. Ibid., 171.
5. Lewis, ix.
6. Ibid., 6.
7. Some of this material is adapted from *Heaven and the Afterlife*. For a full description of how demons afflict and possess people, see *Heaven and the Afterlife* (Minneapolis: Bethany House, 2009), chapter 10.

Chapter 10 Dueling in the Dark

1. Ephesians 6:12

Chapter 11 Evil Comes Home to Roost

1. Matthew 8:28–34

Chapter 12 Kitchen Table Conflict

1. 1 John 4:3–4

Part Four Fond Farewells

1. Acts 6:15
2. Acts 7:55–58
3. 2 Samuel 12:22–23

Part Five Many Happy Returns

1. "A Conversation with Frederick Buechner," *Image: A Journal of Arts and Religion* (Spring 1989): 56–57.
2. Deuteronomy 18:10–11
3. Isaiah 8:19–20 NLT
4. For information about this study, see: Dianne Arcangel, *Afterlife Encounters: Ordinary People, Extraordinary Experiences* (Charlottesville, VA: Hampton Roads Publishing Company, 2005).
5. Matthew 17:1–4
6. Hebrews 12:1

Part Six Do You Believe in Ghosts?

1. Mark Twain, *The Adventures of Tom Sawyer* (New York: Harper & Brothers, 1917), 80.
2. Brian Righi, *Ghosts, Apparitions and Poltergeists: An Exploration of the Supernatural Through History* (Woodbury, MN: Llewellyn Publications, 2008), 88.
3. For a fuller discussion on the subject, see our book *Heaven and the Afterlife*, chapter 5, "Things That Go Bump in the Night: Yes, Virginia, There Really Could Be Ghosts in the Attic."

Part Seven An Eye Toward Eternity

1. Acts 9:3–8

Chapter 25 "Tonight I'm Going to Take You to Heaven"

1. See Job 13:15.

Afterword

1. Matthew 7:13–14

About the Authors

James L. Garlow is the coauthor of *Cracking DaVinci's Code*, with a half million copies in print. He is the senior pastor of Skyline Wesleyan Church in San Diego and a speaker at pastors' and leaders' conferences. Jim has master's degrees from Princeton Theological Seminary and Asbury Theological Seminary and a PhD in historical theology from Drew University. He speaks nationwide and has appeared on CNN, MSNBC, CNBC, FOX, and NBC. His daily radio commentary, *The Garlow Perspective*, can be heard on nearly 850 radio outlets. Jim has four children, and he and his wife live in San Diego, California. For more information, please visit www.jimgarlow.com.

Keith Wall, a twenty-five-year publishing veteran, writes full-time in collaboration with several bestselling authors. He lives with his children in Manitou Springs, Colorado.